AN ECONOMIC HISTORY OF NORTH EAST INDIA 1826 – 1947

AN ECONOMIC HISTORY OF NORTH EAST INDIA 1826 - 1947

Jalad Baran Ganguly

AKANSHA PUBLISHING HOUSE
NEW DELHI-110002

AKANSHA PUBLISHING HOUSE
4649-B/21, Ansari Road
Darya Ganj, New Delhi - 110 002
Email: ektabooks@yahoo.com
Ph.: 23263193/9811582579
Fax : 011-23263193

AN ECONOMIC HISTORY OF NORTH EAST INDIA 1826 – 1947

First Published 2006
ISBN 81-8370-054-3
Edn. 2018

[The responsibility for the facts stated, conclusions reached etc. is entirely that of the author. The publisher is not responsible for them, whatsoever.]

PRINTED IN INDIA

Published by M.P. Misra for Akansha Publishing House, New Delhi and Printed at Tarun Offset Press, Delhi

To Chitra

PREFACE

Economic changes and growth in North East India from 1826 to 1947 under colonial rule reflect the processes of structural changes in political, social, cultural and economic organizations of production impacting on the region's economic growth and distribution of goods and services among different classes of people.

This work is an endeavour to capture the forces of these changes and evaluating their consequences on the wellbeing of the people in the colonial period. Economic pursuits of people and their advancement are conditioned by the prevailing social, cultural and political, institutional architecture and past history. These aspects have been highlighted in appropriate places in respect of the different sub-regions constituting the region.

In 1997 I took up the work of writing the economic history of North East India inspired by the Omeo Kumar Das Institute of Social Change and Development, Guwahati. It was felt that in the field of historical studies relating to the causes of economic change and growth in this region in the colonial period there existed some gap which need be addressed. It was Professor Atul Sarma, of the Indian Statistical Institute, New Delhi and member of the Governing Body of the Institute who first broached this project to me. Thereafter, Professor Atul Goswani, the then Director of the Institute, urged me to undertake this research assignment which I did in the same year. How I wish Goswami had lived to see this work! I state with profound sadness that he passed away on June 4, 2004.

In the initial stage for a few months Mousumi Saikia, a research scholar of the Institute, helped me in collecting some data for the work. Thereafter I went ahead with the hard task of collecting the required source materials for writing this history almost singlehandedly. First, Professor Atul Goswami, now no longer living, and later Professor Abu Nasar Saied Ahmed, who became the Director of the Institute in March 2000 after Goswami's retirement, the Deputy Librarian, several distinguished faculty members and a good few staff-members of the Institute extended all help and cooperation to me in carrying out my work. I am grateful to all of them. I record my unbounded gratitude to Late Professor H. K. Barpujari, my teacher and doyen of historical studies of this region. From him and his writings I got inspiration.

For consulting various reference books, taking notes and borrowing relevant books I have depended on the National Library, Kolkata, the libraries of the Anthropological Survey of India and the Centre for Studies in Social Sciences in Kolkata, the libraries of the Centre for Historical and Antiquarian Studies, the Assam Secretariat's Records Department, the Census Department and the Omeo Kumar Das Institute of Social Change and Development in Guwahati. The staff members of all these libraries extended help and cooperation to me for which I remain grateful to them.

I have been helped, encouraged and advised by many well-wishers and scholars, among whom especially are Amalendu Guha, B. K. Roy Burman, D. P. Barooah, Renu Devi, Atul Goswami, and A.N.S Ahmed.

I gave three seminars at the Omeo Kumar Das Institute of Social Change and Development, Gauwahati and a fourth at the North Eastern Hill University, Shillong where I had interactions with several scholars and benefited by their observations and comments on my work. Pulak Majumdar, my former student, graciously helped me in many ways in completing this work and getting it edited and typed.

Deepak Datta, conventional typist, Ratan Das, Computer typist, and Anupam Chatterjee, who did proof reading of computer – typed first Chapter and Sayantani Biswas, who did proof reading of the rest of the Chapters and the Appendix, deserve my sincere gratitude for completing their assigned tasks enthusiastically.

In the final stage Professor P. K. Mitra, retired Professor of English of Kalyani University, West Bengal, very kindly edited the manuscripts. And he did it meticulously even though it entailed his withdrawal from other urgent academic pursuits to find time for editing the manuscripts. I am deeply grateful to him for his graciously agreeing to undertake and completing this task. Despite his thorough editing work, if any error or pitfall remains, I am wholly responsible for any such blemish and not Professor Mitra.

From 1997 to 2003, for a period of six years, one person who silently but steadfastly stood by me when I was carrying out this work often neglecting my duties in the domestic sphere is my wife Chitra. Despite her glaucoma of both eyes afflicting her, she attended to domestic chores to keep the household running and maintaining a congenial environment in the house to enable me to complete this work. No words are adequate which can express my love and sense of gratitude to her.

P.S. I also acknowledge the help I received from my friends B. Batta Ray and Arabinda Basu in writing this book.

Thanks are also due to Kalpana Digital of Kolkata for correcting the original C.D. It may be noted that certain additions and alterations to this work were made after August 2004. When I first made this book ready.

Omeo Kumar Das Institute
of Social Change and Development,
Guwahati

Jalad Baran Ganguly

CONTENTS

LIST OF TABLES

APPENDIX

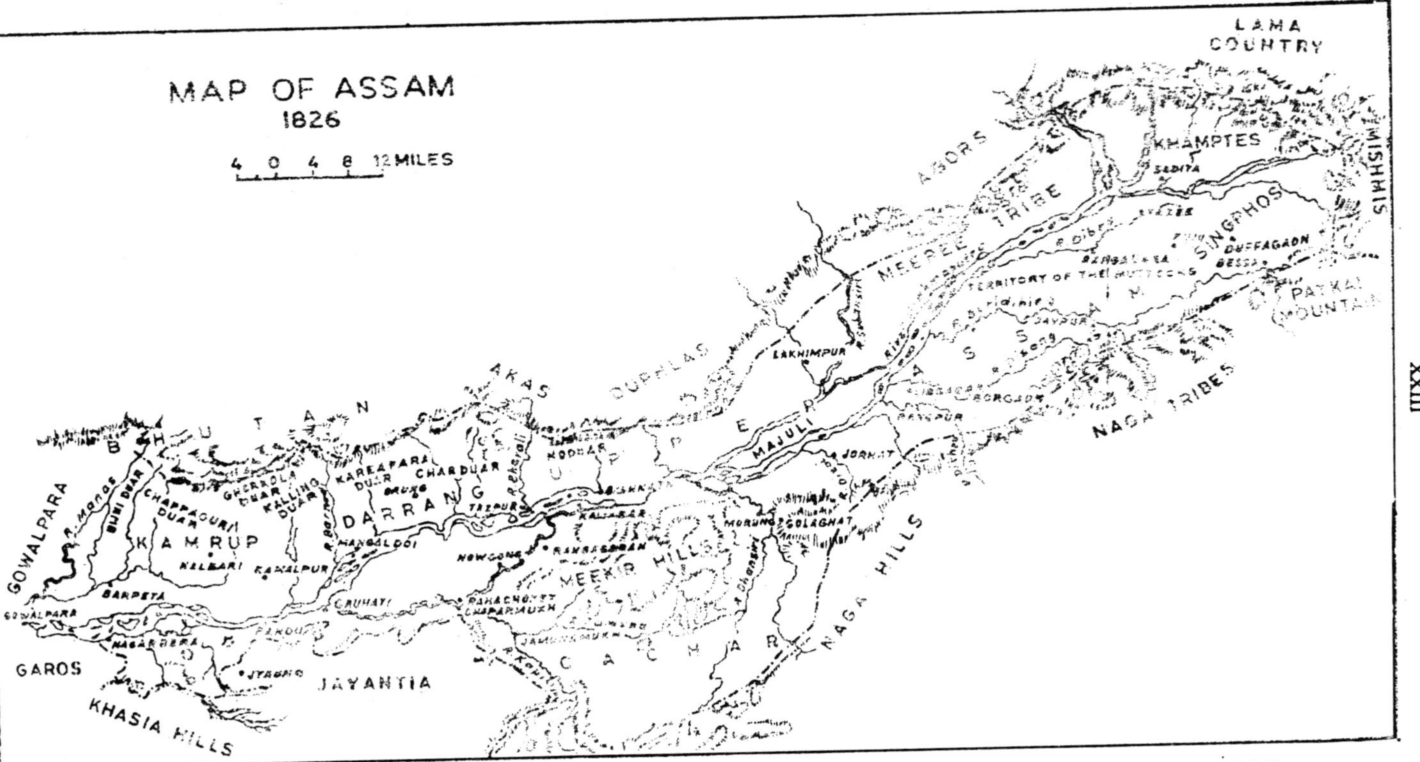

Source: H.K. Barpujari (Ed), The Comprehensive History of Assam, Vol.IV, Publication Board, Assam, Guwahati (1992), P. facing page 1.

PART – ONE
THE REGIONAL PERSPECTIVE

1
THE APPROACH TOWARD WRITING AN ECONOMIC HISTORY OF NORTH EAST INDIA

1. North East India as an Economic Entity

The North Eastern Region as we know it to-day consists of seven political units designated as states in the Constitution of India. These are: Arunachal Pradesh, Assam, Manipur, Meghalaya, Mizoram, Nagaland and Tripura. During the colonial period, political division of this geographical region was different. In 1826, in terms of the Treaty of Yandabo (24 February, 1826), Assam was annexed by the British after defeating the Burmese invaders, who occupied the entire area of the Brahmaputra valley after vanquishing the Ahom rulers. The Burmese had also overran the kingdoms of Cachar, Jaintia and even Manipur. And in accordance with the terms of the same treaty the Burmese agreed to give up their domination over Cachar and Jaintia and to let Gambhira Singh to resume ruling Manipur as its king.

After taking over Assam the British proceeded to annex one after another the states of Cachar, Jaintia and the tribal states of Khasi Hills. They pursued their forward policy of establishing step by step their domination over the adjoining tribal areas, such as, Sadiya and Muttock, the Naga Hills, Garo Hills, and Lushai Hills. In the process they encountered fierce and stiff opposition of the tribal people. Ultimately of course the British raj overcame the stubborn resistance of the hill people and subdued them.

Extension of British control over the north-eastern hills

(presently Arunachal Pradesh) inhabited by the Abors (Adis), Mishmis, Khamptis, Daflas, (Nishis), Apatanis, Konyaks, Wanchos, Monpas, was made possible much later, by mounting a number of armed expeditions. The constitution of the North East Frontier Agency covering the 'Abor or Central Section, Mishmi and Khampti or Eastern Section' and Western Section extending from the Subansiri to the border of Bhutan took shape in 1912 when the proposal sent by the Government of India was accorded approval by the Secretary of State of the United Kingdom.

Tripura came under the British sway much later. In 1858 the Company's rule ended and the country came under the rule of the British Crown, the Paramount Power of India, and the successor to the Mughals. Under the Company the Princely States were treated as 'foreign states' but the Government treated them as 'feudatories' or vassal states.

The British Government took upon itself the responsibility of maintaining 'good government' in the states by making them adopt the British model of administration. To carry out this objective, Political Agents were appointed for the princely states.

In the case of Tripura, the British intervened on the ground that the Indian villages in the districts of Sylhet, Cachar, Chittagong and Tipperah bordering Hill Tripura were raided by the Lushai-Kuki tribesmen. Finally, in 1871 the Political Agent was appointed for Tripura when Birchandra Manikya was the ruling king of that state.

Evolution of the constitutional and administrative arrangements for the different units during the British rule will be outlined in Chapter II in so far as they are relevant to the comprehending economic changes in the respective territories.

Our knowledge about the political history of this part of the country has of late been enriched by the authentic works of some noted historians. But by contrast, there exists a void in the field of writing economic history of the region as a whole. Some political historians, of course, have in some measure dwelt on economic institutions, facts, activities, and the causes that lay behind specific political movements and events[1]. But a close study of the economic system and changes having a bearing on the well-being of different social groups is an imperative need.

The common geographical features of the north-eastern states account for striking similarities in the *modus operandi* of natural resource use for productive purposes. The region is bounded by high mountain ranges on the north (Arunachal Pradesh), east (Nagaland and parts of Manipur) and south (parts of Manipur and Mizoram). Within the area capped by high mountain ranges there are mountainous zones, such as, Meghalaya and Karbi Anglong and North Cachar Hills districts of Assam. In Tripura five hill ranges run parallel to each other from north to south. Moreover, there are innumerable hills and hillocks scattered all over these states. No wonder, more than 70% of the total area of the region is hilly and nearly 50% is under forests. Major part of the forests comprises tropical rain forests.

Assam, Manipur and Tripura have considerable areas of valley lands. They are the Brahmaputra and Barak valleys in Assam, Imphal valley in Manipur and the Gomati, Khowai, Howrah, Manu and Muhuri valleys in Tripura. Some flat valley lands between hills and hillocks are there as well in all these states.

In adaptation to physiographical features different systems of agricultural practices have been developed – while the hill forests have been the sites of shifting cultivation, the valley lands have been in use for practising settled wet rice cultivation. In some parts of Naga Hills an effective system of settled cultivation has been indigenously developed by terracing hill slopes and irrigating the terraced fields by building diversion channels from the nearby hill streams and directing the flow of stream water along the terraces. On the Apatani plateau of the north-eastern hills (Arunachal Pradesh) the Apatanis have devised a unique system of building terraces and irrigation networks for practising cultivation of settled wet rice.

Shifting cultivation is less efficient than settled cultivation in terms of productivity per unit of land as well as labour-year. In most cases, people dependent on shifting cultivation have been unable to attain self-sufficiency in food production. Therefore, they have to procure food from the plains where wet - rice cultivation system yields sufficient quantum of rice, the staple food- grain of the people both in the plains and in valleys. In the past, periodically the hillmen raided the villages in the foothills and looted food stock and other necessaries and even took away men and women as captives to use them as their slaves. The Ahom rulers introduced a system of paying in cash and / or kind some 'compensation' called 'posa' to certain border tribes in exchange for a pledge that no such plundering raids would be committed by them anymore. Even the British Government continued to pay 'posa' to some tribes after entering into fresh agreements with them. The hill farmers produce some non - food crops and collect forest products for which there is a great demand from the plainsmen. This pattern of production explains how a relation of economic interdependence for the hill-dwellers and the plain-dwellers has developed.

This economic factor has traditionally bound together, the different population groups of the north - eastern states for their well-being. Besides, various other features of commonality obtain among these states, such as, territorial contiguity, similar ecological infrastructure, power and mineral resource base, crop - soil - rainfall matrix, etc. Excepting for Manipur, Mizoram and Tripura, the river systems of the remaining four states are connected with the mighty Brahmaputra which runs from the east to the west of Assam. The southern districts of Assam (Cachar, Karimganj and Hailakandi) are drained by the Barak river system with which are related some of the rivers of Manipur, Mizoram and Tripura.

In term of resource endowments, economic interdependence of hills and plains and historical commonality the seven political units comprise a broad economic unit (or zone). Economic scenario of each of the seven states manifests certain distinct structural features and differences in sectoral distribution of state domestic products and the trends in economic changes. Despite the uniqueness of certain economic features of each of the seven states, a general pattern in the economic changes that took place in the past in this region as a whole is discernible. This general trend needs to be focused to establish north eastern economic history as a framework that transcends a somewhat random collection of separate economic histories of north - eastern states. Such generalizations are quite in order as explained by Hicks:

"Every historical event has some aspect in which it is unique; but nearly always there are other aspects in which it is a member of a group, often of quite a large group. If it is one of the latter aspects in which we are interested, it will be the group, not the individual, on which we shall fix our attention, it will be the average, or norm, of the group which is what we shall be trying to explain. We shall be able to allow that the individual may diverge from the norm without being deterred from the recognition of a statistical uniformity. This is what we do, almost all the time, in economics"[2].

2. What is Economic History : An Analytical Framework

Economic history of a country or a part thereof may be broadly reckoned as an account of the economic conditions of its people in the past and changes thereof over the chosen period of time denoted by the trend of growth, stagnation or decline in the gross domestic product. For simple non-monetized barter exchange economies or for economies having a mix of barter and monetized exchanges systems statistical estimation of GDP would be difficult to make, if at all. In such conditions some surrogates for roughly assessing the direction and order (higher or lower) of change in the total output of goods and services might be used. Explanations of the occurrence of particular courses of changes need to be articulated in terms of economic laws/ theories. For this purpose the structure of the economic system that exemplifies organization of economic activities, such as, production, distribution, exchange, accumulation, need to be outlined. The economic system operates within the given social, cultural and political parameters. In fact, political and economic aspects of life are symbiotically related with each other. Economic changes cannot be comprehended ignoring political and socio-cultural changes affecting the living conditions of the people. This is borne out by Hicks who observes: "A major function of economic history, as I see it, is to be a forum where economists and political scientists, lawyers, sociologists, and historians – historians of events and of ideas and technologies - can meet and talk to one another"[3].

The process of production is the outcome of application of human labour for converting the mobilized resources to useful items of immediate consumption (consumption goods) or to that which can be used for production of item now or later in increased quantities (capital goods). Technology applied for producing goods and services is an important determinant of the productive efficiency of human labour. Technology is not a gift of nature, it is developed and adopted by human beings and the ability to do so is dependent on the level of development of human resource itself. Education, training, experience, culture, ideology et al. largely shape the potential of human resource. The growth of population itself, as asserted by Ester Boserup[4], promotes technological change. In analysing the problems of development and growth of agricultural production in primitive communities, in particular, Boserup has cogently outlined the positive impacts of growth of population, which is taken as an autonomous change, on such growth. Population growth has actually been an important element of change in the structure of the north eastern economy.

Institutional factors and ideology also play an important role in determining the pace and direction of economic change and distribution of its gains among the different socio-economic groups in the society[5]. This happens through changes in relative prices of goods and services and the factors of production. Such a course of change takes place mainly through the market mechanism. In other words such a mechanism of economic change presupposes the milieu of the market economy.

As we see large parts of north east India during the period under study did not yet develop into a market economy. Extension of colonial rule over this area and the colonial policy of bringing changes by imposing the required political, administrative, legal and juridical structure entailed basic institutional changes. A market economy started taking shape. Yet the major part of people's activities for survival could be reckoned, what Fernand Braudel has termed, as the structures of every day life[6]. Market economy covers "mechanisms of production and exchange linked to rural activities, to small shops and workshops, to banks, exchanges, fairs and (of course) markets. It was on these 'transparent' visible realities, and on the easily observed processes that took place within them that the language of economic science was originally founded. But there is another, shadowy zone, often hard to see for lack of adequate historical documents, lying underneath the market economy: this is that elementary basic activity which went on everywhere and the volume of which is truly fantastic. This rich zone, like a layer covering the earth, I have called for want of a better expression *material life* or *material civilzation*"[7]. This covers eating habits, luxury and the foods of the masses, drinks, stimulants and drugs, houses throughout the world, interiors, costume and fashion, the spread of technology: sources of energy, metallurgy, transport, money, towns and cities, etc. From an account of the material life of the people one can have an idea about "the limits of the possible" level of social and economic development of the people in the period. These facts need to be noted, for they represent the varied dimensions of social and economic development. Most importantly, Braudel has also emphasized the impact of material progress on population growth. To quote him: "World population doubled during the four centuries covered by this book (15th to 18th centuries); nowadays it doubles every thirty or forty years. This is obviously the result of material progress. But the number of people is itself as much a cause as consequence of this progress"[8].

Braudel has concluded from his studies that the capitalist process has been facilitated by 'a vigorous and expanding market economy', favourable social environment for the 'continuous process of wealth accumulation' and finally the liberating action of world trade[9].

3. Historical Perspective of the North Eastern Economy

The economy of North East India during the colonial period was far from being an expanding market economy. 'Material life' as exemplified in the structures of everyday life and the 'economic life' as it evolved along with institutional changes in North East India need be analysed while writing its economic history. The study will be, in Braudel's words, 'on the borderlines of the social, the political and the economic'[10].

In the beginning of the nineteenth century, that is, in the precolonial period, North Eastern Region, excluding Assam, Manipur and Tripura plains, was predominantly inhabited by tribal communities bearing different names. They mostly migrated into this area from different parts of South Asia. Contrary to the claims of the colonial administrators and writers the people of the region, including tribals, were not a fossilized lot in the cultural, political, and economic spheres of life, waiting for the colonial rulers to bring dynamism into their socio-cultural and economic life. Transition from shifting to settled cultivation had been taking place in some parts of the region already. Higher technology of production than that entailing the primitive form of shifting cultivation was being adopted by a few tribes as manifested in the construction of irrigation works, running of water mills, manuring of fields, terracing of hill slopes for farming practices, diversification and specialization in the field of productive activities and so on. New crops, such as, maize, pineapple, chilli, tobacco were raised. And animal power was harnessed for agriculture practice.

The indigenous population in Khasi and Jaintiya Hills and the Nagas had acquired the art of smelting iron ore into iron. This enabled them to use iron hoes and even iron-tipped ploughs.

The opening of trade routes between the hills and the plains of Assam and between Assam and Bhutan, between Tibet, Burma, and even China, brought forth opportunities for producing more and also new goods for exchanging with the goods needed by the tribes. People of the region – tribals and non-tribals alike – were also getting familiarized with the system of exchange economy.

The economic system related to shifting cultivation was not a wholly non-surplus generating subsistence economy. The shifting cultivators raised surplus crops like oilseeds, cotton, vegetables for exchange. Trade was a source of income for them. It is a myth that this system of forest-farming is destructive of natural resources just as it is a myth that the shifting cultivators had no concept of ownership of land by individual households. These myths have gone against the interest of slash and burn agriculturists and enabled certain vested interests to grab their lands for private gain. The colonial rulers too took advantages of these myths in depriving these cultivators of free access to lands and forests. More fundamentally, as pointed out by Michael R. Dove, these myths "have generally facilitated the intention of external administration and exploitation into the territories of the swidden agriculturists and hence can perhaps best be explained as a reflection of the political economy of the greater societies in which they dwell"[11].

The upshot of these factual details of the tribal people's economic pursuits is that studies in *economic* history of the North Eastern Region by explaining the past performances of the people of this region, when a large segment of population is categorized as tribal is quite in order. In fact there exist several scholarly works on the economies of primitive people. Raymond Firth in his famous book, *Primitive Polynesian Economy* has referred to 'the problem of the existence of market conditions in the economist's sense'. He has noted that market conditions are regulated by prices and that there is no price system in the Tikopia community, a fact that forms the subject of his study. The price system brings about the adjustment between wants and scarce resources having alternative uses. For Tikopia "it is relevant to inquire what processes of exchange exist, what notions of value there are, what part they play in the economic system, and whether there are any objects the functions of which approximate to that of money. If there are not, how is production organized and how are the wants of consumers met, since the rationale of an economic system is to satisfy wants by the production of consumer goods?"[12].

Such inquiries have been made by H. N. C. Stevenson of the Burma Frontier Services, in respect of the Central Chin Tribes located in Burma on the India-Burma border adjoining the Mizo Hills (the then Lushai Hills).[13] Following the suggestion of Firth (*op.cit.*), Stevenson has methodically analysed, supported by factual evidence, the dominant technique of production, the system of exchange, the price system, the control of the means of production, the system of regulation of consumer's choices and the ties between participants in the economic process. Besides, he has also very appropriately dealt with the facts about accumulation of capital to improve production. His finding is that the process of capital formation does not yet exist among the Chin tribes. For there does not exist any scope for application of capital goods in production in the given nature of physical background. But "there is scope for profitable investment in improved methods of carriage, threshing and storage of grain, and it is to these aspects of agriculture that we should first turn in our efforts to teach the Chin the benefits of improved technique".[13]

4. Capital Accumulation Process

We shall look into historical records to find out the realities about the process of accumulation of capital (without quantification in money terms) among the people of the North East during the colonial regime. For capital accumulation is a vital propellant of economic growth and hence an important criterion of assessing performance of an economy. In the extremely primitive society capital formation is generally unknown. But as this society evolves into a peasant economy, production of surplus income and saving of income with the objective of increasing the volume of consumption in future periods through increased production becomes a possibility. But Firth cautions that the level of peasant economies cannot "be raised effectively by some dramatic increase in capital formation by peasants in their traditional and customary activities. The scale of individual operations is too small and income levels are too low for that"[14]. Firth has, however, opined that one of the important ways of setting in motion the process of capital formation may be through mobilization of peasants' savings by taxation and utilizing that for undertaking public works and increasing 'social capital' of various kinds.[15]

Boserup, on the contrary, maintains that in communities excepting for the most primitive ones, 'a high rate of population growth necessitates a high rate of investment'[16]. She points out that a large share of such investments can be "carried out by the cultivators themselves" by putting in extra labour which may come from reducing the periods of leisure enjoyed by them. When current agricultural work is at a minimum, working capital for 'additional investment is normally available'. According to her it does not depend on the cultivators' ability and willingness to reduce consumption in order to save and invest but on the effective incentive to additional work put in by the increased number of family members. If the land tenure system provides the cultivators with access to additional cultivable land or if they enjoy sufficient security of tenure so that benefits of land improvements are reaped by them, they will have the incentive to work more. She has, of course, noted that in rapidly growing tribes, a large part of the investment work might have been carried out by slave labour.[17]

5. Modes of resource use

Geographical features, climate, environment and the kind and quality of available natural resources, such as, flora, fauna, water and minerals in a region largely determine in the initial stage what kind of commodities should be produced there. These geo-environmental features constitute the ecological infrastructure of the region, like the basic economic infrastructure (social and economic overheads) the ecological infrastructure also influences economic performance of the people. The thrust of productive endeavour of the people is conditioned by, what Madhav Gadgil and Ramchandra Guha have called, modes of resource use.

In compiling an ecological history of India, Gadgil and Guha have rightly emphasized the need for appreciating the role of ecological infrastructure in shaping progress of human society. They have conceptualized the modes of resource use related to (i) gathering, including shifting cultivation; (ii) nomadic pastoralism; (iii) settled cultivation and (iv) industry. Each mode is distinctly characterized by its respective 'aspects of technology, of economy, of social organization and of ideology'[18].

"With respect to relations of Production", according to Gadgil and Guha, the mode or resource use is conditioned by "the forms of property, management and control, and of allocation and distribution, which govern the utilization of natural resources in different societies and historical periods.

And with respect to productive forces, it analyses the varying technologies of resource exploitation, conversion and transportation that characterize different social orders"[19]. Generally agreeing with this approach, in constructing economic history of the North Eastern Region, which is richly endowed with a wide variety of flora, fauna, water courses, minerals, etc, changes in the mode of natural resource use having a bearing on the trend of economic performance will be taken into account.

6. Women's Role in Economic Activities

Historians are to look at the past in terms of the present because past illuminates the present, which in turn illuminate the past. In recent decades the output of scholarly works on gender and development has grown steadily. Ester Boserup's work, *Women's Role in Economic Development* published in 1970 actually started the process. In India also a number of field-work based studies in women's position in society and change in their economic entitlement resulting from economic growth, women's contribution to national income, etc. have been published. Bina Agarwal in her well-researched work,

A Field of One's Own, Gender and Land Rights in South Asia, has dealt with women's land rights in traditionally matrilineal and bilateral communities including that of the Garos, Khasis, and Lalungs of North-East India. Her findings confirm that "Women played a major role in crop production and the gathering of forest produce. Their labour input in *Jhum* was greater than that of the man; and their knowledge of indigenous crop varieties was extensive"[20]. She also notes that there was considerable equality in class and gender terms at the turn of the century. These observations need to be verified more thoroughly before assessing women's role in conducting and shaping economic changes during the colonial rule.

7. Periodization of History

Change in history, be it political or social or economic, is a continuous process, which, strictly speaking, cannot be divided into distinct periods. Yet periodization of historical changes serves, what Carr has said, as a 'necessary hypothesis or tool of thought, valid in so far as it is illuminating'[21] The extension of the British colonial rule over Assam and the adjoining areas, now known as Arunachal Pradesh, Meghalaya, Mizoram and Nagaland and the establishment of British colonial suzerainty over the princely states of Manipur and Tripura began taking shape after 1826.

The colonial rule engendered significant structural changes in social, cultural, political and economic dimensions of lives of people of the region, besides administratively integrating the areas in varying degrees of effectiveness into the rest of India.

The colonial policy of imposing state monopoly over land and forest resources and regulation of and or even stopping of access of the local people to forests and pastures in certain circumstances in order to facilitate the process of commercialization of forest resources critically disturbed the traditional mode of resource use which maintained the resource stock in tact. These developments resulted in basic economic changes in the region. The entire period of the colonial rule had been a period of integration of the region's economy into the colonial economy of India. And therefore this coloniai phase of economic changes in the region merits an intensive study in the appropriate historical context.

8. Source Materials

An important advantage of writing the economic history of North East India during the colonial period is the availability of written records and studies related to natural resources. Books on people and their socio-economic conditions written by bureaucrats, missionaries, travellers, scholars, etc., administrative reports prepared and submitted by local officers throw light not only on the administrative development in the region but also on changes in the economic condition of the people. There also exist several ethnographic and anthropological accounts of the tribes of the region based on field studies conducted by trained anthropologists and administrators. Reports and studies of the colonial administrators and scholars cannot, however, be taken as infallible, coloured as their views were by their objective of using these materials for effectively enforcing colonial domination. Even more importantly, some of their findings were based on the wrong premise that these people were a fossilized tribe in every sphere of life and the colonial rulers were there to modernize and civilize those subjugated by them.

The first census of population of India including this part of the country had been taken in 1872 and it was published in the same year. Thereafter the process continued regularly as a decadal exercise. These census reports are a store-house of information about demographic as well as economic changes which must be useful for our study.

Reports of different committees appointed by the government from time to time, such as, the Banking Enquiry Committees, Labour Enquiry committee which contain data that are pertinent to the assessment of socio-economic changes in the region shall also be referred to.

Legislative proceedings, enactment of laws and regulations, press reports and observations on the contemporary scenario constitute another important area to be explored.

Several works by noted historians like H.K. Barpujari, Amalendu Guha, et al. throw light on the economic and revenue policies of the British rulers as also on the development of Assam. These works are of considerable consequence which might be profitably made use of in constructing economic history of Assam and the adjoining areas. Moreover, quite a good number of young teachers, scholars and researchers do present learned papers on different aspects of economic history of the region at the annual conferences of the North East India History Association. Some of them have also to their credit well-researched publications on several themes pertaining to economic changes in this region.

9. Constructing Economic History of North East India: Summing Up

Economic History of North East India during the colonial period, that is, from 1826 to 1947, is proposed to be written by studying the changes in political and economic institutions, structures of everyday life of the people (growing of grains, eating habits, foods, drinks, stimulants and drugs, dwelling houses, costume and fashion, spread of technology, sources of energy, metallurgy, transport, money, towns, etc), demographic development and technological change, particularly that involving switching over from shifting to settled cultivation, growth of market economy, trade – both internal and external – process of accumulation and investment of capital, changes in modes of resource use, women's role in economic performance, trend of human development, etc.

The thread that links the parts of the chain of these events needs to be perceived as the movement, though at a slow pace, towards approximating the capitalist system of production, distribution and resource use under colonial imposition, and for serving ultimately the colonial interest. The growth of the capitalist system in this region has, therefore, been sectorally, territorially and ethnic group-wise of an uneven spread over the region. What is more, the basic foundation for facilitating the process of accumulation and investment of capital for sustained growth of the economy was not built up. The colonial economic model was that of developing only a few selected industries through the involvement of the British capitalist entrepreneurs who were provided with access on preferential basis to the locally available cheap natural resources that ensured earning of high rates of profits. As a result, colonialism ushered in 'enclaves of capitalism' where the indigenous people did not have any significant involvement. The colonial rule also failed to effectively stimulate the creative and productive drives of the people of the region whether in the plains or in the hills. This then is the major thrust of our hypothesis and we shall endeavour to test it with available data and application of economic theory.

Conceptualization of North Eastern economic history in terms of patterns and tracing the continuity and change in the economic conditions of the people of this region during the colonial period will form the basic aspects of these studies.

NOTES AND REFERENCES

1. H.K. Barpujari's edited volume, *The comprehensive History of Assam,* vol. IV contains some papers written by him on different economic aspects for the period, 1826 to 1919.

Amalendu Guha's *Planter Raj to Swaraj (1826-1947)* and *Medieval and Early Colonial Assam: Society, Polity, Economy,* besides S. D. Goswami's work on *British Revenue Policy and Administration* and works of some other scholars represent such attempts. There are also other works of relevance in this field. However, a systematic analysis of economic activities and growth having a bearing on the well-being of different social groups remains to be undertaken.

2. John Hicks (1969), *A Theory of Economic History,* Clarendon Press, Oxford, p. 3.

3. *Ibid.*, p. 2

4. Ester Boserup (1965), *The Conditions of Agricultural Growth (The Economics of Agrarian Change under Population Pressure),* George Allen and Unwin Limited, London, and the Foreword by Nicholas Kaldor.

5. Douglas C. North (1981), *Structure and Change in Economic History,* W. W. Norton and Company, New York, London, Structure of an economy is composed of economic institutions, demography, technology and ideology. Any change in any one or more than one element of the structure may cause a change in the performance of the economy. North has formulated a theory of demographic change, and that of growth in stock of knowledge and of institutions. He has depended on the existing literature on demography including the thesis of Boserup. The general theory of institutions propounded by him includes a theory of property rights to account for the individual and group incentives in the system, a theory of the state and a theory of ideology. He presumes that changes in the stock of knowledge are related to changes in the structure of incentives.

6. Fernand Braudel (1986), *Civilization and Capitalism: 15th - 18th century,* vol. I, *The Structures of Everyday Life,. The Limits of the Possible* (Translated from the French. Revised by Sian Reynolds), 2nd Reprint, William Collins Sons & Co Ltd, London, Glasgow

In the three - volume work Braudel has presented 'an economic and social history, of the world from the Middle Ages to the Industrial Revolution'.

7. *Ibid.*, p. 23.

8. *Ibid.*, pp. 31.

9. Fernand Braudel, *op cit.* vol. II : *The Wheels of commerce*, pp. 600-01.

10. *Ibid.*, p. 21
11. Michacl Dove (1983), *Theories of Swidden agriculture, and the political economy of ignorance, Agroforestry Systems: 85-89*, The Hague.
12. Raymond Firth (1965), *Primitive Polynesian Economy*, Routledge & Kegal Paul, London, (originally published in 1939), p. 16.
13. H. N. C. Stevenson (1986), *The Economics of the Central Chin Tribes*, (originally published by the Government of Burma in 1943) reprinted by Tribal Research Institute, Government of Mizoram, Aizawl, p. 188.
14. Raymond Firth and B. S. Yamey (ed.) (1964), *Capital, Saving and Credit in Peasant Societies*, George Allen and Unwin Ltd, London, the essay by Firth, p. 21.
15. *Ibid.*, p. 29
16. Ester Boserup (1965), *The Conditions of Agricultural Growth: The Economics of Agrarian Change under Population Pressure*, George Allen and Unwin Ltd., London, p. 88.
17. *Ibid.*, p. 90.
18. Madhab Gadgil and Ramachandra Guha (1992), *This Fissured Land : An Ecological History of India*, Oxford University Press, Delhi, P. 14.
19. *Ibid.*, p. 12
20. Bina Agarwal (1994), *A Field of One's Own, Gender and Land Rights in South Asia*, Cambridge University Press, London, p. 104.
21. E. H. Carr (1961), *What is History*, Penguin Edition, London, p. 60.

2
THE GEOGRAPHICAL AND HISTORICAL BACKGROUND OF NORTH - EAST INDIA

A. The Geographical Background :

1. Introduction

North East India comprises seven political units, namely, Arunachal Pradesh, Assam, Manipur, Meghalaya, Mizoram, Nagaland and Tripura. Presently all these units have the constitutional status of state of the Indian Union. But during the colonial period, excepting for Manipur and Tripura, all the other units were parts of Assam Province. Of course administrative arrangements for the hill areas were different from those of Asam plains. Both historically and geographically, these political units have assumed the characteristic of a single region having a narrow land connection (like a chicken neck) with the rest of India through northern Bengal. Such a regional perspective has been buttressed by the commonality of resource base and low level of development of basic infrastructure. Therefore in 1972 the North Eastern Council was constitutionally created for the purpose of formulating plans of development and channelling additional resource flows from the centre in order to execute the North Eastern regional plans.

In the colonial period Assam comprised two main geographical divisions, namely, the Brahmaputra valley in the north and the Surma valley in the south. At the time of partition of India in 1947 the latter, excluding Cachar district was transferred to East Pakistan, now Bangladesh. Besides the Surma valley, during the colonial period Assam's geographical boundary included Barak valley (Cachar plains), the Brahmaputra valley having six plain districts, namely, Goalpara, Kamrup, Darrang, Nowgong, Sibsagar and Lakhimpur, five hill districts known as United North Cachar and Mikir Hills, Khasi and Jaintia Hills, Garo Hills, Naga Hills, Lushai (Mizo) Hills, besides the three frontier tracts Sadiya, Lakhimpur and Balipara Frontier Tracts.

2. Physical Divisions

The region has two broad physical divisions – the hills and mountains of different heights and the plains or river valleys. In the north of Assam in the eastern flank of the Himalayan range, stretching from Bhutan in the west and parts of China (Tibet) and Myanmar (Burma) in the east lies the north-eastern mountainous territory (present day Arunachal Pradesh) covering an area of 83,743 sq.kms. In the hills and narrow strips of flat foothill areas of this territory live successively the tribes from west to east which are known by the names of Bhutias, Akas, Daflas (Nishis), Miris, Apa Tanis, Adis, Mishmis, Khamptis, Singaphos and various Naga tribes. In 1919 these hill areas were divided into the Sadiya Frontier Tract covering the eastern and central sections, the Lakhimpur Frontier Tract and the Balipara Frontier Tract covering the western section. In Manipur nearly 92 per cent of the area of the State consists of hilly and mountainous terrain while the Manipur (or Imphal) valley accounts for only 8 per cent of the total area. The Meiteis live in the plains, besides some tribal people who in course of time came down from the surrounding hills and settled down in the plains. The hill dwellers of Manipur mainly belong to the Naga and Kuki tribes. Some other smaller tribes are also there.

The Naga Hills are bounded by Burma (Myanmar) and the north-eastern hills in the east, Manipur in the south and Assam plains and the Barail Range in the west. They cover an area of 16,488 sq. kms. having hill ranges of different altitudes varying between 914 metres and 3,048 metres. These hills having a scattering of narrow valleys are inhabited by several Naga tribes, the more important among them being the Angamis, Aos, Chakesangs, Konyaks, Lhotas, Phoms, Rengmas, Semas and Sangtams.

The Khasi and Jaintia Hills where live the Khasis and Jaintias, lie in the south-west of Assam. These hills having an area of 14,262 sq.kms. have in their western border the districts of Sylhet and Mymensingh (now in Bangladesh).

Shillong situated on a high plateau (1496m above sea level) in the Khasi Hills has the distinction of being called the 'Scotland of the East'. Because of its salubrious cold climate the capital of Assam was located in Shillong. The highest peak of Khasi and Jaintia Hills is the 1,965m high Shillong Peak.

In the west of Khasi and Jaintia Hills we have the Garo Hills (area: 8,167 sq.kms). The river Brahmaputra flows down the west of these hills. The district of Mymensingh of British India (now in Bangladesh) borders upon Garo Hills on the south. Its highest peak is Nokrek (height 1,403m) in the western end of the district.

In the south-eastern part of Assam bordering Nagaland lie the Mikir Hills (now called Karbi Anglong) and further down south bordering Manipur lie the North Cachar Hills - homelands of the North Cacharis and the Mikirs (now known as Karbis) respectively. These two contiguous hill areas were combined to constitute the district of United North Cachar and Mikir Hills having a total area of 15,222 sq.kms. These hills have an average height of 915 metres. Garo Hills, United Khasi and Jaintia Hills, and United Mikir and North Cachar Hills are all on the Shillong plateau.

The Lushai (Mizo) Hills district of Assam is bounded by Cachar district of Assam and Manipur in the north, Burma (Myanmar) in the east and Hill Tipperah and Chittagong Hill Tracts (now in Bangladesh) in the west. The hills running in ridges from north to south with an average height of 900 metres cover an area of 21,081 sq.kms.

Tripura (area: 10,486 sq.kms) lies in the south of Assam bordering Cachar. In the colonial period it was known as Hill Tipperah and its boundary was defined by Sylhet district in the north, Tripura district in the west, Noakhali in the west and Chittagong Hill Tracts and the Lushai Hills district in the east. Five main hill ranges of Hill Tipperah run parallely from north to south. Heights gradually decline in the southern direction. Average height of ranges rises successively from west to east. The hill ranges are separated by flat valleys having an average breadth of about 20 kms.

Proportions of hill areas in the different territorial units vary from 54.34 per cent in Assam and 92 per cent in Manipur. Narrow flat valleys lying between hill ranges and mountains notwithstanding, the present day states of Arunachal Pradesh (north-eastern frontier hills), Meghalaya (Khasi and Jaintia and Garo Hills), Mizoram (Mizo Hills) and Nagaland (Naga Hills) consist of nearly cent per cent hill areas.

The Brahmaputra valley "is an alluvial plain, about 450 miles (725 km) in length, with an average breadth of about 50 miles (80.4 km), lying almost east and west in its lower portion, but in its upper half tending somewhat to the north-east"[1]. The valley covers an area of approximately fifty-five thousand square kilometres.

The Barak valley or the Cachar plains "approximately 3000 sq. miles comprises alluvial level stretches except where broken up by isolated hillocks and low ranges of hills which project from the surrounding mountains. The chief river is the Barak which is from 100 to 200 yards (91.4 to 182.8 metres) in width and in places over 70 feet (21 metres) deep. Despite some differences in land formation and climate, these plains closely follow the broad pattern of the Upper Brahmaputra valley"[2]

3. Climate

As for climate, North East India is a high rainfall zone. Climate of the plains of the region is generally hot, humid and damp in the spring and monsoon months (March to September), but less so in autumn (October and November), and then quite cold in the months of December, January and February. "The copiousness of the spring rains, and the steady prevalence of moisture throughout the year, are extremely favourable to the two great crops of the province, rice and tea"[3]. Besides, the region also abounds in extensive tracts of tropical rain forests. For cultivation of Kharif crops in the plains as also in the hills, where swidden (shifting) cultivation is practised, the farmers totally depend on rain waters. In the monsoon because of heavy rainfall many rivers burst their banks and inundate the valleys with different intensities. Heavy floods occasionally cause considerable damage to crops. Soil erosion on the hill slopes in the upper reaches of the rivers results in collection of silts on the river beds causing consequently rise in their levels. The phenomenon has made this region highly flood-prone.

The climate of the hills of higher elevation is quite healthy. "The whole of the central plateau of the Shillong range is very salubrious, and the same is the case with the Naga Hills. The Garo and North Cachar Hills, on the other hand, are low and feverish"[4].

The region seldom faces widespread drought and general scarcity on account of failure of monsoon. But uneven distribution of rainfall in some months on occasions reduces yields of food crops causing scarcity and bringing suffering to the people in some parts of the region.

4. Health

The damp, humid and generally unwholesome climate, large tracts of marshes, wastelands thick with bushes and other vegetations make many parts of the region extremely susceptible to a number of deadly diseases of epidemic proportions. *Kala-azar*, malaria, dysentery, cholera, and pox epidemics occurring in different parts of North-East India in some years wreaked havoc in terms of death and persistent morbidity. These also caused depopulation and fall in the outputs of staples. The intensity of havoc caused by epidemics is recorded in Assam's Administration Report for 1921-22. To quote: "The first epidemic of *Kala-azar* of which we have knowledge commenced in 1881 and in the decade 1881-91 the mortality attending its progress up the Assam valley from the Garo Hills, where it was first observed, through Goalpara, Kamrup and Nowgong to the Golaghat subdivision of Sibsagar, where the plague was stayed, was terrible. Whole tracts which before its advent were covered with thickly peopled and prosperous villages, were left by it deserted and uncultivated, while villages disappeared, and large areas of land were thrown out of cultivation. Between 1891 and 1901 the population of Kamrup decreased by 7 per cent, and in Nowgong the population declined by more than one-fourth"[5]. Carrying out vigorous preventive measures and the discovery of an effective treatment for this disease in 1920 ultimately brought about success in controlling this epidemic.

"Next to *Kala-azar*, Malaria is probably the most active destroyer of health and of life. It is most prevalent in low hills, and in the jungle covered land at their foot, while in open country, which is under cultivation, it is usually less potent for harm"[6].

In some years cholera and pox epidemics also caused heavy losses of life and reduced prosperous villages into wastelands covered with tall grasses, bushes and various weeds.

5. Earthquakes

North Eastern region is also an earthquake prone zone; the recorded history of earthquakes during the colonial period indicates that earthquakes caused heavy damages to property and even loss of life in several parts of the region in certain years. Report on the Administration of Assam, 1921-22, gives an account of the incidence of earthquakes and losses caused by them (pp.12-13). This account shows that on 10 January 1869 Cachar (in Assam) was rocked by an earthquake. "Another severe shock occurred in September 1875, which did some damage to houses in Shillong and Gauhati, and Silchar was again visited by an earthquake in October 1882, but all previous seismic disturbances were completely thrown in the shade by the earthquake of June 12th 1897, which was the most severe and disastrous" as per record in Assam, or, indeed, in India. The station of Shillong was levelled with the ground, nearly all masonry buildings in Gauhati and Sylhet (now in Bangladesh) were completely wrecked, and much damage was done in Goalpara, Nowgong and Darrang. Two Europeans and 1,540 Indians lost their lives, the majority of the latter being killed by landslips in the hills and by falling in of river banks in Sylhet. In the plains large tracts of land subsided and were covered with sand and water, and the levels of the country were so affected that the towns of Goalpara and Barpeta became almost uninhabitable during the rains. The total cost incurred on special repairs to public works necessitated by the earthquake has been over 37 lakhs of rupees, but this sum falls short of what is required to restore them to the former condition. To this must be added the damage to private property of which it is difficult to form an estimate"[8].

On 18 July 1918 another severe earthquake occurred which caused considerable damage to property, particularly in Sylhet (now in Bangladesh).

Like heavy monsoon downpours resulting in flooding of river valleys, earthquakes are also a great cause of destruction. Of course earthquakes, unlike floods, occur at 'distant intervals'. But the damages to life, property and land surface and river beds caused by earthquakes remain as permanent scars on the topography adversely affecting prospects of farming operations and maintenance of assets such as buildings, bridges, roads, embankments, towns and forest wealth.

6. Minerals

Important from the economic point of view are the mineral resources which include coal (mainly in Assam, Eastern Naga Hills, Khasi Hills and Garo Hills), limestone in Khasi and Jaintia Hills, iron ore in Assam, Khasi Hills and, in small quantities, in beds of small streams in Manipur, corundum in Khasi Hills, kaolin in Garo and Jaintia Hills, and Upper Assam, gold mixed with river sands in upper Assam and salt springs in Upper Assam, Cachar and Manipur. Mainly minerals based manufacturing industries were developed during the colonial period. But in the precolonial period also iron smelting and forging of tools and weapons from iron, extraction of coal, limestone and washing of gold from rivers were of considerable value. The Khasis, notes the Administration Report for 1921-22, smelted iron of excellent quality which was exported to Surma and Brahmaputra valleys. There used to be extraction of large quantities of iron ore in upper Assam during Ahom rule. In that period 'that great iron cannon for which Assam was once famous were forged'[9]. The Khasis were also expert manufacturers of agricultural tools and implements in their forges.

7. Forests

The North Eastern Region is 'physically and climatically' essentially a forest - rich region. In the precolonial period, about 50 per cent of the region's geographical area was covered by forests. The types of forests have been classified as tropical, semi-evergreen, Eastern Himalayan wet temperate, Assam sub-tropical pine, sub-tropical wet hill forests, etc. Considerable areas also had different varieties of bamboos and grass brakes of a number of species. Forests were rich in different good timber species, such as Sal (*shorea robusta*), *Khoir, Ajhar, Gomai, Bonsum, Sonaru, Simalu, Bola, Koroi, Gamar, Jarul, Nageswar*, India -rubber, oak, ash, and so on. The eastern part of Manipur bordering Burma had luxuriant teak trees over a considerable area.

The forests of North East India are rich in bio-diversity having a wide range of species of flora and fauna many of which are found rather uniquely, only in these forests. Many rare orchids and useful medicinal and dyeing plants are also found in these forests. Elephants, rhinoceroses, deer, rare birds, beetles, butterflies etc. make biotic life rich in these forests.

People's life has been intimately associated with forests. In the hills the main method of cultivation of food crops, vegetables, cotton, oilseeds, pulses, etc has been that of swidden (shifting) cultivation in forests. The hill people cannot survive without depending on forests. They collect fuel wood, building materials (such as timber, bamboo, cane, grass) for dwelling houses, materials for suspension bridges over hill streams and rivers, canoes, weapons, implements, furniture, utensils, besides many other useful articles. Forests are also an important source providing people with eatable wild roots, tubers, arum, green leaves, fruits, nuts, berries, bamboo shoots, honey, hunting games for meat, etc. Lac, latex, *agaru*, medicinal plants (like Mishmi tita), dyeing plants like madder and some other forest products were important items of commercial value to the hillmen.

Forests in some parts of North East India were particularly suitable for rearing *mithuns* (*Bos Frontalis*), a semi - domesticated species of cattle which is a highly valued animal reared by the tribal people as an important source of wealth and of meat on ceremonial occasions and for community feasts.

The economic life of the people living in hill villages was overwhelmingly based on the use of forest wealth both as inputs for carrying out productive activities and also as final consumption goods. In the villages in the plains also dependence on forests and forest products was quite considerable though not as much as that in the hill villages. Moreover both the hill and plain villages enjoyed clean environment on account of forests which influenced climate, weather, health, waterflows in the rivers.

Development of tea industry in the colonial period signified the beginning of wide ranging economic changes in the region. This was possible because tea plants grew wild in the forests in the uplands of lower elevation in Upper Assam, Naga Hills, Manipur, North Cachar and the Lushai Hills. Discovery of the plant by Robert Bruce, Agent of Purandar Singh, in 1823 and later also by captain Charlton in 1832 led to the establishment of the first tea plantation on an experimental basis by the Government in 1835. Extension of area under tea cultivation was possible only by converting waste lands into tea gardens.

8. Agriculture

In Assam, Manipur and Tripura there are considerable areas of valley lands consisting of the Brahmaputra and Barak valleys in Assam, Imphal valley in Manipur and narrow valleys of Gomati, Khowai, Howrah, Manu and Muhuri rivers in Tripura. Some flat valley lands between hills and hillocks are there in all the north - eastern states. These lands are very fertile where wet rice cultivation was generally practised.

In adaptation of cultivation to the physiographical features, different systems of agricultural practice were evolved. While the forests in the low hills and hill slopes were the sites of swidden (shifting) cultivation, the flat valley lands were in use for settled wet rice cultivation. In some parts of Naga Hills as also of Manipur hills where Nagas live, an effective system of settled cultivation was indigenously developed by terracing hill slopes and irrigating the terraced fields by building diversion channels from the nearby hill streams and springs for ensuring the flow of stream water over the terraces. Also on the Apa Tani plateau of the north-eastern hills (Arunachal Pradesh) the Apa Tanis devised a unique system of building of terraces and irrigation networks for settled wet rice cultivation.

In both the systems of cultivation – in the upland swidden cultivation and settled cultivation on terraced fields as well as in the plains in the valleys – besides rice, which is the main staple food for all population groups in the region, a number of other crops, such as, cotton, oilseeds (sesame), corns, maize and vegetables in the swidden farms and oilseeds (mustard), sugarcane and some pulses and vegetables in the plains settled farms were raised.

The swidden cultivation was generally less efficient than the system of settled cultivation in terms of productivity per unit of land as well as labour-year. Many hillmen dependent on swidden cultivation were unable to attain self - sufficiency in food production on a sustained basis. The system lacked accumulation of stock and consequently following crop failures on account of natural calamities and / or pest attacks the hillmen faced acute shortage of food. In such situations they had to procure foodgrains from the plains where the settled system of cultivation normally yielded sufficient quantum of rice. The plains cultivators also faced natural calamities and pest attacks. But in such emergencies they were not as helpless as their hill neighbours as they could build up buffer stocks from the surpluses produced during good years.

Since the hill farmers produced some non-food crops and collected forest products for which the plainsmen had the demand, trade between the two groups provided the channel for exchange of their surplus produces for mutual gains. This pattern of production had brought about a system of economic interdependence among the hill and plain - dwellers.

9. Manufactures

Handloom weaving of cotton, silk and woollen textiles was the most important and extensively pursued cottage industry in the region. In Assam where handloom weaving was a household craft 'loomshed was as common to every family as the kitchen'. Gandhiji aptly observed: "Every woman of Assam is a born weaver... And she weaves fairy tales in cloth"[10]. Besides cotton textiles, women in some parts of Assam specialized in the art of rearing three varieties of silk worms, namely, *eri*, *muga* and *pat*. By weaving these three kinds of silk fabrics of different cost structures the demands of people different in economic state and condition could be satisfied.

The Meitei women of Manipur also excelled in the art of handloom weaving of textiles of exquisite designs, patterns and textures. Their textile products were traditionally an important commodity for exchanging with other products, therefore, it was the core item of the exchange economy of Manipur.

In the hills the tribal communities having a nearly self - sufficient economic system, handloom weaving was a common occupation of every woman as in Assam. Since they wove textiles on their loin looms, the width of the cloth sheet was narrow and the volume of output was low. Their handloom products were, however, very colourful and attractively designed. As trade relations with the non - tribals developed and demand structure became dispersed variegated demands for textile products of the hills increased. A part of the colourful and brightly designed textile products, such as, cloth pieces, quilts, wrappers, was for self consumption of the hill - dwellers. The demand of the plainspeople for these products also went up considerably.

Since the region had in it an extensive forest area including bamboo forests, handicraft like basketry, mat making, bamboo - walling and roofing, making bamboo utensils, various artifacts, such as, box, comb, hand - fan, umbrella, sun and rain hats, musical instruments, fishing baskets and nets, were common in hill villages as household units. While the people in the plains used both bamboo and timber for house - building the hill people used bamboo as the main building material even though use of wooden poles and planks was not very uncommon. For roofing they used sun grass, bamboo mats, leaves, etc.

In the plains and the hills alike various dyes – red being the most widely used – were prepared from forest and agricultural products, such as, leaves, roots, barks, latex, flowers, fruits. Some of these were collected from forests in the neighborhood or grown locally. There were some raw materials for dye - making which were procured even from outside through barter exchange. One important item was *Majathi*, a creeper that grew in the hills only. People of Assam procured that item from the Bhutias and Daflas in the north and also from the Khasis in the south [11]. Lac was another important forest product used for dyeing purpose.

Wood - carving and ivory - carving were well known crafts of the region. But the number of artisans engaged in these crafts were small as the demands for these products came mainly from the nobility.

Gold washing in different gold - dust bearing fast - flowing streams in upper Assam yielded quite a considerable amount of gold every year. This was the craft of a small number of people belonging to a particular professional caste known by the name of Sonwals. This trade gradually died as the gold - dust borne by the river streams became insignificant. The crafts of gold-smithy and silversmithy (silver was imported mainly from Tibet and Bhutan) provided occupation to about two thousand artisans during the Ahom period.

Nagaland, Manipur and Khasi Hills have iron deposits from which iron was extracted by using indigenous processes of smelting. The Nagas and the Khasis had their own ironworks where they manufactured various tools, implements, weapons and so on. The Meiteis of Manipur also had their own indigenously developed system of recovering clay iron and iron - smelting process for producing various tools, weapons, farm implements and the like. In the colonial period the growing practice of importing pig iron and steel bars from Bengal led to a gradual abandonment of the indigenous system of ironsmelting.

To meet the growing demand for farm tools and implements, and for various iron and steel products of domestic use blacksmithy became a growing specialized trade of a class of artisans whose number was estimated at more than two thousand persons by the end of the nineteenth century [12].

Pottery has been a common cottage industry in the region. Even as Assam developed bell metal pottery of exquisite quality, it was earthen pottery that was more extensively produced in the plains of the region. This industry turned out a variety of earthen pots and pans, toys, rings for well, etc. Even the tribal artisans produced earthen pots in their indigenously devised potter's wheel.

10. Trade

In the Ahom period Assam had a flourishing trade in several export and import goods with Bhutan, Tibet, Yunnan province of China, Burma (Myanmar) and the north-eastern tribal communities (of present-day Arunachal Pradesh). In these pre-market economies external trade transactions were carried out mostly by exchanging goods for goods and in a few cases goods for services and vice versa. The composition of this transborder trade depended on the level and structure of the economies of the trading partners. Besides having mainly an agrarian economy, Assam had an extensive secondary sector of handloom weaving of cotton and a variety of silk textiles and brass and bell metal utensils making cottage industry. Assam was also endowed with a rich stock of forest wealth. It being a land-locked region, people's requirement of salt was met from indigenous sources like salt-wells, ashes of some plants, etc. But the demand for salt could not be fully met from these sources. Therefore, until Assam's trade with Bengal opened up, it had to depend on rock salt supplies from the neighbouring countries in the north.

The chief items of exports from Assam were rice, cotton, oilseeds, dried fish, timber, lac, munjeet (Indian Maddar), black pepper, elephants, ivory, cotton textiles, *eri* and *muga* silk, brass and bell-metal utensils, and so on. Main items of imports were salt, woollens and blankets, beads, ponies, several other animal husbandry products, besides the luxuries like Chinese silk, silver bullion, gold dust, precious stones, etc which were consumed by the members of the nobility.

The narrow passes through the hills and mountains that separated Assam from its northern and north-western border countries served as the channels through which the transborder trade flowed. These passes were known as *dooars*. Trade and migration of population flowed through such passes from ancient times.

At Bhamo in northern Burma bordering Yunnan Province of China a big trade fair was held every year in the cold season. The Chinese traders came to this fair to sell manufactured and raw silks, spices, Chinaware, spherical masses of stamped gold and silver, cast-iron, culinary vessels, bell-metal gongs, vermilion, tea, rhubarb, honey, hams, musk, verdigris, dried fruits, etc.[13] The Chinese merchants procured various local products of Burma, Manipur and of Assam in exchange for their imported articles, but the most important item that they purchased was cotton.

Some parts of Assam's trade transactions with Bhutan, Tibet, China and Burma were conducted through the participation of the north-eastern frontier (Arunachal Pradesh) tribes, such as, the Khampas, Nishis, Mishings, Mishmis, Singphos and Khamptis, who acted as the go-between. They imported goods from Tibet and also procured some items from the neighbouring tribal producers for reselling to the traders from Assam from whom they bought items required by Tibet and other tribals.

There was a network of markets in the foothills of the Khasi, Jaintia and Garo Hills, Naga Hills, Mizo Hills, Karbi Anglong and North Cachar Hills bordering Assam plains. In these markets the hillmen mainly sold their surplus products, such as, cotton, sesame, vegetables, various forest products like timber, dyeing materials, medicinal plants, handloom products and even iron tools, and implements. Their chief purchases consisted of food-grains, salt, metal utensils, beads, bangles, readymade garments, firearms, etc.

Assam's trade with Bengal mainly involved imports of salt (amounting to five to six hundred tons annually)[14] and some quantities of betel and tobacco in exchange for silk, muga, ivory and timber. Besides, the Garos exchanged their products, such as, cotton, agar, lac and some other forest produces for various consumable items including cloths and household necessaries. Such transactions took place in their foothill markets. As J.B. Bhattacharjee observes: "Like Goalpara in Lower Assam, Sylhet in Surma Valley was an important trade centre for the Khasi-Jaintia hills, Cachar, Manipur, Mizo (Lushai) hills and Tripura."[15] Lime stone and iron 'of a very superior quality' were the two important items of export of Khasi Hills. Cachar's exportable items were timber, ivory, lac, wax, elephants, cotton, agar, bamboo, rattan, etc.

With the involvement of the colonial administrators and traders the volume of trade transactions between Assam and Bengal was boosted by removing restrictions and reducing the effective rates of import and export duties. On the basis of customs returns at Kandahar Chokey, it was estimated that in 1808-09 Assam's imports and exports amounted to Rs. 2,28,300 and Rs. 1,30,000 respectively.[16]

In the pre-colonial period the Ahom rulers maintained a custom-house (*chokee*) at Kandahar lying on the north bank of the Brahmaputra opposite Goalpara for collecting custom duties levied on all items of imports into Assam and exports from there. An officer designated as Duaria Barua was posted at the *chokee* for collecting custom duties. He paid an annual rent of Rs. 45000 to the king for enjoying the right of realizing custom duties.[17]

B. The Historical Background

1. The genesis of colonialism in North-East India

The Ahoms, a branch of the Tai or Shan race, conquered Assam and established the Ahom kingdom early in the thirteenth century. They first established their kingdom in the upper Brahmaputra valley and over the centuries extended their rule into the entire Brahmaputra valley and resisted the Mughals from extending their empire into Assam. The Ahoms ruled over Assam for about six hundred years and built up a moderately prosperous kingdom having a growing rice economy characterized by expanding area of wet rice cultivation and rising volume of rice output and a steadily growing population. The arts and crafts were diversified as the number of artisans and the output of different artefects and textiles, silk fabrics, etc increased. And there was an increase in the volume of trade with neighbouring hillmen, Bengal, Bhutan, Tibet, Manipur and Burma.

The decline of the Ahoms began in the late eighteenth century as their once strong state structure was severely weakened by the bloody civil war, known as Moamaria/Matak rebellion that continued for 40 years from 1769 to 1806 AD. With the help of the Company's troops under the command of Captain Welsh, who came to the help of the Ahom ruler in response to his appeal to the British authority for such assistance in 1792, the Moamaria rebellion and its atrocities were quelled. But before the Moamarias could be totally pacified Captain Welsh and his troops had to withdraw in July 1794 as directed by the higher authority. The direction was in accordance with the policy of non-interference in the affairs of foreign states as propounded by Sir John Shore who succeeded Lord Cornwallis as Governor-General in 1793. This step was taken much against the repeated entreaties of the Ahoms who wanted their continued stay in Assam. "The Raja (Gaurinath Singh) and his ministers were unanimous in asserting that, if they were withdrawn, the country would inevitably return to a state of anarchy"[18]. And they were not wrong in their anticipation. Moamarias and some tribal chiefs again raised their heads against the Ahom rulers and continued their incursions and acts of plundering and committing cruelties to the people of Assam.

Even more disastrous was the intervention of the Burmese army sent by the king of that country under different commanders on the invitation of disgruntled and feuding Ahom princes. In different phases the Burmese troops overran almost the entire Brahmaputra valley and the neighbouring kingdoms including Manipur. They even reached the borders of the British territory some parts of which were threatened to be annexed by the Burmese. At that point of development the British had to actively and determinedly intervene and resist the Burmese troops, fighting against them. After successive battles were fought by the British and the Ahom, Manipuri, Chachari and other allied forces with the Burmese armies and following the effective British armed operations in Burma, the king of Ava (Burma) had to accept the terms of peace offered by the British. Accordingly the Treaty of Yandabo was concluded between the British authority and the king of Burma on 24 February 1826. In the same year Assam (the Brahmaputra valley) was annexed to British India. In accordance with the terms of the same treaty the Burmese agreed to give up their domination over Cachar and Jaintia and to let Gambhir Singh resume his rule over Manipur as its king.

After taking over Assam, the British proceeded to annex

one after another the states of Cachar, Jaintia and the tribal states of Khasi Hills. They pursued their forward policy of establishing step by step their domination over the adjoining tribal areas such as, Sadiya and Muttock, the Naga Hills, Garo Hills, and Lushai Hills. The process was not an easy and smooth one; they encountered fierce and stiff opposition of the tribal people. Ultimately, of course, the British Raj overcame the valiant resistance of the hill people. "The boundaries of the British Power in Northeast India", aptly observes Amalendu Guha, "were in fact always moving, always in a flux right up to its last days in India. Nevertheless, the British province that came to be known as Assam took shape more or less by 1873"[19].

Extension of British control over the north-east frontier hills inhabited by the Abors (Adis), Mishmis, Khamptis, Daflas (Nishis), Apatanis, Konyaks, Wanchos, Monpas, etc. took place much later, of course, by mounting a number of armed expeditions some of which were even repulsed by the brave hillmen.

British rule was extended into these north-eastern hilly tracts in stages generally after violent massacres of British officials who visited these areas for establishing contact with the tribal people dwelling in these hills. Sadiya in upper Assam and its neighbouring areas constituted the territory of Khampti chief. In 1839 the Khamptis attacked the station of Sadiya and killed the Political Agent Colonel White. Following this event Sadiya along with the area around it was brought under direct British rule as a part of the Lakhimpur district in 1842. In 1911 Williamson, the Assistant Political Officer at Sadiya, Dr. J.S. Gregorson and their party were murdered by the Adis at Pangi, north of Pasighat in Siang district of the present day Arunachal Pradesh. Consequently in 1912 the Central and Eastern Sections of the North East Frontier were made to constitute a new administrative charge having headquarters at Sadiya. A second administrative unit, comprising the western section was created covering the area inhabited by the Bhutia, Dafla, Aka, Apa Tani and other tribes. Each was under the charge of a Political Officer who functioned directly under the Government. In 1914 these two administrative units were renamed 'Sadiya Frontier Tract' and 'Balipara Frontier Tract'.

In Assam and the adjoining principalities the British Government started the process of directly introducing administrative, judicial and revenue reforms in order to modernize these systems. Even though Manipur and Tripura were not directly ruled by them, the British authority persuaded and motivated the respective feudal rulers to reform their traditional archaic systems. For this purpose political agents were appointed and posted at Imphal and Agartala, capitals of Manipur and Tripura respectively. In Manipur the British political agent was appointed for the first time in 1835 and in Tripura in 1871.

Manipur's relations with the British underwent change following the occupation of the state by the latter in 1891. In that year the British intervened to settle the succession dispute between the rival claimants to the throne. The armed forces of Manipur under the rebel price Tikendrajit Singh clashed with the British forces and inflicted heavy losses on them. But ultimately defeating Manipur's forces decisively the British authority virtually took over the administration of the kingdom of Manipur on 27 April 1891 even though it was not annexed to the British Indian Empire. The British permitted the establishment of native rule defining the position of the Raja as subordinate to that of the Queen Empress of India. Rs. 50000/- was stipulated for an annual tribute to be paid by the Raja and his successors to the British Government. Henceforth the British Political Agent was also made the Superintendent of Manipur State.

Tripura was never formally incorporated into British India, and therefore the Manikyas (kings of Tripura) were not required to pay any tribute to the British. They, however, paid a token 'nazarana' to the British at the time of any prince's accession to the throne. Right from the time of the Mughal rule the Manikyas held a zamindari estate known as Chakla Roshnabad in the plains on the west of the hilly terrain of Tripura.

After coming on the scene, the British had not changed this arrangement. When the system of permanent settlement was introduced in 1793, that zamindari was also made a permanently settled one in favour of the Manikyas. Thanks to this zamindari settlement, a king at the time of his accession to the throne paid nazarana to the British in order to get his accession recognized by them. Of course, the Manikyas paid annual revenues to the British for holding the zamindari as per the permanent settlement terms.

The hilly part of Tripura was left to be independently ruled by the Manikyas. This position has been also confirmed by Mackenzie according to whom ".....the Rajah who is an ordinary Bengali zamindar on the plains, reigns as an independent prince over 3000 square miles of upland and was for many years a more absolute monarch than Scindia or Puttiala - owning no law but his own soverign will, bound by no treaty, subject to no control, safe in his obscurity from criticism or reform"[20]. The hilly part of Tripura was accordingly known as 'Independent Tipperah' (later just 'Hill Tipperah'). However, with the appointment of the Political Agent by the British at Agartala in 1871 some form of indirect rule over the state was imposed.

Through the political agents posted at Imphal and Agartala the British intervened into the affairs of Manipur and Tripura. The political agents advised the princes to bring about reforms in the systems of administration of law and justice, ensured maintenance of peace and orderly fiscal management in order to curb unwarranted profligacy of the princes. The rulers were also persuaded to take steps to open up their closed politico - economic structures and develop the infrastructure for providing to their subjects access to the modern medical and public health services, educational facilities, postal services, etc and effect reforms of the social evils like slavery, *sati* (particularly in Tripura), the cruel methods of inflicting punishment on the criminals, etc. Development of external trade was also especially encouraged.

2. The British Tribal Policy in North-East India

As already noted (p. 27) the hillmen practising shifting cultivation were unable to attain self-sufficiency in food production on a sustained basis. They exchanged some of their non-food surplus farm and forest products to procure from the plains the foodgrains, salt and sundry other commodities they required. There was also demand from the plainsmen for the hillmen's surplus products. Therefore markets for exchanging goods produced by the hillmen as well as by the plainsmen were set up in the foothill areas by the rulers of the different political units.

Despite such trade relations, periodically the hillmen raided the villages in the nearby foothill areas and looted food stocks and other materials they found in the villages and even took away men and women as captives to use them as their slaves. Some of the highlanders claimed that the foothill villages fell within their jurisdiction and hence they had the right to collect some sort of a royalty of the products gown there by the plains villagers. To restrain the hillmen from plundering the villages in the plains the Ahom rulers sometimes closed the passes used by the hillmen for coming down to the markets in the plains. These steps, however, could not completely stop such raids from the hills. Therefore to protect the villagers the Ahoms introduced the system of payment of some compensation in kind called *posa* to the Chiefs of border tribes in the North Eastern Hills as a *quid pro quo* for the chiefs to ensure that no such plundering raids were committed by them anymore In respect of the tribes of the North Eastern Hills, such as, the Bhutias of Char Duar (Rs.1,740), the Thebangia Bhutias (Rs. 146), the Akas (Rs.700), the Daflas (Rs.4,130), the Miris (Rs.1,118) and the Adis, the British also followed the policy of *posa* payment in cash against the pledges of the respective tribes to refrain from realizing the so-called tributes from their neighbouring foothill villages falling within the Government administered territory. The amounts of *posa* paid to the different tribes were as indicated within brackets against each.

As the colonial power consolidated its rule over the plains of Assam, it had to deal with the border tribes like the Garos, Khasis, Nagas, Mizos, Kukis, Karbis, North Cacharies and also the tribes of the North Eastern Hills who had economic and other kinds of transaction with the plainsmen. The British took upon themselves the task of maintaining law and order and protection of life and property within the territory under their administrative control. In the beginning they followed the policy of non-interference in the affairs of the tribes. But as and when the tribals raided and plundered the plains villages, the local administrators took steps to stop such raids and even made armed interventions to capture the offenders and punish them, if necessary, even entering into the hill villages concerned. Such expeditions into tribal territory were often resisted strongly and violently by the tribals causing deaths to the military personnel of different ranks.

On some occasions the British even intervened in settling inter-tribal disputes and massacres. The tribal people, in their turn opposed the expansion of British rule and the presence of the foreigners in areas so close to their own territories. They were apprehensive of losing their freedom and control over their domains as the foreign power would be bent upon capturing their hills and villages unless resisted. As time passed relations between the Government and the tribes soured causing frequent clashes and losses of life and property. For example "Ten military expeditions were led into the Naga Hills between 1835 and 1851", as recorded in the Administration Report for 1921-22," the greater number of which were to punish raids"[21](p.43). In the course of such expeditions often tribal villages were burnt down as a measure of inflicting punishment. In the wake of these events, the Government of India took the stand, as spelt out in the Governor General's (Lord Dalhousie) Minute of 20 February 1851, that the Government would not interfere into the internal affairs of the tribes unless they committed 'mischief' within the British territory. But they would be encouraged to trade with the plainspeople 'as long as they are peaceful towards us'. Should they become 'turbulent or troublesome', this facility would be totally stopped.[22]

This policy did not work. Tribal raids into the so-called British territory occurred and violent resistance to British armed expeditions into tribal villages caused loss of lives on both sides and burning down of villages. The process culminated in the annexation of Naga hills to British India as a district of Assam in 1881.

This largely defines the common pattern of British relations with the tribes that ultimately led to the annexation of the tribal polities and territories into British India as a part of Assam but these were kept outside the normal administrative jurisdiction of the elected executive authority of the Provincial Government of Assam. It was decided that the tribal people should be "governed in a simpler and more personal manner than those of the more civilized and longer settled districts. It was, therefore, provided by the Frontier Tracts Regulation II of 1880, that the operation of unsuitable laws might be barred in all the hill districts (of Assam), in the North Cachar sub-Division, the Mikir hills tract in Nowgong and the Dibrugarh frontier tract in Lakhimpur."[23] Accordingly by issuing an order under this Regulation the areas just mentioned were excluded from the operation of the Civil Procedure Code and exemptions were made in regard to payment of stamp duties, court-fees, fees for registration, for transfer of property, etc. Moreover, a simpler system of administration of justice in civil and criminal matters was prescribed under the Scheduled Districts Act.

3. The Inner Line Regulation

The usual transactions and intercourse between the people from the plains and the hill people across the frontier often led to disputes and serious disturbances. In the 1860s the traders from the plains keenly competed with each other for procuring India-rubber brought down by the hillmen. These transactions caused frequent disturbances. Extension of tea plantations to areas beyond the border-line into the tribal territory also led to clashes and destructions that created problems for the Government relating to maintenance of peace and order in the region. "In order to prevent the recurrence of these difficulties," writes Gait, "power was given to the local authorities by the Inner Line Regulation of 1873 to prohibit British subjects generally, or those of specified classes, from going beyond a certain line, laid down for the purpose, without a pass or license, issued by the Deputy Commissioner and containing such conditions as might seem necessary."[24]

Accordingly, an Inner Line was laid down in the following districts: – In the Balipara Frontier Tract towards the Bhutias, Akas, and Daflas; in the Sadiya Frontier Tract and Lakhimpur, towards the Daflas, Miris, Abors, Mishmis, Khamptis, Singphos and Nagas; in the Sibsagar subdivision of the Sibsagar district, towards the Nagas. For some time the Inner Line was also maintained along the Lushai border."[25]

Even as the Inner Line Regulation did not completely stop the inter-ethnic intercourse and trade transactions causing flow of forest and other natural resources out of the hills resulting in some loss of bio-diversity, this measure proved in the long run quite effective, rigidly regulating the migration of plainsmen to tribal areas and eliminating any possibility of alienation of tribals from their lands, forests, water, mineral and other resources. This has been the most crucial factor in the differences between the tribal communities of North East India, excluding those of Tripura and the Assam plains, and those in other parts of India in respect to the preservation of indigenous social and cultural institutions and practices and economic power of maintaining indigenous system of community or other forms of ownership and command over land and other productive resources. To such resources the individual members of the community enjoyed equitable access as informed by their traditional egalitarian ethos.

The British Government also exerted influence, and in some cases even used pressure, on the rulers of Manipur and Tripura to follow similar policy in order to preserve the tribal identities and to eliminate the possibility of alienation of tribals from their lands and other natural resources. After quelling the Kuki rebellion and the upheavals in the hills of Manipur which continued for two years, from 1917 to 1919, the British Government devised a new arrangement for administration of hill areas. These areas were placed under the direct jurisdiction of the Maharaja who would decide matters on the advice of the Political Agent.

Another significant aspect of British policy was to ensure investments of funds for social and economic development of tribal people and to bring about changes in the administrative and judicial structure and to build up public health services and communication facilities without opening up these areas for unrestricted entry of outsiders for trade and exploitation of natural resources and settlement in land.

C. The Political Economy of Imperial Intervention in Assam

The historical events that opened up the opportunities for the British to intervene in the affairs of "the north -east frontier of Bengal" and ultimately to occupy the entire region could not be considered just a fortuitous combination of circumstances[26] making it unavoidable for them to assume the responsibility of bringing peace and order into the trouble-torn region by driving out the Burmese and quelling the different local rebel groups who were indulging in plundering, killing and creating all sorts of disorder and indulging in lawlessness. Even admitting the justification of British involvement in restoring peace and order in Assam, Manipur and the neighbouring principalities, one could not say they were wholly motivated by a disinterested interest, for the British themselves also stood to gain from these developments. In fact, they sought to boost their trade transaction with Assam and the adjoining territories on favourable terms[27]. When Captain Welsh was deputed with the Company's troops in 1792 to put down the Moamaria rebellion he was asked by the Governor - General in Council to submit a report on Assam giving information about the monarchy, aristocracy, civil, military and ecclesiastical departments of government, military strength, etc. and also to furnish details about the prospects of commercial intercourse between British India and Assam. As directed, Welsh prevailed upon the Ashom Raja to agree to his proposal for effecting 'Commercial Regulations' in terms of which the Raja's monopoly custom *Chawkey* at Candahar on the Assam - Bengal border was abolished. This was done to facilitate free flow of trade between Bengal and Assam. Welsh mentioned in his report that this arrangement resulted in yielding 'great pecuniary advantage' to the British and led to 'the improvement of trade between the two states'.

Welsh was directed to indicate the possibility of maintaining 'beneficial commercial intercourse between the two states' in the event of Welsh's withdrawal from Assam. The report was also to mention 'to what extent and in what articles' trade between India and Assam might be carried on. Accordingly Welsh submitted detailed lists of importable and exportable articles pointing out the 'problem, extent and actual state of commerce'[28].

The East India Company began assessing prospects of advancing their commercial interests by promoting trade transactions with the north eastern frontier territories even before Welsh's entry into Assam in 1792. For the company was aware of the fact there was a regular trade of considerable volume existing between Bengal and Assam during the Mughal period. It made them interested in exploring the prospects of entering into north - eastern trade. "The structure and the quantum of trade in the region," observes Bhattacharjee, "attracted the attention of the English East India Company to North East India when they were engaged in Bengal trade in the medieval period"[29]. And Welsh after assessing the prospects of expanding trade transactions with Assam wrote to the Governor - General that he was confident that "with the restoration of peace and order in Assam a new source of wealth and riches must flow to the Company"[30]. With this end in view, on 28 February 1793 he persuaded the Ahom King Gaurinath Singha to enter into a commercial agreement with him as the representative of the English Government at Ahom court with the object of establishing "a reciprocal and entire liberty of commerce between the subjects of Bengal and Assam for all singular goods and merchandizes"[30].

In the initial phase the British, it seems, overlooked the 'economic worth or surplus revenue - yielding potentiality of this region' which prompted them to pronounce: "We are not led into your country by the thirst of conquest but are forced, in our defence, to deprive our enemy of the means of annoying us" - British proclamation to the Assamese, March 1824.[31] But soon they realized that they underestimated the economic worth of the region as a base for expanding the volume of trade with this region as also with the neighbouring countries. It further dawned on them that by overhauling the indigenous land management system they would be able to mobilize surplus revenues. Following the discovery of the fact that there were vast areas of uncultivated and uninhabited wooded lands in these sparsely populated territories they started the process of identifying the most productive (and, of course, profitable) system of resource use for economic development that would serve the interests of the colonial power and also, of course as a fallout, those of the local people.

Amalendu Guha has interpreted these happenings as the colonial intention of turning "Assam into an agricultural estate of tea-drinking Britons and to transform local traditional institutions in such manner as to suit the colonial pattern of exploitation".[32] In Great Britain by the beginning of the nineteenth century capital accumulation for investment in industrial development in addition, indeed in preference, to that in commercial ventures assumed decisive economic importance. This economic change had a significant impact over the British trade policy vis-à-vis India and ipso facto Assam. "In 1813 the monopoly of the East India Company for British trade with India was abolished, and twenty years later its monopoly of British trade with China also came to an end. 'John Company' ceased to be a trading concern, but retained until 1858 the shadow of political power, of which the substance had long since passed to the Ministers of the Crown".[33] The Government became specially concerned about creating conditions favourable for investment of British private capital in India and expanding market opportunities for British manufacturers as well as those turned out by the industries started and managed by British entrepreneurs in India.

In Assam from this time on the Government initiated the process of colonisation primarily for the development of tea plantations. For this purpose by 1871 in more than 3 lakh acres of so-called 'waste lands' were settled the tea planters in Assam.

This was the beginning not only of settlement of land in favour of European planters but also immigrants from other parts of India. Sanjib Baruah has, therefore, rightly observed that British conquest of Assam turned this state into a 'land frontier attracting large-scale immigration'. He has also opined that the colonial state designated large areas of Assam as "waste lands" available for tea plantations or for peasent settlers, was the reward of conquest ......". This entailed dispossession of the local gentry, peasantry and the hunting-gathering and shifting cultivating community[34]. Baruah has, however, questioned colonial rationale of designating unoccupied wooded lands 'wastelands' and the right of the colonial power to give away 'wastelands' as it pleased. This approach violated the 'social meanings' of land to the people of precolonial Assam.

Several studies in the history of the British occupation of Assam and the rest of North East India conclusively prove that the prospect of development of tea plantation and tea manufacturing in Assam, Cachar and some neighbouring areas was one of the very important factors motivating the British to adopt the policy of occupying Assam and the rest of North East India.

J.B. Bhattacharjee has claimed that the British estimation of the possibility of commercially growing tea in North East India got confirmed by the discovery of tea plants growing naturally in Cachar.[35]

Priyam Goswami has analysed the significant economic circumstances that prompted the British to look for an alternative source of supply of tea under their own control to end their dependence on exclusive source of tea from China. Since the time the Europeans began taking tea and developed it into a habit, they had been depending solely on the Chinese supply.

Following the ban on import of tea into England from Europe imposed in 1669, it was the English East India Company which enjoyed the monopoly of operating tea trade in England.[36] In 1833 the East India Company's monopoly of British trade with China was rescinded by the Government and thereby the import of tea into England was thrown open to competition in order to bring down the price of tea for the benefit of the consumers there. For 'Tea was a question for every Englishman's breakfast table'.[37] Importance of tea trade in England's economy and also in the fortunes of East India Company would be evident from the fact that it accounted for "about 1/10th of the total revenue of England and the whole profit of the East India Company."[38]

Earlier the East India Company did not show any interest in exploring the possibility of development of tea plantation in India when it was approached by some English tea enthusiasts for ending England's total dependence on the

Chinese tea. But after 1833 the Company earnestly wanted to provide opportunities for investment of British capital and enterprise to grow tea in India where the soil, topography, climate, and a number of other conditions were favourable for tea cultivation. And since indigenously grown tea plants were already discovered in Upper Assam in 1823, prospects of tea plantation in the sparsely populated cultivable lands in Assam appeared very bright. To translate such possibilities into realities the British went in for the occupation of Assam and its neighbouring areas by any means, fair or foul.

We must not also overlook the primary politico-historical aspect of British involvement in the affairs of the North East frontier of their Indian empire. Burmese invasion of Assam and some other parts of north-east India actually sounded an alarm signal for the British who were themselves an imperial expansionist power. Roy Burman therefore thinks that the British got an excuse in 1824 for imperial aggrandisement and colonial expansion eastward, where prospects of tea cultivation, so highly coveted and lucrative in the sphere of international commerce existed, and where, if necessary, pressure could be exerted on China from the vantage point on its frontier to grant favourable terms to the British traders in their overseas trade with Canton".[39]

Internally, the colonial power pursued the policy of extending the boundary of its empire towards the northeast so that by occupying this vast resourceful and sparsely populated region, where the people followed the pre-capitalist subsistence mode of productive activities, it could not only encourage and patronize the metropolitan capitalist entrepreneurs to turn the virgin forests and the so-called waste lands into tea plantation areas by introducing the capitalist agrarian structure but also expand markets for British manufacturers and provide preferential opportunities for investment of surplus accumulated capital from the home country in the downstream and complementary industries entailing exploitation of mineral resources and development of transport and communication lines. Such enterprises, it could be visualized, would be mutually sustaining and yielding economies of scale and profits from both vertical and horizontal combinations of enterprises.

NOTES AND REFERENCES

1. *Report on the Administration of North East India (1921-22)* (hereafter Admn. Report 1921-22), p. 1.
2. Amalendu Guha (1991), *Medieval and Early Colonial Assam, Society Polity Economy,* published for Centre for studies in Social Sciences, Kolkata, by K. P. Bagchi & Company, Kolkata, New Delhi,. p.15
3. *Admn. Report 1921-22,* p.12
4. *ibid.*
5. *ibid* .p.. 11
6. *ibid.* p. 12
7. *ibid.*
8. *ibid.* p. 12-13
9. *ibid.* p. 24
10. Rajen Saikia (2000), *Social and Economic History of Assam 1853-1921,* Manohar, New Delhi. pp. 73-4.
11. *ibid.* p. 52
12. *ibid.* p. 64
13. R. B. Pemberton (1835), *Report Upon the Countries on the Eastern Frontier of the British Territories,* Reprinted in 1979 by Mittal Publications, New Delhi, p. 134-35.
14. K. K. Datta (1961), *Survey of India's Social Life and Economic Condition in the Eighteenth Century,* Calcutta, as referred to by J. B. Bhattachrjee (2000), Trade and Colony, *The British Colonisation of North East India,* North East India History Association Shillong, p. 42.
15. J. B. Bhattacharjee, *ibid.* pp.10-11
16. *ibid.* p. 42
17. Francis Hamilton (reprint edn. 1963). *An Account of Assam,* Guwahati, referred to by S. D. Goswami, Department of History, Dibrugarh University, Assam, Bengal Trade in the early nineteenth century: Role of the Custom - House, unpublished seminar paper, p. 2.
18. Sir Edward Gait (1997), *A History, of Assam,* Seventh Edition, Lawyer's Book Stall, Guwahati, p. 200.
19. Amalendu Guha (1988), *Planter - Raj to Swaraj Freedom Struggle and Electoral politics in Assam, 1826 -1947,* Peoples Publishing House, New Delhi, Reprint edition. p. 2
20. Alexander Mackenzie (1995), *The North -East Frontier of India,*

first published in 1884 entitled "History of the Relations of government with the hill tribes of the north-east frontier of Bengal", reprinted by Mittal Publications, New Delhi. p. 272.

21. *Admn. Report* 1921-22, p. 43
22. *ibid.* p. 43
23. Gait, *op. cit.*, p. 316
24. *ibid,* p. 317
25. *Admn. Report* 1921-22, p. 91
26. In the concluding chapter of his work, "History of the relations of Government with the hill tribes of the north-east frontier of Bengal" Alexander Mackenzie observed : "Fate seems determined to prove that there shall be no rest for the English in India till they stand forth as the Governors or advisers of each tribe and people in the land". Mackenzie, *op. cit.* p. 369.
27. S. K. Bhuyan interpreted the objective compulsions and objectives of British intervention in Assam as follows:

    "In Assam, as in other theatres of commercial adventure, the British had to compete with other European merchants. The trade was profitable, but not very flourishing, owing to the quarrels and disputes amongst the merchants, and to the civil strife then raging in Assam. The British who had become masters of the neighbouring province of Bengal were ultimately compelled to interfere in the affairs of Assam in their own interest, and this eventually led to their occupation of the country". (*Anglo-Assamese Relations 1771-1826,* Third Lawyer's Edition, Guwahati, 1990, Preface, vi)
28. Welsh's Report on Assam, 1794, quoted in Mackenzie (1995), *op. cit.* pp. 377-378.
29. Bhattacharjee, J. B. (2000), *op. cit.* P. 6.
30. Bhuyan, S. K. (1990), *op.cit.* pp. 339 and 340.
31. *ibid.* p. xiii
32. Guha, Amalendu (1988), *op. cit.* p. 2.
33. Trevelyan, G. M. (1963), *A Shortened History of England,* published in Pelican Books, 1959, reprinted in 1960,1962, and 1963, p. 504.5.
34. Sanjib Baruah (1999), *India against itself, Assam and the Politics of Nationality,* Oxford University Press, New Delhi, p. 47.
35. Jayanta Bhusan Bhattacharjee, *Cochar under British Rule in North East India,* Radiant Publishers, New Delhi, p. 189.

36. Priyam Goswami (1999), *Assam in the Nineteenth Century: Industrialization and Colonial Penetration*, Spectrum Publications, Guwahati: Delhi, p. 17-20.

    She has pointed out that the East India Company financed the procurement of tea from China by illegally exporting opium from Bengal to China. In order to check the menace of opium consumption China had prohibited import of opium into China as early as 1800. Yet the East India Company continued to import opium to China clandestinely even by bribing the officials. The dispute over trading in opium in China ultimately led to the waging of the Opium War of 1840-42.

37. Flora Annie Steel's observation is quoted in Montfort Chamney, *The Story of the Tea Leaf*, p. 30. Here it is reproduced from Priyam Goswami, *op.cit.* p. 18.

38. Priyam Goswami, *op.cit.* p.18, foot note No. 45.

39. B.K. Roy Burman, *Prefatory Introduction to Alexander Mackenzei*, (1995). op. cit. p. 7.

3
THE PRE - COLONIAL SYSTEMS OF LAND DISTRIBUTION AND LABOUR UTILIZATION

The Paik System in Assam; Lallup System, the Lois and Kei-roi-thau in Manipur and the Tripura Model - Slavery in North East India, that is in Assam, Manipur and Tripura - Abolition of slavery in these States - Women's role in Economic performance in Assam, Manipur and Tripura.

1. The Paik System in Assam

In the early part of eighteenth century when the British extended their domination over the North-East India, Assam, Manipur and Tripura were monarchal states. Productive activities of the people were almost wholly concerned with agriculture and allied activities. In a milieu such as this land and land-based resources and labour force were the most important means of production, the level of capital accumulation being almost negligible. In all the three states the monarchy exercised absolute control over both land and the subjects who were a source of labour. Therefore they devised specific systems of enforcing this right to distribution and to productive activities like building of homesteads, temples and monasteries and mobilization of labour for producing goods and services including military services and services for building social overheads (public utilities). The feudal control over their subjects was also exercised for engaging them to perform domestic duties for the kings and their relations, nobles, high civil and military officers and favoured religious establishments.

For all these purposes the Ahoms introduced the *paik*

system. Under this system excepting for the nobles, priests and persons of some selected high castes and "those engaged in replaceable occupations the whole adult population were liable to render service to the state as labourers and soldiers"[1]. They were known as paiks who were organised by forming *gots* consisting of three or four *paiks* so that one member of each could be asked to render services to the state in rotation enabling the remaining members of the got to cultivate that paik's land and make available food for his family. Each *paik* was allotted 2 *puras* (about 3 acres) of wetrice land (*rupit*) free of rent. He also had his homestead land (*bari*) rent free. While over such land he enjoyed hereditary and transferable rights, the 2 *puras* of *rupit* land called *gamati* was the absolute property of the state over which the paik enjoyed no hereditary or transferable right at all.

The *paiks* were employed in peace time for public works, such as construction of tanks, embankments and roads.

Above the *gots* stood the *khels* consisting of 20 and more *paiks* controlled and managed by designated officers of specific hierarchy. An officer known by the name of *Bora* commanded 20 paiks, a *Saikia* 100, a *Hazarika* 1000, a *Rajkhowa* 3000 and a *Phukan* 6000 paiks who were subjected to as rigid a discipline as that of a regular army. These officers were recruited from the high nobles of Ahom clan. The Ahom Kings did not pay any remuneration to any of their officers but assigned a certain number of *paiks* to each instead. These *paiks* were required to render services to their respective officers as they did to the king before they were placed under their officers.

Paiks were treated by the king as his alienable subjects who were also assigned to the high priests and *Brahmans* for managing temples. "Some paiks purchased exemption from services. In no other way could a man escape from the control of the officers of his *khel*, whose jurisdiction was personal and not local"[2]. The *paiks* were of two categories, namely, *Kanripaik* and *Chamuapaik*. Though both were grouped into *khels* a *Kanripaik* had to render manual services of any kind to the state. A *khel* of the *Chamuapaik* was required to pay taxes in the form of their specialised products or their skilled services. Such *Chamuakhel* represented the artisan classes like goldsmiths, gold washers, braziers, fisherman and oil pressers. These *khels* were like guilds. But paiks_belonging to such guilds were much fewer in number than the *Kanripaiks* who constituted the bulk of the peasantry.

Besides giving 2 *puras* of land, to the paiks over which they had no permanent right of holding, the Ahom kings donated considerable areas of land to the privileged few like the nobles, priests and subjugated chiefs or kings of vassal states. Over such lands the donees enjoyed permanent and heritable rights of holding. Besides land the donees were also assigned *paiks* and slaves for cultivation of their lands and for performing other kinds of duties. Vast estates of farms known as *khats* were also owned by the King himself, his queens, brothers, princes and princesses along with *paiks* assigned to them for cultivation of the *khats*. The above system of distribution of land rights and mobilisation of labour power for public works was not a unique one. Similar systems obtained in the Kingdom of Manipur, where it was known as *lallup*.

2. The System of *Lallup* in Manipur

The command structure of the King of Manipur over his subjects for harnessing their services both for military and for civil duties represented the basic component of the political-economic system. In this system it was compulsory for every man aged between 17 and 60 to render free services to the state for ten days in every forty. As an individual attained the age of 17 he became entitled to have one *pura* of cultivable land (roughly 3 acres) for his and his family's support. He had however to pay taxes in kind, like lallup service, for instance, to the king for this piece of land. The system had some flexibility; an individual could avoid rendering *lallup* services for the required period when his turn came by providing a substitute in his place or by paying a certain sum of money to someone or to a group of lallup workers who would agree to do the work assigned to him under *lallup*. This amount was not payable to the state but only to the substitute workers. Also, a man suffering from serious illness or becoming permanently disabled before attaining the age of 60 was exempted from performing *lallup* duty.

The system covered all civil and military services that were to be rendered by the subjects. In times of peace emphasis was given to the public works. *Lallup* workers were also commissioned to meet personal needs of the King, members of his court and of nobles for building and maintenance of the palace and for running the palace workshop and so on. Even the tribal subjects living in the hills were required to render free *lallup* services so as to enjoy their right of access to forest and hill lands for shifting or terrace cultivation in accordance with their traditional community management system. Many public works – building of public roads, river embankments, channelling of the flows of streams for irrigating paddy fields etc. were carried out with the help of *lallup* labour. The whole of Manipur valley was divided into 6 *pannas* or divisions to facilitate administration and management of the functioning of the *lallup* system.

Besides *lallup*, there was also the system of division based on professional functions or occupations among the specified households known as *yumnak mashin*. Some families were assigned the work of maintenance of temples and worshipping of deities (as priests). Other professionals included weavers, dyers, artificers, goldsmiths, blacksmiths, carpenters, brass and bell metal workers, etc. Surnames of the families of different professional groups were decreed by royal edicts. There were seven *salais* (clans) who were divided into 538 *Yamnaks* or surnames[3].

3. The Lois: The Kei-Roi-Thau

Pottery, sericulture and silk-cloth weaving, boat-making, salt manufacturing, iron smelting, distilling of *yu* (country liquor), cutting of posts and beams of timber, making of canoes, cutting grass for Rajas etc. were exclusively operated by the *Lois* who held the status of the lowest caste or division in the society.

Another class of people named *Kei* (originally slaves of the Raja) also had a lowly position in the society. Their duties were to provide rice for the Raja's household. In the 19th century when the supply of rice under this arrangement became insufficient a new system called *kei-roi-thau* or work of *Keis* and *Lois* was introduced. This work was imposed on the residents of all places outside the capital. It was not confined to the supply of rice alone; any work or the supply of any other article could be demanded under orders of the Raja. This arbitrary and oppressive system was commonly resented by the affected persons.

Within the *lallup* system the structure of an occupational division of the population was built up by royal edicts. These divisions were not absolutely rigid; some flexibility was permitted in order to meet the needs of the King and his household and also of other members of the royal court. Occupational divisions were linked with hierarchical groupings of population on ethnic lines. McCulloch's study reveals that the population of Manipur was divided into the following descending order of hierarchy: the Meitheis, the Phoongnai, the Tengkhul (Naga), the Ayokba (captured slaves made to work for the Raja), the Kei, the Loi and the Mohammedans. The Meithei population was divided into four groups called *pannas* of different ranks which were linked with the nature of work performed by them. All of them had to attend to their assigned duties for every ten days in forty. The members of these *pannas* took part in the skilled jobs of house-building, bridge-building, boatmaking including collection of timber for such building activities, etc. Some of the members also worked as goldsmiths, silversmiths, blacksmiths, carpenters, brass and bell metal artisans, weavers of royal clothes, keepers of Raja's elephants, ponies, etc. "In fact", writes McCulloch, "excepting the lowest description of service, there is scarcely any which is not performed by some part of the Meithei population"[4].

Neither in Assam nor in Manipur land was scarce for the farming population. Vast areas of cultivable waste land were available for extension of area under cultivation. To encourage the cultivators to reclaim waste land for cultivation favourable terms were offered. In such a situation there was hardly any landless agricultural labourer in these states. This was the main reason why the donees of land grants by the Kings had to depend on the paiks (in Assam) and *lallup* workers (in Manipur), besides slaves for cultivation of their lands. The institution of slavery was common in all the north - eastern states, including the hill areas (more about the system later).

4. The Tripura Model

The case of Tripura was somewhat different from these states. Tripura's contact with Bengal under the Mughals and later under the British influenced the administrative structure as also the land management system. The total area of hill Tipperah by which name the state was known at that time was of 4086 square miles out of which about 2869 square miles (i.e., 60% of the total area) consisted of hilly terrain and marshes not fit for settled plough cultivation without reclamation entailing heavy labour costs. Of the remaining 40% of the land only about 100 square miles were under actual cultivation in 1871 as recorded in the administrative report for 1886-87. Thus some area of land in Tripura also remained as cultivable waste land. The indigenous population belonging to different tribes, who practised shifting cultivation on the hill slopes had no separate holdings owned by them individually. Some form of community ownership of forest lands was in vogue. For using the forest land for shifting cultivation they had to pay an annual house tax to the King. Cultivation in the plains was mostly done by Bengali settlers in the state. A few tribal settled cultivators were, of course, also there. As the state was sparsely populated and as the revenues of the government could be augmented mainly by the process of extension of land settlements, the King encouraged the people in the neighbouring province of Bengal to come and settle in the state. This was done by offering attractive terms for waste land settlements retaining the King's ultimate right over the lands.

The Law Research Institute, Eastern Region, Gauhati High Court, Gauhati which conducted a study of the land system of Tripura opined that some system of land revenue assessment of the cultivators was imposed since the Kings had to pay revenue to the Mughals and the British in respect of the plain areas. "But what principles the King followed in assessing the land-revenue and whether the assessment was related to the yield of the land is still shrouded in obscurity. The Kings are known to have made extensive grants of land for religious and charitable purposes free of rent. They are understood to have settled lands most often with the people of the upper classes in perpetuity and on fixed rents. Settlement of land with the actual cultivators at a nominal rate of rent or free of rent in lieu of services rendered to the state was also prevalent, but it was confined to small areas"[5]. W. W. Hunter in his Statistical Account of Hill Tipperah observed that the King of Tripura was the only *zamindar* or 'superior landlord' in Hill Tipperah. Even as he retained very little area of plainsland under his own management, he made many grants of land in perpetuity at a fixed rental. The lands not granted like this were farmed out for revenue collections. "Small *taluks* or perpetual tenures are often granted with only a nominal rent reserved; and, in these cases, where the grantee is the actual cultivator, he virtually enjoys the position of a peasant proprietor. Such cases, are, however, the Political Agent reports, extremely rare, as a talukdar in possession of even 3 *bighas* or one acre of land generally employs labourers to cultivated for him"[6]. This arrangement was possible because of the availability of agricultural labourers who were ready to work as wage labourers. Detailed legal provisions relating to land settlement and land revenue were promulgated for the first time in as late as 1880.

In Tripura's land management system in the plains there was some element of compulsion under which the cultivators had to render services against settlement of land for personal cultivation as in Assam (*paik* system) or in Manipur (*lallup*). Express imposition of obligations on the part of the Raja's hill subjects to render free services to the state known as the "Taithung" and the "Lahar" was also there. The former was the system for compelling the hill people to provide the officials of the government at the time of their tours of hill areas, with free services of guides and labour for carrying their goods and personal effects. The system of "Lahar" required the hillmen to clear the jungles and make the forest paths suitable for movement of the officers-in-charge of the hill areas. In Tripura also, besides the agricultural labourers slaves were employed for cultivation of land owned by the nobles and other privileged few who got land grants from the King. These members of the upper strata maintained slaves for performing their domestic duties also.

5. Slavery in North - East India

The origin of slavery as a form of application of human labour power to productive activities treating humans as an exchangeable commodity can be traced to 'a rather early stage of development of production'. At that stage it became evident that human labour power was able 'to produce considerably more than was needed for the producer's maintenance'. This realization coincided with the growth of 'division of labour and of exchange between individuals'. And then the 'truth' was discovered 'that man, too, may be a commodity; that human power may be exchanged and utilized by converting man into a slave'. Frederich Engels continues to state: "With slavery, which reached its fullest development in civilization, came the first great cleavage of society into an exploiting and an exploited class. The cleavage has continued during the whole period of civilization. Slavery was the first form of exploitation, peculiar to the world of antiquity, it was followed by serfdom in the Middle Ages, and by wage labour in modern times"[7].

The humankind reached the stage of civilization from that of 'Savagery – the period in which the appropriation of natural products, ready for use, predominated". Thereafter came the period of 'Barbarism' when 'knowledge of cattle-breeding and land cultivation was acquired'. Humans learnt 'the methods of increasing the productivity of nature through human activity'. The transition from Barbarism to 'civilization' signified the acquiring of "knowledge of the further working-up of natural products, of industry proper, and of art"[8].

Engels' linking of the institution of slavery with that of civilization well explains the basics of the practice of slavery on an extensive scale both in the plains and in hills of north-east India in the pre-colonial period. Of course the systems of private ownership of property and trade and exchanges of commodities evolved in the hills much later and also on a less extensive scale than that in the plains. There was, however, an important distinction between the sources of slaves in the two sub-regions. In the plains the poor, destitute and heavily indebted persons became slaves of the well-to-do propertied and politically privileged persons in the society including functionaries of religions institutions. Both the slaves and slave-owners were in most cases members of the same ethnic community but belonging to different castes or professional classes. In the hills most of the slaves were the captured plainsmen who were the victims of occasional raids carried out by the hillmen in the foot-hill villages. In the course of inter-tribal wars also captured tribals of the defeated groups were treated as slaves though such cases were few. In the tribal villages in a few cases, the persons who committed crimes were punished; they were made to serve their fellow victims as their slaves. Economic, social or political compulsions under which freemen became slaves varied from one part of north – east India to another. The relations between the slaves and their masters and the duties performed by the former also were not of the same kind everywhere. Nor were the social status of the slaves and scope and opportunities for the slaves to become freemen same all over the region. All these aspects of slavery had important impacts on the productive activities and the economy of the sub-region concerned. Therefore it should well be in order to portray all aspects of slavery in this region state by state.

6. Slavery in Assam

The Ahom rulers of Assam introduced the novel system of enlisting every male adult as a *paik* who was required to render services to the state in the sphere of public works, to attend to the private services of the King and his nobles and to take part in military service at the time of war. It was strictly prohibited to make any *paik* a slave. Only the prisoners of war, criminals under sentence of death and some freemen could be assigned by the King to the nobles for working in their estates as slaves[9].

The institution of slavery was an important element of the Ahom system of management of the economy. Since labour force was the main source of creation of wealth, land being nearly abundant for the given size of the population at that time, the upper classes, including the priestly class and temples were allotted *paiks* and slaves by the government to enable them to get their farm lands cultivated. The slaves were also employed for attending to domestic services and gardening in their homestead and temple compounds.

The slave force in Assam also consisted of children,

victims of distress sales by their parents, to discharge their debts and / or even to meet their subsistence needs. Children of existing slaves and those born to slave mothers became slaves even if their fathers were freemen.

Adult men and women sold themselves as slaves for discharging their debt obligations or even to secure bare maintenance. This class of slaves could be freemen after serving for an agreed period of time to repay the debt. Though formally they were bondsmen, seldom could they clear their debts within the stipulated period of time and therefore they were ultimately reduced to the status of slavery.

A substantial number of slaves were, of course, prisoners of wars and criminals who could escape death sentence by becoming slaves of the nobles and priestly classes.

"Again", writes N. K. Barooah, "many Assamese had been enslaved by the hill tribes advancing from the Burmese borders towards the Sadiya frontier after the outbreak of Ahom civil wars in 1814. The Burmese invasion merely enlarged the opportunities for such slaving by the Khamptis and Singphos who accumulated many thousands of slaves"[10].

7. Population of Slaves

Several estimates were formed of the population of slaves in Assam by different authorities in the early colonial period. Captain Adam White's survey put the number of slaves in Upper Assam for 1830 at 11,000 slaves and 4,000 bondsmen. According to him in the districts of Kamrup, Darrang and Nagaon about the same time there were 27,000 slaves. "In 1853, in Kamrup or Guwahati district alone, according to statistics furnished by the Collector, out of a total population of 193,331, the number of *pykes* were 122,216, slaves 3,396 and bondsmen 24,700; of 70,286 females, 25,206 were slave girls"[11]. These facts reveal that slaves and bondsmen, who were quasislaves, constituted 14.5 per cent of the population. In the case of women the picture was worse as nearly 36 per cent of them were slaves.

Amalendu Guha noted that thousands of slaves and bondsmen were liberated after the occupation of Assam by the British. Even then in the 1830s out of the estimated population of 271,944 of Kamrup district about six per cent were slaves and about three per cent were bondsmen.

Presuming that the figures for the other districts would be similar, he concluded : "at the close of the Ahom period, some nine per cent or so of the total population were slaves and bondsmen"[12].

8. Slavery in Manipur

Slavery was also extensively practised in Manipur as an institutional form of employment of a considerable proportion of total labour force in productive activities in the field as well as for rendering personal services to the slave-owners and performing their domestic duties. Brown, Mc Culloch, Hodson, et al have observed that slavery in Manipur was of milder form and not comparable with that in the western countries in respect of harsh treatment of the slaves. Mainly there were two classes of slaves in Manipur : some had to become slaves in order to repay their debts taken from their would be masters. And a slave remained a slave until the debt including interest was fully repaid. A similar kind of bondage could be the fate of a person who, in utter helplessness, needed money for meeting some unavoidable expenses and to obtain that from a person of resources he offered himself to be the latter's slave. These slaves, or more appropriately, bonded labourers, were fed and clothed by their owners. There were cases of parents in abject poverty selling their children for money to avoid starvation. Such slaves lived almost as members of the family and they were generally treated well by their masters. Cases of ill treatment must have been also there, otherwise why were there instances of slaves running away from the owners' houses? Some even escaped into British Indian territory where they were immediately set free.

Also having been unable to pay compensation for committing a crime as decreed by the court, some people became slaves. When a thief was caught but the stolen goods could not be recovered from him, he and other members of his family could be seized and sold. They would be performing duties as slaves until the stolen goods were fully recovered. A defaulting debtor and the members of his family faced similar fate. Also, any culprit involved in an adultery case who was unable to meet the claim for damages would be subjected to slavery[13].

The Raja himself had battalions of slaves numbering from 1200 to 1500. The social classes of such slaves after they were liberated came to be known as *Ayokpa, Tengkul* and Kei. When the rulers changed, the slaves of the outgoing rulers, according to the traditional practice, were redistributed among the incoming rulers. In the 1860s the King ordered that the slaves would remain the property of their owners under all circumstances[14].

All slaves in Manipur were broadly grouped into two classes: 'the one, the absolute property of the buyer, called *meenai chanaba* (meaning "to belong to and be fed by a man") the other *asalba*, or a slave for such time as the money paid to him, or advanced on him, may not be paid back"[15].

Slavery in any form depresses labour efficiency and productivity. It not only severely restricts civil liberty but also narrows the space of choice of the persons in bondage and thereby hampers human development.

9. Slavery in Tripura

To sustain the system of slavery as existed in Tripura in the premodern period, slaves were procured from the neighbouring states who were captured there and offered for sale to outsiders. It was an old practice of engaging slave eunachs in the King's palace for different specific duties.[16]

The magnitude of the problem of slavery in Tripura was considerably less than that in Assam and Manipur. In the plains of Tripura majority of the King's subjects were immigrant Bengali cultivators and middle class professionals. Slavery among these classes of people was practically non-existent. But the *thakoors* who were relations of the King and enjoyed several official privileges maintained slaves for doing their domestic duties. T.E. Coxhead, officiating Political Agent of Hill Tipperah, in his report of 1876 as submitted to the Government of Bengal stated that it was a common thing "for a hillman when in difficulties to sell himself for a period in consideration of the debt incurred being liquidated. Sometimes he sells himself without any restrictions as to the term of his slavery, sometimes he sells himself with his wife and children. Women also dispose of themselves for the same reason".[17] The children of slaves who died without discharging the debt or fled leaving them behind became slaves. The position of girls who were such slaves was the most pitiable. The system was obviously resented by the hillmen at large. The Political Agent cited the case of two women slaves kept by Gour Chandra Thakoor, who were released from slavery on the intervention of the Raja himself to whom the case was referred by the Political Agent. A similar order of release was passed by the Raja on receipt of a complaint from a Hillman, who was a resident in British territory, whose wife and children were detained in slavery in Hill Tipperah. "They had been living as slaves in the house of the Raja's son-in-law, a young widower; and the Raja's interference shows that even family bias will not always prevent him from seeing that justice is done when a case demanding it is clearly laid before him."[18] The Raja told the Political Agent that he disapproved of the custom of slavery, for which reason there were no slaves in his own household.

10. Abolition of Slavery in Assam

Low technology-based subsistence farming was the main foundation of Assam's economy having a feudal structure of socio-political hierarchy. Labour productivity was at a low level and the system of slavery was an important factor in dampening labour efficiency. The feudal environment did not foster entrepreneurial skill in organizing productive enterprises. These factors contributed to the prevalence of the vicious circle of low labour productivity, low level of income, low savings - income ratio, negligible capital accumulation and investment resulting in the continuance of low level of income. The ruling oligarchy considered their slaves as their main assets which they acquired mostly as free gifts, from the ruler and hardly paying anything for procuring slaves.

Therefore, as the colonial rulers started consolidating their rule in Assam and mobilizing revenue by reorganizing the revenue system, abolishing some of the privileges enjoyed by the upper classes during the Ahom rule, raising revenue rates, both the upper and the poorer classes were economically very hard hit. The slaves were almost the sole asset of the former class; therefore they were involved in selling away their slaves to overcome distress. On the other hand many tenants fled their farms and habitats to avoid paying higher rate of land rent and many others offered themselves or their children to be slaves so as to survive the ordeal.

The famine of 1825 made the plight of the cultivators, that is the paiks, particularly deplorable. Particularly, because they had to pay land revenue and taxes from which they were earlier exempted by the Ahom kings.

Being unable to pay taxes they sold themselves as slaves so that they might claim exemption from such payments. David Scott, the Governor General's Agent in Assam, in the face of such a grim situation issued a proclamation permitting such enslavement of *paiks*. This led to a fall in the collection of revenues. "To make up the losses, innumerable extra cesses were levied and a host of farmers of revenue were scattered over the district (Kamrup) whose extortion and oppression compelled many of the *pykes* to conceal themselves amongst the slaves of those who could afford them adequate protection. In fact there had been so much concealment of *pykes* that the Agent had to institute an enquiry into the title by which slaves were restored to their original rank of *pykes*".[19]

Scott's Proclamation was, however, denounced by authorities in England who considered slavery in every form "an evil of great magnitude and particularly revolting to the moral feelings of Englishmen".[20] Scott believed that slavery was so much ingrained in the socio-political structure of Assam that its abolition in a hurry would adversely affect the upper classes in Assam who depended on their slaves and bondsmen for their livelihood. He even argued that such a step would imply infringement of their right to hold private property. Slavery, he opined, was socially, culturally and even legally acceptable to the people of Assam. Moreover, the slaves of Assam were not harshly treated as elsewhere. "In poor and middling families, the slaves and bondsmen were treated like the other inmates, the same kitchen serving for the whole household, and both mistress and maid being entirely clothed in home-spun-dress. Among the rich they often obtained great influence and ruled their master's affairs in the capacity of *ghar-giris* or dewans".[21] The picture of slavery in Assam was somewhat confirmed by the Indian

Law Commission on Slavery. "It appears to be the general opinion", they wrote, "that the slaves in Assam were on the whole well treated".[22] Scott's Assistant, Adam White, after enquiring into the condition of the slaves reported that slaves were more or less on par with the agricultural labourers. "They were employed in cultivating the lands of their masters and received a fair amount of clothing. If a person possessed many slaves he only required the labour of a few in rotation and allowed the others to engage in the cultivation of lands, for the rent of which he became responsible, reserving to himself what profit there might be after allowing the slave a fair maintenance".[23]

Scott and contemporaries in Assam believed that any attempt to abolish the system of slavery abruptly would be wrong. They were not blind to the evils of the system, but aware as they were of the organic nature of the society opined that the process of reforms should be slow and without infringing the proprietary rights of individuals.[24] But mounting evidences of human sufferings caused by the continuance of the system impelled some officials to contemplate positive actions for ameliorating the conditions of the poor and helpless humans who had no other alternative for survival than becoming slaves/bondsmen.

T.C. Robinson, Scott's successor, received the following report on slavery from Rutherford in Civil Charge of Nowgong: "The system of slavery now existing and which is daily obtaining a greater hold in Assam must be abolished or restrained. It appears astonishing the number of people who from the pressure of rent have sold themselves for trifling sum and become bondsmen with their wives, families and descendants until the original sum which they can never have the means of realising is obtained".[25] In 1832 the Government of Bengal made the sale and purchase of slaves from one district to another illegal. Robertson accordingly issued an order "prohibiting sale or mortgage of a native of Assam to a foreigner". Any infringement of the order would attract punishment which was imprisonment for a period of six months.

About the same time the Governor General in Council had to take steps under the Chartered Act of 1833 to abolish slavery as and when it would be "safe and practicable". Accordingly rules were promulgated in August 1837 to facilitate the gradual emancipation of slaves and bondsmen in Assam. "Slavery however continued until 1843 when it was abolished under Act V of the Regulations".[26]

The abolition of slavery however caused disruption in the field of agricultural production and economic losses to the members of the nobility and priestly classes who depended on the services of slaves and bondsmen for getting their estates cultivated. On the other hand the emancipated slaves also suffered as they had neither land nor any savings with which they could acquire land and be free farmers. And for survival many of them returned to their masters to "servc as *bandhas* (bond *labourers*), *bherunias* (agrticultural labourers), and *marakiyas* (landless wage labourers). Slavery in a less rigorous form thus survived even when trafficking or keeping slaves became an offence in the Indian Penal Code 1860".[27]

11. Abolition of Slavery in Manipur

Investiture of Churachind Sing, who was a minor, as the Raja of Manipur was celebrated on 29 April 1892. On the same day, Maxwell, the then Political Agent and Superintendent of the state, announced the abolition of the system of slavery. He proclaimed, "all persons at present in slavery to private individuals shall cease to be slaves in five years from the 29th April (1892), or any previous date on repayment of the purchase money". The system was so much deeply ingrained in the socio-economic structure of Manipur, particularly in its rural areas, that it continued to operate, there in some form or other till the British paramountcy over the state came to an end in 1947.[28] It is obvious that without determined follow-up actions in liberating the slaves and enabling them by providing necessary resources to take up productive activities on their own, the system could not be completely abolished. Of course, the formal abolition of slavery certainly enabled many such unfortunate persons to cut off their ties of bondage and become free labour with human dignity.

12. Abolition of Slavery in Tripura

Slavery was abolished in British India by Act V of 1843. In Tripura, however, on the insistence of the British Government through their Political Agent the Rajah of Tripura Bir Chandra Manikya finally issued a Proclamation in 1877 "forbidding the sale, purchase, receiving in pledge, or forcible detention as a slave, of any human being, under penalties to be awarded by the criminal courts, but authorizing the making of contracts of service for a period not exceeding three years".[29]

The slaves then existing were thus given the option of leaving their masters or staying with them for a period up to three years but all future dealings in slaves were forbidden. This provision was made in order to give time to the slave-owners to be accustomed to manage their domestic duties without the services of slaves. It was also advantageous for the slaves who could find time to seek gainful employment elsewhere as free humans.

By the time slavery was abolished in Assam, Manipur and Tripura administrative, judicial, land settlement and land revenue systems were restructured by the British either directly as in Assam or through the respective Rajas by applying persistent pressure and with persuasion. The basic thrust of these reforms was to create peasant proprietorship so as to enable the peasants to get plots of land settled in their name for which they were required to pay land revenues as fixed by the Government. These were temporary settlements, revenue rates for which varied from time to time. The Paik and Lallup systems were abolished. In Goalpara district of Assam and in some parts of Tripura land settlements were on a permanent basis. Not all the cultivating households, however, could become peasant proprietors. Some of them could become tenant and sub-tenant farmers on payment of rent to the landowners and others became landless agricultural labourers. Most of the former slaves who did not have the means to get land settled in their names on payment of revenues became agricultural labourers and only in a few cases sub-tenants of peasant proprietors. On the whole the transition from the system of slavery to that of peasant and landless tenant farming and wage farming as landless agricultural labourer was an important development in the matter of land and labour use management. This change led to an augmentation of investment in land improvement and an increase in labour productivity, as also total agricultural output.

13. Women's Role in Economic Activities

The women of North East India were free from the handicaps of the *purdah* system. They enjoyed freedom of movement both inside and outside their homes. This environment was conducive to their actual participation in the different sectors of productive activities. They played an active role in agricultural operations, animal husbandry, collection of forest produce, running of household industries like spinning and weaving of cotton, silk and woollen textiles and preparing cloths besides managing housekeeping. The people of both the plains and hills of North East India had predominantly subsistence economies based mainly on cultivation of food and non-food crops partly by practising the system of settled cultivation in the plains, and partly by that of swidden (shifting) cultivation in the hills. The agrarian sector also covered collection of forest produces, hunting, fishing and animal husbandry. Of course, this primary economic sector could not be sustained without having the secondary sector consisting of household industries to produce necessaries like cotton, woollen and silk clothes and to process agricultural crops, forest products, dairy and poultry products, etc. The region had also some surplus over subsistence for disposal of which the people carried out some volume of trade and exchange (mostly of barter type), both internal and external. In this paradigm of economic activities the women's role was of vital importance since they were involved in productive activities in all the three sectors of the economy. Many women, particularly of Manipur and of some hill areas, took part in trading activities with much acumen that helped boost total volume of productive activities and family incomes.

In fact, women constituted nearly fifty per cent (if not more) of the total effective strength of the economy's labour force. While the menfolk were frequently required to render military service to the state, their participation in agricultural and allied activities on a sustained basis was minimal. Had the women not regularly participated in farming and non-farming productive activities these economies would not have endured. Given the extremely low level of capital acc-umulation, if at all there was any, capital output ratio was nearly nil. Given also the fact that technology of production was of a very low level, labour-output ratio by contrast was very high. And in this situation the women labour power played the most crucial role in keeping the economic system going. Even though this was the picture common throughout North East India, there were some variations in the specificities of involvement of women in economic activity in different parts of the region.

14. Assam

"The women of Assam", writes Hem Barua, "have a distinct place in the economy of the family; they take an active part, mostly in eastern Assam, in the rearing of crops. They transplant the paddy seedlings and reap the harvest when ripe".[30] In Assam there was no separate weaver class or caste. All Assamese women, irrespective of caste or creed or social position, took part in weaving and every house did have at least one loom. Weaving constituted the most essential part of a girl's education and she who did not know this art was looked down upon by her neighbours and relatives. Observing this aspect of Assamese culture Gandhiji commented in *The Young India* in 1921: "Every woman of Assam is a born weaver. No Assamese girl who does not weave can expect to become a wife. And she weaves fairy tales in cloth".[31] The women wove silk and cotton cloths with beautiful designs of indigenous art in their home looms. They remained busy carrying out agricultural operations, processing of agricultural crops like husking and winnowing of paddy and cooking food for the family, fetching drinking water and collecting minor forest produce, feeding pets and poultry, fishing, etc. Therefore, they remained very busy almost the day. In addition to such strenuous works they devoted much of their hard-earned leisure time to weaving. This was possible because it was a kind of creative leisure for them.

15. Manipur: Position of Woman in Society, Economy and Civil Society

Meitei women have been the solid bastion of traditional Meitei culture and civilization. The Meitei kings were engaged almost in constant warfare with the neighbouring powers and the hillmen of the hills flanking the Imphal Valley. Under the *Lallup* system, every Meitei male between the age of 17 and 60 was required to render free service to the king for ten days in every forty. Besides every male could be conscripted by the kings for waging wars with other powers. This was possible because the Meitei women, who were extremely industrious, used to perform the productive activities related to agriculture, animal husbandry, cottage industry and internal trade besides the domestic chores. These constituted the mainstay of the Meitei economy and, therefore, the role of women was of vital importance in keeping up the superstructure of Meitei state going and expanding.

Rice was the main agricultural crop which was grown mainly by using the method of transplantation of seedlings. Women worked in the paddy fields from early morning for preparing fields, sowing seeds, nurturing seed beds and transplanting seedlings, weeding, etc. These activities were generally performed by women of a particular village in groups, the system being known as *khut lang.*[32] For harvesting crops, which called for mobilization of large work force, men joined women in completing the work quickly. Kitchen gardening for growing vegetable both for self-consumption and for exchange fell within the sphere of women's activities.

They did the work of feeding and taking care of domestic animals – cows, buffaloes, ponies, goats, fowls, ducks, pigeons, etc.

Meitei women have been traditionally very good spinners of cotton yarn and weavers of cloth. Every woman irrespective of her family's political and economic status took part in these activities. Every family's common requirement of cloth were met by women of the family who produced the materials on their own looms.

Selling surplus agricultural, horticultural and household industrial products and buying goods for family's consumption and meeting other needs were jobs exclusive to women. In fact the markets were run by women themselves. As the Meitei women worked more hours in farming than men it was a 'female farming system' as defined by Ester Boserup.[33]

The gamut of women's activities further included 'embroidery, rice pounding, fishing and helping in house-building' etc.[34]

Meitei women value cleanliness. They keep their houses spic and span and the court-yards clean. Cloths and utensils are regularly washed. Naturally the level of sanitation and hygiene in Meitei villages is generally good.

Despite the important role played by Meitei women in productive and other activities which constituted the core of Meitei culture and civilization, their status in society was not commensurate with it. They had little say in the decision-making process whether in the affairs of the family or the spheres of society and state. This position further worsened after the Meiteis embraced Vaishnav cult of Hinduism in the 18th century. The position of women in society was affected by the custom of polygamy common among the well-to-do Meiteis. The treatment meted out to women by their husbands according to Brown was virtually no different from that associated with 'domestic slavery'. He observes "women are really the slaves of their husbands; they are sold in satisfaction of their debts, and it is said that men often pawn their wives to purchase some office or even a pony".[35]

Meitei personal law was heavily weighted against the interests of women. This law was based on the *Puyas*, i.e., the accepted law or the command of the ancestors. This has been stated in detail by Sanabam Raghumani in his paper, 'Meitei Personal Law'[36] which claims; "The husband is the master and is entitled to deal with the women in the light of his title inherited in his cattle or slaves".[36] Inheritance of ancestral property was traced through the male line. A woman's property in Meitei law could consist of the presents given by her parents at the time of her marriage or after it. 'Movable property' records Raghumani, 'is women's real property'. Any property (movable) given to a wife by her husband after her marriage with him could be retained by her even after divorce from her husband. Any piece of property purchased with a woman's own property remained her property. The basic deprivation of women related to the fact that they had no title to land even though, rather paradoxically, 'female farming system' obtained in Manipur.

Without playing down such social infirmities of Meitei women, it may be asserted that their energy, skill, enterprising sprit and hard-working habits found their expression in increased production of goods and services in the farm and non-farm sectors as also in the trade they carried on as they were free farm living in 'purdah' and, more, enjoyed the rights of free-mixing and unrestricted movements in the fields, roads, markets. Women's contributions to the growth of Meitei economy as reflected in increased production of goods could be considered very high. Their participation in trade and exchange served as an important incentive to production of surplus over family's own consumption needs. And this was the significant propellant of growth and accumulation of wealth.

Launching organised protest movements by women against state policy to influence state actions and policies at different points of time both before and after 1891 marks an important feature of Manipur's economic history. In the configuration of Manipur's civil society, women's mass movements stand out as an important component.

16. Tripura

In the plains of Tripura the population consisted of the immigrant Bengali peasants, middle class professionals, and some tribals who settled down in permanent wet rice cultivation in the plains. The distribution of population religion-wise shows sizeable Muslim population which consisted of immigrant peasants and artisans. Since the Muslim women, other than the elderly ones, were kept behind the *pardah* they were unable to take part in agricultural and other activities in the fields. The Hindu component of population was caste ridden and women of the upper caste did not take part in field operations. It was only the women-folk of the lower peasant caste who took active part in agricultural operations and in animal husbandry. Weaving of cloth was the monopoly of the weaving caste. In weaving women belonging to these families did take part though not exclusively. It was largely the work of menfolk. Women of all classes, castes, and religions, of course, did manage house-keeping which entailed cooking, washing, cleaning, etc.

In the hill economy of Tripura women's role was very important, indeed, as important as in other parts of North East India. They practised shifting cultivation; in the model of this form of cultivation they followed the principle of division of work on the basis of sex. Women's exclusive participation involved husking rice, pressing oil, collecting fire wood, fetching water, feeding pigs & poultry, carding cotton, spinning yarn, weaving cloths, cooking food, brewing rice beer, cleaning house, etc. There were some activities which involved the joint participation of women and men, such as sowing, weeding, watching, harvesting, transporting jhum products from the field to the house, fishing and marketing of *jhum* products, if any, threshing paddy, shelling sesamum.

NOTES AND REFERENCES

1. Edward Gait, *A History of Assam,* Calcutta, 1967, p. 249
2. *ibid.* p. 250.
3. Details of the system of *lallup* have been culled from the following sources:
   (i) R. Brown, *Statistical Account of Manipur,* first published in 1874 reprinted in 1975, Sanskaran Prakashak, Delhi, p.83.
   (ii) T.C. Hodson, *The Meitheis,* reprinted edition, Neeraj Publishing House, New Delhi 1984 (first published by David Nutt, London 1908), p. 59.
   (iii) Gangmumei Kabui, *Glimpses of Land and People of Ancient Manipur,* published in Naorem Sanajaoba, Manipur Past and Present Vol. I, Mittal Publications, New Delhi, 1988.
4. W. McCulloch, *Account of Valley of Manipur and of the Hill Tribes,* Calcutta, 1859, parts of which are quoted in Hodson, 1984.
5. Law Research Institute, Eastern Region, Gauhati High Court, Guwahati Directed by J.N. Das, *A Study of Land System of Tripura,* Guwahati, 1990.
6. W.W. Hunter, *Statistical Account of Hill Tipperah,* 1876, p. 503.

7. F. Engels, *The Origin of the Family, Private Property and the State,* Foreign Languages Publishing House, Moscow, 1952, pp. 286-87.
8. *ibid,* p. 46.
9. H.K. Barpujari, *The Comprehensive History of Assam,* Vol. V, Publication Board Assam, Guwahati, pp.209-10.
10. N.K. Barooah, *David Scott in North-East India 1802-31: A Study in British Paternalism,* New Delhi, 1970. p.161.
11. H.K. Barpujari, *op. cit.* p. 213.
12. Amalendu Guha, *Medieval and Early Colonial Assam: Society Polity Economy* Centre for Studies in Socieal Sciences, Calcutta, 1991, P. 56.
13. R. Brown, *op. cit.* p.91.
14. *ibid.*
15. T.C. Hodson, *op. cit.* p. 90.
16. Nalini Ranjan Roychoudhury, *Tripura through the Ages, A Short History of Tripura from the Earliest Times to 1947 A.D.,* Sterling Publishers Private Ltd. New Delhi, 1983, p. 51.
17. T.E. Coxhead, Officiating Political Agent, *Hill Tipperah, Administrative Report for 1975-76,* reproduced in Dipak Kumar Chaudhuri (ed), *Administrative Report of the Political Agency, Hill Tipperah (1872-1878),* Government of Tripura, Vol. I, 1996, pp.79-80.
18. *ibid.*
19. H.K. Barpujari, *op.cit.* p.211 (based on the Report of Francies Jenkins).
20. H.K. Barpujari, *ibid,* p. 212.
21. H.K. Barooah, *op. cit.* p.162.
22. Quoted in N.K. Barooah, *ibid,* p.163.
23. *ibid.*
24. *ibid.* p.170.
25. H.K. Barpujari, *op. cit.* p. 213.
26. *ibid.* p. 214.
27. *ibid.* p. 214-15.
28. Gangmumei Kabui, Socio Religious Reform Movement and Christian Proselytism, Published in Lal Dena (ed), *History of Modern Manipur (1826-1949),* Orbit Publishers, New Delhi, 1991, pp. 98.

29. C.W. Bolton, *Political Agent, Hill Tipperah, Administration Report on Hill Tipperah for the year 1877-78,* reproduced in Dipak Kumar Chaudhuri, *op. cit.* p.134.
30. Hem Barua, (1962), *The Red River and the Blue Hill,* Lawyer's Book Stall, Guwahati, pp. 87-88.
31. Quoted in Rajen Saikia, (2000), *Social and Economic History of Assam, 1853-1921,* Manohar, New Delhi, pp. 73-74.
32. Ksh Bimla Devi (1988), Manipuri Women - A Study, published in Sanjaoba (Ed), *Manipur: Past and Present,* Vol.I, p. 167.
33. Easter Boserup, (1970), *Women's Role in Economic Development,* George Allen and Unwin, London, p. 16.
34. Ksh Bimla Devi, *op. cit.,* p.167.
35. R. Brown, (1975), *Statistical Account of Manipur,* first published in 1874, reprinted in 1975, Sanskaran Prakashak, Delhi, p. 77.
36. Noarem Sanajaoba (Ed), (1988), *Manipur: Past and Present,* Vol. I, History, pp. 329-348.

4
TRIBAL ECONOMIC FORMATIONS IN NORTH EAST INDIA IN THE PRE-COLONIAL INDIA PERIOD

1. Introduction

About 200 tribal communities[1] lived in the hilly areas spreading over an area of over two lakh square kms and covering the present day states of Arunachal Pradesh, Assam, Manipur, Meghalaya, Mizoram, Nagaland and Tripura[2]. They were at different stages of economic formation. Most of the tribal communities practised shifting cultivation in order to produce their food crops, such as, rice, millet, maize corns, job's tears, besides vegetables of many kinds, oil seeds (mainly sesame seeds), some tubers like tapioca, arum, ginger, etc, as also their main fibre crop, namely cotton. But some tribes were still dependent mainly on hunting and gathering for meeting their subsistence needs. Among their other occupations was collection of forest products, such as, timber, bamboo, thatch, for building houses, medicinal plants, lac, wax, ivory, and a number of other minor items of forest produce including fruits, nuts, eatable green leaves, bamboo shoots, etc. The Apa Tanis, Bhutias, Khampties, and a few other tribes such as, some of the Naga tribes, viz. the Angamis and Chakesangs, practised settled cultivation by terracing hill slopes to produce food and other essential crops.

Besides agriculture, horticulture, animal husbandry, fishing, poultry farming, animal husbandry and simple manufacturing activities at the household level also comprised the bases of the tribal economy.

The semi-domesticated *mithun* (Bos Frontalis) was the

animal most commonly reared by the tribal communities since the animal thrived in the bio-climatic features of large parts of North-east India which were most conducive to its growth and living. The animal was sacrificed as a ritual in some of the religious festivals.

Further, this animal flesh was an important item in the feasts hosted by the chiefs and others who could afford. Some of the well - to -do tribals accumulated wealth in the form of *mithuns*. It also served as a medium of exchange in many transactions.

Even being at a comparatively high level of economic formation many of these tribes continued to pursue the traditional practice of hunting and gathering for their livelihood. Often the highlanders carried out predatory raids on the villages of settled cultivators in the plains and looted their movable properties, such as, agricultural and manufactured products. They even forcibly carried off persons - both men and women - to use them as their slaves. The permanently settled cultivators living in dispersed villages in the plains could not effectively resist such raids of the fierce hillmen. After making such raids the tribesmen swiftly retired to their hills along with the looted goods and the captives. It was not always possible for the Ahom rulers to conduct punitive expeditions into the tribal villages in the north- eastern hills to bring to book the guilty ones. Nor could the Ahoms build up strong defences around the threatened villages of the plains against such intruders descending from the hills. In order to conciliate the tribes Ahom King, Pratap Singh (1630-1641 AD) reached an agreement with the Akas, the Daflas, the Miris and the Adis of the north-eastern frontier hills (present - day Arunachal Pradesh) granting them the right to collect annually a part of the produce of certain villages of the plains and enjoy the benefit of labour-services of the specified numbers of *paiks*. These *paiks*, of course, got remission from rendering equivalent quantum of labour services to the Ahom ruler.

The Bhutias grew barley and wheat in their farms located in the highlands as well as valleys. They also cultivated mustard, pulses, maize, sugarcane and fruits. Productivity per unit of land was low on account "of infertility of the soil" and their "primitive method of cultivation"[3]

2. Models of settled cultivation as Practised by Tribes

The Angamis and Chakesangs of the Naga Hills, the Tongkhul Nagas of Manipur (hilly part), the Apa Tanis, the Khamptis and the Monpas (of Towang) in the north eastern frontier hills practised settled cultivation by terracing hill slopes. All these tribes adopted highly effective systems of irrigating the rice fields by suitably channeling of waters of their respective hill streams into the successive rungs of terraces. As required for raising crops year after year they also used different kinds of manures in such fields of theirs. The farm tools used by these tribes were different only in some cases from those used by the shifting cultivators. The Monpas used plough for preparing land for cultivation and they applied a mixture of oakleaves and nightsoil as manure to produce wheat in the terraced farms. The Khamptis practised settled cultivation in the plains of the Lohit valley to grow rice in plenty. They had their own indigenously developed plough which was drawn by buffaloes and even at times by elephants.[4]

The system of settled cultivation on terraced fields as practised by the Apa Tanis living in about 20 square miles of area located in the present- day Subansiri district of Arunachal Pradesh is by far the most successful and efficient system of wet- rice cultivation. They have succeeded in ensuring irrigation of their ricefields on a perennial basis. The Apa Tani valley is surrounded by hills inhabited by other tribes. In their isolated single broad valley they practised a highly advanced system of irrigation for growing paddy in plenty yielding surpluses which they could exchange with their neighbouring tribes for their necessaries not produced by them.

The elaborate system of tapping stream water for flooding their terraced rice fields shows their masterly skill in utilizing the stream waters to the maximum extent possible for growing rice, which is their staple food crop. C. Von. F. Haimendorf has given detailed description of the system.[5]

"Every one of the larger streams rising on the wooded heights that ring the Apa Tani country is tapped soon after it emerges from the forest and reaches a gully wide enough to accommodate a series of narrow terraces. A short distance above the terraces occurs the first diversion from the stream but usually only a little water is here deflected; the stream continues on its course while the feeder channel, branching off at an angle, leads water along -side the series of terraces so that by blocking or opening the connecting ducts any field can be flooded or drained as required. ...." (p. 25). Different varieties of paddy are grown on the terraces of different elevations and moisture-content capabilities. On some of the terraces the stubble is left to rot to serve as fertilizer. Such terraces are not ploughed or hoed. " In their planting season women go over the field planting seedlings in between the old stubble but the entire field remains undisturbed for many years, and manure is only scattered over the surface" (p. 27).

The other terraces not kept under water for the whole year are prepared for transplanting paddy seedlings before the cropping season begins. Fields are cleaned and hoed and then irrigated by directing the flow of water from the nearby channels until water seeps through the soil to make it soft and muddy. Then the field is "puddled by young men, who supporting themselves between two poles, tradle the mud underfoot, so that to a depth of two or three feet the soil is churned to a smooth thick paste. On these fields the three varieties of early ripening rice (......) are grown"[6]. They build terraces as high as it is possible to build, even though these cannot be irrigated by connecting them with channels to obtain stream water. These fields are almost entirely rain-fed, which is why their yields are lower.

They meticulously prepare the nursery beds for growing paddy seedlings for transplanting to the terraced fields. They weed the permanently flooded terraces two or three times, and the others not so flooded 'as much as five times'.

Different varieties of paddy crops ripen at different times beginning from August and continuing up to September or October. Millet and maize are their dry season crops. Separate fenced plots are used for growing a variety of vegetables, millet seedlings and tobacco. Bamboo groves, pine trees and orchards are located in the gentler hill slopes.

They are very particular about the sustainable use of

soil for cultivation by maintaining its fertility unexhausted. "Throughout the winter and spring months, from the end of harvest until the time for transplanting, women and men are to be seen daily carrying baskets of rice chaff, pig and chicken droppings, ashes and kitchen refuse to heap on their fields"[7].

Their villages are built on higher ground lying above the flooded rice-fields. Dwelling houses are built on wooded piles ' but constructed mainly of bamboo and thatched with rice straws.' "Space is limited in an Apa Tani village and the houses stand wall to wall in streets and narrow lanes. Here and there a street broadens to form a small piazza, in the centre of which stands an open assembly platform (*lapang*). The houses of the wealthy stand in the reasonably broad main streets and usually near the assembly platforms, whereas those of humble folk are crowded together in back lanes".[8]

The well - stocked granaries are built on piles and fitted with some devices to make these rat-proof and are located in the outskirts of the villages to ensure their safety from the spread of village fires.

The Apa Tanis have well-defined system of private ownership of land. Besides some 'clan-land' and 'common village land' all cultivated land such as "irrigated rice-fields, land suitable for dry crops, garden plots, groves of bamboos, pines, fruit trees and other useful trees, as well as house - sites and sites for granaries" are privately owned. No wonder the influence and social prestige of an Apa Tani depends largely on the size of his land holding. 8 (a).

Since the Apa Tanis specialized in agricultural and horticultural farming, animal husbandry had a secondary role in their economy. They grew surplus of food grains which they exchanged with Nishi and Miri neighbours for *mithuns* and pigs. They ran their highly developed weaving industry by importing almost the entire quantity of cotton they required from the Nishis. 8 (b)

The Apa Tani tribe have a genius for organizing economy. The model of land use they developed in their plateau received approbation from every visitor to their plateau- for ecologically sound and sustainable technique of settled wet rice cultivation. Therefore they could maintain mutually beneficial trade transactions with their neighbouring tribes who practised unsustainable and deficient shifting cultivation to meet their subsistence needs.

Verrier Elwin has referred to the account given by a tea planter named H.M. Crowe who was probably the first visitor to the Apa Tani plateau where he spent Christmas in 1890. He was ' charmed and astonished' to find that in such a remote valley the Apa Tani society was highly organized, people were industrious and had developed an " extensive system of irrigated fields and, though ignorant of the plough, succeeded with their hoes in raising two annual crops for themselves and their neighbours." They lived fairly prosperous and happy life in their remote and isolated village.[9]

The Angamis of the Naga Hills also practised a highly developed system of settled cultivation by terracing hill slopes on higher elevations than that of the Apa Tani plateau. Several early British explorers of the Naga Hills in the nineteenth century were greatly impressed by the highly efficient and environmentally sound method of terracing high hill slopes and also irrigating and manuring the fields for growing rice on a permanent basis.

H.H. Godwin-Austen, who conducted the survey operations in the Naga Hills in 1872-73 observed: " Where the steep rise in the slope commences, the spurs are at once more level, and are terraced for rice cultivation; not a square yard of available land has been left, and the system of irrigation canals is well laid out"[10] According to him the rice is 'exceedingly fine and very nourishing containing much sugar and gluten' .... .They manure the fields before ' the first water is let in upon the fields.' They first raise rice seedlings in nurseries and then transplant in the fields just before the rains.[10]

R. Brown, a member of the Survey Party observed[11] that immense quantum of labour needed to be applied for making the terraces "and the skill manifested in irrigating them would do credit to a trained engineer." Terraces were built on the slopes of steep hills of great height starting from the highest level where water was available and were 'continued down to the base of the hills.' He further noted that- the terraces were at places 'relieved by patches of open jungle' and that the slopes of the hills below the villages were 'well wooded'. These features definitely helped conserve soil and maintain the terraces intact for years. The terraces varied in conformity with the varying nature of the ground. The height of 'the interval or step between the terraces' varied from 'a few inches to five or more feet.'

In his 'Rough Notes on the Angami Nagas' John Butler[12] highlighted the fact that the terraced lands were extremely productive being well- irrigated and well-manured. Irrigation channels constructed by the Angamis " often covered ' long distances by means of aqueducts ingeniously constructed of hollowed out trees, and sometimes bridging deep ravines'.

The Angamis use only a few simple farm tools for constructing terraces very ingeniously and irrigating, manuring, preparing nurseries, transplanting paddy plants, cultivating rice and other crops, weeding fields and harvesting crops. Besides the all purpose *dao* (big forest knife) and a small sized axe which are almost commonly used by all the tribes in north-east India, they use a light hoe with a crooked handle measuring about 18 inches to 2 feet in length with an iron tip of about a foot long. With these tools the Angamis require to put in much arduous manual labour for farming operations.

The Angamis carefully manure their terraces with cowdung wastes which they spread on the soil and mix with it with their hoes. The crooked and short hoe necessitates a very bent down position to operate it.

Complementary to cultivating crops they rear cows, pigs, goats, dogs and fowls 'both for the purpose of food as well as for sale and barter'.

Rice is, of course, the main crop cultivated in the terraces but they also grow millet (*jawar*) on higher terraces where irrigation water is scanty. They use this grain mainly for making their sour beer which they consume so freely. They also grew 'a kind of coarse dal or field pea', Indian corn , several varieties of small grains similar to what the Assamese call *koni dhan*, various kinds of yams, chillies, ginger , garlic, pumpkins and other vegetables, cotton 'in the lower ranges and low valleys', etc. Some of these crops are grown on their *jhum* farms.

In the Angami model of settled terrace cultivation, private ownership of land is well-recognized. They can freely sell and buy terraced fields just as they sell or buy a pig or a cow. Not all Angami households exclusively practise settled terrace cultivation. Many of them also practise shifting cultivation on hill slopes under forests where terracing is not possible and the method of slash and burn cultivation is only preferable. This is also done to produce some of their necessary crops, which cannot be grown on terraced fields. Their economy is thus organized for producing food grains, vegetables, fibre crops, oilseeds and other cash crops and for managing animal husbandry utilizing land, forest and water resources to the maximum extent possible whether by operating terrace cultivation or by shifting cultivation depend as it does on each system's suitability.

Land used for shifting cultivation is not, of course, privately owned in the same sense as it is owned in the case of terrace cultivation. Land distribution for such cultivation is controlled by the community, that is, the village council.

The Angami women represent the backbone of their economy. They play the most laborious and crucial role in running their economy as against men who spend most of their time in fighting and hunting excepting for building terraces in the initial period. Women work in the fields for cultivating various crops such as rice, cotton, tobacco and vegetables. All weaving of cotton and nettle - fibre materials is done by them. They also manufacture salt from the salt springs near their villages. Besides cooking, pounding rice, washing, fetching water, collecting fire wood and doing all other household works, they tend cows, goats, pigs, fowls, etc[13].

"The Angami villages are almost always large ones, Kohimah, the largest containing 900 houses. Many streets contain 400 or 500 houses, smaller houses being generally young offshoots from the others." [14]

The Angamis not only evinced their technological skill in designing and building terraces and irrigating them by drawing channels in the high hills, they also designed and built wooden sledges for carrying heavy loads such as stones. The sledge is " shaped like the prow of a boat, the keel curving upwards. Into this sledge the stone is levered, and carefully lashed with canes and creepers, and to this the men, sometimes to the numbers of several hundreds, attach themselves in a long line ,and putting rollers beneath the sledge, they pull it along until it has been brought to the spot where the stone is to be erected."[15]

The settled cultivators in the hills such as the Apa Tanis, the Bhutias, the Khamptis of the North eastern frontier hills, the Angamis and the Chakesangs of the Naga Hills, the Tongkhul Nagas of Manipur et al had as a rule much better and sustainable method of using land, water and forest resources for production of food and other crops. As a rule they were economically much better off than the other hill people whose economies were organized around the practice of shifting cultivation. We may now note the basic features of the economic model of shifting cultivation.

3. The Typical Jhum Model

Most of the tribes of North -East India practised *jhum chash*, that is the slash and burn or shifting cultivation. Excepting for some of its minor aspects the system of using forest land for their subsistence economy was broadly similar to those prevailing among all these tribes. The variations reflected the difference in their ecological settings and the techno- cultural efficiencies. The common feature of the system was to cut down the forest plants, mainly bamboo and a few small standing trees, bushes, creepers, reeds, etc. The bigger trees, if any, were generally left standing where they were. Cutting of jungle was done in the cold season and the debris was left to dry to be burnt to ashes which would serve as the fertilizer for the crops. In the period between mid- April and mid - June, that is, before the onset of monsoon, seeds of paddy, maize, millet, and a few other coarse grains, sesame, cotton, pumpkin, brinjal, chillie, beans and some other vegetables were dibbled into ash-filled holes dug by the blunt top of the dao (big hill knife). It was a system of mixed- cropping as a number of crops were grown in the same plot of land in a given crop year. The different crops became ready for harvesting in different time sequence.

Therefore growth of one crop did not interfere with the growth of other crops.

The jhum fields required frequent weeding out operations and constant watching to prevent wild animals and birds from damaging the crops. For this purpose a simple watch house on bamboo was built where usually the jhumia couple lived some months and operated indigenously made contraptions to scare birds away from crops, and also set up traps for rats, wild animals, etc. After harvesting all the crops that would continue up to the middle of the cold months the *jhum* plot was abandoned and left fallow to allow regeneration of bamboo and other forest plants which were burnt down for jhuming. In some parts of the region a given *jhum* plot was cultivated for two crop years in succession. If sufficient accessible forest land was available for *jhuming* by the villagers, then a plot once *jhumed* would be left fallow for ten years or so which was the normal time for the natural growth of vegetative cover to make it a suitable site for slash and burn cultivation.

Besides cultivation and processing of crops, productive activities of the shifting cultivators included horticulture, animal husbandry, such as raising poultry, piggery and rearing of semi-domesticated *mithuns* (*Bos frontalis*), fishing, collection of eatable and non-eatable forest products, hunting of games, weaving cloth, making nets, mats, baskets, manufacturing other handicrafts and agricultural, fishing and hunting tools, and also house - building. The jhumias did not produce every thing they consumed. They, however, produced certain surplus crops and collected forest products in excess of their own requirements. Therefore they took part in trading activities involving exchanges of goods with both fellow - tribals as well as non -tribal traders who visited tribal villages for buying surplus products of the tribals as also for selling goods - both agricultural and manufactured-to the tribals. Parts of such exchanges were of the barter type and parts involved cash as the medium of exchange.

Credit supply was an essential input for the less resourceful jhumias who depended on crops advance provided by the money lenders (mostly non-tribal *mahajans*) to meet their requirements of food and other essential items of subsistence during the lean months. Generally they repaid the advance after harvesting of the crops was over. The moneylenders charged very high rate of interest on crop advance they paid. Once a *jhumia* family took such advance it could seldom avoid taking it again year after year. In this respect the *jhumias* in Tripura were the worst affected.

The family was the basic unit of the organization of production which operated within the limits set by the village authority. The same authority normally controlled the distribution of forest lands among people around the villages (among the households) for *jhuming*. There was no individual ownership of forest land on a permanent basis. This, therefore, precluded the right to transfer a plot of land by any family which selected its plot every year or once in every two years as the case may be following the customary practice. Disputes, if any, among the families about the right to use a particular plot for *jhuming* were settled by the village council headed by the village chief. The *jhum* farmers were not required to pay any rent for use of forest lands for *jhuming*. However, among certain tribes, such as, the Kukis of Manipur and the Mizos in Mizo Hills, the tribal chiefs allotted lands to the individual household for shifting cultivation and even collected tax from the cultivating families.[16]

In the case of the Khamptis, the chief was ' the lord of the soil'. But he had to distribute the produce among the members of the community in proportion to each one's contribution to the total output retaining for himself only a reasonable portion of it.[17]

The practice among the Padams was such that whatever offerings were made to the chief (Gaum) plus whatever was received as fines, forfeitures and escheats were utilized for the benefit of the community as a whole.[18] In Tripura, the tribal *Jhumia* households were required to pay house -tax (*ghar-chukti kar*) to the Raja.

After the first year of shifting cultivation or, in some cases, after the second year the land was left fallow for regeneration of forest as also to become fit for slash and burn cultivation again. In the period following, access to the plot was restricted to the same household which cleared it. Of course, the village community exercised some control over it and could permit some other household to use the fallowed land for hunting and gathering activities and even for farming at the end of the fallow period in special circumstances. This custom of managing the fallow land was somewhat vague and flexible. Some writers maintain that the household which first cleared a plot of land for shifting cultivation enjoyed preferential right of use over that plot during the fallow period. Any village land not under cultivation was the common property of the villagers. Whatever might have been the actual practice, the fact remains that in the shifting cultivation regime so long as population did not exceed the carrying capacity of the village land (each village had its boundary marked by natural features like streamlets, forests, tree lines or the forest paths, etc.) no household was deprived of forest plots for cultivation. When all village lands were exhausted, the village shifted to a new site where enough forest lands would be available for shifting cultivation and hunting and gathering activities.

Next to land, labour was the most important factor of production. All able-bodied male and female members of the household of the ripe age for working took part in different farming operations, such as, preparation of fields for shifting or terrace cultivation, animal husbandry, horticultural farming, fishing, hunting and gathering. Mishra has noted in respect of the Mishings of Arunachal Pradesh that the women were 'the backbone of agricultural operations, from land preparation and sowing to harvesting of crops'[19]. This is also true of many other tribes in North East India with just a few exceptions. For an example, the Adi women of Arunachal Pradesh as Barpujari mentions, were not subjected to the whole burden of the field as was the case with most of these frontier tribes.[20] On the other hand Singpho women's drudgery of work was of the highest degree, observes Barpujari again quoting S.F. Hannay's 'Sketch'. They performed all household duties - cleaning the grain from the husk, spinning, weaving dyeing, etc. besides drawing of water, planting seeds, reaping crops and even cutting and fetching in firewood.[21]

4. Economics of the Jhum Model

"*In a typical jhum model* the system reproduced itself at the end of every production period. *Production was for subsistence only*. In other words, the system produced 'just enough to maintain itself'; it did not produce any effective surplus. There was no accumulation and investment of surplus for '*expanded reproduction*', and so no effective growth of output from year to year. It was a sort of stationary economy. It was also almost a closed system in the sense that the method of production did not entail any substantial use of inputs of production and goods of consumption imported from outside the system to pay for imports and or accumulation.

"The system evolved as the historical experience of the people and in harmony with the ecological environment. The social structure, with a few exceptions, was homogeneous in the sense that it was neither divided into castes nor into classes. The cultural ethos was informed by egalitarianism so that any family in distress was helped by the village community. If any family produced more than its requirement the surplus was used up in community feasts on different occasions. Villages were uni-tribal; mixed villages were almost unknown, customary laws and conventions evolved to inform social relations of the individuals and the families constituting the village society."[22]

5. Manufactures

The products of the primary sector comprising agriculture, horticulture, animal husbandry and forest products were not enough for the tribal people of North-East India who needed manufactured goods for maintaining their standard of living. In their self-reliant economic model they had to produce manufactured goods to meet their needs. Next to food and drinks, textiles, woollen and other fabrics were important items of production for self-consumption. Almost every adult tribal woman took part in ginning, spinning and weaving textiles on their loin looms. In the silk producing areas (very few) women were assisted by men in rearing silk and processing the cocoons for extracting silk yarn and weaving silk textiles. Rearing of sheep and collection of wool were done by men while weaving was mainly the duty of women. The tribals also consumed tobacco and in some areas even opium. Different brews of rice beer bearing different names were produced by the respective tribal households at their own level and mostly for self-consumption as well as ritual observances when the products were shared with other members of the community.

An important aspect of tribal economy was the manufacturing of salt from brine springs wherever those existed. This was done until salt became obtainable through import from outside. In the earlier days, in the absence of brine springs, ash produced by burning some species of banana plants was used as the substitute for salt.

Tribal artisans in different parts smelted iron and the blacksmiths produced iron tools, agricultural implements and other necessary equipment.

Pottery was not common in the north-eastern hills partly because the clay was not suitable in most places and partly because people were accustomed to use large and fine bamboos for almost every purpose. Of course pottery manufactures were there on a small scale in some parts. Elwin notes: "The Apa Tanis have a tradition of making attractive clay models of animals which are used as toys. In northern Siang the Membas and Khambas make beautiful images of the Lord Buddha out of clay."[23]

The Adis practised the craft of casting in brass. The Daflas made their own brass ornaments, dishes and sacred bells. The Sherdukpens and Khamptis turned out silverwork. The Khamptis and the Mishmis also practised ivory carving.[24] Some of the tribes were familiar with carpentry and some had the tradition of wood - carving. "In Kameng bowls, cups and dishes are made; magnificent masks are carved for use in ceremonial dances and Monpa artists make wooden images of the Lord Buddha. The Khambas and Membas of northern Siang carve wooden masks."[25]

In western Kameng a few families of Monpas produced paper from local materials. The paper was " of fair quality and is (was) used by the literate Lamas for their correspondence and religious books."[26] Referring to E.T. Dalton's accounts of the Khamtis, Elwin states that the Khampti priests passed their leisure hours by carving in wood, bone or ivory, making ivory handles of weapons, carved 'high relief twisted snakes, dragons, and other monsters with a creditable unity and gracefulness of design.' The Khampti

Chiefs worked in gold, silver and iron; forged their own weapons and made their wives' jewels. They also manufactured 'embossed shields of buffalo and rhinoceros hide, gilding and lacquering them with skill and taste'. [27]

Carpentry, house-building with materials, such as, bamboo, thatch and wood and decoration of dwelling house, were also the commonly practised craft. Some of the tribals made beautiful toys for their children. Making ornaments even in the interior of hills with locally available materials, such as, bamboo, wood, 'blue wings of birds and the green backs of beetles', etc. and decoration of baskets with the stuffed bodies of highly coloured birds' etc. were the expressions of ingenuity and artistic taste that made life jolly and free from boredom in their remote and isolated habitats.

The Khasis, Jaintiyas and the Nagas acquired the art of smelting iron ore into iron. And using this metal they manufactured iron hoes and even iron -tipped ploughs. It was done partly for their own use and partly for sending out to Assam plains.

6. Trade and Exchange

Trading activity was an important sources of income for some of the north-eastern frontier tribes, such as, the Khampas, Nishis, Mishings, Mishmis, Singphos, Khamptis , et al . These tribes were engaged in importing goods from Tibet and/ or procuring products from fellow tribals for reselling to the traders from Assam.[28]

Some of Assam's trade connections with Bhutan, Tibet, China and Burma could be maintained through these tribal people who acted as middlemen. In the western part of the north-eastern hills (Arunachal Pradesh) live the Akas , on their east the Nishis occupy the hills north of Chaiduar in Lakhimpur. Further east live the Adis and the Mishings. The Mishmis occupy the hills between the Dibang valley and the Indian border with Burma. Their neighbours are the Khamptis living in the Lohit valley. The Singphos dwell on the hills lying between upper Assam and Bhamo in Burma.

Among these tribes the Mishmis have been acclaimed by Wilcox as the most efficient traders: " The Mishmis differ with the other hill tribes in their habit of trafficking - every man among them is a petty merchant" writes R. Wilcox in his *Memoirs of Survey of Assam* as quoted by Elwin.[29] From the same account it is learnt that the Mishmis exchanged *bih* (poison), *gathewan* (an odoriferous root), *manjit* (madder) and *teetah* (a bitter root) for Tibetan cattle , brass pipes, gongs, copper vessels, etc. Later these things were sold to Assamese traders in exchange for Assam's cows, buffaloes, colour beads, etc.

The Miris were also adept in conducting trade with Assam where they exported products of neighbouring highlanders from whom the goods were first purchased. They brought from the hills pepper, ginger, *manjit* (madder) and wax for exchanging with the Assamese inhabitants in the foot hills. The Adis also carried on similar traffic.[30]

The Nagas disposed of their surplus produce in the markets in the plains. W. Robinson recorded[31] that the Nagas frequented the markets at Nagura and Kacharihath and also other markets along the borders for bartering their ' cotton and ginger for minor articles'. They manufactured salt from the brine springs in the vicinity of their hills and a part of that they sold in the said markets at Nagura and Kacharihath and elsewhere along the borders.

A.J. Moffatt Mills observed that the Nagas were ' very keen barterers but at the same time just and open in their dealings'. He further noted that the western Nagas brought " large quantities of cotton and chillies, ginger and yarns, the Eastern Nagas, salt, etc. to be bartered for rice, ducks , and salt in the first instance and for rice etc. in the second"[32]

According to Barpujari , the Bori Nagas were very eager to maintain their intercourse with the Assamese as it yielded good profits and therefore they were opposed to the entry of the Abors (Adis) into the plains; and this was one of the most important causes of their internecine strife with their neighbours in the south'. The tribes, such as the Garos , the Khasis and the Eastern Nagas were so much dependent on trade for their subsistence that blockade of the duars on the occasion of aggressions was speedily followed by surrender of offenders'.[33]

Trade flow between the hills and the plains of Assam and between Assam and Bhutan, Tibet, Burma and even

China was facilitated by the opening up of trade routes between these territories." There were five trade routes from Sadiya and Upper Assam leading to Tibet or China proper. These consisted of the pass of Dibong, the Mishmi route , the Phungan pass to Manchee and China, the route from Manipur to the Irrawady, and the Patkai pass to Bhamo on the Irrawady. The most important and the easy route was on the north-eastern side over the Patkai to the upper districts of Burma and thence to China. ..... Numerous passes and ways known as *Duars* still exist between Assam and Tibet through Bhutan. The route to Tibet runs across the Himalayan mountains parallel with the course of the Brahmaputra". There were numerous forest and hill pathways and riverways connecting the hill areas with the plains of Assam.[34]

The history of trade and exchange between the tribal people of the north-eastern hills and their neighbours in the Tibet region in the north and those in the south in Assam plains is very old. The hill people in the adjoining hills to the south of the Brahmaputra valley had also trade transactions with people in the plains. Such trade and exchange relations clearly highlight the economic interdependence of the tribal and non tribal neighbours for their subsistence and economic advancement. Of course the total volume of such transactions remained perforce restricted because of the small quantity of surplus produce they did have after consumption. There were also other hindrances, such as, lack of infrastructural facilities, insecure movements along trade routes, several restrictions imposed by the ruling authorities, coercive exactions by third parties and the barter system of exchange. Yet such trade and exchange acted as incentives as well as opportunities to the tribals to produce more and new goods to exchange them for the goods they needed from their non-tribal neighbours. This way trade infused some element of dynamism and growth into the tribal economic formations.

7. Technology

Excepting for a negligible few, almost all the tribesmen and tribeswomen were illiterate and innumerate. Barring the Khamptis and Monpas none had their own written language. Tribals used their mother tongue only orally. Therefore, it was not possible for them to acquire technology from outside their respective territories beyond a certain range. Yet thanks to their qualities of ingenuity, initiative and drive technological improvements were being adopted by different tribal communities in North-East India. Transmission of some technological skills took place as trade relations developed amongst the different tribal communities themselves and also amongst the tribal and non-tribal trading partners. In fact intra-tribal and tribal-non-tribal trade relations promoted cultural exchange and transmission of technology, knowledge of new arts and skills in manufacturing of new goods and so on.

The most significant technological change that augmented agricultural output was the transition from shifting to settled cultivation happening in some parts of the region. This change also signified a change in the organization of economic activities, land management and accumulation of assets and economic disparities amongst the households within the tribe. Emergence of stable and settled villages in the place of shifting villages was also an important outcome. The technical change was manifested in the construction of terraces on hill slopes, diversion of water from hill streams to the terraced fields for irrigation, manuring of fields, etc. In some places watermills were operated and in some animal power was harnessed for cultivation and allied activities. In the Jaintiya Hills the drip system of irrigation was developed for horticultural farming.

As already noted in connection with manufacturing activities, the Khasis, Jaintiyas and Nagas were conversant with the technology of smelting iron ore into iron and forging iron tools and agricultural implements.

Innumerable streams and streamlets separate the undulated territories of the North -Eastern hills. Some big rivers also flow down from the north to the south into the Brahmaputra. Therefore the tribal people had to acquire skill in the construction of different types of bridges. The Adis developed spectacular expertise in construction of bridges. The Adi area of the Siang district (Arunachal Pradesh) abounds in several types of hanging brides. "Cane hanging bridges are common over the longer streams and in several places, over the Siang and the Yamne. Other types of bridges are also found all over the region .... There are the cantilever bridges of bamboo weighted with piles of boulders, suspension bridges with rigid bamboo footways, trestle bridges and combination of these types.

"The cane suspension bridges display the Adi engineering at its best. At one end, the canes forming the main support of a suspension bridge are partly thrown across beams supported on a triangle of strong timber, and are partly stretched and fastened to groups of trees, conveniently situated. The other ends of the main supporting canes are then floated across the river and secured in the same way, on the other bank. Once the two main suspenders are secured, they attach to these some minor suspenders. On these are hung elliptical coils of the same material at an interval of [a] few yards. Foot rests of about ten to twelve inches are then woven with cane strips. Lastly below the main suspension cane, the rings are further strengthened with additional canes, which also serve as hand-rests during crossing. Now these structures including the foot-rest and hand-rest are interlaced with cane strips which add to the stability of the suspension strings. These bridges sway considerably during crossing, but are safe and have never known to break or fail other-wise. It is repaired part by part every year, so that after three or four years, the entire bridge gets renewed all over".[35]

The Adis also used bamboo rafts to cross rivers. The rafts were some 6m long and 1.5m wide each of which contained one small platform for passengers and baggage. A raft was rowed by three or four persons with sticks. One of them steered the raft with great difficulty in the face of strong and rapid water currents.[36]

Technologies of production employed by the different tribal communities were learnt by actual application. S. N. Mishra has discussed the scientific and technical knowledge of the Nishis of Arunachal Pradesh in detail. The fundamentals of the level and range of technological knowledge of the Nishis have been indicated by Mishra. These facts are also relevant to the other tribal communities.

Mishra further states: "...the community has built up

and accumulated a repertory of scientific and technical knowledge. Little children carry their *Dao* and knife which are indispensable tools for cutting, shaping, slaughtering, dismembering, flaying, grating and innumerable other processes in the fields, forest and the homes. Elementary physical properties of such organic and inorganic matter as is used by the community for fashioning hand tools, building materials, domestic utility goods, etc. are fairly well-known and the matter is accordingly differentiated and classified"[37]. Even as they knew the principle of lever, they were ignorant of the property of circular motion and the mechanism of transforming circular motion into linear motion as can be construed from the fact that they did not operate pottery wheel or wheeled cart.

The tribal community had a fair knowledge about the chemical properties of plants and the behaviour pattern of animals found in their surrounding forests. This is evident from the facts that they used plants, leaves and flowers for dyeing (textiles , etc.) tanning hides (in a crude manner) extracting poison from plant substance for using it in their arrow tips for hunting, fighting and even poisoning river water for catching fish.

Mishra observed that the Nishis had rudimentary knowledge about the concept of measurement. Concepts of addition and subtraction were known but not the concepts of multiplication and division. For measuring they used baskets, as they had no device for weighing anything. The system of moon-calendar was used for reckoning months, the year being known by the flowering cycle of certain trees. Days were counted ' by tying and untying knots on a rope.' The unit of measurement of value of a Mithun was determined by the finger-length of its horn, ' a mithun calf with horn being a unit of value'.[38]

The level and range of technical knowledge of the tribal communities was such that the productivities of labour, land and other resources were at a low level and therefore the level of their living in material terms was quite low as the full productive capacity of land and labour remained unrealized. The economy was almost at a stationary level and the carrying capacity of land was extremely low which kept the size of population very small. No wonder, the growth rate of population remained nearly at the zero level.

NOTES AND REFERENCES

1. B.N. Bordoloi, (1998), Tribal Land Tenure System and land Alienation in North-East India, published in S.N. Mishra (ed) *Antiquity to Modernity and Control of Resources among Indian Tribes*, Inter -India Publications, New Delhi.
2. Total area estimated by adding up district-wise hill areas as recorded by B.K. Roy Burman, (1970), *Demographic and Socio-Economic Profiles of the Hill Areas of North -East India, Census of India 1961*, Office of the Registrar General , India, New Delhi, pp. 6-7.
3. H. K. Barpujari, (1970), *Problem of the Hill Tribes, North-East Frontier*, North Eastern Hill University Publications, Shillong, p. 13.
4. D. Ering,(1972), The North-East Frontier Agency, published in *The Tribal Situation in India* , ed, K. Suresh Singh, Indian Institute of Advanced Study , Shimla, pp. 56 -57.
5. C. Von. F. Haimendorf (1962), *The Apa Tanis and their Neighbours, A Primitive Civilization of the Eastern Himalayas*, Routledge & Kegan Paul, London, pp. 12 - 45.
6. *ibid* . pp. 27 - 28.
7. *ibid.* p. 31.
8. *ibid.* p. 14.

8 (a) *ibid.* pp. 16 - 17

8 (b) *ibid.* p. 47 ff

8 (c) *ibid.* p. 50.

9. Verrier Elwin, 1988 *A Philosophy for NEFA*, Government of Arunchal Pradesh, Itanagar (Third reprint) p. 14.
10. H.H. Godwin-Austen, Report on the Survey Operations in the Naga Hills and Manipur during the field season 1872-73, p. 82. Quoted in Verrier Elwin (1969). *The Nagas in the Nineteenth Century* , Oxford University Press, p. 588.
11. R. Brown, Narrative Report of the Progress of the Survey Party, Naga Hills, Season 1874, pp.9-10 and p. 34,quoted in Elwin, pp. 588-590.
12. John Butler, 'Rough Notes on the Angami Nagas'. Journal of the Asiatic Society, 1875, Vol. XLIV, No. 4, quoted in Elwin, op. cit. pp. 586-87.

13. H.B. Rowney (1882) , The Wild Tribes of India, quoted in Elwin op. cit. p. 101.
14. R.G.Woodthrope, Notes on the Wild Tribes Inhabiting the So-called Naga Hills on our North-East Frontier of India (1881) quoted in Elwin op. cit. p. 52.
15. *op. cit* p. 54.
16. P. Hungya, (1987) ' Land Tenure system in the Hills of Manipur' Published in *Land Relations in North-East India,* B.B. Datta and N.N. Karna (eds) , People's Publishing House, New Delhi, p .68.
17. H.K. Barpujari (1998), *Problem of the Hill Tribes : North - East Frontier,* NEHU Reprint, first published 1970, p. 10.
18. *ibid.*
19. S.N. Mishra (1983), Arunachal's Tribal Economic Formations and their Dissolution, Economic and Political Weekly, Vol. XVIII, No. 43, p. 842.
20. Barpujari, *op.cit.* p. 11.
21. *ibid.*
22. J.B. Ganguly (1993), 'Development of Peasant Farming in the North -Eastern Tribal Region (A study in Tribal Continuities)', published in *Continuity and Change in Tribal Society,* Mrinal Miri (ed), Indian Institute of Advanced Study, Shimla, p. 300; Some other aspects of Jhum model have been gleaned from this paper.
23. Verrier Elwin, 1988. *A Philosophy for NEFA,* Government of Arunchal Pradesh, Itanagar, p. 99.
24. *ibid.* p. 99
25. *ibid.* p. 101
26. *ibid.* p. 99
27. *ibid,* p. 98-99. (E.T. Dalton's Descriptive Ethnology of Bengal (Calcutta, 1872) contains accounts of the Khamptis, pp.1-9.
28. (a) H.K.Barujari (ed) 1993, *The Comprehensive History of Assam,* Vol.V, Publication Board, Assam, pp. 113-114.

    (b) J.B. Bhattacharjee (ed), 1994. *Studies in the Economic History of North-East India,* HarAnand Publications , New Delhi, pp. 187 -89.
29. Verrier Elwin, (1959), *India's North-East Frontier in the Nineteenth Century,* Oxford University Press, Madras, p. 306.

30. R.B. Pemberton, (1835), Report Upon the Countries on the Eastern Frontier of the British Territories, Reprinted in 1979 by Mittal Publications, New Delhi, p. 78.
31. W. Robinson, (1841), A Descriptive Account of Assam, p.244 reproduced in V.Elwin, 1969, op. cit. p. 599.
32. J. Moffatt Mills, (1854), Report on the Province of Assam, p. xii- iii, reproduced in V. Elwin, op. cit. 1969, pp. 599-600.
33. H.K. Barpuajri, 1998. *op.cit.* p.14.
34. Edward Gait, (1967), *A History of Assam,* Revised and Enlarged by B. K. Barua and V. S. Murthy, Thacker Spink & Co. Kolkata, p. 273.
35. Sachin Roy, (1960), *Aspect of Padam - Minyong Culture,* North-East Frontier Agency, Shillong. pp. 20-21
36. *ibid.* p. 23.
37. S. N. Mishra , *op.cit.* p. 1840.
38. *ibid.*

PART – TWO

5
ECONOMIC HISTORY OF STATES

A. ASSAM

1. Introduction

Geographically Assam's three divisions comprise the Brahmaputra valley, the Barak valley and the Hill Districts. The Brahmaputra valley measuring a total area of 33,800 sq.kms covers the districts of Goalpara, Kamrup, Darrang, Nowgong, Sibsagar and Lakhimpur. The Barak valley comprises the district of Cachar having an area of 6,940 sq.kms. The districts of Naga Hills (area: 16,488 sq.kms), Khasi and Jaintiya Hills (area: 14,262 sq.kms), Garo Hill (area: 8,167 sq.kms), United North Cachar and Mikir Hills (area: 15,222 sq. kms) and Lushai (Mizo) Hills (area: 21,081 sq. kms) are reckoned as hill districts of Assam. The three Frontier Tracts of Sadiya, Lakhimpur and Balipara commonly known as the North Eastern Frontier Hills are also part of the tribal areas of Assam.

Our study in economic history of Assam covers the area of the Brahmaputra valley. The economic formations of all the tribes living in the hill districts of Assam and the North Eastern Frontier Hills have been discussed in chapter IV. Similarly in the Appendix an overview of change and continuity in all the tribal areas has been given.

The geographical features have been treated and a brief historical account given in chapter II. First let us note the conditions prevailing in the pre-colonial period in the Brahmaputra valley.

2. The Polity, Economy and People in the Pre-colonial Period

The Ahoms conquered Assam in the beginning of the thirteenth century and by the end of the eighteenth century the process of transformation of the Ahom tribal formation into a mighty empire, having the characteristics of a feudal system of polity and economic management reached its culmination. Of course, the Ahom rulers encountered series of uprising and revolts of the Moamarias in the 1780's that seriously weakened the Ahom Kingdom's sway and the people were even inclined to accept Moamaria supremacy.[1]

Moamaria uprisings were followed by Burmese invasion causing acute sufferings of the people and the shattering of their agrarian economic system. In the words of Gait, villages were burnt and reduced to ashes, supplies were looted, crops in the fields were wantonly destroyed and the people suffered from terrible famine conditions. People deserted their homes, roamed about in the jungle somehow managing to subsist on wild fruits and roots, and many of them took shelter in the neighbouring tribal hill villages and even in Bengal.[2]

The breakdown of the mighty Ahom empire apparently in the face of external interventions that ultimately resulted in the British occupation of Assam was also attributable to its internal structural weaknesses. Yet during the period of Ahom rule Assam achieved unprecedented improvements in the fields of agriculture, infrastructure, industries, internal and external trade, and social and cultural aspects of people's life, technology of production, etc. And it was possible on account of the political-economic structure gradually built up by the Ahoms.

In the Ahom feudal polity the system of monarchal rule manifested a combination of what Hicks terms 'customary' and 'command' elements.[3] The monarch's commands were not exclusively the means of wielding feudal rights over running of the administrative structure, exercising rights over land distribution, utilizing services of labour, bureaucrats, nobles, the militia, traders, craftsmen, artisans, etc. for ensuring continuity of the feudal rule. In this regard the existing social customs, conventions and practices were also respected. Besides, the feudal power in all respects did not flow only from above, some elements of 'belowness' that is exercise of power by the subordinates vis-à-vis their supervisers also marked the feudal polity. In fact these characteristics sustained the Ahom polity for over five centuries.

The Ahom rulers regarded both land and their subjects as their property and they could utilize them in the manner they chose to do. This approach was the basis of the *paik* system, details of which appear in chapter III.

As the chief executive of the state the Ahom King had five councillors or Patra Mantris, namely, Bar Gohain, Burha Gohain, Barpatra Gohain, Bar Barua and the Bar Phukan who assisted him in running the administration of the Kingdom. They constituted the highest echelon of administration below the King and they were members of designated prominent families. These officers were normally hereditary "but the king had the right to select any member of the prescribed clan that he chose, and he could also, if he wished, dismiss a Gohain."[4] The three Gohains were the highest-ranking ministers and occupied a very exalted position of power in the polity so much so that they could even depose a weak and unworthy King. There are instances of such actions jointly taken by the Gohains, all aimed at preserving the Ahom Kingdom. The Kings took counsel of the Gohains in important matters such as waging war, organizing defence against foreign aggression, finalizing peace accords with other powers.

The Gohains were not paid any salary as such, but a specified number of *paiks* were placed at their disposal for exclusive use of their services in their houses and respective farm estates. David Scott estimated that the Gohains had for their own use 10,000 *paiks*, which was equivalent to a grant of Rs. 90,000 per annum.[5]

The members of the King's family and his near relations were allotted *mels* or estates which were managed by the state officials designated as *phukans* or *Baruas*.

From time to time were appointed local governors each of them distinctly nomenclatured, such as, the Sadiya Khowa Gohain (governor of Sadiya), the Morangi Khowa Gohain (governor of Naga marshes), the Solal Gohain (Governor of

Nowgang and neighnouring areas). Some ruling chiefs 'who had made their submission to the Ahoms were transformed into Governors acting on their behalf.' There were numerous other high ranking officers of the state generally appointed only from the fifteen earmarked Ahom families. Of course, for some of the offices which did not involve military service, "the higher classes of the non-Ahom natives of the country were also eligible, and also the persons of foreign descent, provided that their families had been domiciled in the country for three or four generations."[5] These officials also were not paid any salary but were assigned certain number of *paiks* in lieu thereof.

Large number of *paiks* were also 'assigned for the support of temples or of Brahmans' as well as of the Vaishnava *satras* along with revenue-free land grants.

The composition of the nobility and the systems of appointment of civil and military functionaries of the state and the manner of payment of remuneration in terms of land grants and assignment of *paiks* for performing a variety of duties for the nobles and the officials, show the essential features of feudalism. The main property in the system was land and the holding of this property was not only dependent on performing assigned duties – administrative, judicial or military – but it also enabled the holders to wield political power.

These were the essential features of a feudal order. Of course, the Ahom system differed from that obtaining in medieval Europe where the serfs under the feudal lords were fully dependent on their masters for land grants and were rigidly attached to the respective fiefdoms of the nobles. In contrast, land given to the *paiks* and the number of *paiks* that would be assigned to the nobles and members of the state bureauracy were all determined by the King who was paramount authority in the Kingdom and had owned all land and of course the subjects of the kingdom. The structure of the Ahom polity has been aptly characterized by Guha as a quasi-feudal one built up on a 'largely tribal base'.[7]

In Assam, where rice is the staple food of the people, two main verieties of paddy were grown, namely, *ahu* (a short-maturing dry rice) and *Sali* (a long-maturing wet rice). For raising *ahu* paddy, seeds were simply broadcast on the fields where standing water was not required for the plants to grow. But *Sali* paddy was grown following a method that first needed raising paddy seedlings in the nursery and then later transplanting seedlings into the irrigated fields where standing water was required to be held for a minimum period of time at a certain stage of the growth of paddy plants.

The Ahoms practiced settled plough cultivation of wet rice. During the hey days of Ahom rule, Assam achieved a significant level of economic development the mainspring of which was the expansion of area brought under *Sali* rice cultivation by using higher technology of production. This involved use of iron implements for reclamation and preparation of land for rice cultivation, use of buffaloes for farming operations (as was done in other south-Asian countries from which region the Ahoms migrated to Assam), building and maintaining embankments for protecting farm lands from river floods, erection of ridges around individual paddy fields for holding water there as required for *Sali* rice plants to grow and yield paddy in plenty, etc. In building and maintaining the infrastructure required for rice cultivation as a social good, sufficient quantum of labour-power had to be mobilized which was possible under the paik system. In fact this system enabled the king to have the standing militia not only for performing military duties but also for building the social overheads like roads, embankments, bunds, bridges and so on.Considerable number of paiks were assigned to nobles, state officials, religious institutions, favoured priests, etc. These paiks could be employed for reclaiming more and more areas of wasteland for the purpose of extending area for cultivation.

In the newly introduced system of rice cultivation labour productivity was higher; therefore, the Ahom King and the nobles could extract more surpluses from the agricultural sector. The main form used for the generation of surplus was the exploitation of the attached *paiks* who produced increased amounts of food and other necessaries. About one-fourth to one-third of the total *paiks* population would be engaged by the state, nobles and other state officials for performing specified duties. The remaining *paiks* not engaged were able to produce food and other necessaries to meet the requirements of the total population of *paiks* and their families. Their level of consumption could not have been significantly higher than what it was at the subsistence level since every *paik* had to pay a poll tax. No wonder, then the surplus generated in the economy only enriched the King, the ruling elite, the religious institutions and the clergy.

In the seventeenth century – 'the century of Ahom-Mughal conflicts' – Assam was free from its relative isolation under the Ahoms. The relative closeness of its economy also resulted in some openness, which brought about some element of diversification in production of goods and services and the composition of external trade in Assam's economy. These changes caused growth in the volume of commodity production and tade.[8] In the closing decades of the seventeenth century new crops like pineapple and tobacco were included in the list of horticultural crops grown in the region. These two cash crops occupied an important place in the agrarian economy. Since the late sixteenth century there were definite evidences to indicate that the region achieved growth in trade and crafts and some advance towards monetization and specialization. 'By 1663 their currency consisted of gold coins, silver rupees and cowries'.[9] Thereafter more coins of different denominations were issued that led to expansion of money supply. Rise in money supply was both the effect as well as the cause of growth in the volumes of internal and external trade. A rise in trade transaction in its turn served as incentive to increased production and supply of goods. This trend continued until the onset of the Moamaria rebellion and the Burmese invasion of Assam.

Internal trade flourished during the Ahom rule until the outbreak of the Moamaria rebellion and the Burmese invasion. A number of markets established in the foothills provided facilities for the hill people to exchange their surplus products such as, cotton, sesame, iron and iron tools, forest produce, vegetables for rice, dried fish, salt, cotton and silk fabrics, utensils, beads, etc.

In peace time regular trade between Assam under the Ahoms and Bengal was transacted. The items of Assam's exports to Bengal consisted of stick lac, muga silk cloth, munjeet (Indian madder), black pepper, long pepper, cotton, ivory, bell-metal vessels, mustard seed, iron hoes, 'thaikol fruit' and interestingly, slaves. Salt, fine pulse, ghee, sugar, stone beads, coral, jewel and pearls, cutlery and glassware (European), spices, paints, copper, lead, English woollens, *taffetas* Benares silk or Kinkhaps, *satin*, gold and silver, cloth, shells and muslin were imported in 1808-09. Total value of imports in 1808-09 amounted to Rs.2,28,300 as against the total value of exports which was Rs. 1,30,900. Item-wise break-up of exports and imports for the year 1808-09 as given by Hamilton in his Account of Assam is given in table 5.1 below:[11]

Table 5.1
Foreign Trade Between Assam and Bengal in 1808-09

EXPORTS

Commodities	**Quantity (maunds)**	**Value Rs.**
Stick Lac	10,000	35,000
Muga silk	66	11,350
Cloth	75	17,500
Munjit (Indian madder)		500
Black pepper	50	500
Long pepper	50	300
Cotton	7,000	35,000
Ivory		6,500
Bell-metal vessels		1,500
Mustard seed	15,000	20,000
Iron hoes		600
Slaves		2,000
Thaikol fruit (?)	50	150
Total		1,30,900

IMPORTS

Commodities	Quantity (maunds)	Value Rs.
Salt @ Rs. 5 ½	35,000	1,92,500
Fine pulse		800
Ghee	100	1,600
Sugar		2,000
Stone beads		1,000
Coral		5,000
Jewel and Pearls		500
Cutlery and Glassware (European)		1,000
Spices		1,000
Paints		500
Copper		4,800
Red Lead		1,000
English Woollens		2,000
Tafetas		2,000
Banares Silk or Kinkhap		500
Satin		1,000
Gold and Silver cloth		1,000
Shells		1,000
Muslin		10,000
Total		2,29,200

Source: Hamilton, *Account of Assam*, pp. 45-6
Quoted by H.K. Barpujari, Vol.III, pp.146-7, where total imports have been shown Rs. 2,29,200

The trade figures indicate that Assam heavily depended on imports of salt from Bengal; 84 percent of the total value of imports was expended on this item. The table also shows that Assam had an unfavourable balance of trade with Bengal necessitating export of bullion (gold and silver) to pay for the import of surplus. Part of this bullion came from Assam's favourable balance of trade with Tibet and Bhutan.

Guha has rightly cautioned that these trade figures based on customs check-post returns for the year 1808-09 cannot stand for the exact quantitative dimensions of trade position in the first half of the eighteenth century when Assam's population was nearly double the size of that in 1808-09. And Assam's economy was more or less undisturbed by internal or external disturbances during that period. However, by taking these trade figures as ordinal magnitudes, rough comprehensions of the composition of Mughal-Ahom trade might be made.[12]

The Ahom land revenue system was basically linked with the *paik* system, the essential features of which have been discussed in chapter III. It may be further noted that each *paik* got 3 acres of good rice producing land free of rent. If any *paik* chose not to render physical service he had to pay two rupees in lieu of that. He also got land for his homestead and attached kitchen garden for which he paid one rupee as house tax. If a person reclaimed waste land for cultivation he was allowed to hold the land on payment of one to two rupees a pura (1.5 acres) "so long as it was not required on a new census taking place to provide the paiks with their proper allotment".[13]

The *char* (sandbank) land was generally cultivated by immigrant rayats known as *pam* cultivators. They paid a plough tax while the hill-cultivators paid a house or hoe tax.

The non-cultivating artisans, such as, the gold-washers and brass-workers, had to pay a poll tax of five rupees per head while the oil-pressers and fishermen paid three rupees each.

"The rice lands were redistributed from time to time, but not the homesteads, which descended from father to son. The only other lands which could be regarded as private property were the estates granted to the nobles and in later times to temples and Brahmans, which were cultivated by slaves or servants, or by paiks attached to the estate and granted with it."[14]

Later, as the Ahoms learnt about the Mughal system of land-measurement which helped to estimate correctly the liabilities of the tenants to pay land revenue to the state, a countrywide land survey was undertaken by surveyors employed for the purpose from Koch-Bihar and Bengal. This work was nearly completed by 1751.[15] This development helped to detect excess taxable lands in the occupation of the *paiks*. The new revenue system augmented the amount of land revenue collections. Despite these changes the basic *paik* system for mobilizing manpower for public works, military service, cultivation of farm lands, etc. continued.

Under the *paik* system although the male adults were obliged to take part in state services for three to four months a year, cultivation and other productive activities were not affected as "the home-keeping adults were bound by law to carry on the cultivation and other affairs of their absent comrades". This feature as observed by S.K. Bhuyan, made every subject "take an interest in the affairs of the state; and the peasants being made to work for their co-villagers, and indirectly for the state, developed some degree of civic consciousness and a sense of public duty'.[16]

The Ahom rule is distinguished by the fact that official manuals were compiled in 'the training of elephants, horses and hawks, on civil and military engineering, on the duties and insignias of officers, on the order of precedence in the court, and on the administration of justice'. Another admirable aspect of Ahom rule was the "maintenance of official chronicles of events as they actually took place, based mainly on the dispatches of governors, commanders and ambassadors, and the recorded proceedings of the king and his ministers".[17]

The Ahoms were free from the pernicious caste system of social divisions, but they were tolerant of the caste system among their Hindu subjects. They also officially disallowed the settlement of Ahoms in lower Assam but considered upper Assam as their home country. Over time, of course, settlement of some Ahoms took place in lower Assam.

3. Population Profile

Assam in the beginning of the Ahom period was a sparsely populated state which abounded in large tracts of cultivable waste-lands. In this condition the pace of economic development much depended on the growth of population that could lead to the reclamation of more waste lands by harnessing more labour power that engendered some capital formation. It also resulted in the establishment of new village settlements in remoter areas and opening up of the countryside. There were some inventions of such developments in the different accounts of Ahom rule and its achievements. The rice economy built up by the Ahom rulers raised rice output that could provide support to the rising population.

The growth of population was, however, halted and the size of total population drastically fell during the period of civil war from 1770 to 1809 and the process of depopulation further worsened as Assam fell under Burmese occupation that lasted from 1817 to 1825. This trend was reversed only after some decades of the annexation of Assam by the British in 1826.

In the absence of any reliable census of the population in the pre-colonial period, guess estimates made by some historians about the total population in the early decades of the 18th century ranged from 2.08 million to 3.20 million.[19]

In the early colonial period, in 1835 the population of the Brahmaputra Valley was estimated at 7,99,519. Gait, however, opined that this estimate based on the official returns about assessment of land revenue could not be wholly reliable.[20] Yet assuming that the population of Assam under the Ahoms fell by more than 50 percent in the wake of the civil wars and the Burmese occupation, we may presume that the size of Assam's (Brahmaputra Valley) population on the eve of the British annexation of Assam was a little less than one million.

The population was composed of multi-ethnic, multi-religion identities. The Ahoms belonged to the Sino-Tai linguistic group. They represented only about 5.45 per cent of the total population (as was the position in 1921). Ahom population in 1921 was 2,10,380 out of the total population of 38,56,000 of the Brahmaputra Valley.[21] Nearly three-fourths of the population were Assamese Hindus. There were a number of tribal ethnic groups who belonged to different linguistic families and were at different levels of socio-cultural and economic development. Their main productive activities were related to shifting cultivation although some of them also practised settled cultivation. The religious divisions of population included the Hindus, tribals having their own faiths, Buddhists, Muslims and even Sikhs (though not many). The Khamtis, Phakials, Aiteneong, Turungs, and a few other tribal groups were Buddhists. The Muslims were the descendants of the Muslim invaders and of some skilled artisans invited from Mughal India for settlement. The Sikhs were the descendants of either Guru Nanak or Guru Teg Bahadur who visited Assam in the 16th and 17th centuries respectively.

The Vaishnava reformation movement initiated by Sankaradeva and Madhavadeva in the 15th century emphasizing the path of salvation through faith and prayer rather than by animal sacrifices, etc. had a great impact on the Assamese psyche and socio-cultural and economic practices. In the wave of Neo-Vaishnavism in the 16th century large masses of people belonging to tribal faiths and other non-Hindu clans came under this influence and became liberal Hindus.

In Assam's population mosaic the *bhuyans*, 'a high-caste migrant adventurers from north India', occupied an important position. There were some non-Hindu bhuyans also. The bhuyans actually were a powerful class of big land-holders. They played a leading role "in the cultural life as well as in communal dyke-building activities for water control".[22]

Many of the Muslims were skilled artisans, such as, inscribers, embroiderers using gold and silver threads, dyers and painters, cotton cloth weavers, manufacturers of gun-powder, musicians and tailors. The Muslim population finely adapted themselves to the indigenous Assamese socio-cultural environment.

The rigidity of caste distinctions even among the Assamese Hindus was much diluted under the impact of the Neo-Vaishnava movement. Considering weaving, spinning, oil-crushing, rice-pounding, basket-making, etc. were usually operated as normal household activities, these activities were not cast-specific. The Kalitas who approximated to the characteristics of a caste, were not a homogeneous professional group. There were diverse occupation groups among them, such as, potters using wheels, blacksmiths, goldsmiths, bell-metal artisans, carpenters, boat-builders and weavers. Sonowals (gold-washers), Telis (oil-men), Nadials (fishermen), Haris (scavengers) were also professional communities. Only the Hiras (potters not using wheels) were an untouchable caste. Additionally, almost all the groups just mentioned also took to cultivation as a subsidiary occupation.

Slavery was prevalent on an extensive scale, holding men and women in bondage for performing domestic and agricultural duties for their masters. This institution has been discussed elaborately in chapter III.

The traditional Ahom social system, we have already noted, was free from caste division. And they were not at ease with local practices of making distinctions between one group of their subjects and another.[23] But as years passed, they slowly adopted the local practices of maintaining distinctions among the people of different economic strata which meant discarding the traits of tribalism so marked by the values of egalitarianism, social equality, free mixing etc. among all members of the society.

The Ahoms gradually adopted the feudal superstructure as it existed elsewhere in India. In sharpening the social distinctions based on political status, it was decreed that only the members of the nobility could exclusively wear ornamental turbans, coats, shoes, etc. and use specially decorated palanquins and umbrellas and fans, ornamented with gold or silver, embroidered carpets, and so on. In the royal court, distinctions were made in allotting seats to the different strata of the nobility and to the gentry in hierarchical order. Similar distinctions were also observed when building dwelling houses for the monarch, the different ranks of the aristocracy and for the commoners. Only the royal palace was built of bricks and mortar with both ends rounded; the house of a noble having one end rounded was distinguished from those of the commoners. Besides, the houses of the masses were to be smaller and built on markedly lower plinths than those of the nobles.[24]

4. The Material Life of People : "The Limits of the Possible"

Excepting for the craftsmen engaged in different

traditional crafts, such as, silk and cotton weaving, pottery, basketry, gold washing and jewellery, simple carpentry, brick-making, stone-carving, etc. for the masses of common people the only occupation was cultivation and processing of agricultural crops. Many of the craftsmen made cultivation their subsidiary occupation. Under the paik system adult males of working age had to render military and public service to the state for certain period of the year. Excepting for such obligatory application of labour, no class of wage labourers existed. "Unless forced by circumstances the people of Assam," writes Barpujari, "....... Loath to work on hire or as wage earners".[25] He deplored that the people were generally indolent on account of the enervating climate. The condition further worsened after they became addicted to opium-smoking in the later years of the Ahom rule. Skill formation was at an extremely low level. Therefore, skilled labourers and artisans, such as, carpenters, blacksmiths, wheel-wrights and masons hailing from Bengal and Upper India had to be hired.[26] The peasant women were an important component of the work-force.They did most of the transplanting of paddy plants and harvesting of rice. They even took part in fishing at times.

Assam's economy was essentially a subsistence one based on agricultural production. Anandaram Dhekiyal Phukan has brought out the features of Assam's self-sufficient agrarian economy in the following words: "There is not a single family in Assam that is not engaged in the culture of lands, and every family provides itself by agriculture with almost all the necessaries of life. They cultivate rice, pulses, fruits and vegetables to supply their table, mustard to light their houses, and silk or cotton to provide their garments."[27]

Every Assamese family had handlooms for producing cloth, a task its women undertook to meet the requirements of the family. Cloth was produced mostly for self-consumption.

Processing of agricultural produce, such as, extracting oil from mustard and sesame seeds, crushing sugarcanes for *gur* (molasses), pounding of paddy for separating husk from grain, etc. were technologically at a very low level. And in the sphere of agricultural production, there was no urge to bring more fertile waste lands under cultivation for producing enough surplus for accumulating wealth and capital.

No wonder, the standard of living of the large majority of people was poor and it was reflected in their food habits, dress, living houses, etc. Boiled rice, soup of pulse, vegetable curry, some milk and curd and a little quantity of fish or meat of pigeon or duck constituted the usual menu for lunch and dinner. Only the Hindus of *Sakta* faith and Muslims took mutton. But venison, which was eaten occasionally subject to availability, was acceptable to all.

A typical village cottage of a cultivator consisted of two or three detached rooms standing on low mud plinths around the courtyard. The walls made of reeds were plastered with mud. The courtyard was not sunny or airy as the huts were huddled together. Two sheds were erected in the corners of the courtyard, one for operating the handlooms and the other for housing the cattle. At the back of their houses they had their kitchen gardens where vegetables and some other useful plants were grown. Plantain, coconut and bamboo groves were raised around the house. "The presence of these trees and plants, though picturesque made the entire area damp and ill-ventilated".[28] Excepting for a few brass and bell-metal utensils, they mainly used earthen pots and pans, besides banana leaves as plates from which to eat on some occasions. They slept on mats spread on the floor or on small bamboo platforms. Quilt made of old cloths was used in cold weather. Bamboo and cane baskets were used for keeping in them their quilt, cloths and other useful articles. No wooden or steel boxes, suitcases or trunks were used.

The usual dress of a man consisted of a *dhuti* and *chaddar*. In winter they wore home-made jackets or coats and *eri* (endi) *chaddar* (wrapper) when required. Shoes were seldom used. Woman wore a '*mekhala* or long flowing skirt down to the ankles', a breast cover called *riha* and also a *chaddar*, and she used thin gold necklaces and earrings made of amber. Sometimes men covered their heads with home-spun napkins. When going out in the sun or rain or working in the fields both men and women used broad-beamed large hats made of bamboo, cane and palm leaves which served the purpose of an umbrella.

Sankardev who preached neo-vaishnavism, or purified Vaishnavism, developed the Vaishnava monastery system called *Satra* system, which since then had occupied a key position in the Assamese social structure. The spiritual heads of the followers of Vaishnavism known as *Gossains* or *Satradhikaras* possess the respective *satras*. Their position in the religious and social hierarchy of Assamese society is quite high. In the villages the *Namghars* affiliated to *Satras* serve as the place of religious congregations where people assemble and take part in devotional songs. The *Satras* received liberal grants of land and *paiks* made by the Ahom Kings for their support.

The low level of subsistence living of the majority of the people in Assam is also reflected in the low level of urbanization. In fact, even the original capital of the Ahom Kings, Garhgaon, was nothing better than a concentration of some villages with 'tilled fields and a walled palace complex'. The wall surrounding this complex consisted of live bamboo plantations. Comparatively, Rangpur a brick city, which became the Ahom capital during the reign of Rudra Singh (1696-1714) was a large and thickly populated town twenty miles in extent as described by Captain Welsh in his Report. "The surrounding country had been very highly cultivated. The nobles held large tracts of land, which were tilled by their slaves, but the produce was never brought to the market, and it was all but impossible to buy grain. Salt and opium were found more serviceable than money as a means of procuring supplies". Welsh found that Gauhati was "an extensive and populous town. It was situated on both banks of the Brahmaputra and extended to the neighbouring hills."[29] The other towns of the time, each built around a fort, were Dhubri, Ghila and Hajo – all in the western part of the region.

The prices of necessaries reflect to some extent the common people's income level and their purchasing power to procure goods they did not produce but needed for consumption. From a copper plate deed of grant made in 1739 A.D. we get an idea of the prices of various commodities prevailing then which are noted below:[30]

	Rs.	annas	
1. Rice	2	1/5	annas a maund
2. Milk	2	½	annas a maund
3. Gram	0	4	annas a maund
4. Salt and oil	4	¾	annas a maund
5. Gur	1	¼	annas a maund
6. Black pepper	20	0	annas a maund
7. Betel leaf	0	1	for 40 bundles
8. Earthen pots or Kalsis (pitcher)	643 pieces for one rupee		
9. Areca Nut	5,120 Nos. for one rupee		

Drawing upon a number of other records of the same period, Gait has mentioned the prices of the following articles:

10.	Goat	Re. 1 each
11.	Ducks	One anna each
12.	Pigeons	One pice each
13.	Dhutis	5 annas a piece
14.	Gamchas (towels/napkins)	6 pice each

"The price of salt appears to have ranged from 5 to 10 rupees per maund; it stood at the latter figure in Capt. Welsh's time."[31]

Gait further notes that after Rangpur was looted, rice in the husk was sold at the rate of 600 pounds for a rupee, buffaloes fetched 5 rupees and cows 2 rupees each.[32]

Such low prices seem to have ruled during the transitional period between the end of Ahom rule and the beginning of British occupation, owing to severe shortage of money supply and the economic hardships of people, which impelled them to make distress sales of their agricultural products and domesticated animals.

From the account of the material life of the people given above we may note that the common people during the closing period of Ahom rule before the Moamaria trouble and Burmese invasion could just make do with their subsistence level living after paying taxes to the rulers which they could afford to do by exchanging for money the little surplus of their agricultural and handicraft products. In this milieu at the level of common people there was no accumulation of capital and no investment either, and they were fetered in the midst of the circular flow of economic activities at the static subsistence level.

It was because of natural fertility of Assam's soil and also abundant rainfall during the agricultural season, suffering of people on account of crop failures caused by drought was rare. The year 1665 however, was an exception when an exceptionally severe drought resulted in 'a complete failure of the crops'.[33]

In periods of distress, however, the traditional system of some kind of social security took care of the poor, who could seek help of the co-villagers 'in the shape of doles of paddy'.[34]

Compared to the extremely low level of living standard of the peasantry the economic condition of the ruling aristocracy headed by the Ahom King was immensely good. During the Ahom rule agricultural production, manufacture of crafts and mineral production increased. Large parts of such increased output and income were appropriated by the rulers through collection of revenues, taxes and duties (on exports and imports) and directly engaging the assigned *paiks* and slaves in cultivation of lands under their control. Free labour of artisans was also mobilized in the royal *Karkhana* (workshop) for production of several articles of use and arms and ammunitions.

Next to the ruling aristocracy the monastaries were also the favoured beneficiaries of the system. They received large tracts of farm lands and a large number of *paiks* as royal grants which were instrumental in yielding huge quantities of agricultural and horticultural products. There were also collections of offerings of the devotees. In the process the *Satradhikaris* and *Gossains* amassed lot of wealth.

Wealth accumulated by the rulers was mainly in the form of idle assets like gold, silver, jewellery, and imported costly articles of dress, furniture utensils, etc.

There was no accumulation of capital through savings out of current income and its investment by the king or by the nobles for increasing production of agricultural and non-agricultural goods and services. Some investments were made in building the infrastructure, such as roads, embankments, buildings and temples and monasteries. Expenditures were also incurred on conducting land survey and streamlining the revenue assessment system.

The Ahom rulers took special care in accumulating knowledge by "reducing every branch of useful knowledge to writing. They had official manuals on the training of elephants, horses and hawks, on civil and military engineering, on the duties and insignia of officers, on the order of precedence in the court, and on the administration of justice. The maintenance of official chronicles of events as they actually took place, based mainly on the dispatches of governors, commanders and ambassadors, and the recorded proceedings of the King and his ministers, distinguished the Ahom from the races of India."[35] These chronicles, called *Buranjis* were initially written in Tai-Ahom language. Later some of these *Buranjis* were also written in Assamese.

An important consequence of Ahom rule was the improvement brought about in 'the wet-rice culture of the *Sali* variety in the extensive and undulating plains of eastern Assam'. They popularized the use of improved varieties of iron implements for reclamation and preparation of rice fields. Sufficient number of these implements could be imported from Burma to which area the Ahoms had regular access. They also brought Buffaloes for using them as the major source of animal power, which was common in south-east Asia. The *paik* system of mobilizing manpower for cultivation of paddy, besides using it for military service and public works, was an important element of the structure of the rice economy developed by the Ahoms.

In the Ahom administrative structure special emphasis was put on public works which included the building of economic infrastructure, such as, construction of embankments, ridges around farm lands, roads and bridges. Besides, construction of palaces, public buildings, tanks, burial mounds, temples, etc. was undertaken. An important officer, designated as Chang-rung Phukan, headed the public works department. He maintained records of all constructional works executed by his department. Some of the buildings, roads, bridges, temples, tanks, or their remains have been in existence for a long period of time till to-day. The records maintained by the head of the public woks department are known as *Changrung Phukanar Buranji*. Some of the stone bridges built during the Ahom rule, such as, those over the Namdang, Darika and Dijai rivers are reportedly still intact.[37]

NOTES AND REFERENCES

1. Edward Gait (1977), *A History of Assam*, Lawyer's Book Stall, Guwahati, p. 189.
2. *ibid.* p. 189.
3. J. Hicks (1969), *A Theory of Economic History*, Oxford University Press, p.14.
4. Edward Gait, *op.cit.*
5. *ibid.* p. 225.
6. *ibidi.* pp. 26-7.
7. Amalendu Guha, 1982, "The Medieval Economy of Assam", Published in the *Cambridge Economic History of India*, vol.I, Appendix, Orient Longman, Delhi, p.504.
8. *ibid.* p. 480.
9. *ibid.* p. 488.
10. *ibid.* p. 489
11. H.K. Barpujari (ed), *The Comprehensive History of Assam*, Vol.III, Publication Board, Assam, Guwahati, pp. 146-47.
12. Guha, *op.cit.* p. 491.
13. Edward Gait, *op.cit.* p. 229.
14. *ibid.*
15. Guha, *op.cit.* p. 485.
16. S.K. Bhuyan (1990), *Anglo-Assamese Relations 1771-1826*, Lawyer's Book Stall, Guwahati, p. 589.
17. *ibid.*
18. Guha, *op.cit.* p. 496.
19. Guha, *ibid.* p. 497.
20. Gait, *op. cit.* p. 284.
21. *ibid.* p. 140.

22. Guha, *op.cit.* p. 480.
23. S.K. Bhuyan, *op.cit.*, p. 592.
24. S.L. Baruah, (1997), *A Comprehensive History of Assam*, Munishiram Manoharial Publishers, New Delhi, pp. 418-19.
25. H.K. Barpujari (1993), *The Comprehensive History of Assam*, vol.V, Publication Board, Assam, Guwahati, p.132.
26. *ibid.* p. 133.
27. Observations on the Administration of the Province of Assam by Anandaram Dhekiyal Phukan contained in A.J. Moffat Mills (1854), *Report on the Province of Assam*, republished by Publication Board, Assam in 1984, Guwahati, p.102.
28. H.K. Barpujari, *op.cit.* p. 136.
29. Edward Gait, *op.cit.* p. 206.
30. *ibid.* Foot note: Gait has referred to similar other records of the same period quoting prices of these commodities which vary from the prices indicated in the copper plate. Prices of goats, ducks, pigeons, dhuties, and gamchas (towels) are taken from such records.
31. *ibid.*
32. *ibid.*
33. E. Gait, *op.cit.*p. 144.
34. Edward Gait (1967), *A History of Assam*, Revised and Enlarged by B.K. Barua and H.V.S. Murthy, Thacker Spink, Kolkata, p. 270
35. S.K. Bhuyan (1990), *Anglo-Assamese Relation 1771-1826*, Third Lawyer's Edition, Guwahati, p. 589.
36. Amalendu Guha (1982), *op.cit.* pp. 481-82.
37. S.L. Baruah (1997), *op.cit.* p. 429.

6
AGRICULTURE IN COLONIAL ASSAM

1. Post-Annexation Reorganization of the Revenue System

In 1826 when the British established their supremacy over Assam by driving out the Burmese invaders agriculture was in an extremely shattering condition. Assam in the words of Anandaram Dhekial Phookan, a noted Assamese Government official, 'groaned under the oppression and lawless tyranny of the Burmese', that destroyed more than one-half of the population the size of which had already greatly fallen in the course of the internecine civil wars and commotions that preceded the Burmese invasion.[1] The Burmese took away not les than thirty thousand Assamese as slaves. And in that oppressive and uncertain condition the surviving but famished peasants "had almost given up cultivation, and lived chiefly on jungle roots and plants; and famine and pestilence carried off that had escaped the sword and captivity".[2]

Immediately after annexation of Assam, the British started exploring the methods of reorganizing the system of assessment and collection of revenue to the maximum extent possible. David Scott[3], Agent to the Governor General of the North-East Frontier of Bengal and Commissioner of Revenue and Circuit in the District of Assam, had been instrumental in building the revenue administration structure in Western Assam since 1824 when the British first occupied this part of the region. He did not favour any radical change in the existing system but wanted at the same time to streamline it by removing the loopholes and widening the bases of such collections for ensuring additional revenue demands. Such measures aggravated the sufferings of the peasants and hampered the process of agricultural recovery.

David Scott retained the pargana system of assessment and collection of revenue in Kamrup and its adjoining areas and the *Khel* system of the Ahoms in other parts of the occupied region. The Mughals introduced the pargana system in the lower Assam area of their occupation and the Ahom King retained the system even after the Mughals had vacated their occupation. In his restructured revenue system Scott made use of the existing land survey and settlement records until fresh measurement of lands was conducted.

Settlement began in 1824-25 in the occupied territory comprising Kamrup, Naduar, Demorua, Rani and Beltola. In Kamrup there were 26 parganas for each of which settlements were made with the *Chawdhuris*. The *Chawdhuris* enjoyed no ownership right over such lands. But they got rent-free lands and were assigned some *paiks*. No other remuneration was paid to them. "They were assisted by *Patwaris* (accountants) and *Thakurias* (subordinate collectors) who were remunerated by the grant of rent-free lands."[3]

Besides land revenue other sources of revenue retained by the occupation authority were : a tax of two rupees payable by the *paiks* against three *puras* of land (*igamat*) given to them; poll tax varying from one-half of a rupee to one rupee; professional tax on the braziers, silk-weavers, gold-washers, fishermen, etc. and also the usual duties on hats, ghats and fisheries. Moreover, for *devottar, dharmottar* and *brahmottar* lands also land revenue was assessed at half the rate that applied to other arable lands. In the earlier regime these were rent-free lands.

"In upper Assam the *khel* system was retained for administrative purposes, but the liability to render personal service was abolished except when a limited number of *paiks* were assigned to a prince and ex-function-aries. All *paiks* outside this special group had to pay a poll-tax of three rupees for the cultivated lands, homestead and garden. This tax was collected by the old staff of the *khel*. The *chaudhuries* and the junior officials were elected by the cultivators – a system particularly in existence in former days."[4]

Amounts of revenue assessed and its collection in lower Assam were obviously higher than in Upper Assam. In 1824-25 in Lower Assam the total collection amounted to Rs.1,18,723 against the total assessment of Rs.1,17,824. In Upper Assam for the same year the actual collection was Rs.28,058 as against the assessed amount of Rs.1,39,162. In 1828-29, the respective figures for Upper Assam were Rs.78,452 and Rs.1,53,835. In Lower Assam the assessed amount subsequently went up to Rs.3,00,383 but the actual collection was Rs.1,78,686 only.[5]

The new British system of revenue administration, within a few years, replaced the Ahom *khel* system almost totally. This process of change caused a decline in the area of land under actual cultivation as many liberated *paiks* failed to cultivate land so intensively as to be able to pay the amounts of assessed revenue and consequently left their lands and fled to neighbouring areas of Bhutan and Cachar where tax rates were nominal.[6]

Since the existing Ahom records of land survey made in the mid-eighteenth century 'afforded little insight into the existing order of things' a fresh survey of land was conducted 'by a party of local surveyors under an officer named Mathews'. The inadequacy of Scott's revenue measures became apparent from the fact that two-thirds of the land remained fallow as was revealed by the survey conducted by Mathews. The survey also brought out the fact that about 20 per cent of the arable land was held under the provision of rent-free lands. Moreover remissions of revenue dues amounting to Rs.28,376 and Rs.33,278 in two years "had to be granted for desertion of lands by the cultivators, deficiency of assets, mistakes of the collectors, etc."[7] This shows that the peasants were unable to resume cultivation of all the deserted and fallow lands as they were reduced to a state of penury having been burdened with rent liability that was beyond their capacity. No wonder, Scott's estimate of the prospect of annual revenue collection of rupees three lakhs in Lower Assam remained unfulfilled.

The mismanagement of the revenue administration and rampant corrupting practices of the *chaudhuris* and their extortions from the peasants caused distress of a number of peasants and their fleeing from homes to escape the burden of tax, and other forms of hardship. Lieutenant Rutherford and Lieutenant Bogle were deputed to investigate into the prevailing disorders in Lower Assam.

Their report revealed that the operation of the system of assessment and collection of land revenue and other taxes "has been hurtful in the extreme....its direct tendency has been to reduce the *ryots* to a state of poverty and dejection of the most distressing nature, to cause a decrease in the population, to impede cultivation, to ruin those resources whence the Government might soon have derived a handsome revenue, to create constant dispute and anxiety in the minds of the people, to eradicate every feeling of gratitude towards their rules, and to enrich a few worthless beings at the expense of the whole population of the country."[9]

The investigators also noted that the system was abused by a few Chaudhuris in concert with the corrupt amlah who enjoyed 'loosely defined fiscal powers' and as a result people 'placed completely at their mercy suffered severely'.

With their recommendations accepted the ryots received settlement of lands directly from the Government. Duties to collect revenue were assigned to Tahsildars who received as their remuneration a fixed rate of commission that ranged from 7 to 15 percent. This arrangement came into force in Lower Assam in 1833 and it was decided to extend it into the remaining areas. In 1835-36 two changes were made in this arrangement. Leases were to be granted for a number of years and the Tahsildar became a revenue contractor in the sense that he was to meet the contractual obligations to pay the amount of revenue settled by the Government. He could on the one hand 'reap what benefit he could from extending cultivation, and on the other hand he was responsible for ordinary losses occasioned by diminished cultivation'.

Anandaram Dekial Phukan had a skeptical attitude toward this system. He observed that this would neither help the process of advancement of cultivation nor would it bring about general improvement of the country. "In general the lands of the Ryots are measured either annually or after every two or three years, and public assessment being fixed on the basis of the Ryots' cultivations for a term extending generally from one to five years, the Chowdrees and Bisyas are entrusted with its collection from the Ryots for the same term, and are allowed a commission of from ten to seventeen Rupees percent as charges of collection."[10] If the area of cultivation was extended additional assessed revenue was retained by them, and if it shrunk because of desertion or for any other reason the resulting loss of revenue was to be borne by these fiscal officers. On the expiry of every period of contract, a fresh survey would be made and the revenue fixed for the period following it and the subsequent only. Generally the period of settlement throughout the province did not exceed five years.

According to Dhekial Phukan the majority of these fiscal officers seldom gained anything exceeding the percentage allowed them as their remuneration but there were instances of some of these officers, who suffered considerable losses and even condition of 'utter ruin' in the event of desertion by ryots in particular parts of the country where tillage fluctuated and the cultivators were non-resident ryots.

Also, if any collecting officer failed to record any prospect of raising revenue at the expiration of his short lease without assigning 'good reasons' for the same he was liable to suffer dismissal from his charge, a punishment that would be meted out to him without considering the situation in which he did not have sufficient 'means and inducements to incite him to exert himself in the improvement of his charge'. In such an atmosphere of uncertainty these officers of his kind were indifferent to the expansion of, or shrinkage in cultivation since any rise in revenue from expansion, if any, would 'only swell the public treasury without adding to their own gain'. Therefore Dhekial Phukan proposed a modification in the system by granting "long lease to the officers now employed as collectors of the several fiscal divisions". The modus operandi for this change would be to "let out farms or *ijarahs* for terms extending upto 20 or 25 years, on the basis of an assessment that was to be fixed on an accurate survey and would continue invariable till the expiration of the lease; it further provided that the farmers would be permitted to appropriate to their own use any increase in the Revenue which they might effect during the period of their lease, holding them at the same time responsible for any deficiency caused by other than accidental or natural causes, that at the expiration of the lease, the assessment might be fixed on a re-measurement and survey of the farms, and the lease continued to the original farmer; and that the farmers be allowed to let out all the unoccupied and waste lands within their farms on such terms as they deemed best conducive to their interests, a measure which alone was likely to reclaim the vast wastes of the country."[11]

Dheikial Phukan was categorically against the introduction of the permanent settlement system as was done in Bengal. He said in unequivocal term that the preservation of the ancient 'Ryotwaree' system in Assam and the recognition of the proprietory right of the Ryots of their respective holdings were the 'greatest boon' the British Government conferred on the country. He was of course aware of some of the abuses of the system perpetrated by the revenue farmers and Mufussil Revenue officers that caused alienation of the lands of the poor Ryots on some pretexts as also levying a general cess or other forms of illegal impositions for their private use. He also proposed several measures for the protection of the Ryots' rights to their lands.

The revenue reform of 1832-33 implied that the entire burden of tax liability of the peasants was limited to land and capitation taxes. But there was no uniformity in the rates charged in the different districts nor in the classification of land according to fertility and productivity in different parts. The rates in the different districts were given as under:

(i) Kamrup: revenue ranged from Re.1 to 0.37 per plough

(ii) Darrang: revenue ranged from Re.1.25 to 1.50 per plough

(iii) Nagaon: revenue ranged from Re.0.50 to 1.00 per plough

(iv) In Raha, Morung and Chapari mahals in lieu of land tax plough / hoe taxes varying between Re.1 and Rs.2 were charged.

(v) Sibsagar (1839): 0.25 per bigha (1/3rd acre) on *rupit* land (best arable land for rice cultivation) and 0.125 rupee for other lands.

(vi) Lakhimpur (1842): rates varied between 0.25 and 0.125.

The poll tax that was imposed on one's caste and profession was discontinued from 1837-38 and the entire liability of tax payment was fixed and devolved on land.[12]

The district collectors were prone to raise land revenue rates misjudging the capacity of the ryots to pay at higher rate, this was because they found that the peasants promptly met their obligations in this regard. Even the Board of Revenue turned down some of the proposals for enhancement of land revenue rates with remarks that caution was called for in enhancing the land revenue rates 'in a newly but partially cultivated province like Assam'.[13] Despite this consideration the rate on non-rupit land in Lakhimpur was raised from Re.0.50 to 0.75. In Sibsagar the rates for different category of land were raised from Re.1.25 to 1.50. In Kamrup the rate of *bori* land was raised from 0.25 to 0.50 rupee in 1844-45. In 1848-49 it was further raised to full one rupee in order to equalize the rates on all non-*rupit* lands. On similar ground, in Darrang district also rate on non-*rupit* land was raised from Re.0.75 to Re.0.875.[14]

Despite such revenue measures making the burden of land tax payment proportional to the fertility of the different types of land the result was far from satisfactory. Dhekial Phukan observed that the assessment did not appear to have been made according to the actual capabilities of the ryots. Therefore he proposed that *rupit* or rice lands be divided into two or three classes based on quality and capability of the soil for taxing at proportionately lower rates for the less fertile and higher rates for the more fertile lands. He was against any enhancement of the rates prevailing then since they were already excessively high. The Government, he opined, must first take measures for effecting improvement in agriculture and commerce before thinking of considering any rise in the rates of assessment. He estimated that in the poorest-classes of *rupit* lands assessment of revenue equalled half the value of production of those lands. Such exhorbitant assessment would surely cause unhappiness of the people.[15] Dhekial Phukan's proposition failed to reverse the Government's decision to raise revenue demands from time to time.

Raising of revenue demands was sought to be justified by the government on the assumption that the Assamese peasants who were by nature lethargic would of necessity overcome their sluggishness and be induced to produce more for paying higher amounts of taxes to the government. In the process peasants were put under unbearable pressure. It was further aggravated as the peasants and others were required to pay all taxes in cash since in the early years of the colonial rule the economy faced a severe shortage of cash.

2. The Cash Crunch and the Hardships of Peasants

In the pre-colonial period only small parts of government and private transactions involved the use of cash. Most of the taxes were paid in kind, the rest in cash. In the Ahom period cash mainly consisted of gold and silver coins issued by the Ahom rulers and also the coins issued by the Mughals when they occupied parts of Western Assam. During the Ahom rule state officials were paid their remunerations in kind by assigning a number of *paiks* to them. For public works, workers engaged were the *paiks*, who were also paid wages not in cash. Large parts of local materials required for public works could be obtained from the surplus generated by the *paiks*. Major parts of the internal trade transactions could be conducted through the barter system of exchange. Therefore, the overall need of the volume of cash in the economy was small which the available supply of cash could meet.

But under the new regime the demand for cash went up manifold. For, one thing, almost all government functions entailed cash transactions. Remunerations to all civil and military officers and members of the staff were paid in cash. All government purchases were made in exchange of money. Total disbursement of cash by the government was the sum total of all government expenditures, such as, on salaries and wages, purchases of materials for public works and running of government offices, etc. But not the entire amount of public expenditure circulated within Assam as, according to Francis Jenkin's report on Asam submitted in 1833, nearly one-half of the public expenditure on salaries was remitted out of the province, since a large majority of the public servants hailed from outside Assam. Besides, the surplus government revenue generated in Assam, i.e., total revenue minus total expenditure, was deposited into the treasury in Calcutta. Total revenue receipts and disbursements for the year 1824-25 to 1837-38 are given in table VI.1 below. The table indicates that over Rs.5 lakhs of surplus revenue in cash was withdrawn from circulation in Assam and transferred to Calcutta treasury.

In 1835 coins minted by the government were proclaimed the sole legal tender in the country. Obviously this government decision further reduced the supply of cash. And as government spending on public works and purchases of locally made goods was of quite limited amount, infusion of substantial amount of cash by the government into the economy was also lacking.

On the other hand, the demand for cash went up as the government pursued the policy of monetization of all public transactions. The peasants, artisans and others had to obtain cash for meeting their tax and other liabilities to the government. Therefore they sought to sell their products, commodities and services in the market in exchange of cash. But Assam was still in the stage of subsistence economy, therefore, the market for goods and services was very undeveloped. Demand for food and other essential consumption goods in terms of cash was very much low while the supply of such goods was much higher which meant that the sellers were forced to exchange their goods at very low prices. For example: the seized stock of rice of a farmer who became a defaulter in respect to payment of land revenue was sold in public auction at the rate of only twelve rupees for one hundred maunds.[16]

The growth of market was an important prerequisite for economic development of Assam. For facilitating the process of growth in Assam of those days when commercial banking was non-existent, rise in the volume of market transaction required a rise in the supply of legal tender money and an increased velocity of its circulation. Some traders took full advantage of the prevailing shortage of money and provided loans of cash to the needy farmers and others at very high rates of interest, even as high as ten percent per month in some cases.[17]

The sufferings of the ryots became so acute that the government had to decide to accept 'cloths of certain fixed dimensions, salt, iron-hoes and other articles in general use besides gold, ivory, muga silk, munjit, etc. in settlement of land revenue demand.[18]

As the value of money increased and the prices of goods fell, the peasants and artisans had to pay land revenue and taxes to the government practically at higher real rates even though their money rates remained unchanged. This was so even when the revenue could be paid in kind, for quantities of goods required to be handed over to the government must have been determined on the basis of calculation at the low market prices.

The revenue and monetary policy of the government thus caused the peasants untold sufferings. A large number of them were unable to meet the revenue demands of the government and were forced to abandon their lands and homes and take refuge in the remote interior for reclaiming waste lands for cultivation for mere survival. There were also many cases of such wretched peasants selling themselves and their children as slaves. No wonder, many prosperous villages became desolate.

The process of the vital structural change from a subsistence to a monetized economy was beset with miseries of the toiling masses due to shortage of money in circulation. Instead of transferring surplus cash revenue to Calcutta, had the government spent it within Assam to rebuild the worn-out and damaged physical infrastructure and taken up additional projects for public works, the deteriorating economic conditions of the people could well have been overcome.

Assam had favourable balance of trade as its exports exceeded imports in the 1830s. The chief items of exports were mustard-seed, muga thread and lac while the major item of import was salt. During the period from 26 December 1832 to April 1835 the total value of exports and of imports amounted to Rs.7,00,325 and Rs.5,50,455 respectively.

During that period Assam had an export surplus which was to the tune of Rs.1,49,870. This trade surplus also did not augment the supply of cash "since the usual export goods were generally bartered for salt and other essential commodities and since the salt traders were all foreigners....."[20]

The Chowdhuri system of land revenue administration was finally done away with in 1867 and settlements were made by the government directly with the ryots in accordance with a Resolution of the Government of Bengal dated 5 November 1867. The system of waste land grants rule was effectively introduced in 1836 mainly to facilitate the development of tea plantation in Assam. These decisions had far-reaching consequences on the economic growth of Assam, which will be studied in the following chapters.

The revenue policy of the colonial government in the early phase of its occupation of Assam aiming at maximizing revenue collections, when the people were still to recover from the disastrous consequences of Burmese occupation, inflicted much hardship on the poor peasants who had to flee their homes and lands to escape paying taxes to the government. As a result some parts of Assam were depopulated and the growth of production and income was severely affected. This was so also because the government did not take adequate steps to renovate and extend irrigation works nor did it provide specific opportunities for the peasants to adopt better and sustainable technology for agricultural and allied productive activities. Neither any high-yielding variety of crop nor any improved breed for animal husbandry was introduced.

The government also ignored the menace of addiction to opium among the Assamese people that was ruining their health and also their ability to take part in productive activities energetically. Even the need for creation and expansion of educational facilities was overlooked. All this left the people of the province at the low level of stationary subsistence economy.

Table 6.1
Revenue Receipts and Disbursements in Assam, 1824-25 to 1837-38

Assam	Receipts Rs. (Sicca)	Disbursements Rs. (Sicca)	Revenue Surplus/Deficit Rs. (Sicca)
Lower Assam			
1824-25	118,723	29,538	89,185
1825-26	202,601	92,513	109.548
1826-27	178,686	125,015	53,671
1832-33	183,196	n.a.	n.a.
Upper Assam			
1825-26	28,058	27,834	224
1826-27	46,073	40,731	5,342
1827-28*	38,835	61,695	-22,860
1828-29	78,452	36,166	42,286
1829-30	90,060	53,921	36,138
1831-32	72,136	n.a.	
1832-33	n.a.	n.a.	
	Revenue receipts under Rajah Purandar's Management	Tribute Transferred to British North-Eastern Agency	
1833-34+	69,450	50,000	
1834-35	70,150	50,000	
1835-36*	64,254	34,000	
1836-37	54,449	28,000	
1837-38	42,216	--	

*** Cholera epidemic year expains the deficit.**

+ Naduar, yielding Rs.10,000, had been transferred this year to Lower Assam.

This accounts for the fall in revenue in Upper Assam under the Rajah, partially.

Source: Amalendu Guha (1991), Assam: *Medieval and Early Colonial* Assam: Society, Polity, Economy, K.P. Bagchi & Co., Kolkata, p.155.

NOTES AND REFERENCES

1. Anandaram Dhekial Phookan, Observations on the Administration of the Province of Assam, Appendix J of A.J. Moffat Mills, Report on the Province of Assam (1854), reprinted by Publication Board, Assam (1984), p. 93.
2. Edward Gait, (1997), *A History of Assam,* Lawyer's Book Stall, Guwahati, p. 275.
3. A.C. Banerjee (1992), *The New Regime, 1826-31*, published as chapter one of the Comprehensive History of Assam, Vol.IV, H.K. Barpujari (Ed), Publication Board, Assam, Guwahati, p. 31.
4. *ibid.* pp. 31-32.
5. *ibid.* p. 32.p
6. *ibid.* p. 33.
7. *ibid.* p. 31.
8. *ibid.* p. 38.
9. Quoted in Banerjee (1992), *ibid.* p. 45.
10. A Dhekial Phukan (1984), *op.cit.* p. 95.
11. *ibid.* pp. 96-97.
12. H.K. Barpujari (ed) (1993), *The Comprehensive History of Assam,* Vol.V, Publication Board, Assam, Guwahâti, p. 7.
13. *ibid.* p. 8.
14. *ibid.* p. 8.
15. Dhekial Phukan, *op.cit,* p. 102.
16. Amalendu Guha (1991), *Medieval and Early Colonial Assam: Society, Polity, Economy,* K.P. Bagchi & Co., Kolkata, p. 144.
17. *ibid.* p. 144.
18. *ibid.* p. 144.
19. *ibid.* pp. 152-53. The amount of trade surplus has been calculated from table 7.2. This table is a reproduction with slight adaptation from Pemberton, *The Report on the Eastern Frontier, 1835,* Tables 12-14.
20. *The Cambridge Economic History of India,* Vol.2 (1983) Cambridge University Press, p .121.

7
RYOTWARI SETTLEMENTS AND SUFFERINGS OF THE RYOTS

1. Introduction

Land tenure system crucially influences use of land for agriculture and allied productive activities. Since Assam's economy was almost entirely an agrarian one, the land settlement system devised and implemented by the colonial government needs to be studied for understanding the trend of agricultural production and economic conditions of the peasants under the new regime. Therefore in this chapter implementation of the ryotwari settlement of land by the government which caused suffering of the ryots is highlighted.

The Government introduced the ryotwari system of land settlement in Assam, excluding some small areas in its western part (Goalpara district), instead of extending the system of zamindari settlement as it prevailed in Bengal. Under the new system there were three main categories of land tenure, namely, ryotwari, *nisf-khiraj* and *lakhiraj*. Under the ryotwari tenancy, the ryots held land on periodic lease from Government and were free to relinquish the whole or part of the land so held giving due notice and in the prescribed manner. The ryots could take up unoccupied wastelands for cultivation in terms of settlement in their favour in due course. It was not required to give intimation to the Government before reclaiming wastelands for cultivation. Such wastelands lay in the districts of Kamrup, Darrang and Nowgong near the banks on either side of the Brahmaputra which were inundated by floods. Though covered with reeds and high grass, these tracts were cultivable fertile lands. In these areas permanent cultivation was not possible. The peasants raised usually the *ahu* rice and mustard for three years or so and then left the areas fallow for a few years. In the submontane tracts shifting cultivation was practised and these areas too were exempt from the system of regular revenue settlements.

The ryotwari system of land tenure covered the large fertile and populous areas lying between the submontane and riparian tracts. In these plain lands comparatively high-yielding *sali* rice was grown involving transplantation of paddy seedlings. This was the permanent form of wet-rice cultivation. Before introducing the system of granting lands on ten-year lease in 1870, ryotwari lands were held under one - year lease which were not heritable or transferable. But the holdings under ten-year lease were heritable and transferable. Of course, such transfers had to be registered in the Deputy Commissioner's office. Rules for such settlements were framed in the Land and Revenue Regulation of 1870, which became operative in 1883. As noted in the Report on the Administration of Assam, for the year 1921-22, "the general system of ten-year settlements was introduced in all parts of the Assam Valley, where the cultivation and occupation of land are of a permanent character. In the five districts of Assam proper the bulk of the more permanently cultivated land is, therefore, now held under a periodic settlement, during the currency of which the raiyat is guaranteed against enhancement of the revenue rates".[1]

A ryot was, however, entitled to relinquish the whole or any portion of his holding and take up new lands for settlement. Any land under such a holding could be taken up by Government for any public purpose on payment of compensation. The lands held under annual lease system for 'fluctuating system of cultivation' no such compensation was payable for land. Of course, Government paid the ryot 'the value of any trees, houses, crops, etc. actually standing on the land at the time of resumption'.

2. Nisf-khiraj and Lakhiraj Holdings

In the Ahom period some lands were granted as *nisf-*

khiraj and *lakhiraj* holdings. The revenue-free *lakhiraj* holdings were granted as *debottor* or temple lands, like *brahmattar* granted to individual Brahman priests and *dharmattor* granted to religious communities. Jenkins confirmed that the holdings of *bona fide brahmottar* grantees were revenue-free. Other *bona fide lakhiraj* and *nisf-Khiraj* lands were assessed at the rate of 8 annas a *pura* (11/3 acre) as against Re. 1 per *pura* for the ryotwari settlements. The *nisf-khirajdars* were allowed the privilege of holding waste lands of their estates revenue free unless they derived a regular income therefrom. Seventy-five per cent of the total number of *nisf-Khiraj* estates were situated in Kamrup district.[2] The *lakhiraj* and *nisf-Khiraj* estates were 'ordinarily cultivated by sub-tenents'. The system of permanently - settled estates obtained in Goalpara district. There were also four other kinds of special tenures in Assam, namely, *Chamuas*, *Khats*, ten-twenties and six-pie *lakhiraj* tenures. There were nineteen such estates including the nine held by the *Chaudhuries*. The remaining ten estates were originally held revenue-free. But the government finding the titles of these holdings invalid, resumed them and 'settled at a *jama* fixed in perpetuity'.[3]

3. Land Revenue Assessments : 1868 - 69

The ryotwari system which ensured peasant proprietorship of cultivated land was as such, a better one than the zamindari system. But in Assam, it is aptly observed in the Cambridge Economic History, "the government itself exercised the powers of a zamindar, and the way the revenue demand was increased, the context in which such increases were enforced, and their consequences for the peasantry, were distinctive"[4]. The periodic enhancements of revenue enforced by the government actually hit the peasantry very hard and affected the growth of agriculture. As noted in Chapter VIII, the government offered more and more liberal terms for wasteland settlement for producing special crops, tea in particular. But where land was used for cultivation of rice and other ordinary crops the peasants were charged higher and higher rates of revenue for different categories of land. The unit of measurement of land assessed for revenue collection was changed from *purah* (11/3 acre) with effect from 1864-69 and categories of land were reclassified in 1868-69 for assessing revenue at different rates. The most fertile cultivable land where winter crop or transplanted paddy is grown is called 'Rupit'. 'Faringati' stands for dry weather crop lands. Homestead or garden land was known as 'Basti'.

The rates of revenue assessed on different categories of land, after numerous exchanges of communications between the local authorities and the Central Government were fixed for 1864-65 but had to be refixed in 1868-69 as shown in table 7.1 below:.[5]

Table 7.1
Land Revenue Assessments on Different Categories of Land

District	1864-65					1868-69	
	Rupit		Non-Rupit		Basti (homestead or garden land) Re.	Rupit	Faringati (dry-weather crop lands)
	As.	P.	As.	P.		As.	As
Kamroop	6	0	4	0	1	10	8
Darrang	5	6	4	6	1	10	8
Nowgong	5	6	4	6	1	10	8
Sibsagar	5	0	4	0	1	10	8
Lakhimpur	5	0	4	0	1	10	8

Source : Barpujari, op. cit. (1993), p. 35

4. The Assam Land Revenue Regulations, 1886

The Assam Land Revenue Regulations was promulgated in 1886 according to which rules were made for upward revision of land revenue rates in 1892. The Government believed that over the years since 1868-69, when the rates were last revised, the material conditions of the people, including the peasants, much improved and the *ryots'* capacity for payment of revenue also increased. This was because the cultivators were getting higher prices for foodgrains and other crops they produced than before on account of increasing demands for such goods from a rising population, including tea garden workers, while costs of cultivation were easing following improvement in the basic infrastructure - road and river communications, expansion of administrative structure, etc.

The reality was not so favourable for the ordinary ryots in the villages. The development of infrastructure benefited mainly the tea planters, urban-dwellers and people belonging to the upper class in social hierarchy. The majority of the *ryots* could hardly produce any marketable surplus other than that which they were forced to exchange for cash to pay the land revenue and other government dues. Moreover, they were already overburdened with the existing high rates of assessment. Dhekial Phukan observed that "a *poorah* of high roopit land yielding twenty or fifteen maunds of rice valued at from 2 to 3 rupees is loaded with a tax of one rupee and four annas. Unless, therefore, the Government provides the people with better and improved means of cultivating their lands, an increase of assessment will inevitably lead to an increase of the unhappiness of the people".[6]

The pitiable conditions of the ryots were tellingly described by "An Assamese" from Jorhat in a letter dated 5th May 1886 to the editor of The Statesman, Calcutta, which was published on 21st May 1886. He pointed out that the Government's Forest Rules and Regulations were "working mischief to the fullest extent upon the helpless and innocent ryots, who have to procure their fuel and building materials from the forest". Then came the promulgation of the Assam Land Revenue and Regulation Act. The said writer opined that the government's impression about the ryots' plight was wrong. He lamented that for meeting the government's revenue demands, the parents were constrained to be "separated from their children whose services they pledge in order to get a loan for escaping the Government liability and many a ryot incurs debt on this occasion at an exhorbitant interest such as has no ending and such as brings ruin upon himself and his family, it is needless to say".[7]

5. Land Revenue Rates as Enhanced in 1893-94

In October 1889, the Revenue and Agriculture Department of Assam proposed before the Chief Commissioner of Assam that in view of the material advancement of the Assam

Valley, when the reassessment of the decennial settled land would be due in 1893, revenue assessment rates for the better quality of land might be enhanced. It was pointed out that the demarcation between the superior and inferior quality of lands would be possible to make in consultation with the people concerned. Such classification of land was unknown in Assam, even then it was considered feasible as in other parts of India. N. Z. Darrah, Director of Land Records, after studying the relevant conditions obtaining in Burma, as officially directed, submitted a report on the measures to be taken for reassessment of land revenue in Assam Valley. He proposed that taking each village as the unit of assessment, lands in a village should be classified into three categories depending on "the relative value as measured by the proportion of the settled area to the wastes, proportion of fluctuating to permanent cultivation and average size of the fields". The Director also opined that the detailed enquiries should be made into the soil productivity, price of produced crop, costs of cultivation, of carrying produce to markets and the net profit earned by the cultivator.[8]

The then Chief Commissioner, J. W. Quinton in his note of August 1890 did not favour any change in the existing system under which lands were divided into three classes, namely, *basti*, *rupit* and *faringati*. But he wanted to raise the revenue rates.

Quinton's successor William Ward also wanted to retain the above - stated three - fold classification of land. He, however, wanted that these classes of land should be further subdivided at least into two categories taking into consideration (i) the demand for land in a given village or group of villages, (ii) productivity of the land and (iii) facilities for marketing of the produced crops. The quality of land could be ascertained by noting the extent of demand for land as indicated by the proportions of cultivated land as against the uncultivated wastes, that of permanent to fluctuating cultivation and the density of population.

The consensus of official opinion was that rates of revenue on land should be enhanced as there had been considerable extent of economic growth in the province that had benefited the ryots. Accordingly the Chief Commissioner desired that revenue rates should be raised at different rates for different qualities of *basti* (homestead), *rupit* and *faringati* lands. In the villages graded as first class the existing rates were to be doubled, for the villages in the second grade the rates to be increased by 50 per cent and for the third grade villages by 25 per cent. On receipt of the Government of India's directive, rules were formed under the Assam Land Revenue Regulation I of 1886 and new rates of revenue were fixed. These were published in the Gazette on 8 October 1892 for information as also for response of the public.

The new rates were vehemently opposed by several associations, public leaders, and ryots of all the five Brahmaputra Valley districts excepting Goalpara where the Zamindari system obtained. Public criticism was based on the facts that there was no tangible improvement in the economic conditions of the ryots who would be hit very hard if new rates were implemented. Memorials were submitted to the Government by several associations arguing the case against enhancement of revenue rates. The manner of classifying villages and classes of land was also objected to. The noted organization of civil society of those days, namely, the *Jorhat Sarbajanik Sabha* admitted that after annexation of Assam by the British the people were generally better off than in the days of devastation perpetrated by the Burmese invaders. Yet the condition of the people was so bad that large areas of cultivable land lay fallow. The rytos continued to cultivate their land by using the age-old crude implements and weak cattle. If they were made to pay higher rates of revenue they would be driven to the clutches of the *mahajans* and would remain perpetually indebted to them.

One argument against the raising of revenue was that the government had done very little toward improving agricultural productivity. Moreover, the government so neglected the construction and maintenance of bunds and embankments, etc. that the peasants suffered heavy losses of crops and cattle on account of recurring floods. It was also feared that many ryots having been unable to pay higher rates of revenue would be forced to relinquish their lands which would cause fall in the output of rice and rise in prices of foodgrains.

Gunaviram Barua, a retired Extra Assistant Commissioner, made a representation stating that increase in the demand for land be limited to urban areas only. He also doubted if market rate of cultivated produce really exceeded 25 per cent on an average since the latest assessment in 1868. He also apprehended that the proposed hikes in revenue rates would hit hard the Brahmins, Gossains and the gentry whose main occupation was other than cultivation and who generally sublet their lands to underryots. They might be compelled to alienate their holdings to others.[9]

The government stuck to maintain its stand on the classification of villages and lands into different classes as it would be unreasonable to assess two *rupit* plots of land - say, one yielding 12 maunds per bigha and the other 5 maunds, at the same rate. But the people insisted on the continuation of the existing system as they got accustomed to it.[10] As a consequence of such a rigid stand taken by the government and the landholders - ryots, Gossains and others - violent protests were made by the latter against the former's land reassessment measure. In mobilizing the ryots' protest agitations the *Raijmel* (association of the masses of people) took the leading part. "Headed by their respective *Gossains* or leading personalities", writes Barpujari, "the *mels* originally constituted as an authority on socio-religious matters, gradually developed into a *Raijmel* as an organ for redress of general grievances of diverse communities and from their original Khel or clan their jurisdiction extended to the village and even to one or more *tehsils*"[11]. The violent protests and agitations were widespread and suppression of these upheavals by government was also ruthless.[12] According to the official report, there were a dozen casualties.

Finally, in February 1894, the government decided to limit the enhancement of rates for *Faringati* (inferior) lands to 32.7 per cent and even for other lands, in the cases of individual holdings, the hike in assessment was kept nearly within 50 per cent. The revised rates were as given below (Table 7.2)

Table 7.2
Land Revenue Rates as Finally Fixed in 1893-94

Class of Land		Rates proposed			Rates per bigha 1893-94		
I.	Domestic or garden land	Rs.	a.	P.	Rs.	a.	P.
	First class	1	6	0	1	6	0
	Second class	1	4	0	1	4	0
	Third class	1	2	0	1	2	0
II.	Rupit						
	First class	1	0	0	1	0	0
	Second class	0	14	0	0	14	0
	Third class	0	12	0	0	12	0
III.	Faringati						
	First class	0	14	0	0	12	0
	Second class	0	12	0	0	10	0
	Third class	0	10	0	0	9	0

Source : Barpujari, *op. cit.* p. 36

At the fag end of the nineteenth century, following the third Burmese war, famines in some parts of India and the fall in the value of Rupee, etc. caused a severe crunch in financial resources of the Government. The shortfalls in the central allocations for the provinces were sought to be met locally by raising revenue collections, mainly, land revenue[13]. This was the basic reason for the Assam government's decision to enhance land revenue rates. The agrarian scenario in Assam started changing as some degree of dynamism and growth in agriculture were visible in the wake of immigration of peasants from Bengal into Assam. This aspect will be considered in Chapter-IX.

The protest movements of the ryots against the Government's decision to enhance the revenue rates were a reflection of stagnation in the agricultural sector comprising the large masses of peasants living on a subsistence level.

NOTES AND REFERENCES

1. *Report on the Administration of Assam, for the year 1921-22* (reprinted as *Report on the Administration of North East India* (1921-22) by Mittal Publication, Delhi, in 1984, Part II Administration Report, p. 59.

2. *ibid.* p. 60
3. *ibid.* p. 60
4. Dharma Kumar (ed), 1983, *The Cambridge Economic History of India,* Vol. 2 (C.1757 - C. 1970), Cambridge University Press, Cambridge, 1983, p. 119-20.
5. H. K. Barpujari (ed), (1993), *The Comprehensive History of Assam,* Vol. V, Publication Board, Assam, Guwahati, p. 35.
6. Anandaram Dhekial Phukan, op. cit. (1984), p. 102.
7. "An Assamese", from Jorhat, "Published in the Letter to Editor" column titled 'Assam' in *The Statesman,* Calcutta for May 21, 1886.
8. H. K. Barpujari (ed), 1993, *op. cit.* p. 23.
9. *ibid.* pp. 25 and 28
10. *ibid.* p. 30
11. *ibid.* p. 30
12. *ibid.* An account of these agrarian ryots is given in pages 30 to 33.
13. *ibid.* p. 34

8
WASTELAND SETTLEMENT AND DEVELOPMENT OF TEA INDUSTRY

1. Introduction

In the colonial period, extensive area of cultivable wooded land was not used for agricultural production. It was not required to reclaim these lands for agricultural production. The land already under cultivation was sufficient for the small population to meet their needs for food and other necessaries. Such wooded parts of the terrain were not, however, useless. For these were the sources of timber, building materials and many sorts of wild nuts, fruits, berries, etc. Moreover these protected plots of agricultural land from erosion and acted as natural means of conservation of soil. But the foreign rulers considered such areas of land as wasteland. Therefore, the government policy on use of wasteland and its implementation was another decisive factor of shaping the agricultural economy of colonial Assam.

Assam's population was drastically reduced because of the protracted civil wars and also the Burmese occupation of Assam that preceded its annexation by the British in 1826. Natural calamities like floods, earthquakes and outbreak of Cholera and of *Kala-azar* on epidemic scale also further added to the process of depopulation. This trend rendered vast areas of cultivable land fallow. A large number of villages were left desolate and covered with trees, bushes, shrubs and reeds. Besides, the uncultivated lands in the Ahom period also covered a sizeable part of the total area of cultivable land.

After the annexation of Assam the government became concerned about how best to utilize such wastelands for increasing revenue realization and for effecting improvement in economic condition of the people. Therefore the local administrative functionaries formulated several proposals for providing incentives and opportunities to resourceful and enterprising persons willing to seek settlement of wastelands on attractive terms that the government would offer and also to invest capital on development of wastelands for productive purpose. These authorities also considered several possibilities of remunerative uses of such settled lands, even in some cases, with the involvement of the government in such enterprises.

David Scott, the first Agent to the Governor General and Commissioner of Assam (1825-31), submitted a plan to the higher authority for utilization of wastelands for producing light-weight and high-value exportable goods like *Muga* and mulberry silk. Traditionally the people of Assam were skilled in producing *muga* and other varieties of silk. He proposed that the government should incur some expenditure on establishing sericulture demonstration farms in order to provide training to the local producers in method of growing better species of mulberry plants and better breeds of silk-worms which should turn out silk of exportable quality. His initial proposition did not find favour with the government. He repeatedly pleaded for the development of sericulture which he thought held the most bright prospect for revenue augmentation. Ultimately, that should in turn open up employment and higher income opportunities for the people. He even foresaw the possibility in this scheme of establishing "a small commercial Residency superintended by the medical officer of Gauhati, with a view, not so much to securing an immediate profit on the investment, but to create a steady demand for the silk"[1].

Scott estimated that for production of improved and good quality silk, the required amount of government's outlay would be about twelve to fifteen thousand rupees. If the government did not approve of such an outlay, Scott proposed to levy an extra cess upon the inhabitants. "The trifling additional burden to which the people would thus be individually subjected" on account of the cess, Scott assured the government, "would be speedily and amply repaid by the increased value of the land and by the introduction of an article of exchangeable value so much wanted at present to enable them to provide for the payment of revenue"[2]. The authorities considered Scott's proposal "a doubtful experiment" and therefore it could not be pursued. .

Scott had proposed in 1827 a plan of granting wastelands on attractive terms. But the response was far from encouraging. Captain Francis Jenkins, who served as Commissioner of Assam from 1834 to 1866, put forward a more liberal scheme of wasteland settlement to the government of Bengal in 1836. The Governor of Bengal, however, favoured the scheme on the lines of the *Sundarban Grants*. He wished to offer more favourable terms for settlement in order to involve 'foreign enterprise, industry, capital and skill' for utilization of vast potentialities of Assam's resources. According to this scheme as approved, wastelands "(i) amidst cultivated lands were to be granted rent-free for five years, (ii) high reed and grass wastes to be granted rent-free for ten years, (and) (iii) forest and high wastelands to be granted for a term of twenty years"[3].

Jenkins and the District Collectors apprehended that this scheme would pave the way for the zamindars of Bengal ('foreigners") to take up large tracts for settlement and then sublet them which would lead to the emergence of the zamindary system in Assam like that of Bengal[4]. In appreciation of such objections, a few clauses were added to the rules, namely, the grantee would not get any exemption from paying full revenue "for lands broken up without sanction of the Collector" and that 'no grant for agricultural purpose could be made of an extent less than one hundred English acres. The applicant must also satisfy the Collector that he was in possession of necessary capital and agricultural stock or implements to the extent of rupees three per acre".[5] Obviously only the rich European capitalists could avail themselves of such settlement terms.

But Jenkins noted in 1846 that vast areas of wasteland still remained unutilized. He also concluded "that the upper classes in Assam had not the means enough for their reclamation'; therefore 'he urged the Sadar Board of Revenue to consider' if additional incentives could be offered to the speculator to occupy these lands for cultivation of articles of foreign export like sugarcane or the indigo"[6].

Jenkins planned to encourage the Assamese people to develop "an industrial and commercial bias by encouraging increased cultivation of such crops as were easily marketable and by creating a class of speculators to exploit the natural resources of the province(.)" and convert the wastelands into "fruitful fields of sugarcane, mustard, lac, tobacco and vegetables. He felt that a certain amount of compulsion was necessary to rouse the dormant spirit of the people"[7].

In 1856 Jenkins pleaded with the government that even though the people of Assam had not yet been able to take up any sizeable quantity of wastelands for settlement, some of them were, of late, showing their interest in establishing and managing large-sized farms as their career. In accepting Jenkin's proposal, the Government decided in May 1856 to grant wastelands to "Europeans, Assamese, Bengalies and others without distinction and the cultivation of whatever produce the grantee might think proper"[8].

When Jenkins and District Collectors were groping for an effective means for utilization of wastelands for economic development and improvement of the conditions of the people of Assam, a decision had already been taken by the Governor General in Council to appoint a tea-committee in early 1834 for preparing a plan for cultivation of tea-plant in Assam. This came, what Barpujari observed, 'as a god send'[9].

2. Growth of Tea Industry

The political economy of British interest in developing tea industry in Assam has been discussed in Chapter II, Sec. C. It may be reiterated that the discovery of naturally grown tea plants in upper Assam, the problems of having supplies of tea from China dealt with by England and large areas of wasteland suitable for growing tea-plants lying unutilized were the conditions that attracted British enterprise and capital to develop this industry in Assam in the 1830s. Following the appointment of the Tea Committee for Assam in 1834, an experimental tea garden was started by the government in 1836 and tea was manufactured successfully in 1837. In 1838, the Bengal Tea Association was formed in Calcutta. It was a joint venture of the British and Indian entrepreneurs. About the same time some resourceful investors became interested in growing tea here on a commercial basis. Both these groups located in Calcutta and London came together to form the Assam Company in 1839 with a total capital of £500,000 based on 100,000 shares of £5 each[10]. After tea was successfully produced for two consecutive years, the government decided to withdraw itself from directly running tea plantations and growing tea and instead allow the Assam Company or any other concern to grow tea plants by acquiring lands under the Wasteland Grant Rules of 1838[11].

These Rules were as given below:

Table 8.1
Wasteland Settlement Rules 1838

Categories of Wastelands			**Land revenue per acre**
Under grass	Under reeds **and high grass**	Under **forests**	
(i) First 5 years	First 10 years	First 20 years	Nil
(ii) 6th to 8th years	11th to 13th years	21st to 23rd years	9 annas (16 annas make a rupee)
(iii) 9th to 30th years	14th to 35th years	24th to 45th years	Re. 1 – 2 annas
One – fourth of grant revenue – free in perpetuity			

Source : Tabulated from Baden-Powel, *The Land Systems*, Vol.3, PP. 410-15 cited by Guha, vide, Guha (1991), p. 157.

The Government became optimistic about the prospects of development of tea plantations to bring in its wake all-round development of Assam's economy. And it patronized the Assam Company with this end in view by transferring two-thirds of the Government Experimental Tea Gardens to this company in 1840 free of rent for at least the first ten years[12].

The condition of the company in the early years of its formation, "was far from prosperous, but about 1852 its prospects began to improve, and in 1859 it had 4000 acres under cultivation and an outturn of over 760,000 pounds of tea. Its local expenditure exceeded a lakh of rupees a year in 1853, by which time nine other gardens had been started – all in Upper Assam"[13]. There were three private gardens in Sibsagar and six in Lakhimpur. In Kamrup and Darrang districts the gardens were first started in 1854.

Tea was an export-oriented industry and when the world demand fell short of the world supply, price crashed. Since supply-elasticity of tea, being an agricultural crop, is low, the producers suffer great losses, in such an eventuality. In Assam in the 1860s, particularly following the introduction of "fee simple grants" in 1862, and being attracted by the success of the Assam Company there was a mad rush for acquiring wastelands under the Special Wasteland Settlement Rules for raising tea plantations. The situation has been commented upon in the Administration Report for 1921-22 as follows:

"..... although Colonel Jenkins, Commissioner of Assam, recorded a serious warning, no one else seemed able to see formidable dangers into which the too rapid progress of the industry would bring it. Later still, in 1862-63, officials as well as planters seem to have indulged in visions of fabulous prosperity, which only deepened the gloom of the miserable time that was so soon to come on them. ....The evil first fruits of the reckless way in which wastelands have been dealt with, in the belief that Government was fostering tea cultivation thereby, were being gathered in the shape of increasing hostility to Government and its officials, caused by difficulties about surveys, boundaries, title-deeds, and the like which all had arisen out of the mistaken policy of giving vast tracts of land to any one choosing to ask for them, without enquiry and without precaution of any kind"[14].

Gait has also noted that the success of the Assam Tea Company and Jorhat Tea Company, which was formed in 1858, engendered "the most extravagant ideas regarding the prospects of tea cultivation. Fresh gardens were opened in all directions; and a period of wild excitement and speculation supervened. The mania extended even to Government officers; and three Deputy Commissioners, four assistant

Commissioners and several police officers threw up their appointments to engage in tea-planting"[15].

In this situation 'land jobbing and abuse' was indulged in by many grantees of wastelands under the special Land Settlement Rules who started tea plantations not with the objective of manufacturing tea but for selling off to others the estates with mature or immature plantation, or even without any, to earn quick profit. Lands were taken up disregarding their unsuitability for growing tea plants; plantations were opened with insufficient number of bushes and neglecting the problem of insufficiency of labour supply.

As could be expected such mad rush for starting new companies and opening new plantations recklessly resulted in "a general collapse". Many companies became defaulters in meeting their liabilities and had to wound up, and the companies which survived suffered depreciation of their shares as the shareholders sought to get out of tea by selling off their shares in a hurry in the same spirit as they showed in acquiring shares as a speculative venture.

The depression continued until 1869 and the efficiently managed gardens started earning good profit and even some of the defunct gardens reopened under better management. Tea industry recovered from depression and continued to grow steadily for the next thirty years. In 1872 the total acreage under tea in the Brahmaputra valley rose to about 27,000 acres with a turnout of six million pounds of tea. In 1878 the total production of tea in the region including Brahmaputra valley, Cachar and Sylhet was 28.5 million pounds which further rose to 53.5 million in 1885 and to nearly 134 million pounds in 1901. In 1920 the output reached 234 million pounds. "In 1922 owing to fine plucking it fell to 199 million pounds, but in the following year it was 237 million pounds, viz., 160 million in the Brahmaputra and 77 million in Surma valley." The total area under tea cultivation reached 412,000 acres representing 25 per cent of the total area of land taken up for this purpose.[16]

Total investment of capital in tea gardens of Assam was about £14 million. Sixty-eight leading tea companies had £9,654,732 as their share capital and 231,547 acres under tea.[17]

Imports of tea into the United Kingdom from India steadily increased. In 1866 India's share was just 4 per cent and that of China 96 per cent. In 1886 the proportions of imports from China, India and Ceylon were 59%, 38% and 3% respectively. In 1903 India's export of tea to the U.K. accounted for 59% that of China 10% and of Ceylon 31% of the total imports of tea into the U.K.[18]

Expansion of acreage for plantation of tea was encouraged by the Government by progressively offering more and more attractive terms for settlement of waste lands for this purpose. The Rules of 1838 have already been discussed. In 1854 by amending these rules the term of 'the lease was extended to 99 years'. Rates of assessment were also reduced so much that 'during the last 74 years the rent was fixed at only As.6 per acre'. The rules of fee simple grants were promulgated in 1861. Land, under the new system, could be purchased at rates varying between Rs.2.5 and Rs.5 per acre. Those who took lands on lease under the previous system were also permitted to convert those leases into fee simple 'at the twenty years' purchase of the rent payable at the time of commutation'. In 1862, the system of auctioning the grants at an upset price of Rs.2.5 per acre was put into effect. The reserve price for auction was raised to Rs.8 an acre. In 1974 this system was replaced by the system of granting lands on 30 years' lease. The lease was sold at the reserve price of Re.1 per acre. Such lands, at the end of the revenue-free term, were assessed at progressive rates so that in the closing years of the lease the rate might become Re.1 per acre. Gait noted that leases due to expire prior to 1932 could be renewed up to that year 'at rates varying from Re.1-2-0 to Re.1-4-0 per acre'[19].

The growth of tea industry was occasionally affected by the supply exceeding demand and the price of tea falling, but the long-run trend had been one of steady growth. By the end of the nineteenth century, i.e., in 1898 precisely, the supply outstripped demand, even as the cost of placing tea in the market increased on account of the fall in money-supply caused by the closing down of the mints which raised the value of the rupee which was legal tender in which wages to labour and other staff were paid. For a brief period tea industry 'entered once more on a period of depression'. But the industry took measures to reduce cost of production, to open new markets to stop extensions of plantation, etc. The industry thus succeeded in recovering from the slump condition. Again the industry faced difficulty after the First World War ended, but this was followed by a period of remarkable prosperity. In 1923 the average price of tea produced in the Brahmaputra Valley was 15 annas and 10 pies per pound. This price provided good returns to the industry. The demand for tea went up in Great Britain and Ireland as price of tea fell over the years. It increased from about 100 million pounds in 1866 to 255 million pounds in 1903. Also the tea planters of India and Ceylon succeeded in capturing new markets so that their sales of tea outside the United Kingdom went up from 39 million pounds in 1895 to 140 million pounds in 1923.[20]

The industry could achieve steady growth by reducing cost of placing tea on the market by developing improved method of cultivation which made it possible to raise average yield of tea per acre from 224 Ibs. to 448 Ibs. Mechanization of the process of manufacturing tea, amalgamation of small tea gardens, reduction in European staff and expenditure incurred on machinery, stores, tea chests and freight – both local and ocean, resulted in overall reduction in cost.

The industry built up such a strong foundation for itself as could weather many upheavals in the world market for tea and fluctuations in prices. The industry all over the world was affected by the Great Depression of 1929-1931. Price of Assam valley tea per pound fell from 15as 5p in 1927 to 10as 9p in 1929, to 10as 1p in 1930 and 7as 10p in 1931. Areas under tea in the two valleys taken together increased from 360 thousand to 420 thousand acres in 1921 and to 434 thousand in 1931. This shows that increase in the decade 1911-21 was 16.7 p.c which fell to 3.3 p.c in the decade that followed i.e., 1921-31.[21] Following the International Tea Agreement of 1933, under which acreage of plantations and outturn of the quantity of tea produced were restricted, the industry gradually recovered from the shock.

The long-term trend of the growth of tea industry in Assam, in respect of the number of estates, the area in possession of the estates and the total output of tea has been positive despite alternate spells of prosperity and slump. This trend was also reflected in respect to the generation of employment and investment of capital.[22] The trend is indicated in Table 8.2 below:

Table 8.2
Growth of Tea Industry in Assam 1850 - 1947

Years	No. of estates	Area under cultivation (in thousand acres)	Total area of tea estates (in thousand acres).	Output in million lbs
1850	1	2	n.a.	0.22
1859	48	8	n.a.	1.21
1869	260	25	n.a.	4.71
1871	388	59	n.a.	11.46
1880	1,055	154	566	34.01
1885	941	198	922	53.62
1890	867	231	994	82.12
1895	812	276	996	99.52
1900	804	337	1,060	141.12
1905	727	339	1,097	150.74
1910	730	350	1,165	178.72
1915	779	383	1,324	245.39
1925	930	416	1,556	225.17
1935	1,067	436	1,672	226.34
1940	1,130	n.a.	1,678	n.a.
1947	998	375	1,449	297.00

Source: Gowsami 1994, p. 276. Figures for the period from 1880 – 1935 relate to Assam including Cachar and Sylhet districts.

The table shows that by 1935, after the Great Depression, the industry was back on its steady growth path. The rise in demand for tea during the Second World War within the country and abroad yielded good returns to the industry even though there were some dislocations on account of the War.

During the colonial period the tea industry occupied a very important position in Assam and had influenced considerably the Government policy on the management of Assam's economy. It directly and indirectly favoured the planters in promoting and regulating labour-supply, and offered extraordinarily attractive terms and condition for settlement of land for plantations and the government even giving away government-run tea estates in the beginning. The Government also took steps for opening up the river route between Calcutta and Upper Assam, and helped set up other supporting industries. The importance given by the Government toward flourishing of this industry is reflected in the following observation of C. S. Mullan, Superintendent, Census Operation, Assam for 1931. "The tea industry is so vitally connected with the economic life of Upper Assam, Cachar and a considerable part of Sylhet that its prosperity is a matter of the utmost concern to the province. Tea is the true economic barometer of Assam"[23].

As E. A. Gait has pointed out, the development of tea industry yielded many benefits to the people and economy of Assam. The wastelands used for growing tea plants, according to him, were in most cases, not suitable for rice cultivation. The growth of tea industry, which did not entail any diversion of land normally used for growing other crops, opened up wastelands 'hidden in dense jungle' for productive use. The result was a happy one, the generation of employment for 5,27,000 labourers in 1923. It was true that most of these workers came from other states, but local unemployed or underemployed worker, should there be any, could also take up employment in the gardens. Moreover, many educated persons also got jobs in this industry. The rise in demand for rice to meet the needs of the tea garden employees pushed up its price that benefited the cultivators of Assam. A considerable number of internal markets grew up that facilitated the marketing of locally grown agricultural products. Development of road, river and rail transport facilities followed in the wake of the development of tea industry. Many of the immigrant tea garden labourers gradually settled down as cultivators.[24]

3. Social Costs of Developing Tea Industry:

We need to find out the real social costs involved for developing tea industry. First, the Government, in order to attract foreign capital and enterprise for developing tea plantations, offered progressively favourable terms for wasteland settlements along with certain other concessions.

On the other hand, the poor ryots were to pay higher and higher rates of land revenue that hit the rural population very hard (vide Chapter VII). The ryots were debarred from taking up lands under the liberal wasteland settlement rules for traditional agricultural pursuits.

Secondly, raising of tea plantations caused heavy loss of forest wealth to the province. T. J. Campbell who wrote the history of the Forest Department of Assam, pointed out that 'large areas of forest clad land' were leased out to tea gardens, most portions of which were not brought under tea cultivation. "At close of 1896 out of 994, 501 acres held by planters, 276,014 acres only were under cultivation"[25]. He also resented that timber used for buildings, accessories, firewood, charcoal, etc. in the tea gardens did not bring any revenue to the department, 'except that first realized under special conditions, and at rates much below those fixed as royalty for individual trees.' "In many cases gardens saw up their own tea boxes, and in others saw-mills have been established for the purpose, which work under concession from the department........."[26]

Tea planters also caused a colossal waste of timber since they turned timber into charcoal for use as fuel in the tea factories. The Deputy Commissioner of Darrang district estimated that about 1000 trees were annually used for this purpose alone on each garden without planting a single tree to replace them.[27]

In contrast to such special privileges enjoyed by the tea planters, after the promulgation of the Assam Forest Regulation of 1891, which came into force in April 1892, the common people and the ryots were required to procure firewood and building materials from forest on payment of the prescribed royalty. Previously people there had free access to forest produce which they could collect for use.

Even without minimizing the pioneering role of the British entrepreneurs in mobilizing capital and investing it in developing the tea industry in Assam, it needs to be pointed out, following the detailed data-based estimate made by Guha that, "not more than half of the estimated British capital assets in 1859 was of the nature of capital inflow". The other half according to his estimate represented formation of capital through a process of ploughing back and mobilization of locally available savings.[28]

By keeping large parts of the area of land in their possession without growing tea plants, the planters might have cornered land for restricting entry of others, particularly the local entrepreneurs, into tea plantation ventures.

Following the Government's decision to relax waste land grant rules by reducing the minimum area of land for such grants to 200 acres, and in special cases, even to 100 acres, some local entrepreneurs became interested in starting tea plantations. Notable among the pioneers were: Jagannath Baruah, Kali Prasad Chaliha, Bishuram Barua, Radhakanta Handique, Sheikh Sahanur Ali and Munshi Muhammad Ali.[29] The average size of each of their gardens was small and many of these gardens could not afford to have their own factories; therefore, they had to send green tea leaves to the neighbouring European-owned gardens for processing.

In 1903, the proportions of tea plantations owned by Assamese entrepreneurs accounted for only 3.16 per cent of plantations in Nowgong district, 0.4 per cent in Lakhimpur, 3.25 per cent in Sibsagar and 3.62 per cent in Kamrup.[30]

Some entrepreneurs from other parts of India also joined the tea plantation business. In 1928 there were 220 Indian-owned tea estates as against 760 European-owned in Assam. The total area of the estates of the former was 231 thousand acres while that of the latter accounted for 1,399 thousand acres.[31]

4. Exploitation of Labour:

Right from the beginning the planters had to face problems of the dearth of labour for employment in the gardens. There was hardly any landless agricultural labour in Assam; initially some tribal workers like the Singphos and some members of the Naga tribes could be employed for clearing forest and for plantation work. But within a short period of time this source of labour-supply dried up. Some technically skilled labourers from China were employed at higher wage rates and by offering other facilities. They worked only in the initial stage. For the source of adequate labour supply, the planters finally identified the tribal peasants in the provinces of Bihar, Bengal, United and Central provinces,

Madras and even Bombay, for recruitment as tea garden labourers.

The poor and helpless tribal villagers of these parts were actually uprooted from their habitats as indentured labour and were made to work under duress. They were paid very low wages which was decried by the Royal Commission on Labour. The monthly wages in 1929-30 were Rs.13 as.8 and P.7 each for men, Rs.11-1-7 each for women and Rs.7-8-6 for a child worker. These rates were lower than the wage rates in other industries.[32] The Workmen's Breach of Contract Act 1859 was extended to the tea districts of Assam in stages from 1863 to 1867. Taking advantage of this legal provision the tea garden Managers often resorted to force to prevent the illiterate labourers from leaving the gardens and to make them work even by physically torturing them. There were cases of binding even women and minor children under 939 days' contract through making advance payment of a paltry amount of only Rs.4 per head. The new immigrant workers were placed under illegal long term agreements and those who absconded to escape the unbearable sufferings were even illegally arrested.[33] Although the Workmen's Breach of Contract Act was repealed in 1826, the tea garden managers taking undue advantage of the illiteracy, ignorance and powerlessness of these workers (trade unions were yet to be organized with the tea garden labourers), deprived them of their freedom of movement.

In this environment, the labourer-management relations were extremely deplorable. Tea is a labour intensive industry, where maintenance of stable labour supply is very crucial for keeping the industry going. The tea garden managers in Assam resorted to all sorts of cruelty and exercised dictatorial powers for curtailing the workers' basic right to mobility instead of offering favourable terms and conditions for work in the gardens. The uprooted and home-sick workers deserved a sympathetic understanding from the garden managers of their emotional problems. But it appears they seldom received kind treatment of the management to be able to adjust themselves to their new surrounding which was so different from the environment of their home villages.

Almost nothing was done by the management for social

development of the immigrant tea garden workers. The workers living in inhuman conditions in the gardens indulged in drinking heavily and gambling that made them paupers and, what is more, pessimistic about their future. Creation of opportunities in the remote and isolated gardens for their literacy and education as also their children's was almost criminally neglected. The Investigating Committee of the All India Women's Conference observed in July 1946 that they 'did not find satisfactory arrangements for schooling in a single garden they visited either in the Surma or in the Assam Valley'.[34]

5. Growth of Collective Bargaining

Colonial forms of exploitation suffered by the tea garden workers gradually hardened their attitude. They also received inspiration and help from some social reformers of Bengal and Assam. Their pitiable conditions were focussed in the press which created public opinion in favour of the suffering workers. On the floor of the Assam Assembly members started exposing the constant cruelties inflicted on the tea garden workers as also their illegal exploitation by the planters and demanding remedial measures. Even without any outside help and motivation some workers individually as well as collectively opposed, sometimes even violently, the maltreatments meted out to them by the work supervisors, sardars and even the managers. At times they demanded higher wages, both in cash and in kind, and also better living conditions like better housing and medical facilities.

Over the years, the workers gradually gave up the hope of going back to their homes, and as they became more and more inclined to get settled in Assam, they turned to seek political support from outside and get themselves organized for bargaining collectively with the management.

Four registered trade unions of tea garden workers came into existence by 1939. According to Guha,[34] some of the unions were sponsored by the employers, obviously to weaken the hard bargaining strength of the workers. Since then, over the years, more and more trade unions of tea garden workers were established which also joined the all India trade union bodies as members. The growth of labour unions in the tea industry led to the emergence of organized labour as a class for asserting its economic and political rights and countervailing to some extent the pressure of organized capitalists as a class.

6. Tea Industry in Assam's Economy

Tea industry occupied an important place in the industrialization process initiated by the colonial Government in Assam. The area of land used for productive purpose for tea plantations, that is, yielded higher rates than that in the traditional peasant agriculture per acre. It created employment opportunities for both local and immigrant workers and generated increased income, a considerable part of which, of course, leaked out of the province. The growth of tea industry quickened the process of monetization and augmented volumes of internal and external trade. It boosted the growth of other industries, such as, oil, coal, and plywood besides development of steamship navigation, railway transport and road transport facilities in the province. As stated above, the development of tea industry on the other hand burdened the peasants, workers and other sections of society with heavy real costs.

Tea is not only a land – based and labour-intensive industry primarily, it also involves large amount of capital investment and managerial efficiency. To meet the needs for land, the government patronized the planters in their efforts to acquire vast areas of wastelands at highly attractive terms while charging higher and higher revenue rates from the peasants. Moreover, the development of the peasant sector of Assam's economy was quite neglected. The Government wanted, along with the planters, to turn the agricultural peasants into tea garden labourers. This did not happen. But it caused 'stagnation in rice acreage'. In the long term interest of Assam's balanced growth, the Government should have encouraged growth of rice, sugarcane, silk and other crops along with that of tea. "Such a policy could have been adopted," opines Guha, "at least from the fifties, by equalizing the tax burden between tea and rice lands. After the tea industry had begun to make profits, there was no longer any justification in making the peasants pay at four to five times the average rate at which a planter was taxed for his holding".[36]

The Government's policy of going all – out to support the tea industry without caring earnestly for the development of the indigenous agrarian sector, led to the emergence of an enclave capitalist sector in the midst of the traditional subsistence farming operations using very simple technology and generating very little amount of capital accumulation, if at all. This policy of the Government was not conducive to the promotion of balanced economic growth of Assam in the long run.

NOTES AND REFERENCES

1. N. K. Barooah (1970), *David Scott in North-East India 1802-1831, A Study in British Paternalism,* Munshiram Manoharlal, New Delhi, p. 107. This information is based on Bengal Political Consultations, 29 October, 1830, No.36 Scott to Chief Secretary, 6 October 1930.
2. *ibid.* pp.107-8
3. H. K. Barpujari (ed), 1993, *The Comprehensive History of Assam,* Vol. V. Publication Board, Assam, Guwahati, p. 39.
4. Bengal Revenue Proceedings, 9 August, 1836, No. 47; Jenkins 22 June as quoted by H. K. Barpujari, *op. cit.* p. 38.
5. *ibid.* 1837, 30 May, No. 65, also 1838, 6 March, No. 73 as cited by H. K. Barpujari, *op. cit.* p. 39.
6. Barpujari, *ibid.* p. 39.
7. *ibid.* pp. 39-40.
8. *ibid.* p. 10
9. *ibid.*
10. *ibid.* p. 41
11. H. K. Barpujari (1996), *Assam in the Days of the Company,* North East Hill University Shillong, pp. 233-7.
12. Amalendu Guha (1991), *Medieval and Early Colonial Assam Society Polity Economy,* K. P. Bagchi & Co., Calcutta, p. 154.
13. Edward Gait (1967), *A History of Assam,* Thacker Spink & Co., Calcutta, p. 407.
14. *Report on the Administration of North East India (1921-22):* A Mittal Publication, Delhi, 1984 (This is a reprint of the Report on the Administration of Assam, for the year 1921-22), Part II, p. 16.
15. Gait, *op. cit.,* p. 408.

16. *ibid.*
17. *ibid.* pp. 408-9
18. *ibid.* p.409
19. *ibid.* p. 412
20. *ibid.* pp. 410-11
21. C. S. Mullan (1933), *Census of India, 1931*, Vol. III, Assam, Part I Report, p. 7.
22. P. C. Goswami (1994), *The Economic Development of Assam*, Kalyani Publishers, New Delhi, p. 276.
23. C. S. Mullan, *op. cit.* p. 7.
24. Gait, *op. cit.*, pp. 413-4.
25. T. J. Cambel (1898), *Brief History of the Forest Department in Assam*, Published in Home, Foot Note on pp. 38.
26. *ibid.*
27. Cited by Keya Dasgupta (1983), "Plantation Economy and Land Tenure System in Brahmaputra Valley, 1839 – 1914", *Economic and Political Weekly*, Vol. XVIII, No. 20., 16 July.
28. Guha (1991), *op. cit.* p. 171.
29. H. K. Barpujari (ed) (1992), The Comprehensive History of Assam, Vol. IV, Publication Board Assam, Guwahati, p. 368.
30. Keya Dasgupta (1983), *Plantation Economy and Land Tenure System in Brahmaputra Valley, 1839 – 1914*, Economic and Political Weekly, Vol. XVIII, No. 20, 16 July, p. 1290.
31. P. C. Goswami (1994), op. cit. p. 139.
32. M. Reid (1931), The Indian Peasant Uprooted (A Study of the Human Machine), London p. 139.
33. *ibid.* p. 141.
34. Cited in Hem Barua (1960), The Red River and the Blue Hills, Lawyer's Book Stall, Guwahati, p. 156.
35. Amalendu Guha (1981), *Formation of a Working Class in Assam Plantations: A study in Retrospect*, published in Problems of Tea Industry in Northeast India, Shillong, p. 101.
36. Amalendu Guha (1991), op. cit. p. 175.

9
POPULATION GROWTH AND AGRICULTURAL PROGRESS

1. Introduction

We have already noted the importance of population growth in promoting capital accumulation in the land surplus and sparsely populated regions (Chapter I section 5). Here follows an account of population growth and agricultural expansion in Assam in the colonial period.

In the closing decades of the eighteenth century and in the early decades of the nineteenth century Assam's population steeply declined on account of the protracted civil wars, Burmese invasion and plunder, outbreak of epidemic diseases, and also natural calamities like earthquakes and floods. In Chapter V we estimated that about 1826 Assam's population was a little less than one million. The size of this population was nearly one-half of that in the mid-eighteenth century. Following the occupation of Assam by the British as law and order environment improved, the rate of natural growth of population stabilized. But the marked increase in population growth during the colonial period was the result of immigration of population from outside.

In the pre-and early-colonial period the mainstay of Assam's economy was subsistence agriculture combined with household manufacturing of cloth, processing of agricultural crops, etc. for self-consumption. The technology of production in all spheres was very poor and highly labour-oriented. Capital formation in the economy was nearly zero. In such a milieu fall in population meant fall in production. A large area of land, the very basic input of production lay unutilized which in course of a few years became wastes. Therefore, the main sources of growth could be rise in population, productive utilization of waste-lands, capital formation in the economy and improvement of technology.

The colonial rulers pursued the policy of raising revenue collections by encouraging settlement of waste-lands which, therefore encouraged immigration of different groups of people from outside.

In Chapter VIII we have discussed the British policy of offering more and more attractive terms for waste-land settlements for raising tea plantations. Tea plantations are highly labour-intensive operations. But there was shortage of local labour supply as the Assamese peasants abhorred the occupation of wage-labour. Therefore, growth of tea industry entailed immigration of labour from outside in large numbers. Secondly, availability of cultivable land for settlement on easy terms and conditions induced migration of landless peasants from the neighbouring province of Bengal for settlement in Assam and taking up lands for cultivation. A third group of immigrants came from Nepal, some of whom worked in the British armed forces posted in Assam and others used the abundant *char* lands (sandbanks) for rearing cattle (mainly buffaloes) for producing milk and for other dairy products. Some of them had subsidiary occupation. They collected fuelwood which they sold to the urban-dwellers.

Besides the landless peasants, many Bengalis came to Assam to serve as civil officers and office employees (amlahs). In course of time they settled down in Assam. Bengali doctors, lawyers, teachers, businessmen and many others also found avenues for pursuing their professions in Assam on a permanent basis.

The Marwari businessmen, locally called 'Keyas', migrated to Assam to carry on with their wholesale and retail trade in the internal markets considered important and located near tea gardens, on the frontier and in remote areas, in fact wherever the British rule was extended. They operated also in the tribal villages in the hills and plains. Their role in the transaction of external trade was very important as well. Another area where their business throve was the one related to money-lending and inward and outward remittances of money through *hundis* and other instruments.

On account of such immigrations, population of Assam steadily grew. This population growth infused buoyancy in all sectors of economic activities. The process of urbanization got a fillip as also the degree of specialization in productive activities. Of course, agriculture continued to be the predominant sector of productive activities in terms of employment, income and more and more intensive use of the crucial productive input, namely, land. Growth of population led to the growth of capital formation in agricultural sector, extension of area under cultivation through reclamation of cultivable fallows and wastelands, production of new food as well as cash crops in increasing quantities, establishment of new rural markets and growth in the volume of economic transactions.

2. Changes in the Density of Population: 1872 - 1901

The first official census of the population of Assam was taken in 1872. At that time Goalpara was a part of "Kutch Bihar" division. Next decennial census was taken in 1881 when Goalpara and the plains adjoining the Garo Hills were included in the Brahmaputra valley which earlier comprised only the five districts of Kamrup, Darrang, Nowgong, Sibsagar and Lakhimpur.

The areas of the districts were redrawn after 1891 which necessitated the recasting of 1891 census results for the districts in 1901 in order to look into the enumerated figures for 1891 and 1901 critically through the comparative perspective. The earlier censuses had various deficiencies, such as, underenumeration on account of infrastructural difficulties in movements faced by the enumerators and the incompetence of enumerators, themselves. Therefore, it should be more useful for us to review the trend of rise in the density of population per sq. mile in the districts as well as in the Brahmaputra valley as a whole. These are given in Table 9 : 1 below:

Table : 9.1
Changes in the Density of Population from 1872 to 1901

	Density of population per sq. mile			
District	**1872**	**1881**	**1891**	**1901**
Goalpara	98	113	114	117
Kamrup	146	167	164	153
Nowgong	68	82	90	68
	(79)	(95)	(106)	(79)*
Darrang	69	80	90	99
Sibsagar	63	79	96	120
	(102)	(127)	(157)	(197)*
Lakhimpur	29	13	60	88
Total Brahmaputra valley	77	93	102	108

* The figures within brackets indicate the density per sq. mile in the former areas of the district.

Source : Census Report for Assam 1901, p. 10

The density of population in Kamrup and Nowgong districts fell in the years between 1891 and 1901 on account of the ravages of the earthquake of 1897, floods and epidemic of Kala-azar for a number of years which not only caused heavy casualties of life and property but also induced migration of population to other districts. The rise in the density of population in the districts of Darrang, Sibsagar and Lakhimpur, known as the tea districts, was caused by the immigration of tea garden workers.

B C Allen, in his Report on the Census of 1901, has explained the sub – regional variations in the density of population in the Brahmaputra Valley. The Brahmaputra Valley to qoute him, "falls into three divisions – Goalpara, which has many points in common with Bengal .... the greater part of the district being permanently settled, Central Assam consisting of Kamrup, Nowgong and the Mangoldai sub – division of Darrang, which resemble one another, in that they formerly contained a large agricultural population, which has now been much reduced by Kala-azar and floods which followed the great earthquake of 1897, but have not proved particularly suitable for the cultivation of tea, and Upper Assam, consisting of Tezpur sadar, and the Sibsagar and Lakhimpur districts in which the tea industry has attained a position of great importance"[1].

Between 1891 and 1901 population of the Brahmaputra Valley increased by 1,46,596 even as the locally born population declined by 45,409 persons. The increase was on account of the immigration of 1,85,796 people from other provinces.[2] Those who came as tea garden workers constituted the largest proportion of immigrants, while the cultivators from the adjacent districts of Bengal formed the second largest.

3. Large scale Immigration of Peasants from Eastern Bengal

In the following decade, from 1901 to 1911, that is, population in the Brahmaputra valley increased from 26.19 lakh to 31.08 lakh. It works out to an increase of 18.7 per cent. Natural growth of population accounted for 16.7 per cent and the flow of immigration the remainder. The first phase of the decade, from 1901 to 1904, was marked by general improvement in people's health so that 'births exceeded deaths in every district'. But in 1905 the valley was inundated by high floods which was followed by an outbreak of cholera causing 'an excess of deaths in every plains district'. By 1907, the valley recovered from the menace of cholera and population growth showed a progressive trend.[3]

This decade was a turning point in the sense that the number of immigrant tea garden workers was surpassed by "a voluntary stream of settlers, who are at present most in evidence at the outskirts of the Brahmaputra Valley, but have ventured as far east as Tezpur and Nowgong".[4] No wonder, Nowgong district's population rose substantially, i.e., by 16.2 per cent including 14.3 per cent growth of the indigenous population. Following the extension of the Assam Bengal Railway into this district, immigrants from Dacca,

Mymensingh and the Surma Valley began to enter into the district for settlement in lands both fertile and cultivable. The Census Reprt for 1911 notes that these immigrants brought about "considerable development ......in the Kapili Valley, especially in the neighourhood of Lumding junction".[5]

In the decade 1911-21 population continued to grow but the natural rate of growth of population was somewhat retarded because of certain events, such as, 'the universal influenza epidemic of 1918-19', recrudescence of Kala-azar and outbreak of Cholera, small pox and dysentery in different districts at different times.[6]

This downward trend was more than offset by the increased inflow of population from outside Assam. Immigration of "cultivators from Eastern Bengal and colonization by Nepalis and ex-garden coolies increased largely and did much to open up waste land in the Assam Valley".[7] The Census Report for 1921 noted that the immigrants from the six districts of Bengal, namely, Rangpur, Pabna, Bogra, Dacca and Mymensing numbered 258 thousand. The number of settlers in Assam Valley district-wise is shown in table 9.2.

Table 9.2
Immigrants From Eastern Bengal in the Brahmaputra Valley as in 1921.

District	Number of Immigrants (000's omitted)
Goalpara	141
Kamrup	42
Darrang	15
Nowgong	55
Sibsagar	2
Lakhimpur	3
Total in Brahmaputra Valley	258

Note: Parts of thousand under 500 have been omitted and over 500 have been taken as 1.

Source: Census Report for Assam, 1921, p. 40.

88 per cent of these immigrants were 'cultivators of holdings generally under Government, with a sprinkling of field labourers. The reasons for their migration were the growing pressure of land in their home villages and in some cases, 'loss of their lands and even homestead by diluvion' on the one hand, and the easy availability of fertile land in Assam, where the ryotwari settlement system prevailed, 'in place of expensive and uncomfortable holdings as tenants or under-tenants in Bengal', on the other[8]. G. T. Lloyd, author of the Census Report, 1921 was happy to note: "They are hard-working good cultivators who cannot fail to benefit the country"[9].

The then Deputy Commissioner of Nowgong also observed: "They do better cultivation than the local people and as such they are certainly beneficial to the country, since their advent the local people seem to be shaking off their old lethargy and they have created a novel sphere of competition"[10]. Similarly the Deputy Commissioner of Kamrup also praised the industry and skill of these immigrant cultivators. "............They have reclaimed and brought under permanent cultivation thousands of acres which the local cultivators had for generations past merely scratched with haphazard and intermittent crops...." In fact, they transformed the large undulating expanses of sandbanks (char lands) into prosperous agricultural farms. These cultivators produced some new crops and used improved methods of cultivation.[11]

The rate of population growth continued in the next two decades, 1921-31 and 1931-41. As a result the total population increased from 31.08 lakh in 1921 to 48.55 lakh in 1931, which went up further to 59.19 lakh in 1941. The pressure of population on land became perceptible as the density of population per sq. mile increased from 149 in 1921 to 179 and therefrom to 219 in 1941. In the decade 1921-31 the natural growth of population was higher than in the previous decade. Migration of population from outside into Assam continued almost unabated but because of high birth rate among immigrants who settled down in Assam the natural rate of growth was also high. The immigrants belonged to the three main groups, namely, the Bengalis, tea garden workers and the Nepalis.

4. Immigration from Bengal and Its Impact on Assam's Economy and Society

The trend of immigration from Bengal into Assam from 1911 to 1931 is shown in Table 9.3 below :

Table 9.3
Number of Persons Born in Bengal as Enumerated in the Districts of Assam Valley ('000s omitted)

	1911	1921	1931
Goalpara	77 (34)	151 (78)	170 (80)
Kamrup	4 (1)	44 (30)	134(91)
Darrang	7 (1)	20 (12)	41 (30)
Nowgong	4 (1)	58 (52)	120(108)
Sibsagar	14(0)	14 (0)	12 (0)
Lakhimpur	14(0)	14 (0)	19 (2)
Total	120	301	576

Figures within brackets show the number of immigrants hailing from Mymensing district of Bengal.

Source : Census of Assam, 1931, P. 50

In 1931 about 6 lakh people, that is, 12.5 per cent of the total population of Assam Valley, were immigrants from Bengal, the very large majority of whom were cultivators. The trend of this migration changed the traditional ethnic, religious and lingustic composition of population of the province. C. S. Mullan, Superintendent, Census Operations, Assam 1931, observed on this trend as follows:

"Probably the most important event in the Province during twenty five years – an event, moreover, which seems likely to alter permanently the whole future of Assam and to destroy more surely than did the Burmese invaders of 1820 the whole structure of Assamese culture and civilization – has been the invasion of a vast horde of land hungry Bengali immigrants, mostly Muslims, from the districts of Eastern Bengal and in particular from Mymensingh".[12]

Referring to the figures about immigration of this group (Table 9: 3 above), he further observed: "These are startling figures and illustrate the wonderful rapidity with which the lower districts of Assam Valley are becoming colonies of Mymensing. .... Where there is waste land thither flock the Mymensinghias. In fact the way in which they have seized upon the vacant areas in Assam Valley seems almost uncanny. Without fuss, without tumult, without undue trouble to the district revenue staffs, a population which must amount to over half a million has transplanted itself from Bengal to the Assam Valley during the last twenty five years".[13]

Despite Mullan's critical and alarming observations about the immigrant Muslim cultivators, the trend continued in the subsequent decades also. The reasons were both political and economic. 85 per cent of the immigrant settlers were Muslims and their immigration was politically encouraged and assisted with the objective of altering the religious composition of Assam's population. "The Assam Government", writes P. C. Goswami, "which was dominated by the Muslim League leaders from 1926 until 1938 also encouraged the new settlers. As far back as 1920 a special Muhammadan Sub-Deputy Collector was appointed in Nowgong district to look after the welfare of the immigrants. For the settlement of Government waste land with the immigrants, colonization officers were appointed for Nowgong district (1928-29) and for Barpeta (1920-30) and .... Mangaldai (1929-30) subdivisions."[14] No wonder, these were the areas where settlement of these immigrants was the largest.

It is obvious that immigration of these cultivators could not be sustained on such a scale only on religious and political patronage. These settlers contributed substantially to economic improvements of the local population and augmented the supply of rural wage labour for which there was local demand. P. C. Goswami aptly observes: "One welcome result of the influx of these farm settlers is the improvement of the farming practices in the province. The new settlers developed the whole agricultural system in Assam, helped to improve the health of the countryside by clearing the jungles and marshes, and also converted the wild areas into prosperous agricultural regions. The introduction of jute, vegetables, etc., as commercial crops in Assam has largely been due to the immigrants. The local people began to take to other crops besides paddy on commercial basis only after witnessing the success achieved by the immigrants......"[15]

From an economist's standpoint, economic development of such a dimension required huge amount of capital to be invested. In this context it is worth noting what Ester Boserup's observations were on 'The Economics of Agrarian change under Population Pressure'. She opined that in any community, 'a high rate of population growth necessitates a high rate of investment' and a large share of agricultural investment could be carried out by the cultivators themselves without restraining their consumption for the purpose of capital formation by shortening the periods of leisure and working for longer periods. "The question is whether an increasing family provides sufficient incentive to additional work and whether the system of land tenure is such that the cultivators have access to additional cultivable land or sufficient security of tenure to make land improvements a worthwhile investment"[16]. In Assam in the late 19th century as also in the early 20th century there were vast areas of cultivable waste land and the land settlement rules were also favourable for extension of cultivation to additional areas. Since the rate of growth of local population was very low, even negative, such extension of cultivation under pressure of increasing family size was not possible. But capital formation for investment on extension of cultivation by employing additional labour came about in the form of settlement of landless and skilled peasants in the wastelands. This was possible through their hard labour and their use of agricultural implements and cattle that they procured with their own savings or by borrowing money.

The new scenario in the district of Nowgong where such settlements took place on a large scale (between 1924 and 1930 there was an increase of nearly 64 thousand acres of land where they settled) has been candidly described by Rai Bahadur P. G. Mukherjee of Nowgong in his report submitted for inclusion in the Census Report for 1931.

According to Mukhrjee the immigrant farmers opened up extensive areas of dense jungle for cultivation along the south bank of the Brahmaputra. These people brought "in their wake wealth, industry and general prosperity to the whole district", As a result Government revenue increased. By growing and selling jute they earned lakhs of rupees with which they bought their food-stuffs and imported goods, met the costs of litigation and cleared debts taken from *mahajans*[17].

Mukherjee has also pointed out that these immigrants often encroached on Government reserves and even on lands of the local people. They sometimes occupied lands near Assamese Villages by trespass or through purchase and created law and order problems. "Many immigrants" writes Mukherjee, "had to be punished with fines and ejectments, sometimes with the assistance of the police". Government appointed a special Colonization Officer to deal with these problems and to make the settlers obey legal provisions and also maintain good relations with the local neighbours. Gradually the immigrants understood that Government's order were to be respected and they gradually settled down as 'peaceful citizens'[18]. The Nowgong scenario was also the reality in other lower Assam districts where the immigrants settled down.

5. Immigration of Tea Garden Workers and Nepali Graziers

The two other groups of immigrants, namely, the tea garden workers and the Nepali graziers also made substantial contributions toward Assam's agricultural progress. The tea garden labourers, we have already noted in Chapter 8, were the uprooted peasants from Bihar, Orissa, Central Provinces and Berar, United Provinces, Madras, the Central Indian Agency and Bengal. The number of persons, according to Assam's Census of 1931, who were born in the principal recruiting provinces including their princely states, are indicated in table 9: 4.

Table 9.4
Migrant Tea Garden Workers Enumerated in Assam Birthplace – wise*.

Birth Place	Enumerated in the Censuses of (thousands omitted)		
	1931	1921	1911
Bihar and Orissa	472	571	399
Central Provinces and Berar	82	91	77
United Provinces	68	77	98
Madras	58	55	35
Central India Agency	15	18	07
Total	695	812	616

Source : *Census of India*, 1931, Vol. III Assam, p. 45

* "Figures for Bengal are not given as although a considerable number of coolies are recruited from the Western part of the presidency the great majority of people born in Bengal and censused in Assam are Eastern Bengal colonists" (ibid)

The table shows a marked increase in the population of this group in 1921 over that of 1911. According to the Census Report 1931, there was an 'enormous rush of immigrant coolies to Assam in 1918-19 due to distress in their home districts'. But following the depression in tea industry there were labour strikes and violent labour troubles in the tea gardens there, because of which 'a large number must have returned to their homes. Therefore their number fell in 1931 as presumed. As the "industry began to prosper again in 1923 and subsequent years the continued shortage of labour became a most pressing problem". This was sought to be overcome by opening up another area, the Madras Presidency, for recruitment in 1923, introducing at the same time the system of short term recruitment from Bihar and Orissa and, of course, by recruiting whenever possible local workers. In 1930-31 number of tea garden 'coolies' imported was 52 thousand while the number of 'coolies added locally' was 67 thousand including adults as well as children.[19]

Besides taking part in the development of tea plantation and the industry these immigrant tea garden workers also directly cultivated land for production of rice, vegetables, etc. as tenants and / or subtenants of ryots or underryots.

From the early part of the 19th century settlement of Nepalis in Assam took place. Many of them were retired soldiers of the British armed forces operating in the tribal and frontier areas. Besides, many Nepalis migrated to Assam in search of opportunities for gainful employment as graziers. Number of persons born in Nepal and included in the Census enumerations in Assam in 1901, 1911, 1921 and 1931 were: 21,347; 47,654; 70,344 and 88,306 respectively. Decadal increase in Nepali population was mainly due to the steady flow of immigrants from Nepal. The figure for 1931, 88,306, represented only those who were born in Nepal. The total Nepali population including the locally born Nepalis who were identified by languages spoken by them, namely, Rai, Gurung, Limbu, Magari, etc. stood at 1,40,000 in 1931.[20]

The Nepalis settled down mainly in the districts of Darrang, Lakhimpur and Kamrup as buffalo graziers in the *char* (sandbank) lands. Considerable areas of such lands were declared as grazing reserves for the Nepali *Khutiwalas*. Therefore, number of Nepal born persons increased from 35,964 in 1921 to 46,914 in 1931 as shown in Table 9.5.

Table 9. 5
Increase in the Number of Nepali Immigrants

District	Number of persons born in Nepal enumerated in Assam in the census of	
	1921	1931
Darrang	18,997	24,862
Kamrup	8,527	10,101
Lakhimpur	8,440	11,951
Total	35,964	46,914

Source : Census of India, 1931, Vol. III, Assam p. 53

Some of the Nepalis lived in the outskirts of towns in Assam for rearing cattle for producing milk and for other dairy products which they sold to the urban dwellers. They also collected fuelwood from forests to meet the demands of the townsmen. These Nepalis played an important role in meeting the needs of the growing urban population. In fact they were a significant element in the rural-urban linkage in Assam.

The trend of steady agricultural growth following the immigration of population since the beginning of the 20th century may be gauged from the changes in the (i) pattern of land utilization, (ii) extent of irrigation facilities, (iii) areas under different crops, and (iv) outputs of crops. Table No. 9.6, describes land utilizations in the plains districts of Assam including Cachar for the selected years from 1901-02 to 1946-47 are given:

Note:

(a) Included under other uncultivated land excluding current fallow.

(b) In 1901-02 the details for a major portion of the Goalpara District and some portion of Cachar District were not available and hence the comparatively smaller area in the total area.

(c) Up to and including the year 1946-47, the figures for the Sylhet District are adjusted for the portion merged with Assam after partition by taking one-eight of the figures for the Sylhet District. It should be noted that the total area shown in the Table is not the whole area of the province. The data are compiled from the village papers and hence exclude unadmini-stered areas in the NEFA and some portion in other Hill District for which data are not available". (P. C. Goswami, op. cit. (1994), PP. 260-61.

Table 9.6
Land Utilisation in the Plains-Districts of Assam
(including Cachar)
(in million acres)

Year	Forest	Not available for cultivation	Other un-cultiveted land excluding current fallows	Cureent fallows	Net area sown	Total areas	% of net area sown to total area	Area sown more than once	% of area sown in more than once to net area sown
1	2	3	4	5	6	7	8	9	10
1901-02	2.33	(a)	9.93	1.08	2.40	15.5 (b)	15.4	0.21	8.8
1911-12	1.97	3.01	9.48	0.80	3.10	17.36	17.8	0.32	10.3
1921-22	3.07	3.01	7.50	1.09	3.64	18.40	19.8	0.37	10.2
1931-32	2.98	2.25	8.12	1.00	3.87	18.23	21.2	0.52	13.4
1941-42	3.23	2.26	7.24	0.90	4.60	18.23	25.2	0.73	16.1
1946-47	3.21	2.26	6.96	0.91	4.73	18.07	26.2	0.70	14.8

Source : (1) Table of Agriculture Statistics (Assam), Annual;
(2) Annual Report on Crops and Seasons in Assam, Annual. Quoted
(2) in P. C. Goswami (1994), op. cit. PP. 260-61.

Table 9: 6 shows that the net area sown increased from 2.40 million acres in 1901-02 to 4.73 million acres in 1946-47. Decadal growth trend in this respect was maintained throughout this period. Percentage of the net area sown to the total area also continuously increased: it rose from 15.4 per cent in 1901-02 to 26,2 per cent in 1946-47 Similarly area sown more than once also increased from 0.21 million acres in 1901-02 to 0.73 million acres in 1941-42 but it slightly dipped by the year 1946-47 to 0.70 million acres. This fall might be attributed to the disturbances occurring prior to and following the partition of the country. As we know, area sown more than once, net area sown, crops grown, etc depend on the irrigation facilities available as one of the determining factors. Expansion of irrigation facilities promotes growth of the net area sown which in turn advances the growth of agriculture in that region. Since in Assam annual rainfall is quite high agricultural operations predominantly depend on rain-water irrigation. But there are areas where by constructing canals, tanks, wells, etc irrigation facilities have to be provided. Reliable data about growth of irrigation facilities are scanty. Yet, for the years 1929-30 and 1930-31 figures about district-wise irrigated area and crops irrigated can be obtained from the Government of India publication (1933), titled, Agricultural Statistics of India 1930-31. These data are given in Table 9.7.

Table 9.7

Area (in acres) Irrigated and Crops Irrigated

District	Area	Irrigated	from				Crops Irrigated		
	Govt. canals	Private canals	Tanks	Wells	Other sources	Total	Rice	Wheat	Barley
1	2	3	4	5	6	7	8	9	10
Darrang									
192930									
1930-31	—	97,683	—	—	—	97,683	97,683	—	—
Goalpara									
1929-30	—	143,252	—	—	—	143,252	143,252	—	—
1930-31									
Kamrup									
1929-30	10,582	22,661	719	33	11,053	45,048	45,048	—	—
1930-31	—	65,214	181	33	1,063	66,491	66,491	—	—
Lakhimpur	—	—	—	—	—	—	—	—	—
Nowgong	—	—	—	—	—	—	—	—	—
Sibsagar	—	—	—	—	—	—	—	—	—
Total									
1929-30	10,582	263,596	719	—	11,053	285,983	285,983	—	—
1930-31	—	306,149	181	33	1,063	307,426	307,426	—	—

Source : Agricultural Statistics of India, 1930-31, Vol.1, Govt. of India, Manager of Publications Delhi, 1933, pp. 70.

The table shows that it was mainly rice, which was the irrigated crop, and that private canals in the districts of Darrang, Goalparas and Kamrup accounted for the largest areas irrigated. In Kamrup district there were also tanks, well and other sources for irrigating crops.

Areas under different crops are indicated in Table No. 9.8, below:

Table 9.8:
Areas under Different Major Crops
(in thousand acres)

Year	Rice	Cereals and pulses including Rice	Rape and Mustard	Oil seeds including Rape and Mustard	Sugar cane	Tea	Tobacco	Jute	Cotton
1	2	3	4	5	6	7	8	9	10
1901-02	1,789	1,869	162	177	30	275	2	5	3
1911-12	2,573	2,682	238	245	30	288	8	58	35
1921-22	2,945	3,118	283	306	37	334	10	76	36
1931-32	3,198	3,400	293	319	28	352	14	95	37
1941-42	3,699	3,668	368	404	42	362	15	277	38
1946-47	3,913	4,167	293	329	54	367	19	184	30

Note: "The figures above do not include the figures for NEFA"
Source : "Table of Agricultural Statistics; *Report on Crops and Seasons; Statistical Abstract Assam (1951-52); Agricultural Statistics of Recognised States (1956)*; *Indian Agricultural Statistics*, 1954-55". Quoted in P. C. Goswami (1994), op. cit., pp. 264-65.

The table reveals that the total area under the most important major crop, namely, rice went up from 1,789 thousand acres in 1901-02 to 3,913 thousand acres in 1946-47, that is, the increase was more than double (118.7 per cent) in a span of 45 years. This was possible mainly because of the fact that the peasant settlers brought more wastelands (or cultivable fallow lands not under forests) and *char*-lands (sand banks) under cultivation. There were also expansions of areas used for growing of other crops like pulses, rape and mustard and other oilseeds, sugarcane, jute, cotton and, of course, tea. Cultivation of jute on a large scale was mainly taken up by the immigrant peasants who already had the expertise of growing and processing of this crop in their home districts in Bengal. It was purely a commercial crop and its prices fluctuated even as there were variations in the demands for jute and jute products in the international market. Such fluctuations are reflected in the upswings and downswings in areas put under jute cultivation from year to year. The marked increase in area under jute in 1941-42 was presumably due to rise in war-time demand for jute and jute products. The main jute growing districts were Goalpara, Nowgong, Kamrup and Darrang in each of which the immigrant peasants from Bengal settled in large number.

Sugarcane cultivation was also undertaken in larger areas over the decades: it increased perceptively and the area under cultivations increased from 10 thousand areas in 1901-02 to 54 thousand acres in 1946-47. Cotton was grown mainly in the hilly areas and therefore, the total area under this crop remained stable over the decades.

Average yields of principal crops as recorded in the Government of India's 'Agricultural Statistics of India, 1930-31' are given in Table No. 9:9 below.

Table 9.9
Average Yield (lb per acre) of Every Principal Crop in Each District

District	Rice Winter			Rice Autumn	Rape & Mustard	Sugar-cane (gur)	Cotton cleaned	Jute
	Broad-cast	Trans-planted	Both					
Darrang	672	1,008	997	840	504	2,240	—	—
Goalpara	896	1,120	1,064	728	560	2,800	—	—
Kamrup	672	840	784	672	448	2,240	—	—
Lakhimpur	896	1,008	1,008	672	504	3,360	—	—
Nowgong	840	952	896	728	560	2,240	140	—
Sibsagar	784	952	952	616	560	2,800	—	—
Average for the plain districts of the whole of Assam		896		706	504	2,576	200	1,400

Source : *Agricultural Statistics of India, 1930-31,* Vol. I, Published by order of the Governor General in Council, Manager of Publications, Delhi, 1933, p. 346.

Yields of some of the principal crops as indicated in Table 9.10 almost consistently increased during the first half of the twentieth century. Output of rice, the most important cereal consumed by people, more than doubled but per capita availability of rice declined from about 1820 kg in 1901 when population was 31.5 lakh to only about 189 kg as population increased to 62.87 lakh in 1941. This was the reason why during the Second World War large quantities of rice had to be imported into Assam. On the other hand production of jute, an important item of export, increased manifold. The war-time scarcities and disturbances and the campaign launched for growing more food, etc will be discussed in Chapter 15.

Table 9.10
Yields of Some of the Principal Crops
(metric ton)

Year	Rice	Rape & Mustard	Sugar cane (gur)	Jute	Cotton
1	2	3	4	5	6
1901-02	574,106	37,112	35,127	3,181	272
1911-12	825,699	54,523	35,127	36,909	3,181
1921-22	945,077	64,832	43,323	48,363	3,272
1931-32	1,026,267	67,123	32,785	60,454	3,363
1941-42	1,187,042	84,305	49,178	167,272	3,454
1946-47	1,255,717	67,123	63,229	117,090	2,727

Note: Total yield of each of the different crops has been estimated by multiplying the areas under the respective crops by the average yields recorded in *Agricultural Statistics of India, 1930-31*, Vol. I, published by Order of the Governor General in Council, Manager of Publications, Delhi, 1933, pp. 346.

These are only approximate figures but are nevertheless indicative of the rise in the yield of the principal crops over nearly a period of 50 years beginning from 1901-02.

Sources: (1) Table of Agricultural Statistics: Reports on Crops and Seasons, quoted in P. C. Goswami (1994), *op. cit.*,p. 264-65

(2) *Agricultural Statistics of India 1930-31, Ibid*[21].

6. Conclusion

Different groups of immigrant population have contributed to the growth of Assam's economy using intensively available productive resources, particularly the wastelands and sand-banks (*char* lands) and also by augmenting the supply of wage-labour to meet the needs of tea and other industries. There were also professional and educated persons, traders, etc. who came from outside to settle down in Assam. They helped the entire process of diversification of economic activities, growth of markets and expansion and modernization of the administrative infrastructure so essential for economic development. The process added to the plurality of Assam's population – its multiplicity, both ethnic and religious as also linguistic and ended the state of isolation of the indigenous population groups and their age-old low level of subsistence and near stationary productive activities.

But such results of immigration of population, particularly of the landless peasantry, though favourable, had obvious limitations. For, the high rate of growth of rural population without its being associated with proportionate changes in the secondary and tertiary sectors of production affected the prospects of sustainable resource use and generation of employment opportunities for the growing workforce in the non-farm sectors. Moreover, unabated settlement of immigrants from across the western border in large number posed a threat to the ethnic, linguistic, religious and cultural identities of the indigenous communities. This trend seriously circumscribed the advantages of socio-cultural plurality of Assam's growing population.

NOTES AND REFERENCES

1. B. C. Allen (1902), *Census of India 1901*, Vol. IV, Assam Part I Report, Shillong, p. 3.
2. *ibid.* p. 16-22.
3. J. M. Swiney (1911), *Census of India 1911*, Vol. III, Assam, Part I Report, pp. 15-16.
4. *ibid.* p. 23.
5. *ibid.* p. 19.
6. G. T. Lloyd (1921), *Census of India 1921*, Vol. III, *Assam, Part I Report*, p. 6.
7. *ibid.* p.5.
8. *ibid.* p. 41.
9. *ibid.*
10. Quoted in *ibid.*
11. Quoted in *ibid.*
12. C. S. Mullan (1932), *Census of India, 1931, Vol. III Assam, Part I Report*, Shillong, p. 49-50.
13. *ibid.* p. 50-51.
14. P. C. Goswami (1994), *The Economic Development of Assam*, Kalyani Publisher, Ludhiana, New Delhi, p. 24.
15. *ibid.* p. 25.

16. Ester Boserup (1965), *The Conditions of Agricultural Growth (The Economics of Agrarian Change under Population Pressure)*, George Allen and Unwin Limited, London, p. 88.
17. C. S. Mullan (1932), *op. cit.* p. 51.
18. *ibid.* p. 52.
19. *ibid.* pp. 45-48.
20. *ibid.* p. 53.
21. *Agricultural Statistics of India, 1930-31*, Vol. I Published by Order of Governor General in Council, Manager of Publications, Delhi, 1933, p.346.

10
CHANGING SCENARIO OF THE RURAL ECONOMY IN ASSAM (1891 - 1930)

1. Introduction

The effects of the immigration of population on agricultural expansion have been noted at some length in Chapter 9. Chapters 7 and 8 deal with the reorganization of land settlement by the colonial government as theme. These changes as also the starting of co-operative credit societies had led to significant changes in Assam's rural economy. These we review in the present Chapter.

Agricultural growth in the non-plantation sector in Assam in the closing decades of the nineteenth and early decades of the twentieth century was largely stimulated with the immigration of hard-working peasants from Bengal and of the Nepali graziers who brought more and more cultivable wastes into productive use. The ryotwari system of land settlement promulgated by the colonial rulers served as an incentive to the ryots who held land as proprietors directly under the government. But such incentives were somewhat constrained by the Government's policy of imposing high rates of revenue for settlement of land in favour of the ryots. The rates were also enhanced from time to time with the objective of raising revenue earnings of the Government. It was also expected by the rulers that higher rates of revenue would compel many ryots to abandon their land holdings and become landless labourers who then could be employed by the planters as tea garden workers. This is what the planters wanted, and they tried to influence the Government's land revenue policy accordingly. Of course this objective remained almost unfulfilled.

The land revenue policy of the Government adversely affected the process of capital formation in the peasant sector of the rural economy. Guha has rightly observed : "the State as landlord took away by and large not only the differential rent, but also profits, if any. It even encroached upon the peasant's subsistence in many cases."[1] Changes in the relative prices of cultivated crops also did not quite favour the peasants. Moreover, some of the cottage industries forming an integral part of the peasant's economy were adversely affected by imported manufactured goods, demands for which expanded in the peasant households. Many peasants had to borrow money from the traders, money-lenders, rich peasants, and so on for meeting the revenue demands of the Government. Such borrowings were mainly in the form of crop advances which was doubly injurious to the peasants' interests. With the crop advances the peasants could procure their necessaries at unfavourable prices and the quantity of crops they had to part with used to be larger since prices for crops were lower because calculated on the speculative but not disinterested assumption that these rates would rule the market in the harvest season. Moreover, the rate of interest was also quite high. These factors contributed to the emerging feature, the growing rural indebtedness (discussed below) in Assam that also affected the prospects of savings and investments so vital for indigenously sustaining a steady state of agricultural growth in Assam.

One emerging feature so significant was the rise in the number of tenants, that is, tenants who cultivated land on payment of rent to the actual proprietor of the soil or one who held it on lease directly from the Government. The Census Report for 1891 recorded the fact that excluding the permanently settled districts of Sylhet and Goalpara, tenants were numerous in Kamrup numbering 77,683. For, in that district "a great deal of land is held on *lakhiraj, nisf-khiraj*; and other special tenures......The total number of tenants in the other districts of the province is only 31,024. This number includes persons who cultivate land on conditions of dividing the produce (i.e., cultivators on *adhya* terms), mortgages in possession and also the tenants of the holders of special grants....."[2]

In the whole province only 35, 497 agricultural labourers were enumerated in the 1891 census.

The number of cultivating tenants rose from a little over one lakh in the five districts of the Brahmaputra Valley (i.e., excluding Goalpara) in 1891 to more than one lakh and sixty thousand in 1901. Regarding this increasing trend, the Census Report for 1901 observes: "The increase in the three districts of Darrang, Sibsagar and Lakhimpur is very significant, and is apparently due to a practice which is growing up amongst the Assamese of leasing out the land lying near a tea garden to the coolies, and moving further afield themselves for their own cultivation. The profits are considerable, as the rent is sometimes as much as three times the Government revenue, but as the coolie must have land near the factory, while the cultivator is not so fettered in his choice, the transaction is for the benefit of both parties."[3]

The system of offering tenancy or sub-letting by the land-holders to the actual cultivators who paid rent either in kind or through cash had been in vogue in Assam even in the pre-colonial period. Of course, the tenants were not so numerous and in the initial period they rendered labour services and, in some cases, paid rent in kind to the landlords. As the process of monetization of transactions in the economy progressed during the colonial rule, payments of rent in cash went up in proportion to the payments in kind. This process also expanded opportunities for the absentee landowners living in towns and administrative centres, to get their lands cultivated by tenants on payment of rent in cash and marginally through labour services and in kind. Crop-sharing system of rent payment (adhi) obtained mainly in the case of fertile *rupit* land on which the pressure of population was rising.

Growth of tenancy-farming was attributable to some other developments in the colonial regime. The Mauzadars had to rely on tenants for getting their lands cultivated. Generally the former slaves, some immigrant runaway tea garden coolies and indebted landless peasants became tenants.

Exhorbitant rates of land revenue imposed by the Government also compelled many ryots to become tenants. The Government's policy of allowing resourceful landholders to consolidate their scattered holdings by exchanging their outlying parcels of land for the lands adjacent to their holdings held by poor ryots, who thus lost the possession of their lands and had of necessity to become tenants of those privileged landlords for survival.[4]

The comparative position of the tenant cultivators among the different groups of working population living on cultivation as enumerated in the 1931 Census is given in Table 10 : 1 below :

Table 10. 1
Number per mille (thousand) of Working Population Living on Cultivation by Groups in Assam Valley (Excluding Goalpara)

1.	Non-cultivating owners	4
2.	Cultivating owners	894
3.	Tenant cultivators	56
4.	Agricultural Labourers	41
5.	Jhumiyas (shifting cultivators)	5
		1000

Source : Census of India, 1931 Vol. III, Assam, Part I Report, p. 21

C.S. Mullan, Census Superintendent, deduced from the above facts that Assam (Assam Valley, excluding Goalpara) was mainly a land of peasant proprietors. Of course, he noted that in the permanently settled district of Goalpara the system of tenancy farming was resorted to on an extensive scale. In 1931 there were 117,000 tenant cultivators in Goalpara district. Mullan consulted the Director of Land Records to check if the census enumerations agreed with the results of the resettlement process completed about 1930. "In Kamrup according to the Settlement Report (1930) 5.15 per cent of *Khiraj* land is sublet and the Settlement Officer of Sibsagar in the Settlement Report of that district (1929) has estimated that 2.75 per cent of the total *Khiraj* area is sublet. He states, however, that this figure should really be higher as landlords were often desirous of concealing the existence of subtenancies owing to the idea that, if recorded, they might result later in trouble over occupancy rights."[5] From the observation of the Settlement Officer it may be presumed that the number of tenant cultivators as shown in the census report was somewhat an understimation. The system of subletting land by the landowners, particularly the absentee ones, became very common. This is also evident from the fact that the number of non-cultivating owners, 4 per thousand, was quite a significant number as agriculture was the occupation of 84.3 per cent of the total population in 1931.

Number of agricultural labourers (actual workers) according to census enumerations in 1911, 1921 and 1931 were as follows for the whole of Assam.

Table 10. 2
Number of Agricultural Labourers in Assam

	Number in			**Percentage variation**	
	1931	1921	1911	1921-31	1911-21
Agricultural labourers	74,306	82,395	50,612	-9.8	+62.8

Source : Census Report for 1931 (op.cit.), subsidiary Table IV, p.189

The table containing the figures indicates a substantial rise (62.8%) in the number of agricultural labourers from 1911 to 1921. But there was a 9.8 p.c. decline in the number of agricultural labourers between 1921 and 1931. This was mainly due to definitional reasons as Mullan, Census Superintendent, has opined: "On account of the different method of grouping the agricultural heads I doubt whether it would be of any use to draw any conclusions from this comparison. The figures show that the proportionate figures of both landlords and agricultural labourers have declined. I doubt this and think that the figures of these groups were probably too high in 1921." This was so as Mullan presumed, on account of the fact that in the earlier census Assamese women in the Brahmaputra valley were reckoned as agricultural labourers because they worked as hard as men in the fields at the time of transplantation of rice seedlings from the nurseries into the *pathars* or fields and also at the time of harvesting. According to 1931 census these women were treated as "helpers in the fields" or "helpers in agriculture" as to go by the same census definition, they did not earn any wage for their work.[6]

Mullan's views about women agricultural labourers in Assam are not wholly correct. The practice of employing women of poorer classes followed by the wealthier cultivators for transplanting paddy prevailed even in the 1880s. According to Guha, "Generally, surplus members of large sized peasant families and widows, children and such persons as had been turned into paupers, were available for wage work. Such employment was relatively more in vogue in Kamrup than in any other district for the simple reason that there were relatively more landlords and Brahmans in the former district."[7] Darrah's note as quoted by Guha indicates that rich cultivators regularly employed their poorer neighbours for harvesting paddy and sometimes for ploughing.[8]

Rise in the number of agricultural labourers within the peasant sector was, however, effectively contained on account of the easy availability of land as ryots or as tenants of ryots and/or landlords and the strong traditional preference for subsisting on the self-sufficient base of economic pursuits of the rural households.

2. Rural Markets

As the tea plantations covered more and more rural areas, productive activities in the field of agriculture expanded and there was a rise in population and the volume of internal trade and the number of rural markets also increased. For the 1921 census, enumeration of facts about the conditions of trade in the interior areas was taken up as a subject of special enquiry. Markets located in the district and sub-divisional headquarters were also reckoned as rural markets. The findings are shown in Table 10 : 3 below:

Table 10.3
Rural markets in the Brahmaputra Valley 1921

District	Actural number of markets	Number of markets per 10,000 population	Average area in sq. miles served by a market
1	2	3	4
Goalpara	110	14	36
Kamrup	41	5	94
Darrang	57	12	51
Nowgong	43	11	86

Source : *Census of India 1921*, Vol-III, Assam, Part-I Report, p.167

The Census Report noted that markets run in the headquarters sat daily for sale of fish, vegetables, etc. In those markets daily attendance of buyers ranged from 200 to 300. Markets also assembled on weekly or biweekly basis. There was a 'bazar day proper when trade is much brisker and the attendance becomes often 2000 or 3000'.[9]

An idea about the growth of trade in the whole province may be had from the rise in the number of persons dependent on trade for a living. Trade provided means of living for 268 thousand people in 1921 as against 245 thousand in 1911. Expansion of trade in food is reflected in the fact that in 1921, 185 thousand persons were connected with trade in food stuffs as against 164 thousand in 1911.[10] The Report also revealed that the fish dealers constituted the largest proportion of traders in food stuffs. Number of milk and ghee sellers (mostly Nepali graziers) increased by 4000. "Groceries, grains and pulse, vegetables and betel nut, *gur* and sweetmeat selling occupy some 8,800 or over 1 per cent of the whole population".[11]

The wholesale trade in most of the goods other than tea and mustard seed was almost solely in the hands of the Marwaris who were also the chief suppliers of credit to the peasants and petty traders. "Marwari merchant capital", writes Guha, "established its octopus-like grip over the expanding network of internal trade that linked this important hinterland with the port city of Calcutta. A few native-born Assamese were no doubt there in trade – some of them were new entrants – but their existence was just marginal."[12]

Darrah's note, included in the Dufferin Enquiry,[13] made mention of the trading activities of the Marwari and other merchants operating in Assam in the closing decades of the 19th century. The same situation, of course, prevailed also in the 20th century. The trading community mainly consisted of Europeans, Bengali shopkeepers and Marwari mechants. But the Marwari traders were the most numerous and they were an influential class of people 'with the exception, of course, of the tea planers'. The 'note' further recorded that Marwari traders were to be found in almost every important village. They dealt in salt, cotton twist and piece goods, brass vessels, 'undrained sugar', etc. They transacted these goods both in cash and in kind. By barter exchange against credit, paddy, rice, mustard, silk cocoons, silk thread and silk cloth were procured from the peasants and artisans. The merchants also in some cases provided crop advances charging interest at the rate of 75 percent per month. According to this note, the Assamese peasants preferred borrowing from each other to borrowing from Marwari merchants.

3. Rural Indebtedness

In the precolonial period, rural indebtedness in Assam was a rarity. There were no professional money-lenders as such; the demand for credit from the rural producers for investment in farming operations was also quite limited. Of course, there were many instances of borrowing. Some people who were extremely poor borrowed money or goods for survival by offering their services and thus became bonded labourers or slaves. But as the colonial rule advanced and demands on the ryots for payment of revenue in cash increased, many ryots were forced to borrow cash for meeting revenue demands of the Government. With progress in the process of monetization and commercialization of economic transactions as also in the expansion of trading activities and dilution of the subsistence economic relations in rural areas, rural indebtedness became a significant phenomenon of Assamese rural economy. Professional moneylenders like the Marwaries and non-Marwari mahajans or shopkeepers operating in the villages supplied credit to meet the demands of the peasants and other needy people. But the rate of interest charged was very high. Therefore, the debt burden of the peasants became so unbearable that parts of it plus interests due on that remained unpaid. No wonder, debts accumulated considerably.

The Provincial Banking Enquiry Committee Report for 1929-30 estimated the extent of indebtedness in rural areas. Abstracts of the Committee's findings are given in Table 10: 4.

Table 10. 4
Extent of Rural Indebtedness in Assam Valley

District/Regions	P.C. of indebtedness of the total number of families in the sample	Average Debt per family (Rs.)	Average Debt per indebted family (Rs.)
1	2	3	4
Darrang	81.5	188	229
Nowgong	78.0	183	235
Jorhat Sub-division	83.5	120	145
Goalpara	62.0	111	180

Source : Assam Provincial Banking Enquiry Committee Report, 1929-30, quoted in P.C. Goswami (1994), *The Economic Development of Assam*, Kalyani Publisher, Ludhiana, New Delhi, p.60

As case study the Committee surveyed 4,995 families in the whole of Assam including Sylhet district to which district belonged about 50 per cent (2,500 families) of the total number of rural families included in the samples. Therefore, the Committee's findings about the average debt per family in Assam (Rs. 205) and the amount of debt per indebted family (Rs. 242) were not valid for the districts in the Brahmaputra Valley. From the table given above, it is, however, clear that the extent of rural indebtedness in Darrang, Nowgong, Goalpara districts and Jorhat Subdivision in terms of average debt per family and average amount of debt per indebted family was lower than the provincial average.

As for the overall economic position of the province, the Committee's observations were largely as follows. Of course, as we see, these observations relate to the period of pre-1930's slump that affected Assam's rural economy.

"On the whole we are inclined to think that agricultural indebtedness in the plains districts is increasing. The majority of us believe that cultivators are less hard working nowadays. The desire for social advancement, in so far as it means less manual labour, is a factor of some importance. Then there seems to be little doubt that cottage industries are on the decline, ... Necessaries have risen in price, but against this has to be set the increased price of agricultural produce. Paddy and mustard fetch about twice the price they did twenty years ago. In some districts in the Assam Valley, ... holdings are becoming too small to be economically profitable. Connected with this is the high price that has to be paid for additional land.... Cattle mortality is heavy even in normal times, apart from floods.. It is clear that expenditure on luxuries is on the increase..... So far as we can see the exploitation of the cultivators by the village mahajans, such as Marwaris and Telis, and by village money lenders in both valleys, is on the increase. This is particularly the case where advances are taken on promise of repayment of crop ...... The root of the matter is that the average agriculturist has not learned the importance of saving........"[14].

During the years of depression, 1930 to 1933 the burden of rural indebtedness became very heavy and the Government took some measures for lightening the burden. The Assam Money Lenders Act was passed to restrain the money-lenders from charging exorbitant rates of interest. Lending at compound rates of interest was prohibited and the rates of simple interest were restricted to 9.37 per cent for loans given against security and to 12.5 per cent for unsecured loans. Under the Assam Debt Conciliation Act of 1936, several Debt Conciliation Boards were constituted with a view to reducing the amounts of debt accumulated which the debtors were to pay their creditors through conciliation proceedings. The debtors were also given the option of repaying loans in instalments. "The outbreak of the Second World War", observes P. C. Goswami, "gave a great opportunity to the people of Assam to earn in various jobs arising out of the war efforts in the State. This helped to reduce indebtedness considerably"[15].

The position of rural indebtedness did not, however, improve in the post-war years as the findings of the All – India Rural Credit Survey for 1948-49 indicated. The Survey revealed that the average burden of debts increased, particularly in the case of the land-owning families on account of their higher creditworthiness. Summarising the findings of the Rural Economic Surveys of the districts of Darrang, Sibsagar, Lakhimpur and Nowgong conducted by the Department of Statistics, Government of Assam, Goswami Observes, "Social ceremonies like marriage, *sradha* (funeral ceremonies), etc. account for one-tenth to one fifth of the total loans, and productive purposes like purchase of cattle, seeds, implements, etc and improvement of land, only to 15 to 30 per cent. The proportions of loans for education of children and medical expenses are quite insignificant. Famines and crop failures are the general causes of loans........"[16].

Money-lenders were the chief source of loans for the agriculturists. Along with their friends and relatives the money-lenders provided 80 per cent of the total amount of rural credit. The roles of Government, Co-operative societies, commercial banks, etc were minimal in meeting credit needs of the rural families[17].

4. Co-operative Movement

In the beginning of the twentieth century Government of India decided to provide legal framework for the agriculturists so as to enable them to form cooperative credit societies through mutual cooperation in order to facilitate access to credit at reasonable rates for meeting their needs without depending on the money-lenders and mahajans who charged extremely high rates of interest. Accordingly, the Indian Cooperative Credit Societies Act was passed in 1904. Under this Act two types of societies could be formed, namely, urban cooperative societies having share capital with limited liabilities and the rural credit societies by members contributing deposits to the society of the latter type bearing unlimited liability. This legal provision did not provide enough incentive for members to mobilize sufficient amount of deposits for meeting growing credit demands of the needy members. This was so as the cooperative credit societies were almost wholly dependent on internal resources for meeting credit needs of the members.

In view of such structural deficiencies of the cooperative societies, in 1912 another Cooperative Societies Act was passed laying down the provision for the establishment of Central Banks which could supply credit to the rural primary credit societies and also supervise the functioning of the member societies. Under this new Act primary societies were classified into agricultural and non-agricultural societies.

These two Acts were applicable in Assam also, where as we have noted above, extent of rural indebtedness was rising and the grip of the moneylenders and mahajans on the rural agriculturists was becoming more and more onerous. The agricultural credit in Assam's villages was given mostly in the from of crop advances which the farmers took to tide over difficulties in the lean months between the start of agricultural operations for growing crops in the fields and the time to harvest when the crops matured. Taking long-term loans for a period extending as long as 5, 15 or 20 years for reclaiming and purchasing lands to enlarge the scale of operation, building irrigation works, procuring costly capital equipment, etc was rare among the tenants. Crop advances or short term loans, were taken for meeting consumption needs in the lean months, besides for purchasing agricultural inputs like seeds, manures, etc and for paying taxes and rents on land.

Total demand of the farmers in Assam for medium term loans (for 15 months to 5 years) for purchasing cattle, improvement of land, repairs of implements, irrigation works, etc was also for limited amounts. Primary cooperative credit societies formed in Assam catered mainly for the short term credit needs of the members. A statistical summary of the progress of credit societies in the whole province of Assam is given in table No. 10.5 and an account of the operation of the agricultural credit societies is given in Table No. 10: 6 below.

Table 10. 5
Progress of Credit Societies in a Nutshell

Yearly average	Number	Primary Agricultural Societies	
		Membership	Working Capital in 000 Rs.
1911 – 16	216	11,743	95
1916 – 21	453	16,861	512
1921 – 26	685	29,585	1,044
1926 – 31	1,189	50,308	2,536
1931 – 36	1,283	50,265	3,285
1936 – 41	1,289	40,388	2,770
1941 – 46	1,107	28,317	1,584

Note : The figures relate to the then Province of Assam and hence include the figures for the whole of Assam with Sylhet District.

Source : Annual Report of the Co-operative Department of Assam for the years, 1912-13 to 1945-46. Quoted in P.C. Goswami, *op. cit.*, p. 272.

Table 10. 6
Operation of the Agricultural Credit Societies
(in terms of thousand rupees)

Yealy average	Loans advanced during the year to individuals	Loans re-paid during the year by individuals	Loans due at the end of the year by individuals	Of which over-dues	% of over dues to loans due by individuals	Profit and loss (-)
1912 –16	133	89	280	130	46	16
1916 – 21	140	98	416	228	55	29
1921 – 26	385	223	848	276	33	59
1926 – 31	662	387	2,081	979	47	120
1931 – 36	100	146	2,324	2,051	88	111
1936 – 41	80	164	1,634	1,488	91	(-)3
1941 – 46	50	142	731	680	93	(-)27

Note : Loans still due and loans advanced by Societies and Banks are not shown. The figures for these items will be comparatively less and over dues will also be less.

Source : P. C. Goswami (1994), *op. cit*, p. 274.

Even though quite a good number of cooperative societies were formed, the cooperative movement itself suffered from various limitations and it failed to solve the problem of exploitation of agriculturists by the mahajans. Amounts of loans advanced increased from the quadrennium of 1912 to 1916 to that of 1926-31. But after that it declined on account of the depression of the' thirties. On the other hand, percentage of overdues to just loans due increased over the years and so also increased profits earned. From 1936 to 1946 the cooperative societies incurred losses. Profits shown in the table were not, according to Goswami, the 'actual realizable profits'. "In the absence of adequate audit and proper training of office-bearers, such overvaluation of profits was a common occurrence"[18].

In the light of the criteria of credit classification agreed upon in the Ninth Conference of the Registrars of Cooperatives, in 1926, the Cooperative Department of the Government of Assam classified the agricultural credit societies into first class (category A), and good average grades (B and C) and the hopeless ones (D). The yearly average position of such classification is shown in Table No. 10.7 which indicates the near failure of cooperative movement in Assam as the number of hopeless agricultural credit societies increased from 195 in 1928-29 to 1930-31 quadrennium to 443 during 1936-37 to 1940-41 quadrennium. In the years 1941-42 to 1945-46, the position slightly improved as the movement overcame the economic problems it faced in the wake of the depression of the' thirties. P. C. Goswami has attributed the causes of failure of the agricultural credit societies to the lack of cooperative spirit among the members, and inadequacies of governmental measures for supervising, guiding and controlling the harmful practices of the societies. Many office-bearers were defaulters regarding repayment of loans and therefore were not scrupulous in recovering loans of ordinary members. The practice of auditing the accounts of the societies and giving of directions on the maintenance of accounts properly was neglected.

The very foundation of the cooperative movement in Assam was unsound. In the initial stage primary cooperative societies were organized by the influential local leaders who had to promote and run the societies on honorary basis and were not adept in management of cooperative societies by enlisting the cooperation of all members of ordinary means. The relationship between the influential and resourceful local public figures and the ordinary rural ryot members was something like the patron-client relationship. Therefore, the spirit of democracy and exercise of equal rights by every member in running cooperative societies was conspicuously absent.

Table 10.7
Classification of Primary Agricultural Credit Societies into Different Grades (Nos)

Year by average	GRADES				Unclassified or not working	Total
	A	B	C	D		
1928 – 29 to 1930 – 31	9	142	764	195	166	1,276
1931 – 32 to 1935 – 36	6	91	712	361	113	1,283
1936 – 37 to 1940 – 41	7	63	669	443	146	1,328
1941 – 42 to 1945 – 46	6	52	577	346	87	1,068

Source : P. C. Goswami, *op. cit*, p. 113. The table has been compiled from the Annual Reports on the workings of the cooperative societies in Assam.

NOTES AND REFERENCES

1. Amalendu Guha (1991), *Medieval and Early Colonial Assam: Society Polity Economy.* K. P. Bagchi & Company, Kolkata for the Centre of Studies in Social Sciences, Kolkata, p. 247.
2. E. A. Gait (1899), *Report on the Census of India, 1891, Assam,* p. 300.
3. B. C. Allen (1902), *Census of India 1901*, Vol. IV, Assam Part-I Report, pp. 162-63.
4. Detailed analysis of the causes of growth of the system of tenancy in Assam under the British rule has been made by Amalendu Guha, vide, *op. cit.* p. 256.
5. C. S. Mullan (1933), *Census of India, 1931*, Vol. III, *Assam,* Part. I, Report, Shillong, p. 121.
6. *ibid.* p. 122.
7. Guha, *op. cit.* p. 253.
8. *ibid.* Darrah's note on the 'condition of the people of Assam' contained in *Dufferin Enquiry Proceedings*, No. 10, pp. 8-13.
9. G. T. Lloyd, *Census of India, 1921*, Vol. III, *Assam,* Part-I, Report, p. 167.
10. *ibid.* p. 162.
11. *ibid.*
12. Guha, *op. cit.*, p. 265.
13. Govt. of India, Proceedings of the Revenue and Agricultural Department for December, 1888; Famine Reports on the Condition of the Lower Classes of Population in India, Proceeding 9 and 10 NAI (referred to as Dufferin Enquiry) quoted in Guha, *op. cit.*, p. 278 and p. 301.
14. Extracts from the Report of the Assam Banking Enquiry Committee, 1929-30, quoted in C.S. Mullan, *op. cit.* p. 10.
15. P. C. Goswami (1994), *The Economic Development of Assam,* Kalyani Publishers, New Delhi, Ludhiana, etc. p. 60.
16. *ibid.*
17. *ibid.* p. 61 table 14 in the Appendix, pp. 257-8.
18. *ibid.* p. 111.

11
ASSAM'S FOREST WEALTH AND ITS MANAGEMENT

1. Importance of Forests in Assam's Economy

Assam is aptly described as 'essentially a forest country' in the Administration Report for 1921-22. The forests in Assam are very rich in commercially important timber species, fruit trees, berry bushes, medicinal, aromatic and sundry other useful and exotic plants and orchids. Also, the forests abound in a large variety of fauna, such as, elephants, rhinoceros, different species of deer, reptiles, beetles, butterflies, insects. Assam, therefore, is rich in bio-diversity, for which it is well – known.

Its extensive areas of forests served as the basic ecological infrastructure for cultivation of land on a sustained basis. There was no private ownership of forests, but community control over village forests regulated the access of individuals to forest resources. This ensured conservation of forests without which people's economic pursuits could not have been maintained on a stable basis. Even as the Ahom King "extended his prerogative of ownership over all woods, forests, ferries, mines, etc"[1], villagers were nevertheless free to collect forest produce for their use. They collected from forests some of their building materials, firewood, a variety of raw materials for making agricultural implements, baskets, fishing nets, and also for boat making. Forests also provided, besides fodder for cattle, many eatable leafy vegetables, arum and various other roots, fruits, nuts and berries. Wild banana plants were of great use to the villagers.

"In the history of human progress, the mode of resource use or the manner of maintenance and making use of the ecological infrastructure has played a significant role in shaping the material and cultural aspects of human living. Therefore, the study of the history of any people of any country or region should also include the study of its ecological history. Madhab Gadgil and Ramchandra Guha (1992)[2] have divided the modes of resource use into four historical modes, namely, gathering (including shifting cultivation), nomadic pastoralism, settled cultivation and industry. Each mode has distinctive characteristics about the aspects of technology, of economy, of social organization and of history".

To elaborate: "In the society of settled cultivators although majority of the people consume 'natural resources largely for subsistence — e.g., for food, clothing, shelter, implements, fodder and manure' a small group of people may use resources for large-scale consumption which may not be directly related to subsistence. There may be also exports of resources from out of the village and even out of the region. The peasants generally live together in a given place for generations and therefore maintain approximate equilibrium relations with the environment by developing 'co-operative behaviour among themselves' and subjugating individual interests to long term group interests. In such a milieu the individuals practise restraint in the use of land, water and forest resources for agricultural purpose as they value the prospect of sustained use of the resources for their subsistence more than that of maximizing immediate profit"[3].

Assam's dense forests lying beyond its village forests contained abundant timber species of commercial value, such as, *Sal, Khoir, Ajhar, Gomaw, Bonsum, Sonaree, Simalu Bda,* and *Korsi*,.

In the precolonial period excepting for the use of timber wood for building houses, boats, some items of house furniture, etc., other forms of its use for commercial purposes were very few. During the Ahom period, the big and beautiful wooden palace built at Gorhgaon and some wooden houses built by some nobles received the attention of Shihabuddin Talis, the Mughal Chronicler. Thrones, chairs, boxes, chests, trays, etc generally 'carved out of a single piece of wood' were also appreciated by the visitors to the Ahom capital at Garhgaon. The Ahom rulers appointed an officer called *Kath-Barua* who looked after the royal carpentry works.

Every year, in winter, wood – cutters came from Bengal to collect timber from these forests. But the logs were transported down the water courses in the rainy season when the water levels in the hill channels and streams and also in the Brahmaputra river rose. The logs which floated down the rivers were stacked at different points on the bank of the Brahmaputra wherefrom the timber merchants coming from Bengal bought the logs of timber and rafted them down to different river ports in Bengal. At the Kandahon or Hadira Chokey (custom collecting station) on the Brahmaputra (opposite Goalpara) one custom officer known as Duaria Barua was stationed by the Ahom Government for collecting duties on all goods including timber that were exported through those custom points.

That the Ahoms valued trees so much is evident from the fact 'that the coronation of the Ahom King used to begin with planting of a tree (Ficus Religiosa)'[4]. Even as the Ahom Kings treated forests as royal property and realized royalties on timber and elephants, they did not follow any well – conceived forest policy for maximizing revenue collections from forests. Of course, absence of such an objective indirectly promoted conservation of forest resources.

2. The British Forest Policy in Assam

The British rulers, following the policy of maximizing revenue collections from land and land-based resources, imposed taxes on timber, some minor forest products like reeds and on grazing of animals in forest. "The tax on timber was farmed out to the highest bidder; the farmer being allowed to manage the tracts of the forest uncontrolled by any condition. He was, therefore, free to cut any timber of any size he liked"[5]. This policy encouraged indiscriminate felling of trees, wastage and loss of forest wealth. By 1850 it was noted that in the lower Brahmaputra districts reckless extraction of *sal* trees resulted in widespread denudation of forest wealth. With the objective of putting a brake on this trend the Government decided to impose a tax at the rate of

15 rupees on every one hundred logs of *sal* timber in Kamrup district. In 1852, the system of 'dividing the forests into a number of *mahals* and the system of farming them to the highest bidder for a period not exceeding five years' was implemented.[6] Later the districts of Nowgong and Darrang were also brought under this system. Unrestricted extraction of forests in Sibsagar and Lakhimpur districts still continued.

The forests in Goalpara district were owned and managed by the Zamindars who enjoyed the privileges of the system of permanent settlement of land. They imposed levies on timbers procured by the merchants in the *hats* (markets) or from timber stacks. Though this arrangement restricted the practice of wanton exploitation of forest wealth, in the absence of any planned afforestation programme, the exhausted stock of timber trees was not replenished. Secondly, settlement of immigrant peasants from Bengal in Goalpara also caused extension of cultivation into forest lands.

In the non – permanently settled areas the Government further raised the rate of tax on timber for augmenting revenue earnings and also for enforcing some measure of disincentive for overusing timber resource. Even as by 1864 the rates of tax were fixed at 8 rupees for a log of *sal* timber, 6 rupees for other first class wood stock and 3 rupees for all second class timber the rapid depletion of the stock of forest wealth could not be effectively counteracted.[7]

After the establishment of the Imperial Forest Department in 1864, the Indian Forest Act was passed in 1865 that enabled the Government to exercise state monopoly over forests. In Assam the Assam Forest Regulation was promulgated in 1891 which was made effective on 1st April 1892. Accordingly, any government land (that is, 'land in respect of which no person has acquired (a) a permanent, habitable, and transferable right of use and occupancy under any law; ...... or (b) any right created by grant or lease made or continued by, or on behalf if the British Government') could be constituted a reserved forest. The Government also got the power to permit or prohibit the practice of shifting cultivation by the tribal farmers. The Government could, in addition, establish village forest in government land to which access of the villagers for collecting forest products and grazing cattle was subjected to certain restrictions.

Besides establishing reserved forests the Government also declared 27 species of trees as reserved trees under the Regulation. These trees could not be felled, cut, lopped, tapped or injured in any manner other than what the Government rules permitted.

Forests not included in the categories of reserved forests and village forests were treated as unclassified state forests where also the Government could either prohibit the practice of shifting cultivation or permit this practice subject to certain restrictions. For collection of timber and other forest produce and for 'quarrying of stone, boiling of catcheu, burning of lime or charcoal, cutting of grass, hunting of games, fishing in streams,' etc, the users had to pay fees, royalties, and so on.

Two kinds of permits were issued, namely, permits for collection of timber, for trade and permits for home consumption for the authorized persons, for their own use only. For trade permits some charges were made, while the other one was free of any charge.

Forest (waste) lands settled for ordinary or special cultivation, that is, for plantation of tea, rubber, coffee, etc. were generally subjected to the same restrictions as applicable for unclassified state forests. Or course, the conditions were laid down in each case of lease granted under the Assam Settlement Rules.

The main objectives of the forest policy of the Government were to commercialize the use of forest lands, over which the Government established its monopoly rights. Its accent was on raising plantation crops, carrying out the afforestation programme, and extraction of timber so that the revenue collections from forest resources could be maximized.

3. Establishment of the Forest Department

Assam became a Province under a Chief Commissioner in 1874. Until then Assam's forests were administered by the Forest Authority of Bengal Province. There were two forest sub-divisions in Assam, namely, the Upper Assam Sub-division comprising Lakhimpur, Sibsagar and Naga Hills districts and the Lower Assam sub-division consisting of the districts of Kamrup, Nowgong, Darrang and Khasi Hills.

Goalpara and Garo Hills fell within the jurisdiction of the Bhutan Forest Division. This arrangement was changed after 1874 when five forest divisions were created. They were (1) Goalpara (covering Goalpara and Garo Hills districts), (2) Guwahati (including Kamrup and part of Nowgong districts), (3) Tezpur (Darrang district), (4) Golaghat (covering Sibsagar, Naga Hills and the eastern half of Nowgong district) and (5) Cachar (Cachar and Sylhet districts). Some time later the areas forming the different divisions were rearranged for administrative convenience.[8].

The establishment of the Forest Department gave a fresh impetus to extending the area of reserved forests and exercising of greater control over the uses of forest resources for conserving the existing forest wealth and pushing up the afforestation programme. The total area of the reserved forests increased from 214sq. miles in 1873 to 3,685 sq. miles in 1898. The positive trend of growth is indicated in Table 10:1 below.

Table 11.1
Increase in Area of Reserved Forests, (including that in Sylhet District) 1873 to 1898.

	Year	Area of reserved forests (in Sq. miles)
1873	214	"The forest year terminated on 31 March of each year like the financial year till 1892; since then it was terminated on 30 June".
1878	1,983	
1883	2,177	
1888	3,310	
1893	3,625	
1898	3,685	

Source : T. J. Campbell (1898), Brief History of the Forest Department of Assam, p. 3,

Campbell estimated that the total area of reserved forests measured 12.3 per cent of the total area of the province (including Sylhet district). Observing that since 1874 reservation of forests proceeded rapidly, Campbell opined that there was not "much room for further progress in this direction except where political interests intervene. Some of the most valuable forest tracts have been allotted for tea cultivation ......"[9]

The area of reserved forests was further extended in the subsequent years. A comparative picture of the distribution of reserved forests in 1911 and in 1921 is given in Table 1 0: 2 below.[10]

Table 11.2
Area and Distribution of Reserved Forests in 1911 and 1921 (sq. miles)

District	1911	1921
Cachar	949	1,188
Goalpara	884	897
Kamrup	261	303
Darrang	336	568
Nowgong	198	502
Sibsagar	1,043	1,104
Lakhimpur	333	464
Khasi & Jaintia Hills	114	169
Garo Hills	109	109
Total	4,227	5,304

Source : *Report on the Administration of North East India* (1921-22), Delhi 1998, p. 21.

The unclassified State Forests occupied an area of 15,879 square miles in the whole of Assam including Sylhet.[11] Of course some small proportions of such forests were just "wooded". "The extensive savannah lands bordering the Brahmaputra fall within this class of forest. Cultivation is allowed to extend into the waste lands but steps are now being taken to reserve suitable tracts as village forests for the provision of the ordinary petty requirements of the people."[12] Such village forests covered 9,545 acres of land in the Eastern Circle as noted in the Administration Report. The most valuable forests were the sal (*Shorea robusta*) forests in Goalpara, Kamrup and in Garo Hills yielding considerable quantities of this timber. Sal was also found "in diminishing quantities" in Nowgong and Darrang districts.

Timber and forest produce were mainly required by the tea gardens, Public Works Department, Railways and the external and internal traders of timber. About the tea gardens' requirements, Campbell observes: ".......such large areas of forest clad land have been leased to tea gardens, of which, in most cases, the larger proportion has not been brought under cultivation (at close of 1896 out of 994,501 acres held by planters, 276,014 acres only were under cultivation), that timber for buildings, accessories, firewood, charcoal, etc. bring no revenue to the department, except that first realized under special conditions, and at rates much below those fixed as royalty for individual trees. In many cases, gardens saw up their own tea boxes, and in others saw-mills have been established for the purpose, which work under concessions from the department ...."[13]

Campbell also notes that the total requirements of PWD, railways and that for internal trade were smaller compared to that for external trade. In fact, it was the export of timber that yielded the largest amount of revenue for the government.

Total receipts and total expenditure relating to the operations conducted by the Forest Department in the period between 1874-75 and 1895-96, that is, after Assam was constituted as a Chief Commissioner's Province were as given below:

Table 11.3
Receipts & Expenditure of the Forest Department

Year	Total Receipts Rs.	Total Expenditure	
1874 – 75 to 1895 – 96	55,30,472	i) Conservancy and works	18,97,740
		ii) Establishment	23,53,812
			Rs. 42,51,552

Source : T. J. Campbell (1893), *op. cit.* pp. 54 – 55

The above table reveals that there was a surplus of total receipts over total expenditures which amounted to Rs. 12, 78, 920 for a period of 21 years. The average annual surplus was as much as Rs. 60,900. This was of course a beginning and as the Forest Department expanded its area and range of operations it began to contribute substantial amounts of revenue to the Provincial Government as Table 11.4, indicates:

Table 11.4:
Receipts & Expenditure of the Forest Department and Surplus Yielded by Government Forests

Year	Receipts	Expenditure	Surplus
1911 – 12	11,17,569	8,32,158	2,85,411
1921 – 22	12,97,027	9,91,510	3,05,517

Source : *Administration Report, 1921-22 op. cit.* p. 22

This increase in expenditure, according to the Administration Report for 1921-22, was mainly on account of 'the increased pay of the subordinate establishment'. The Report further observes: "The war prevented any great outlay on the extension or improvement of the forest tramway in Goalpara which continued to be worked: it is intended shortly to connect this tramline with the main line of the Eastern Bengal Railway. The province was sub-divided into two Conservators' charges in 1912, but it is intended to reunite these charges into one charge in the near future"[14].

The forests had been yielding substantial amount of revenue annually to the Government. In the post – depression year of 1931-32 the total income of the Forest Department amounted to 1927,000 rupees and the total expenditure 1613000 rupees and in 1936-37 income and expenditure were Rs.1685000 and Rs.1173000 respectively so that surpluses in the two years just mentioned amounted to Rs.314000 and Rs.512000 respectively.[15]

The Forest Department undertook the afforestation programme by planting trees, such as, *Sisoo (Dalbergia sissoo)* and teak. The progress achieved in this direction was very limited in the beginning on account of shortage of both trained technical staff and unskilled labour. However, the Forest Department's plans for providing training facilities for the youth interested in taking up forestry as an occupation opened up employment opportunities in the growing forests services in the Province.

Shortage of unskilled labour was "a persistent constraint on the expansion of afforestation programme and protection of existing forests from fire hazards, unauthorized grazing of cattle, etc. To tackle this problem, the Government formulated the policy of establishing forest villages mainly with the tribal families. The forest villagers were required to render service for the prescribed period of time as per assignment work made by the forest officials. For the remaining period of time they could work on agricultural and other productive activities. But the scheme was beset by some problems. The villagers disliked to attend to forestry work. They had frequent disputes with the forest officials. Many deserted such villages. Ultimately, in 1931-32 the Government abandoned the policy of establishing forest villages and even cancelled the existing ones."[16]

4. Conclusion

The Government's forest policy was formulated having been motivated by the idea of commercialization of forest management and maximization of revenue collection from forests. Of course, the Forest Department was keen about conservation of forest resources and also raising of new plantations of commercially valuable species of trees. The Government granted special concessions to the tea planters, railways and other industrial ventures in matters relating to the various uses of forest resources for promoting industrial development in the Province. By contrast, the Government put restrictions on the use of forest resources by the villagers, whose traditional system of community management of forests as a result had severely eroded. The hill farmers' practice of shifting cultivation also came under drastic restrictions.

Development and use of forest resources under the overall management of the Forest Department paved the way for diversification of productive activities. "Timber was the major forest product so far, which was mainly used for construction of houses and for building boats. Extraction of lac and some dyeing materials, etc was also made. But with the development of tea industry, opening of railway lines, setting up of plywood factories, safety match factory, etc forest products came to be directly used as industrial inputs, such as, railway sleepers, tea chests and plywood products, match sticks and boxes. Moreover, certain forest trees yielded tanning and dyeing materials, different oils, resins, essence, rubber, etc."[17]

NOTES AND REFERENCES

1. Edward Gait (1967), *A History of Assam*, Kolkata, p. 270.
2. Madhab Gadgil and Ramchandra Guha (1992), *The Fissured Land: An Ecological History of India*, Delhi, p. 14.
3. J. B. Ganguly (1994), Structural Changes in Assam's Economy: 1826-1947, H. K. Barpujari Endowment Lectures delivered at Dibrugarh University, (unpublished MS), pp. 135-36.
4. A. C. Sinha (1993), *Beyound the Trees, Tigers and Tribes* (Historical Sociology of the Eastern Himalayan Forests), Delhi, p. 129.
5. S. Goswami (1987), *Aspects of Revenue Administration in Assam*, Delhi, p. 113.
6. *ibid.* pp. 114-15.
7. *ibid.* p.
8. T. J. Campbell (1998), *Brief History of the Forest Department in Assam*, Published in Home, p. 1.
9. *ibid.* p. 4
10. *Report on the Administration of North East India (1921-22)*, A Mittal Publication, Delhi, 1984, p. 21.
11. *ibid.* p. 21
12. *ibid.*
13. T. J. Campbell (1898), *op. cit.* p. 38.
14. *Administration Report for 1921-22, op. cit.* p. 22

15. P. C. Goswani (1994), *The Economic Development of Assam*, Kalyani Publishers, Ludhiana, New Delhi, pp. 318-319.

16. J. B. Ganguly (1994), op. cit. p. 150. Also, A. C. Sinha (1993), *Beyond the Trees, Tigers and Tribes (Historical Sociology of the Eastern Himalaya Forests)*, Har-Anand Publications, Delhi pp. 60-61.

17. J. B. Ganguly (1994), *op. cit.* p. 149.

12
DEVELOPMENT OF ECONOMIC INFRASTRUCTURE AND INDUSTRY; ECONOMIC DEPRESSION OF 1930'S AND PROBLEM OF UNEMPLOYMENT

An elaborate economic infrastructure was built up during the Ahom rule in the forms of embankments about the Brahmaputra and many of its tributaries and ridges around paddy fields. These were in large number in Sibsagar district "where the country was protected from floods of the Brahmaputra, the Disang, the Dihing and the Darika"[1]. The embanked road built on the south bank of the Brahmaputra linking Upper and Lower Assam facilitated movements of troops, people and transportation of goods. It also protected rice fields from floods. Most of these vital public works were damaged, and even destroyed, during the Burmese invasion of Assam.

In the initial years of the British rule, public expenditures on building, repairing and maintenance of the existing infrastructural works were negligible. Moreover, the system of employing *Paiks* as was practised by the Ahom rulers for public utility works was not continued. And there was shortage of wage labour for repair and maintenance of bunds and embankments. As a result, recurring floods damaged crops as also took heavy tolls of cattle wealth.

1. Roads

The Government, however, built some roads and opened lines of communication for the movement of troops for conducting military expeditions into some tribal areas. In fact the development of infrastructure consisting of roads, riverways, railways, communication system, etc was undertaken on a large scale to meet the needs of the tea industry in the mid-nineteenth century. In 1868 the Department of Public Works was established for the purpose of carrying out the public works programme. In 1880 Local Boards were constituted to build roads, etc for meeting the local needs. For such works resources of the Local Boards came from their share of 'half the proceeds of a local rate of one – sixteenth the annual value of all landed property', tolls collected from pounds and ferries and some government grants.

Over the years the local boards became actively involved in development works at the local level in the fields of education, roads, medical services, etc, Towards the close of the year 1920-21 there were ten Local Boards in the whole of Assam each having elected a non-official Chairman, and later three more Boards followed suit. According to the Administration Report for 1921-22, "the aggregate opening balance of all Boards was Rs. 9,28,053, the total receipts amounting to Rs. 30,67,407 and total expenditure by a little over four lakhs and a half (excepting for Nowgong Board)"[2].

Government grants rose from Rs. 13,50,955 to over 16.7 lakh rupees which accounted for 57.4 p.c. of the total income of the Boards. "Of their 'free' income the Boards (except the Nowgong Board) spent 27 per cent on education, 27 per cent on roads and 23 percent on medical aid, while the remaining 23 per cent was either devoted to other objects or held over as unspent balances"[2].

In 1866 the PWD took up the work of constructing the trunk road from Dhubri in the western part to Sadiya in the far eastern part of Assam. The progress of the work, however, was slow on account of both financial constraints and labour shortage. Since there was hardly any landless peasant, agricultural wage-labourers were very few. Only during the slack agricultural season some local rural workers were available for hire. "Therefore the PWD had to depend on imported laborers and contract-expired tea garden labourers. This resulted in competitions between the planters and the PWD for employing the immigrant labourers"[3].

The undulating topography, heavy rainfall and frequent floods, alluvial soil requiring stones for metalling which had to be carried over long distances, etc. slowed down the road construction work. In 1911-12 the total length of roads in the whole province was 3,559 miles including 375 miles of metalled roads.[4]

Besides effecting improvements of local roads, by the end of the nineteenth century, "the Trunk Road on the North and the South and the Military road linking Golaghat with Manipur" were completed. "The Trunk Road was gradually raised, metalled and improved by replacement of temporary with masonry bridges. The Gwahati-Shillong road, 63 ½ miles, had been carefully aligned, metalled and bridged throughout enabling pony – *tonga* to perform the journey in 8 to 9 hours. This was extended to Cherrapunji and Sylhet thence to Cachar. At convenient places for convenience of officials and non – officials inspection bungalows were erected, and ferry – boats plied at the crossings of all important rivers"[5].

In 1920-21 a sum of rupees 16.5 lakh was spent on the maintenance of 448 miles of metalled roads, 1,588 miles of unmetalled roads, and 2,304 miles of bridle roads"[6]. Road building works were boosted after the constitution of the Road Board in 1926-27. A Tea Cess Fund was created by raising local rates on land under tea plantations for improvement of roads. This Fund was managed by a separate Board Constituted for this purpose. From this time onward emphasis was laid on the application of mechanical methods of road construction. A proposal was mooted for raising separate loans for construction of bridges over 300 ft. span. By 1929 the length of metalled roads went up to 565 miles. In that year Kaccha (earth) roads measured 4,362 miles.[7]

Availability of funds for Assam's road building works was augmented following the creation of the Central (Indian) Road Fund in 1929-30 by levying an additional tax of two annas (12 paise) a gallon on motor spirit. About 20 per cent of the total collection was earmarked for 'works of special or all – India importance' and the balance was distributed to the provinces on the basis of the amount of motor spirit consumed in each province for approved works. "From 1929-30 to 1937-38 Assam received Rs. 21-8 lakhs from the General Fund and Rs. 36.8 lakhs from the Reserve Funds"[8].

In 1928-29 the Road Board of Assam drew up a plan for construction of permanent bridges and metalling and gravelling of roads covering a total length of 1,118 miles. Moreover, the plan also included bridging, where necessary, raising and widening of 617 miles of *Kuchha* roads. These plans were approved by the Provincial Government. Another project in this plan was to construct a motorable road connecting Shillong with the Surma Valley at an estimated cost of Rs. 20 lakh which was to be obtained as a special loan from the Government of India.[9]

Several road building projects were undertaken by the Road Board which had received approval of the Provincial Government. Funds were mobilized from the Provincial budget allocations drawing upon the Tea Cess Fund and from allotments received from the Central Fund. In 1937-38 lengths of different types of road stood at 737 miles of metalled, 1,104 miles of gravelled and 3,571 miles of untreated earth roads; that is, all – told there were 5,412 miles of roads in Assam, including Sylhet district[10].

In 1937-38 the Provincial Government sent up a proposal to the Central Government for the construction of a road – cum – rail bridge over the Brahmaputra that could connect Pandu with Amingaon. But on account of the Second World War that broke out in 1939, consideration of this and some other proposals remained suspended. Of course, following the advance of Japanese forces near Assam, building and maintenance of roads in Assam to facilitate movements of troops, transportation of arms and ammunitions and stores and other provisions to meet military and other exigencies assumed great importance. During this period to cope with defence needs, the South Trunk Road from Goalpara to Saikhowaghat was widened and also changed into two lanes, metalled and black – topped for easy flow of traffic. Bridges on this road were also strengthened. It was during this period that the Assam Approach Road linking Sliguri in Bengal, the nearest broad – gauge railhead, to Jogighopa on the north bank of the Brahmaputra opposite Goalpara was constructed.

The defence engineers rapidly executed the project to improve the Dimapur – Kohima – Imphal Road and its extension up to Tomu on the Indo – Burma border. Another very famous road built was known as the Stilwell Road, running from Ledo in Assam to Bhamo in Myanmar (Burma) and therefrom, to Yunan Province in China, covering a distance of 1,043 miles. This road was built by the American General Joseph Stilwell across inhospitable terrain. He employed Chinese labourers for the purpose many of whom sacrificed their lives to complete that project.

As it is mentioned in the Imperial Gazetteer of India, water communications in Assam make it "less dependent upon its roads than other parts of India".[11] Following the development of tea plantations and railway transport system and of steam navigation services, the most important roads built in the state led to the steamer *ghats*, or to railway stations. "Numerous roads have also been made in the tea Districts, connecting the various plantations with one another and with the main lines of communications, whether water, road or railway. Apart from the trunk roads, the most important routes are: the road from Tura in the Garo Hills to the Brahmaputra, the road that runs from opposite Gauhati to Darranga at the foot of the Bhutan Hills, the roads from Rangamatighat to the north of Mangaldai subdivision, the road from Sibsagar to Disangmukh on the Brahmaputra, and the Dhodar Ali, which runs along the south – east of Sibsagar District"[12].

2. Waterways

Despite building a network of roads the 'chief means of communication in Assam' were still its waterways. The Brahmaputra was navigable by large steamers up to a few miles of Dibrugarh and most of the trade of the Assam Valley flowed through this riverway. In the rainy season, 'tea and other produce' were brought down the tributaries flowing into the mighty Brahmaputra on either side. Of course the river ports were also connected by roads with the interior[13].

In the pre – colonial period, for both external and internal trade in goods the river Brahmaputra served as the 'great highway of traffic'. *Bajras* and *panshis* (country boats) plied on the river for transporting goods and also passengers. These were slow moving boats and it took about a month to cover the distance from Goalpara to Calcutta. But the journey upstream from Calcutta to Gaulpara took eight days more. Still more time was taken going upstream up to Guahati and further up to Dibrugarh. With the development of tea industry along with growth of productive activities in general, the need for steam navigation service was felt for reducing time taken for the movement of goods and of passengers between the river ports of Assam and those of Bengal. Therefore, in 1847 "a steamer service on the Brahmaputra river was established by Government, but the boats ran only at uncertain intervals and they did not proceed beyond Gauhati"[14]. After some years to meet the needs of the tea industry, river steam service was extended up to Dibrugarh. Two private companies were formed' for the purpose of navigating the Brahmaputra'. But the services run by them were irregular and time-consuming as the steamers towed large flats loaded with goods and it took much time in loading and unloading goods at the different steamer *ghats* (stations) enroute. "In 1883, aided by a government subsidy, the two companies established a service of daily steamers on the Brahmaputra river". This service was improved over the years and by the beginning of the nineteenth century the fleet consisted of large, powerful and well-equipped boats so that the upward journey from Goalundo to Dibrugarh could be completed in less than a week[15].

Small ferry services were also introduced on the Brahmaputra at Dhubri and Gauhati. Elsewhere, in other *ghats*, the 'river was crossed in canoes, or rafts made by fastening two or three canoes side by side and laying planks across them'. Even as a good number of minor streams on the important roads were bridged, for the unbridged ones ferry services were maintained.[16] The Pandu – Amingaon ferry service was maintained by the railway company while the Tezpur-Silghat service was maintained by the Joint Steamer Company. The other minor ferry services for crossing the Brahmaputra and its tributaries were run either by the Public Works Department or by the local Boards or even by private parties on payment of an annual fee to the Government as fixed by public auction. In some rivers the ferries plied only in the summer months, and for the cold season, that is, from November to May, when the water level fell, temporary bamboo bridges were made for crossing rivers.[17]

3. Railways

The first railway line, from Bombay to Thane, was opened in 1853. After that over the decades the railway transport system was developed mainly to link the three ports, namely, Bombay, Calcutta and Madras with their respective hinterlands. Development of this transport system became imperative for the expansion and growth of internal and external trade flows so essential for boosting economic growth of the country. Development of this transport system required huge investments of capital and in the early stages such investments by private companies depended on commercial viability and also on government's support. Assam's growing tea industry's urgent needs in the 1850s and the decades following that period were for importing tea machinery and other inputs like coal foodstuff for workers etc. These besides, there was the need for sending the tea produced to Calcutta for the sale at auctions and exporting it aboard. The river ports and steam navigation services somehow satisfied these needs. The tea gardens in that period were located mostly in Dibrugarh and Jorhat subdivisions close to the south bank of the Brahmaputra. Their needs were served by the river ports at Dibrugarh and Kakilamukh. But as the tea gardens spread to areas further and further from the Brahmaputra, sending the produced tea to Calcutta and bringing imported foodstuff for labour, as also coal from Bengal to the gardens become more and more difficult. For these reasons development of railway transport facilities in Assam became an urgent necessity particularly to meet the growing needs of the tea – gardens.

After an abortive attempt initially at forming a railway company in 1879, the first railway company named the Assam Railways and Trading Company, was formed in 1881 which took up the work of laying Dibru – Sadiya rail line. "The first railway line", notes P. C. Goswami, "was opened in 1882 from Dibrugarh Steamer Ghat to Jaipur Road. The Coalfields were connected by railway lines in 1884.........

.... The Dibru – sadiya Railway System was only

seventy – eight miles in length at this time"[18] Later this railway was extended up to 91 miles in order to cater to the needs of about 50 tea gardens lying on either side of the Sadiya road, which was built in 1865. The gardens ware thus enabled to transport their produce to the Dibrugarh steamer ghat and bring food stuff therefrom for the garden staff.

In 1885 two small state railways – one in Jorhat sub – division and a second connecting Theriaghat with Companyganj – were started. While the former, having a length of 32 miles, continued to serve the needs of the tea industry, the latter had to be closed down having been affected by the earthquake of 1897. One railway company privately owned started a railway transport service from Tezpur to Balipara – a distance of 20 miles – on the north bank of the Brahmaputra.

It was in 1905 that the biggest railway company, namely, the Assam – Bengal State Railway began operating railway transport service connecting Chittagong port with several places in Assam. This line passed through the districts of Tipperah, Sylhet and Cachar. From Cachar across the North Cachar Hills it linked Lumding and ran up to a point on the Dibru – Sadiya Railway. This section was connected with Gauhati by a branch line which took off from Lumding.

The hill section of this railway, that covered a distance of 113 miles "contains 24 tunnels, 7 covered ways, and 74 major bridges, the longest being 650 feet, and the highest 113 feet above the river – bed, while many of the banks and cuttings approach 100 feet in height and depth respectively"[20]. Construction of this section of the rail line was indeed a great engineering feat and it also entailed overcoming severe logistics – related obstacles owing to the absence of local labour and food supplies. Besides the railway material, "food for more than 25,000 men had to be carried into the hills on elephants, bullocks, ponies, and other pack – animals"[21]. Therefore, the cost of construction was extremely heavy.

Laying of this railway line in the plains also had to face engineering difficulties, "The principal engineering difficulties in the plains were the bridge, 500 yards in length, which crosses the Kapili and the marshes which fringe its banks;

and the bridge over the Barak at Badarpur, which, though shorter, was even more costly, as its foundations had to be carried 80 feet below the river-bed. The line, which is on the metre gauge has a total length within the Province of 571 miles, and has been constructed by a company working under a Government guarantee. The greater part of the capital has, however, been found by Government"[22].

Besides this main railway artery (Assam-Bengal Sate Railway), there came up some other feeder lines of commercial importance. One metre-gauge line was opened in 1885 to link the steamer *ghat* of Dibrugarh with Margherita through a branch line up to Talap. Though its length was only 78 miles it tapped a large number of flourishing tea gardens and provided an outlet for the coal and oil of Makum to the Brahmaputra. This line was constructed and run by a private company with a Government guarantee. In the same year a small state railway, 30 miles in length and of 2 feet narrow gauge type was opened in Sibsagar District, that linked Kakilamukh on the Brahmaputra to Mariani and Titabar, to meet the needs of the numerous tea gardens in the neighourhood. A branch of the Eastern Bengal Railway was opened in 1902 that connected Dhubri with the Bengal system. It was a metre gauge line and its length within Assam was of 25 miles.[23]

The progress in developing railway transport system in Assam was quite notable in the beginning of the twentieth century. The total length of railway in Assam, including Sylhet district, was only 114 miles in 1891 but by 1903 it went up to 715 miles including 617 miles of state run lines. The total investment of capital up to 1903 in building the minor railways within the Province namely, the Dibru – Sadiya, Tezpur – Balipara, and Jorhat Railways, amounted to Rs. 94.69 lakhs. In 1903, these railways carried 5.67 lakh passengers and 3.17 lakh tons of goods and minerals and incurred gross working expenses of Rs. 5.95 lakh in that year.[24]

By 1921-22 the total mileage of railways in Assam (including Sylhet district) went up to 989.64.[25] Construction of more rail lines continued. By 1931 branches of the Assam – Bengal Railway were opened. There was one between

Katakhal and Lalaghat via Hailakandi. Another connected Furkating Junction with Jorhat via Badlipar; still another linked Simulguri Junction with Khowang via Sibsagar; and then extension was made from Karimganj up to Longai Valley, followed by an extension from Senchoa Junction (near Nowgong) to Mairabari. Moreover, construction of an extension line from Tangla to Rangapara on the north bank of the Brahmaputra was taken up by the Eastern-Bengal Railway.[26]

The steady growth of the railway transport service provided by the minor railways and the Assam-Bengal State Railway remarkably strengthened the economic infrastructure of Assam. It helped growth of the tea industry and development of other industries like coal, mineral oil, etc and postal communication system. This development resulted in the easy flow of goods and movements of people within Assam and between Assam, Bengal and other parts of India. Also it opened up Assam to the immigrant peasants, workers, professionals and others. Flow of capital into Assam from outside for investments in different sectors by both government and private entrepreneurs was also facilitated.

The railway system built up so far was still inadequate to cover the remote areas and meet the needs of all parts of Assam. Even then it increased employment opportunities not only in the tertiary sector but also in the primary and secondary sectors. In short, within the limits it paved the way for all - round growth of productive activities by expanding the market and ensuring greater utilization of natural and human resources.

After 1932-33 till the outbreak of World War II the railway network in Assam remained stable and continued to provide uninterrupted services for passengers, mail and goods movements. During the Second World War, the railways services were streamlined and improved for which purpose the rolling stock was expanded by adding in particular heavier and speedier engines. This system served the war needs by carrying military stores, foodstuff and provisions and army personnel. For bringing the operations of railways under one single line of control, the Assam Bengal Railway and the Eastern Bengal Railway were combined into one railway system named Bengal Assam Railway. The utilization made of the railways was up to its fullest capacity for meeting the war needs.

4. Postal and Telecommunication Services

Along with railways, another important aspect of the development of communications related to the provision of postal and telecommunication services. For this purpose, a Postal Circle was created in the Province. Progress in utilization of this service by the people from 1880-81 to 1903-04 may be noted from the table given below:

Table 12.1
Growth of Postal Business from 1880-81 to 1903-04

	1880 - 1	1890-1	1900-1	1903-4
Number of Post Offices	143	276	344	344
Number of Letter Boxes	107	195	423	452
Number of miles covered by Postal Communication	2,221	3,843	4,230	4,576 ½
Total number of Postal articles				
Letters delivered	2,115,436	2,991,462	4,979,070	5,044,936
Postcards	249,895	1,284,826	3,006,531	3,437,122
Packets	52,638	338,876	965,711 *	872,586
Newspapers	417,742	755,785	1,049,453**	943,254
Parcels	37,256	74,903	136,406	173,994
Value of stamps sold to the public	Rs. 82,369	Rs. 2,04,478	Rs. 2,44,198	Rs. 2,58,583
Value of money orders issued	13,46,130	52,11,700	98,76,590	92,98,498
Total amount of savings bank deposits	—	13,99,347	30,74,356	36,28,721

* Including unregistered newspapers**. Registered as newspapers in the Post Office.

Source: *Imperial Gazetteer of India, op. cit.* p. 81

The figures given in the table "relate to both the Imperial post and the local or District post. "The latter system was maintained by Local boards to provide postal communication between the head - quarters of Districts and subdivisions and revenue and police stations in the interior, in cases where the maintenance of the necessary lines of communication would not be warranted by the commercial principles of the Post Office. The expenditure from Local funds averaged Rs. 48,000 per annum during the five years ending with 1902-3. The number of District post offices on March 31, 1904, was 58 and the total length of District post mail lines 1,387 miles. In 1906 the whole of this system was transferred to the Imperial post"[27].

The Department of Post and Telegraph was upgraded and put in the charge of a Deputy Post Master General under the Post Master General of Bengal and Assam Circle. The Telegraph Engineering Department was headed by a Director. These positions were not subordinate to the Local Government.[28] Development and steady expansion of Postal and Telecommunication services facilitated economic transactions, remittances of money to different places at affordable costs, promotion of small – scale savings, etc, and also provided access of the people of Assam to books, journals, magazines, dailies published within and outside Assam. People living outside Assam also benefited from this having had access to publications originating in Assam. For quick inflow and outflow of postal materials, mail steamer and rail services were operated. This also acted as time saver both for passengers and for movements of goods not only within the Province but also between Assam and places outside it.

5. Industries

As already noted in Chapter 5 (Sec. 4), Assam's traditional manufactures were weaving cotton cloth, rearing silk worms for weaving of three varieties of silk cloth, namely, pat, muga and eri., gold-washing, small quantities of iron-smelting and production of a few implements and tools, making of brass and bell-metal utensils, jewellery, pottery, besides various handicrafts. Most of these productive activities were organized commonly as household industries and there was no caste-wise specialization of artisans as in other parts of India.

Development of modern organized industries, besides tea, was taken up by private companies following the development of transport and communication services. Mining of coal in the Makum fields lying in the foothills of the Naga Hills (Lakhimpur district) began in 1882. The information about coal deposits occurring in that area was available in about 1825 and some quantity of coal was actually mined in 1828. It was after the encouraging results of the geological survey of the region's coal deposits in 1865 and subsequently from 1874 to 1876, that the commercial exploitation of this mineral was started. These findings encouraged the Assam Railways and Trading Company which was incorporated in 1881, to take up the venture of coal mining in the foothill areas of Naga Hills while opening the Dibru-Sadiya Railway in 1882. The coal industry having seven mines was located in Lakhimpur district and it registered some growth in production in the decade 1921-1931. In 1930, more than 300,000 tons of coal were extracted. There was another important coal mine located in Borjan in the Naga Hills.

At Digboi in Upper Assam, petroleum was found in the course of construction of the railway line in 1882 from Dibrgarh to Ledo. Of course the existence of hydro-carbon deposits in some parts of Upper Assam in dense jungles was recorded as early as 1825. As the economic importance of petroleum as a fuel for running motor cars and other vehicles as a new means of road transport assumed importance by about 1860's, the Assam Railway and Trading Company took up the work of drilling mineral oil in 1889.

In 1899 the Assam Oil Company was promoted by the Assam Railways and Trading Company, which started producing petroleum on a large scale. But because of financial constraints steady growth of production of oil could not be sustained. The rate of growth even became negative as the output level fell from 18000 gallons a day in 1919 to 14000 gallons daily in 1920. Production of petroleum in Assam was boosted following the taking over of the management of this Company by the much more resourceful Burma Oil Company in 1921. The daily production of oil went up to 30,000 gallons in 1925 and it increased further to 180,000 gallons a day in 1931.[29] The Assam Oil Company operating as a subsidiary of the Burma Oil Company "Considerably extended their field of operations during the last ten years (1921-1931) and 146 new wells were drilled during the period. Modern plant and equipment have been installed both in the field and in the refinery and the output of crude oil which was just over 5 million gallons in 1921 rose to 53.4 million gallons in 1931. In Badarpur and Masimpur in the Cachar district there were oil fields managed by the Burma Oil Company. The crude oil output of these fields was small compared with that of the Digboi fields, only 2.8 million gallons in 1930 and little below 2 million gallons in 1931"[30].

On account of 'the declining Digboi fields' annual production of oil by the Assam Oil Company remained nearly static at the level of 63 to 67 million gallons from 1934 to 1952[31].

Among other manufacturing industries in the 1930's, mention may be made of a Swedish Match Factory at Dhubri which employed about 300 workers. There were also a few saw mills, edible oil mills (i.e., Cooking Oil, mainly mustard oil), engineering workshops and printing presses, etc.

The tea industry met its requirement of tea chests by importing them from abroad. But such import became difficult during the First World War (1914 – 1918). Therefore, in 1918 the Assam Saw Mill and Timber Company was floated as the first plywood factory in Assam. Later, in 1924, the Assam Railway and Trading Company started its own plywood factory. However, the growth of this industry was affected because of the keen competition it faced from foreign manufacturers of plywood products.

The trend of industrial development was positive until the world-wide great depression of the 1930's. With organized industries (each employing 20 or more persons) developing, employment opportunities also increased appreciably in the decade 1911-1921. Details about ownership of industries, given in table 12.2 below show that in the case of tea industry, more and more Indian Capital and enterprise were getting involved in its development.

Table 12.2
Ownership Pattern of Industrial Establishments each Employing 20 or more Persons

Pattern of Ownership	INDUSTRIES					
	TEA		COAL		RICE & OIL MILLS	
	1911	1921	1911	1921	1911	1921
TOTAL NO OF UNITS	609	782	6	4	4	11
REGISTERED COMPANY	506	629	6	4	-	1
PRIVATELY OWNED						
I) EUROPEAN OR ANGLO INDIAN	55	55	-	-	-	-
II) INDIAN	48	98	-	-	3	11

Source: *Census of India, 1921* Vol. III, Assam, p. 197

From Table No. 12.3 it may be gathered that total employment in organized industries went up by 5.74 per cent, that is, from 501,606 to 530,435 persons. Of course the largest number of persons were employed by tea industry.

Table 12: 3
Growth in Number of Persons Employed in Industries from 1911 to 1921

Years	All Industries	Growing of special products (mainly tea)	Collieries	Petroleum	Wood Industries
		No of persons employed			
1911	501,606	493,761	2810	1010	1172
1921	530,435	519,225	3158	2087	2106

Source: Census of India, 1921, Vol. III, Assam, P. 197

Industrial development during the decade 1921–1931 was structurally the same as in the earlier two decades. But there were some improvements and expansions in the case of the three main industries, viz., tea, oil and coal. According to the Census Report for 1931, the total number of workers including working dependents in the occupation of tea production were 338,000 men and 299,000 women against 336,000 men and 316,000 women in 1921. These figures represent the position for the whole of Assam, that is, including Sylhet district[32].

In oil (petroleum) industry the number of male earners increased from 1,686 to 8,377. This increase was on account of a rise in the output of crude oil in the Digbol Oil Fields from 5 to 53 million gallons. "Compared with the Digbol Oil fields the oilfields in Cachar (Badarpur and Masimpur) are of small importance and employ less than a thousand men[33]".

In coal industry, as the Census Report of 1931 noted, in Lakhimpur district male workers employed were 5,387 as against 3,529 in 1921. In Borjan in the Naga Hills nearly one thousand men were employed. Thus the total number of workers in the industry were nearly 6,400.[34]

Output of industrial goods and employment of labour in organized industries indicate the low level of industrial development in Assam in 1930s. This position was indicated in the memorandum submitted by the Government of Assam to the Royal Commission on Labour in India in 1929. In it was mentioned that Assam was not an industrial province, and did not have any large towns or industrial centres. Tea industry, the largest and most important industry, was mainly an agricultural operation. The only two other large labour employing concerns were coal mines and oil fields and a match factory. There were a few scattered saw mills, rice mills, oil mills, engineering workshops and printing presses, but they were small and of little importance in that province. Regarding availability of industrial labour, which is an indication of the industrial culture of the population, the Memorandum noted that 'as an agricultural province with land still available for settlement and no pressure of population, Assam had no indigenous industrial classes'. Of course, there was 'some indigenous casual labour, both skilled and unskilled, in the small towns and villages to meet the ordinary needs of the people, viz., agricultural labourers, porters, carpenters, black-smiths, etc.' For the few organized industries that came up labour had to be imported from other parts of India. The Memorandum also emphasized the fact that the main difficulty which industry in Assam faced, was in regard to labour supply. The labour employed in Assam's industries was a 'heterogeneous mixture of races and creeds drawn from every part of India'[35].

6. Cottage and Rural Industries

Viewed against most of the local traditional cottage industries, the main organized industries developed within Assam were not competitive. Yet the conditions of the traditional cottage and rural industries and their prospects were affected by the structural changes occurring in Assam's economy. Coming up of a few modern industries, expansions of transport and communication facilities leading to growth in both internal and external trade flows, phenomenal growth of immigrant population groups, such as, peasants, industrial workers, professional classes and the rise in the number of urban centres and in urban population caused by internal (from rural to urban areas) and external immigrations etc. brought about shifts from demand for the products turned out by the traditional cottage and rural industries to the imported products.

The most important household product was cloth woven by women of almost every Assamese family in the Brahmaputra Valley for their own consumption. For this purpose cotton was procured from the neighbouring hills and yarn made of such cotton was spun and then cloth woven within the family. Parts of the silk textile produced as a household enterprise were also for self consumption. But in the closing decades of the nineteenth century, Assam began to import substantial quantities of foreign mill-made twist and yarn and piece goods. At the same time Assam began to re-export cotton brought from the neighbouring hill people to Bengal as the use of raw cotton for spinning yarn for weaving cloth declined in volume. Data compiled by Keya Dasgupta from the Reports on Trade carried by Rail and River of Assam show that for the quinquennium 1880-81 to 1884-85 Brahmaputra Valley's imports of European cotton goods amounted to 34,755 maunds of twist and yarn and 225,392 maunds of piece goods for the quinquennium 1915-16 to 1919-20. Correspondingly, the Brahmaputra Valley exported 85,330 maunds and 164,512 maunds of raw cotton during the quinquennia 1880-81 to 1884-85 and 1915-16 to 1919-20 respectively[36].

Cottage industry manufacturing brass, copper, and bell-metal utensils was also affected as it faced competition with the imported enamelled wares which were much cheaper.

For an evaluation of the overall position of the cottage and rural industries, a census of cottage and rural industries was conducted by the Government in 1921. This census covered the existing cottage and rural industries and their number, details of which are given below in table No. 12.4.

Table 12.4.
Census of Cottage and Rural Industries 1921

Item No.	Name of Cottage Industry	Number of Units
1	2	3
1.	Handloom at work, without fly shuttle	355,096
2.	Handloom at work, with fly shuttle	2,471
3.	Spindles or charkhas at work	145,114
4.	Hand cotton ginning machines at work	58,194
5.	Oil ghanis	9,227
6.	Sugarcane pressing mills	9,072
7.	Tailoring establishments composed of two or more tailors	1,011
8.	Sewing machines	1,887
9.	Brass workshop	636
10.	Bell metal workshop	421
11.	Potter's establishments composed of two or more potters	1,065
12.	Carpenter's workshop composed of two or more carpenters	942
13.	Smithy workshop composed of two or more blacksmithy	1,535
14.	Dairy establishments	1,193
15.	Modern cream separating machines	949
	Total =	588,813

Source : Census of India 1921, Vol. III Assam, Part – II, Provincial Table-5.

The census reveals that in 1921, there were 588,813 units of cottage and rural industries engaged in over 15 different items of productive activities, such as, agri-processing activity; forestry (carpenter's workshop), processing of animal husbandry products (dairy establishment and cream production) and processing of non-agricultural products. Most of these cottage industries used traditional tools and technology. Assuming that an average of two workers participated in running these units, then the cottage industry sector provided direct employment to nearly twelve lakh peoplc.[37] In the absence of any earlier census of such industries, the growth of this sector cannot be quantitatively assessed, but that some cottage industry units started using some modern technology (6,318 units) and there was the growth of population and of transport and communication facilities, which could be taken as evidence that this sector certainly expanded to some extent during the last few decades.

7. Impact of the Great Depression of 1929:

The world–wide great depression of 1929 that afflicted the economies of many countries continued up to about 1934-35. India's as well as Assam's productive activities, which were particularly export-based, were severely affected. The economic slump in these activities spread over the economy as a whole causing unemployment and fall in income and resultant decline in demands for many goods and services. In Assam, the growers of tea and jute were directly affected as world demand for these products declined. Other economic activities directly or indirectly linked with tea and jute productions also suffered as capacity remained underutilized and unsold stocks accumulated. The condition of the tea industry in the depression years and its recovery have been discussed in Chapter 8.

The crises facing the jute growers is evident from the fact that total acres of land under jute (for whole of Assam) declined from 167 thousand acres in 1926-27 to 95 thousand acres in 1931-32 and it increased to 144 thousand acres in 1933-34. Toward the end of 1930s, that is in 1939-40, the total area used for growing jute went up to 286 thousand acres.

The great depression caused the severe problems of the educated unemployment in Assam. Therefore for the 1931 population census it was decided to enumerate the educated unemployed and also record their educational qualifications. There were 825 educated unemployed in the whole of Assam including 339 in the Assam Valley. Detailed findings are shown in table No. 12.5 below.

Table No. 12.5
Number of Unemployed by University Degrees and Certificates

	Indian Degree / Certificates							
British Degree	**Medical**	**Commerce**	**M.A**	**M.Sc**	**B.A**	**B.Sc**	**B.E or LCE**	**I.A. or I.Sc**
1	13	1	2	2	82	15	3	98
						Matriculation		Total
						609		825

Source : Census of India, 1931, Vol. III, Assam, Part I Report, P. 147

In terms of absolute figures, the number of different categories of educated unemployed may not *prima facie* appear very acute but considering the fact that only over the last few decades youths had been joining institutions of higher education, and the total number of such educated people was not many, the reality of the problem was quite a serious one as it almost shattered the aspirations of the emerging middle class. The *Times of Assam* in a leading article published on 16 May 1931 highlighted the acuteness of sufferings of the middle class. An excerpt from it follows:

"The problem of unemployment among the educated young men of the middle class even in this province is now getting increasingly acute. Until a few years ago the employment market in this province was wide enough to absorb the increasing numbers of young men that were turned out annually by the educational institutions. Times have, however, greatly changed, and the supply has now far exceeded the demands in the employment market ....".

Regarding the disastrous impact of slump in tea industry on Assam's economy the article continues to state:

"The slump in tea which is one of the principal industries in Assam and with which is bound up the very existence, not to speak of the prosperity, of many small business, has had, as one of its disastrous consequences the throwing out of employment of a considerable number of men"[38].

The suffering of the people on account of unemployment and loss of earnings and a general decline in income exposed the failure of the Government in providing social security measures of some kind and / or in organizing public works as a succour for the unemployed and other self – employed people affected by the Great Depression. In any economy dominated by an export oriented industry, such as tea, which was subjected to fluctuations in world demand for the product, some provision for unemployment relief was necessary to be included in it. Part of the total cost of production was to be borne by the industry. Also was needed a provision in the Government's budget for bearing part of the costs of social security measures for the workers.

NOTES AND REFERENCES

1. Edward Gait (1967), *A History of Assam* (Revised and Enlarged by B. K. Barua & H. V. S. Murthy), Thacker Spink & Co., Kolkata, p. 267.
2. *Report on the Administration of North East India (1921-22)* (Reprint of the *Report on the Administration of Assam for the year 1921-22*), A Mittal Publication, Delhi, (1984), p. 105.
3. J. B. Ganguly (1994), *Structural Changes in Assam's Economy (1826-1947)*, H. K. Barpujari Endowment Lectures delivered in Dibrugarh University (unpublished MS), P. 118.
4. H. K. Barpujari (1992), (ed), *The Comprehensive History of Assam*, Vol. IV, Publication Board, Assam, Guwahati, p. 299.
5. *ibid.* pp. 299-300.
6. *Administration Report for 1921-22, op. cit.* p. 112
7. P. C. Goswami (1994), *The Economic Development of Assam*, Kalyani Publishers, Ludhiana, New Delhi, etc. p. 183 f.n.
8. *ibid.* pp. 183-84.
9. *ibid.* p. 184
10. *ibid.* p. 184 f.n.

11. *Imperial Gazetteer of India*, Vol. VI, New Edition, 1908, Oxford at the Clarenden Press, p. 79.
12. *ibid.*
13. *ibid.* p. 80
14. E. A. Gait, (1967), *op. cit.* p. 399.
15. *ibid.*
16. *Imperial Gazetteer of India, op. cit.* p. 81.
17. P. C. Goswami, *op. cit.* p. 172 f. n.
18. *ibid.* p. 173 and the foot note.
19. Edward Gait, *op. cit.* pp. 399-400
20. *Imperial Gazetteer of India, op. cit.* p. 78
21. *ibid.*
22. *ibid.*
23. For all these details of extension of railway lines in Assam refer to *ibid.* pp. 78-79
24. *ibid.* p. 29.
25. *Administration Report for 1921-11, op. cit.* p. 112.
26. *Census of India, 1931*, Vol. III, Assam, Part I – Report, p. 9.
27. *The Imperial Gazetteer op. cit.* p. 82.
28. *Administration Report for 1921-22, op. cit.* p. 55.
29. For the historical aspects of coal and oil explorations and their production figures given here we relied on P. C. Goswami, *op. cit.* pp. 147-49.
30. *Census of India, 1931, op. cit.* pp. 7-8.
31. P. C. Goswami, *op. cit.* p. 149.
32. *Census of India, 1931, op. cit.* p. 122.
33. *ibid.* p. 124.
34. *ibid.*
35. From the Assam Government's Memorandum written for the Royal Commission on Labour in India (1929) as quoted in *Census of India, 1931, op. cit.* p. 124.
36. Keya Dasgupta (1988), "Industrialization in the Brahmaputra Valley (1881-1921", *Proceedings of the North East India History Association*, 9th Session, Shillong, p. 502.
37. J. B. Ganguly (1994), *op. cit.* pp. 123-25.
38. Extracts from the article quoted in Census of India, 1931, Report, *op. cit.* p. 127.

13
LITERACY, EDUCATION AND URBANIZATION IN ASSAM

The prolonged civil war and the disastrous Burmese invasion of Assam under the Ahoms in the pre-Annexation period depopulated the region and rendered large areas under prosperous farming operations desolate and unproductive. Even more harmful consequence was the weakening of the moral fibre and virility of the people of all ranks. The loss of nerve and the enterprising zeal of the masses of people were palpably reflected in their growing addiction to the locally produced opium. The people at large resigned themselves to pessimism, indolence and poverty.

Shortly after the occupation of Assam, the Government restored law and order and reorganized administrative, judicial, and land settlement systems. But the vital need for creating opportunities for education of people and enhancing literacy was ignored. Education shapes attitudes, generates optimism and enhances productive efficiency. Also spread of literacy and education might free the people from the debilitating habit of consuming opium.

As Gunner Myrdal aptly observes, "Literacy is needed, for acquiring higher skills in all occupations, including agriculture, and for developing more efficiency in all the various types of local and functional operation............"[1]. Therefore, a review of the growth of literacy and education in Assam in the colonial period should throw light on the corresponding process of economic growth in the province during the British rule.

During the rule of the Ahoms literacy and education was

limited to the 'priestly classes, scribes and a few others connected with the government'. For the ruling Ahom aristocracy, 'it was not a necessity to have literary education for their respective calling'[2]. But Since the colonial rulers maintained elaborate written records of all administrative, judicial, legal, developmental, military and other official transactions, the need for appointment of educated government staff went up manifold. As few educated persons for such appointments were available locally, educated Bengalis coming from the neighbouring districts of Bengal were appointed for running government offices. In the initial period Bengali was even made the 'language of the court and the schools', which took away the urgency of launching a government programme for spreading literacy and education through mother tongue among the Assamese population.

The Ahom noblemen and the gentry became unemployed and were deprived of the official positions held by them earlier. The Government gradually realized the need for remedying the situation by taking effective measures towards providing educational opportunities for the Assamese youths. In 1834, Francies Jenkins, Commissioner of Assam (1834-60) sought the approval of the higher authority for opening schools at Sadar stations, namely, Goalpara, Guwahati, Nagaon, Darrang and Biswanath. Some youths of rank were to be sent to Calcutta for receiving education and training to e able to teach in English and Bengali in school. To start with, however, teachers were recruited from Bengal for running the schools. Jenkins opined that in the provnce of Assam, which was backward then the Government had to bear the responsibility of spreading literacy and education among the people.

Till the Charter Act 1813 was passed by the British Government, the East India Company was quite indifferent toward education of the people and hence spending any money on it. But the new Act made it incumbent on the Company's Government to incur public expenditure on "the revival and improvement of literature and the encouragement of a knowledge of science amongst the inhabitants of the

British territories in India"[3]. Actually, however, effective steps were taken for promotion of education in the country with the appointment of the General Committee of Public Instruction in 1823. In Assam, opening of schools began under the Governments initiative after 1934 with the objective of imparting modern education. Financing was done by the Government, but not entirely; public donations were also invited for opening and running schools.

Earlier, David Scott, the Governor General's Agent immediately after the Annexation of Assam in 1926, had set up eleven schools of the traditional system where teaching of Sanskrit was the main curriculum.

Purandar Singh, Ahom ruler of Upper Assam from 1833 to 1838, was a man of vision who created educational opportunities on a massive scale for the local people in the territory of his jurisdiction. He decided that no illiterate person would be eligible for working as *Kheldar* or *Mowzadar* (revenue-collector). He also made it obligatory on every *Khelder* to start a school in his area. Of course, his plan of developing literacy and educational opportunities in upper Assam came to an end with the resumption of British rule there in 1838. The Government, however, established one school in Sibsagar in 1841 for the education of the descendants of the Ahom ruling dynasty and 'sons of the gentry'. Two more schools of this category were later opened in Jorhat and Jaypur. All these schools were in Upper Assam.

Steps taken by the Government to provide opportunities for literacy and education were limited. Following the 'Filtration Theory' the Government involved itself in supporting only a few schools for the members of the upper stratum of society and expected that the educated class would help those of the lower stratum to be educated over time. Obviously this was a faulty proposition and therefore the expectation of progress in education of the people had turned into deep frustration.

The situation improved after 1854 as this theory was rejected by a Despatch of Charles Wood in that year, consequently the system of supporting public efforts too to establish schools of high, middle and primary levels by sanctioning grant-in-aid was initiated.

Initially the amount of grants-in-aid was very meagre and public donations and initiative for opening schools was also limited. In 1871-72 the quantum of the Government's grant-in-aid to self-supporting schools was enhanced which paved the way for starting more schools. "In 1873," writes Barpujari, "on the strong support of the higher officials backed by the American Missionaries, George Campbell, Lioutenant Governor of Bengal, made Assamese the language of the court and the schools. As a result at the end of the century the number of Primary Schools rose from 204 in 1871-72 to 1351 with an enrolment of 38, 182 in 1882-82. A number of Lower Vernacular Schools also came into existence as intermediaries between Primary and Middle School. During 1897-1902, the number of Primary schools, went up from 2800 to 3534 with a corresponding increase in the number of pupils from 83,000 to 103,541"[4].

The overall system of education was not, however, mass-based. Comparatively well-off people only could afford to pay for the education of their children. The poor peasant families were hard hit by the enhancement of revenue by the Government from tome to time. For them mere survival was their main concern. Education should have been made free at least at the primary level. In the beginning the medium of instruction was Bengali, which was also a predicament the rural children had to suffer to acquire literacy and receive school education. No wonder, in 1881 only 2.41 per cent of the male population and 0.07 per cent of the female population of all ages in the Brahmaputra Valley were literate. In fact, growth curve of literacy and education started slowly moving in upward direction only since the closing decades of the nineteenth century.

The 1891 census showed population divided into three broad classes: the learning, the literate and the illiterate. Those at school or otherwise under instruction were shown as learning, 'those able to read and write but not under instruction as literate and those who were unable to read and write and were not under instruction as illiterate'. District-wise distribution of literate population in the Brahmaputra Valley is shown in table 13.1 below.

Table 13.1
Percentage of Persons, Learning and Literate in 1891

District	Learning		Literate	
	Male	Female	Male	Female
Goalpara	1.27	0.07	4.48	0.14
Kamrup	1.16	0.05	4.64	0.11
Darrang	0.98	0.03	4.24	0.13
Nowgong	1.22	0.07	4.58	0.14
Sibsagar	1.44	0.08	5.70	0.18
Lakhimpur	1.08	0.07	6.52	0.27

Source : Census of Assam, 1891, P. 145.

In every district literacy rate went up compared to that in 1881. But there was some variations from district to district. Male literacy ratio was the highest in Lakhimpur district (6.52%) and lowest in Darrang district (4.24%). In respect of Female literacy, Lakhimpur returned the highest percentage of literacy (0.27) and Kamrup the lowest (0.11).

No separate category of learners was shown in the 1901 census. Those who knew to read and write were regarded as literates. "The return of literacy" observes B. C. Allen, "is beset with a certain amount of difficulty. In the first place it is not always easy to determine what the expression should include. A considerable number of people can read and write, but only ...... 'with difficulty' and it is not easy to say at exactly what stage the claimant to the title should be described as literate. The standard of knowledge exacted was probably low, as the average enumerator is not a man of great literacy attainments himself, and would be contented with but little in others; but any excess in this direction must have been to some extent corrected in the abstracting office, as literates may have been occasionally overlooked, but never improperly inserted in the tables"[5].

The scene of literacy reflected in the Census Reports needs to be reckoned as indicative of the trend of changes without quantitative exactness. And here we use the literacy figures published in the different census reports as broad pointers to the growth of education in the province in very general terms.

In 1990 number of male literates in the Brahmaputra Valley in every 1000 went up from 49 to 50, and that of female literates per 1000 went up from 1 to 2. In both the cases the rates of change were less than one per cent.[6] "In the Assam Valley", the census report notes, "the proportion of literates is low, ranging from 68 in Kamrup to 49 in Goalpara, — but nearly all the inhabitants are cultivators, who, after all, do not require to go to school to learn to follow the plough". Such an attitude of the Government toward providing educational opportunities for the rural people affected development of the villages through application of higher technology of production. Education of the farmers would have empowered the farmers to stand against exploitation by the middlemen, mahajans, etc.

Progress of literacy after 1901 and till 1931 as reported in the Censuses of 1911, 1921 and 1931 is indicated in Table 13: 2.

Table 13.2
Number of Literates per mille (one thousand) in Brahmaputra Valley in Certain Periods from 1911 to 1931.

	All aged 10 and over		15 – 20		20 and over	
	Male	**Female**	**Male**	**Female**	**Male**	**Female**
1911	116	06	129	10	119	05
1921	140	12	161	20	143	10
1931	161	16	185	22	169	13

Source : Census of Assam Report, 1911, P. 151

C. S. Mullan, Superintendent, Census Operations, Assam observes that although there had been a steady progress in literacy, the rate of progress in the 1921-31decade had been slower than in the previous decade. This happened even as total expenditure on public instruction increased. While in the entire province of Assam, Mullan notes, the total number of literates between 1911 and 1921 increased by 50 per cent, between 1921 and 1931 the increase was only about 40 per cent[8].

Mullan sought the cause for this lower rate of progress despite the Legislative Council's, continual interest in the spread of education and continuing increase in total expenditure on public instruction. For Assam as whole, in 1921-22 the total expenditure on this account including the expenditure incurred by local bodies amounted to Rs, 34,84,000. It went up to Rs. 53,59,000 in 1929-30. In 1930-31 there was a decline in expenditure as it stood at Rs. 52,62,000. "Most of this increased expenditure", writes Mullan, "has been spent (Sic.) on secondary and collegiate education but primary education has by no means been neglected as will be seen from the fact that the total expenditure on primary education rose from 8.27 lakhs in 1920-21 to 13.62 lakhs in 1930-31 and the number of primary school pupils rose from 179,754 to 266,346"[9]. But Mullan also points out that the great majority of these pupils did not attain literacy as they dropped out after a year or so.

There had, however, been positive and definite progress in general education in the province but without any sign of acceleration of the process. The reasons, according to Mullan, were attributable to 'the economic and political disturbances of the decade'[10]. Although the Non-Cooperation Movement caused closing down of village schools and fall in enrolment in 1920-21, "with the restoration of normal political conditions in 1922-23 the general equilibrium in the primary schools was not once restored, hence it appears that non-coöperation movement did not affect the primary schools to any very great extent"[11]. The causes were rather the economic difficulties suffered by common people on account of inflation that began in 1917 in the wake of the First World War. Even though education in primary schools was free, parents had to spend 'an appreciable sum in providing school materials'. The influenza epidemic of 1918 also caused a fall in enrolment in school in the affected areas. Finally, economically the whole country was worse off in the 1921-31 decade and particularly during the great Depression. It had its impact on the progress of education not only in Assam but also in the country as a whole.

In the 1941 census literacy data were recorded to indicate the difference between the progress of literacy in rural area and that in the urban. In Table 13.3 census counts of literates, both male and female, are indicated:

Table 13.3

Literates in Brahmaputra Valley in 1941 per 100

Total Population		Urban Population		Rural Population	
Male	Female	Male	Female	Male	Female
40.99	8.8	48.9	28.0	17.8	2.8

Source : Census of Assam, Report, 1941, P. 64

The census data clearly bring out the sharp differences between the growth rate of literacy in the urban area and that in the rural; marked differences in male and female literacy levels also persisted.

Growth of literacy and enrolment in primary and secondary level schools underscored the necessity of providing opportunities for the students successfully completing their school education to prosecute higher studies at the under-graduate level and ultimately at the post-graduate especially open to the deserving scholars. The Government granted a limited number of scholarships to enable the selected scholars to join colleges and Universities in Bengal. But as years passed the citizens of Assam persistently moved the Government to start a college within Assam so that more students of the province might get opportunity of receiving higher education. A plan for starting was approved by the Government in 1866 [college level teaching classes in the Guwahati High School]. The expenditure per student per annum in the collegiate section was to the extent of Rs. 1086, which was considered very high by the Government. Moreover, col. Keatings, Chief Commissioner of Assam, opined that the youths of Assam should go to "Bengal where they would come in contact with a higher standard of culture and wider interest"[12]. Therefore, collegiate classes in the school were abolished in 1876. This step curtailed the opportunities for the students of Assam who successfully completed the Entrance Examination to join colleges. For few Assamese students could afford to be admitted to any college outside Assam without scholarship.

From 1894 to 1899 every year on an average 22 students passed the entrance examination out of whom only 15 students received scholarships. Very few students passed the first Arts and B. A examinations every year in that period. "The principal cause for the educational backwardness of Assam Valley", observed Rao, "was the comparative absence of the upper and middle classes which generally supplied the material to the colleges elsewhere. Thus, higher education in the Assam Valley languished and it was maintained artificially by the State Scholarships"[13]. Such a view is not acceptable because higher education itself helps emergence of the middle class comprising teachers, administrators, professionals, etc. We said elsewhere: "Higher education — — that is, education at the undergraduate and post-graduate levels —— liberates the mind and widens the world view... It promotes creative thinking, research and writing. It also enhances the power of perception and articulation of independently formed points of view. For these reasons development of higher education improves cultural, social and economic conditions of the community concerned. Growth of higher education also augments the process of specialization and diversification in productive aqctivities"[14]. Therefore, there should have been more liberal grant of Government scholarship to Assamese students to enable them to prosecute higher studies outside Assam since there was no college in the province.

The Cotton College, named after Sir H. J. S. Cotton, Chief Commissioner of Assam from 1896 to 1902, started in 1901 at Guwahati, Sir Cotton took the momentous decision to start this government college and laid the foundation stone on 17th June 1901. This decision was taken in response to the repeated public representations on the urgent need of a Government college in the Brahmaputra Valley. The college was affiliated to the University of Calcutta. The second, a private college named Jogennath Barua College was stared in 1930. During the period from 1940 to 1947, seven more private colleges were established. The resourceful persons of the province took effective steps to mobilize funds, and acquire lands and other resources for starting those new colleges. Opportunities for prosecuting higher studies expanded which helped the process of overall progress of the people of Assam.

During the Second World War, huge amounts of war – oriented public investments were made in Assam which caused increased flow of private income and more savings for the people of Assam. Presumably parts of such savings were invested in the development of higher education with a view to overcoming Assam's economic backwardness.

Most of these colleges had arts faculties and only a few had commerce and science faculties as well. Development of engineering, medical and professional colleges was also very important for building up of the scientific – technological base considered so vital for the adoption of higher technology of production. But this aspect of higher education was long neglected.

The first medical school was established in Dibgugarh in 1900 with 38 students on its roll. This was possible as Brigadier-Surgeon John Berry White, Civil Surgeon of Dibrugarh, donated rupees fifty thousand for this purpose. In his will he laid down the condition that only the students who were natives of Assam or whose parents were residents of Assam for a period of not less than ten years would be eligible for seeking admission to this college. Besides this facility of getting medical education, the students of Brahmaputra Valley were given a few scholarships for taking medical courses in Calcutta Medical College. Later students from Assam also studied in Mitford School and Hospital Dacca.

The first law college, Earle Law College, was started in 1915 at Guwahati. But during the period of the colonial rule neither any agriculture college was established of course, some students were granted scholarship for prosecuting such courses elsewhere in the country. Some scholarships were also provided for studying abroad.

The overall development of higher education in Assam enabled educated youths to join government services as administrators, teachers and technical personnel. Increasing number of youths took to the professions of law, medicine, journalism, creative writings, etc and also braced us themselves to run commercial and industrial enterprises. All this led to the emergence of a progressive and creative middle class, which took initiatives in promoting political consciousness, assertion of Assamese identity and conducting political movements protesting against colonial oppressions and demanding independence. Many took up politics as profession and successfully fought elections to become members of the legislative bodies and if possible join the cabinet of ministers.

Educational development — general, professional and technical - led to the occupational diversification and a general rise in the standard of living of the middle class.

Urbanization

During the Ahom rule urban centers were built up where the capital was situated. These were nothing better than overgrown villages with the palace building and its surroundings reflecting some characteristic urban features. But even these urban centers were in ruins in the wake of the Moamaria rebellion and the Burmese invasion. The oldest Ahom town, Garhgaon on the bank of the river Dikhow, was the capital of the Ahom King Suklenmung who reigned from 1539 to 1552. The brick city of Rangpur on the west bank of the Dikhow was the capital of Rudra Sinha (1696 - 1714). During his rule masonry bridges were constructed over the Namdang and Diman rivers by masons brought in from Bengal. An important landmark of the capital was the *Rang-ghar*, or the pavilion from where the king would watch animal fights and other kinds of sports. There was a big tank named *Jay Sagar* on the bank of which stood two temples. It was a flourishing town, no doubt, but in 1786 when the Moamarias were advancing to the Capital Guarinath Singh fled to Guwahati. Then the Burhagohain (Prime Minister), who continued to resist the Moamarias, shifted the capital to Jorhat on the bank of the Disoi. Jorhat remained the capital of the Ahom rulers till 1839. That year when the British took over the administration of Upper Assam from Purandar Singh, the administrative headquarters was shifted to Sibsagar on the perennially navigable river Dikhow. In 1905 the district headquarters was shifted back to Jorhat as it was at the centre of the district and, to boot, had railway and riverway connections.

When the British occupied Assam, economic activities

promoting urbanization were nearly absent. The colonial structure of governance and economic management helped processes of specialization, marketing of surplus produces, monetization of transactions and expansion of internal and external trade. Supply of money and credit instruments expanded. These processes led to the distinctive divisions of population into two classes those pursuing agricultural occupation and those engaged in non-agricultural pursuits. All these developments brought about concentration of trading and commercial activities, transport and communication, services, professional occupations, running of artisans' shops, etc around the administrative centres where institutional and supporting facilities had already been created. These changes reflected the growth of city or town-centric economic activities. This process of urbanization started in several parts of Assam under the colonial rule in the first half of the nineteenth century. The pace of urbanization, however, was slow during the nineteenth century. One could trace the reason to the colonial neglect of the traditional agricultural sector. Assessment of land revenue at higher rates left practically very little surplus produce in the hands of the cultivators. Therefore expansion of productive activities in urban sphere to meet increased demand from the rural sector was extremely limited.

Growth of tea industry also, rather paradoxically, did not boost the urbanization process. This was a Government – patronized land – based and export-oriented 'enclave' industry (vide, Chapter VIII supra). Growth of tea plantations did not bring about basic structural changes in the traditional peasant economy which continued being mostly a non-surplus generating economy. Of course marked growth of towns like Dibrugarh, Jorhat and Tinsukia in upper Assam was correlated with the growth of the tea industry. However, this trend thwarted the growth of other urban centres, B. C. Allen explained this phenomenon in his census Report of Assam for 1901. Each large garden was itself an urban centre where the Marwari businessmen (Kayah) functioned as a general merchant and money-lender. If possible the garden had its own market where garden workers could obtain their supplies brought by the neighbouring villagers. Local Assamese population were almost all agriculturists and trade and the crafts were almost entirely in the hands of 'foreigners' (immigrant settles). There was nothing to attract the people to the small towns every one of which was the headquarters of a district or subdivision and in many cases "were the magistrate's court removed, the place would not claim to the status of a town at all"[16].

In another sense also growth of tea industry did not accelerate urbanization in terms of the census enumerations. Tea garden labourers were almost cent per cent immigrants. In 1901 the total population of the tea gardens was 6, 57,331 out of whom 6,23,417 were "labourers and subrdinates'[17]. These immigrants represented 19 p. c. of the total population of Assam. Tea garden inhabitants were regarded as rural population and therefore the proportion of total urban population of Assam was lower than what it would have been in the absence of these immigrant tea garden workers. In 1901, only 1.9 per cent of the population lived in towns as defined for the census enumeration. This proportion was 1.8 per cent in 1891.

For the purpose of census enumeration a town included (i) every municipality, (ii) all civil lines outside municipal limits, (iii) every cantonment and (iv) every other continuous collection of houses inhabited by not less than 5000 persons, which the provincial census superintendent naturally decided to treat as town. In 1911 total urban population of the Brahmaputra Valley constituted 2.4 per cent of its total population. Dibrugarh, Guwahati and Barpeta were the only three towns each having a population of more than 10,000. The average population per town was only 6,923. Dibrugarh was the 'headquarters of the most important tea district in the province' and the growth of this industry boosted the growth of population of this town by 100 per cent since 1881 and by nearly 30 per cent since1901 census. To go by the census of 1891 and of 1901, there was a decline in population of Guwahati town because of the exclusion of North Guwahati (on the North bank of the Brahmaputra) from the Guwahati municipality. But the population of the town in 1911 was larger than that of the undivided town in 1881[18].

The proportion of urban population rose up to 2.9 per cent in 1921. This increase was 'a little more in proportion than general population'. Average population per town, however, declined to 5794. 4.2per cent of urban population resided in towns each with a population varying between 10,000 and 20,000, 3.55 per cent resided in towns each with population ranging from 5,000 to 10,000 and 2.43 per cent in town[19] having a population of less thus 5000.

By 1931 the proportion of urban population rose to 3 per cent and the average population per town went up to 7,442. Of course, as C.S Mullan, Superintendent, Census operations, Assam, observed that the so-called small towns had few urban characteristics and were really no better than large villages which had the only distinction of being sub-divisional headquarters. Mullan has also noted that towns were expanding in size and the increase in urban population occurred at a higher rate than the increase of general population of Assam as a whole. The increase in urban population was more pronounced in Guwahati, Nowgong, Tezpur, Dhubri and Jorat in the Assam Valley. These were all district headquarters and 'favourably situated for the purpose of trade". The growth of Dibrugarh town was affected as it began to feel the competition from Tinsukia town which was rapidly developing being excellently situated 'at a railway junction in the very heart of the Tea Industry of the Sadar Subdivision'[20].

Larger towns with their increasing population developed more urban atmosphere and six of the nine towns (constituting the whole of Assam) each having a population of over 10,000 were lit up (lighted) by electricity[12].

Guwahati was steadily expanding for the last twenty years as it had excellent river and railway communications and also educational facilities. It was 'the real capital of the Brahmaputra Valley', although Shillong was the capital of the province of Assam[22].

Proportion of urban population slightly went up by 3.1 per cent in 1941, and the population per town rose up to 9,318. The total number of towns was 19. Distribution of urban population among towns size- wise was as follows.[23]

Table 13.4
Percentage of Urban Population in Towns, each with a Population of:

20,000 and over	10,000 to **20,000**	5,00 to **10,000**	Under **5, 000**
2.95	3.78	1.95	1.32

Source : *Census of India, 1941*, p. 6

The above table of contents is an indication of the steadily growing urbanization in Assam though at a slow pace. But urban population was shifting to larger towns as the towns were becoming larger in size.

With growth of urbanization came about significant structural changes in the occupational patterns of the people. Development of education, medical, communication, financial and other services was somewhat accelerated. Many towns had municipalities, which provided water-supply, sanitation, street lighting, conservancy etc. Laying down town street and road building activities also expanded. The process also led to acquisition of new skills, adoption of higher technology of production, growth of trade and commerce and changes in the consumption pattern. What is more, Transactions between persons / or on the personal level became more and more market determined in place of traditional non-monetary value-based interactions between individuals in social relationships.

NOTES AND REFERENCES

1. Gunnar Myrdal (1970), *The Challenge of World Poverty: A World Anti-Poverty Programme in Outline*, A Penguin International Edition. P. 182.
2. H. K. Barpujari (ed) (1992), *The Comprehensive History of Assam*, Vol. IV, Publication Board Assam, Guwahati, Pp. 348-9.
3. Quoted in *ibid*, p. 348.
4. *ibid*. p. 357.
5. B. C. Allen (1902), *Census of India 1901*, Vol. IV: Assam Part I Report Shillong, p. 97.
6. *ibid*. p. 104.

7. *ibid* p. 97.
8. C. S. Mullan (1932), *Census of India 1931*, Vol. III, Assam, Part I, Report, Shillong, p. 97
9. *ibid.* p.152.
10. *ibid.* p.152.
11. *ibid.* p.153.
12. V. V. Rao (1985), "A Century of Higher Education in North East India", *The North Eastern Hill University Journal of Social Sciences and Humanities*, Vol.III No. 1, January, March, p. 18.
13. *ibid.*
14. J. B. Ganguly (1994), "Structural Changes in Assam's Economy, 1826-1947", Prof. H. K. Barpujari Endowment Lectures Delivered in Dibrugarh University, Assam, (Unpublished MS), p. III.
15. H. K. Barpujari, *op. cit*, p. 328.
16. B. C. Allen, *op. cit.* p. 6.
17. *ibid.* p. 163.
18. J. M. Swiney, *Census of India*, 1911, Vol. III Assam, p. 9.
19. G. T. Lyoyd, *Census of India*, 1921, Vol.III, Assam pp. 30 - 32.
20. C. S. Mullan, *op. cit.* p. 38.
21. *ibid.*
22. *ibid.*
23. K. W. P. Marar, *Census of India, 1941*, IX: Assam p. 2 & p. 6.

14
DISTRIBUTION OF POPULATION OCCUPATION – WISE 1881 - 1951

During the Ahom rule the main occupation of the common people (paiks) was cultivation and military service to the state combined with it. Paiks were also employed in public works like roads, embankment, etc. Other occupational groups were artisans, nobles, civil and military officers, slaves, traders, religious priests and preachers *et al.* Of course such occupational groups hardly constituted exclusive classes earning livelihood. Same persons performed several such duties for meeting their subsistence needs and also under the order of the royalty. In an economy that was at the non-monetized, pre-market subsistence stage, combination of productive activities by individual workers was a unie (?) phenomenon.

After the British occupation of Assam, the ryotwari system of land settlement and payment of revenue in cash were introduced. The processes of modernization, diversification and specialization in productive activities, monetization of transactions, commercialization of production, development of a market economy, etc got under way. Individual ownership of property in various forms–land, houses, farms, money and other financial assets, also came into being and the economy began turning into a market-priented one.

From 1840's tea plantation and industry began to

dominate the economy of Assam. The river, rall and road transport systems assumed the importance of basic infrastructure of Assam's economy. Coal and petroleum industries in the organized sector and many small cottage and household industries in the unorganized sector expanded productive occupations in the secondary sector of the economy. These were the signs of structural changes cutting place in the economy, as the distribution of working population among different occupational categories began to alter the relative inter-sectoral contributions to the gross national product of Assam. Such changes could be regarded as an important indicator of the trend of economic growth of Assam during the period under review. Therefore, in the pages following we propose to record and analyse the changes taking place in the system of distribution of population occupation–wise during the period 1881-1951. For this purpose we shall depend on the relevant census Reports which contain valuable statistics about the occupational structure and livelihood classes of population.

In the 1881 census the occupations of people recorded were divided into 'six great classes, professional, domestic, commercial, agricultural, industrial and indefinite". Under the sixth class (indefinite or unspecified) were grouped not only those people who returned "labourers", "gentlemen", "beggars" or "vagrants", but also people against whom 'no return at all' was entered, and they included even children 'and a large number of women'[1]. For more definite identification of the occupational pursuits of persons in class VI, this class was subdivided into VI (a) representing labourers, gentlemen etc and class VI (b) representing the children and women against whom no occupation entry was made. Distribution of population into these occupational groups is indicated in table XIV:1. The figure in absolute and percentage terms relate to the whole of Assam excluding the Garo and Naga Hills. People, male and female, living in towns and villages are included.

Table 14.1

Occupational Distribution of Population in 1881 (whole of Assam Excluding the Garo and Naga hills)

	Occupation	Total Male		Total Female	
		Persons	P. C	Persons	P. C
1.	Professional	25,641	1.1	1,279	0.05
2.	Domestic	14,356	0.6	2,311	0.10
3.	Commercial	50,457	2.1	10,773	0.45
4.	Agricultural	1,333,437	55.5	677,474	29.80
5.	Industrial	44,998	1.8	43,292	1.90
6.	(a) Labourers, Gentlemen, etc	40,693	1.7	12,467	0.50
	(b) Children & Women against whom against whom no occupation entry made	890,319	37.2	1,530,001	67.20
Total =		2,399,901	100.0	2,277,597	100.0

Census of Assam, 1881, pp. 115 – 16.

The accuracy of occupational groupings as shown in the census report is open to question. Daniel and Alice Thomer rightly pointed out that 'the patterns of life and work of village families' were such that they could not be divided into the defined industrial sectors. "The characteristic unit is not", they opine, "an individual worker doing a particular job, but an entire household which may carry on a round of related activities extending through the full economic spectrum"[2]. Moreover, in many cases of artisans, such as, blacksmiths, brass workers and potters, the same individual or even the same family who produced there arte facts also sold them. This reality then obliterates the line separating manufacturing from trading activities. And it is welt nigh impossible to show any individual member under the class, industry or commerce[3].

Table 14.1, notably shows that only 32.8 per cent of women followed an occupation. This was clearly an underestimation. And the census report admits the inaccuracy of this finding as there was "a good deal of arbitrariness in the practice of returning a woman as following or not following her husband's profession and this is especially the case in regard to agriculture"[4]. Among some tribes and communities women work in the fields as hard as men. But among many other communities women labour took part in certain portions of the work, such as, transplanting rice and reaping harvest as without their participation those time-bound agricultural operations could hardly be completed. Therefore it was a ticklish question that the census workers faced as to whether to include a wife who only went out into the fields on such occasions as one employed in agriculture or not.[5]

The system of categorization of occupations was somewhat changed in 1891. The aggregate of various means of livelihood were divided into the following main classes;[6]

A – Government

B – Pasture and Agriculture

C – Personal and domestic services

D – The preparation and supply of material substances

E – Commerce and transport of persons, goods, and messages, and the storage of goods.

F – Professions, learned, artistic, and minor

G – Indefinite occupations, and means of subsistence independent of occupation.

In 1881, census only those workers actually practising an occupation were included but in 1891 the dependents were also added to indicate 'the total number of persons subsisting by each occupation.

The results of the census are given in Table 14.2

Table No. 14.2
Distribution of Populations of Brahmaputra Valley per 1000 of the Occupational Classes 1891.

Occupation		Per 1000 of Population
A.	Government service	5.32
B.	Pasture & agriculture	849.51
C.	Personal & domestic service	12.14
D.	Preparation & supply of material substances (food & drink, light, firing & forage, building, vehicles & vessels, supplementary requirements, textile fabrics & dress, metals & precious stones, glass, pottery & stoneware, wood, cane & levels, drug, gums, etc & leather)	81.95
E.	Commerce (including transport & storage)	13.23
F.	Professions (Learned & artistic, sports & amusements)	12.67
G.	Indefinite occupations	25.18
	Total =	1,000,00

Source : Census of India, 1891, Assam, P. 294

A summary of the results should help indicate the population groups that belonged to the three major economic sectors, namely, the primary (occupation 'B'), secondary (occupation 'D') and tertiary (occupations 'A' 'C', 'E', 'F' and 'G'). It follows in a tabulated form.

Table 14.3
Sector-Wise Classification of Population 1891.

Sector		Percentage of population (workers and dependents)
1.	Primary	84.95
2.	Secondary	8.19
3.	Tertiary	6.86
	Total =	100.00

Source : Estimated from the census data.

The primary sector obviously provided subsistence for the highest proportion of population since development of manufacturing industries remained at a low level. Tea production was considered an agricultural operation, i.e., cultivation of a special crop; only processing of tea leaves in the factory was treated as a manufacturing operation.

In the census of 1901 occupations were classified into eight main group, i.e., — A. Government B. Pasture and Agriculture, C. Personal Service, D. Preparation and Supply of Material Substances, E. Commerce, Transport and Storage, F. Professions, G. Unskilled Non-agricultural Labour, and H. Means of Subsistence Independent of Occupation. Population was also divided in terms of workers and dependents. Women who took art in planting and harvesting paddy, weaving cloths or marketing fish or other products were treated as workers. But women engaged only in household work like husking paddy and weaving cloths for home consumption simply and, not for sale, were shown as dependent. All children under twelve including those who were school students and lived with their parents or guardians and even did light work like buffalo and cow-herding were classed as dependents. The results of the census of different major occupational groups are summarized in Table No. 14.4.

Table 14.4
Distribution of Population per cent Based on main Occupations in Bramaputra valley 1901.

Occupation	Percentage of population supported by occupation in col.1	Percentage working population included in occupation category in col.1	Percentage of dependents of population included in occupation category in col.1
1	2	3	4
Agriculture	87.00	57.10	42.90
Industry	5.40	56.20	43.90
Commerce	0.80	61.38	38.62
Professions	1.05	38.56	61.44
Others	5.75	—	—

Source : *Census of Assam, 1901*, pp. 161 and 162 and abstraction from Subsidiary Table II.

Agricultural population included as per census 'landholders and tenants', 'agricultural labours' 'growers of special products' (such as tea, coffee, rubber, etc) and 'agricultural training'. In the whole province of Assam 67.9 per cent of the state population were cultivators who held land direct from the state (ryots), 1.7 million persons were cultivating tenants, the majority of whom were in Cachar, Sylhet and Goalpara districts. Also, in Kamrup district in the Brahmaputra Valley there were lerge number of *nisf-khiraj* and *lakhiraj* estates. The census revealed a significant growing trend in subletting of land in the raiyatwari districts of the province. This development has been analysed in Chapter X above.

Classification of the population of workers including their dependents, into the three broad economic sectors namely 'primary', 'secondary' and 'tertiay' have been worked out from the census results of 1901 as follows:

Sector		Percentage of Population
I.	Primary	87.00
II.	Secondary	5.4
III.	Tertiary	7.6
		100.00

For an overwhelmingly large majority of population means of livelihood was agriculture and B.C Allen in his Census Report, therefore, observed : "The occupations of Assam in fact begin and end with agriculture. The only manufacture of importance in the province is tea and the other factories are represented by fourteen saw-mills and the brick and pipe works at Ledo. The mineral industry of the province consists of lime quarries and coal-measures in the Khasi Hills, the coal mines of Margherita and the oil wells of Digboi .."[7]

From 1911 onward the system of classification of populations as recommended by the International Statistical Institute was followed in India with modification to a slight degree. The new scheme enlisted four main classes which again were divided into twelve sub-classes as shown below:

Class	Sub – Classes	
A. Production of raw materials	I.	Exploitation of animals and vegetation
	II.	Exploitation of minerals
B. Preparation and supply of materials substances	III.	Industry
	IV.	Transport
	V.	Trade
C. Public administration and liberal arts	VI.	Public force
	VII.	Public Administration
	VIII.	Professions and liberal arts

(Condt..)

D. Miscellaneous
- IX. Persons living on their own income
- X. Domestic service
- XI. Insufficiently defined occupations
- XII. Unproductive

"The classed and sub-classes have remained the same since 1911 but the orders and groups into which these sub-classes are divided have been modified from time to time" [8].

Grouping together the appropriate sub-classes, five major livelihood classes are identified as agriculture, industry, commerce, professions and miscellaneous (domestic service, insufficiently described occupations and unproductive activities). Population shown in the census (Returned) under these five classes in 1911, in 1921 and in 1931 is presented percentage terms in Table No. 14.5.

Table 14.5

Distribution of population per cent in the Five Main Occupations in Brahmaputra Valley in 1911, 1921 and 1931.

Occupation	**Population (per cent) supported by Occupation**			
	1911	**1921**		**1931 Earners (principal occupation and working dependents)**
1	**2**	**3**		**4**
Agriculture	87.7	89.3		81.82
Industry	2.2	2.0		10.47
Commerce	4.1	3.8		4.35
Professions	0.9	1.0		1.19
Miscellaneous	5.1	3.9		2.17
Total =		100.0	100.0	100.00
Source: Census Report, 1911		ST III 1921: P. 168[9] (1911)	ST III 1931: P. 185[10] (1921)	ST IIA P. 136[11] (1931)

In 1931 Census earners and working dependents were returned under the livelihood classes instead of all dependents. Therefore, the results of this census are not strictly comparable with those of 1911 and 1921 censuses. In 1931 out of every 1000 persons in the Brahmaputra Valley, 494 were non-working and 150 working dependents and earners were 356. Co. 4 table 14.5 indicates the percentage of earners and the percentage of working dependents (506) pursuing different occupations. This change resulted in a significant fall in the proportion of population living on agriculture and in pushing up the proportion of industrial population. The rise in proportion of commercial and professional classes in 1931 as against a drop in the proportion of miscellaneous occupational groups in 1921 may be construed as a sign of some progress achieved in the fields of industrial production, trade, commerce, transport and communication services, etc.

By estimating the quantum of the state (provinces) domestic product (SDP) relative contributions of the three basic economic sectors, namely, the primary, secondary and tertiary to the aggregate amount of goods and services produced could be measured. The changes in relative shares of the three sectors are indicative not only of structural changes in the economy but also of the prospects of sustained growth of income of the people. Generally as the economy grows, the relative shares of the three sectors of the state domestic product go on shifting first from primary to secondary and finally to the tertiary sector. In the absence of time series data about changes in the state domestic product, structural changes in the pattern of absorption of labour in the three sectors over time might throw some light on the direction which the economy was heading for.

For this purpose occupation termed agriculture in the census represent the primary sector, that in the category of industry stand for the secondary sector and the rest, such as, commerce professions and miscellaneous belong to the tertiary sector. We have already noted the limitations of the census classification of livelihood classes, and subject to that we may study the relative growth of the three sectors in terms of absorption of workers (earners, working and non-working dependents) by the respective sectors. This trend in he period 1881 – 1931 is shown in the Table below.

Table 14.6
Sectoral Distribution of Population from 1881 to 1931 (per cent)

	Census years					
Sector	**1881**	**1891**	**1901**	**1911**	**1921**	**1931***
Primary	91.23	84.95	87.00	87.70	89.30	81.82
Secondary	4.00	8.19	5.40	2.20	2.00	10.47
Tertiary	4.77	6.86	7.60	10.10	8.70	7.71
Total =	100.00	100.00	100.00	100.00	100.00	100.00

* Workers and working dependents only

Source : Compiled form the relevant census reports.

There was no steady trend from one decade to another in the relative shares of the secondary and tertiary sectors in providing livelihood for the people. But one of the reasons could be definitional variations and also the manner of taking census of the livelihood classes. Yet a trend of the relative growth of the secondary and of tertiary sectors may be discernible of course, the predominance of the primary sector continued. From 8 to 9 persons out of every ten depended on agriculture and allied activities for their livelihood.

With central movements overarched in the sphere of the occupational distribution of population, the basic structural changes in economic activities were in relation to the growing trends of specialization, monetization, commercialization, urbanization and diversification of occupational pursuits. In short, a market economy was emerging covering not only the urban but also the rural areas. As a fall-out of these developments economic inequalities and class formations struck roots in the province.

Incidentally, we may note that G.T. Lloyd, Census Superintendent of Assam for the 1921 census, had estimated the provincial Domestic Product of Assam for the year 1921-22. His estimate is given in Appendix to this Chapter. As we see, he had not at all followed a rigorous method of statistical estimation of provincial domestic products. Yet considering the low level of monetization of economic activities and that of the market economy, his estimate throws some light on the extremely low amount of per capita income of the people of Assam. This reflects the economic backwardness of the people at large.

On account of the Second World War, the 1941 census report was the results of a very limited operation. Population of livelihood classes was not enumerated. We shall, however, take note of the occupational distribution of population as reported in the 1951 census, which was the first census in post-colonial Assam when the hangover of Assam's economy in the colonial period still persisted in some measure. The area of the Assam Plains, the livelihood pattern of which is discussed below, covered the Brahmaputra Valley and a portion of the Surma Valley (mainly district of Cachar) or what is also known as the Barak Valley. For the 1951 census eight Livelohood Classes were identified as follows[12]:

Agricultural Classes

I. Cultivators of land wholly or mainly owned; and their dependents
II. Cultivators of land not owned wholly or mainly, and their dependents
III. Cultivating labourers; and their dependents
IV. Non-cultivating owners of land; agricultural rent receivers; and their dependents

Non - Agricultural Classes

Persons (including dependents), who derived their principal Means of Livelihood from:

V. Production other than cultivation.
VI. Commerce.
VII. Transport
VIII. Other Services and Miscellaneous Sources.

In 1951 the population of Assam Plains belonging to the eight livelihood classes was a follows: (Table 14: 7)

Table 14.7
Livelihood Pattern in Assam Plains in 1951.

Livelihood Class	Total Population	Per cent
I	4,278,031	54.8
II	1,104,618	14.2
III	123.338	1.6
IV	75,597	0.9
Agriculture I – IV	5,581,584	71.5
V	1,282,133	16.4
VI	324,708	4.2
VII	107,373	1.4
VIII	509,760	6.5
Non – Agriculture V - VIII	2,223,974	28.5
Total Population =	7,805, 558	100.0

Source : *Census of India, 1951*, Vol. XII, *Assam, Manipur and Tripura*, Part 1- A Report. p. 102

The results of the 1951 census also confirm that an overwhelming majority of population (71.5 p.c) depended on agriculture for livelihood. In this census in contrast with the practice of earlier censuses, "the tea garden population forming about 12 per cent of the total population of Assam are excluded from agriculture and counted under non – agriculture". It was argued that this change was justified because "tea is an industry and has some features in common with other industrial undertakings"[13]. Of course it was also admitted that tea industry was "predominantly agricultural in character and rural in atmosphere requiring a very small factory population, though needing a large labour force for the actual plantation of tea"[14]. And if the tea garden population was treated as agricultural workers and their dependents then the proportion of population in the agriculture sector would rise to 85 per cent. This proportion confirms the fact that even at the end of the colonial period and that of the Second World War, people of Assam continued to depend very much on agriculture for their subsistence.

It might also be noted that a large proportion of agricultural population (54.8 p.c. out of 71.5 p.c) belonged to the class of cultivators who wholly or mainly owned it and their dependents. As we discussed elsewhere,[15] the peasant economy of Assam was therefore, a stable one "being based on self-sufficient and subsistence system of household productive activities .... The behavoiur of the peasants was generally informed by the ideology of the self – contentment at the subsistence level of consumption of food and clothing. There was little urge to earn higher income through increased productivity *per capita* with the objective of saving more and investing more in land improvement and adoption of higher technology for further increase in production. The peasant economy was a sort of stationary economy without accumulation and growth"[16].

APPENDIX – I

Estimate of Production and Average Individual Income at Prices Prevailing in 1921-22*.

.... (Crops according to estimates of Agricultural Department)

	Outturn (000's of) maunds)	Average Wholesale price at Chief marts			Values of producce (Rs. Lakh)
		Rs.	a.	p.	
Rice (husked)	54,443	5	5	0	28,92
		(per md)			
Mustard	1,574	6	11	0	1,05
		(per md)			
Gur	867	900			78
Jute	752	7170			57

(Condt..)

	Outturn (000's of) maunds)	Average Wholesale price at Chief marts	Values of producce (Rs. Lakh)
	Rs.	a. p.	
Other crops (cotton, sesamum, pulses, millets, roots vegetables, fruits, etc) Value estimated according to areas reported cultivated	—	—	5,23
Tea (value of exports Rs. 878 crores; value to Assam taken at half this)	—	—	4,39
Coal, taken at anna 7 per maund ex-mines	8,441	—	37
Petroleum, taken at anna per gallon of crude oil ex-wells	9.5 million gallons	—	06
Fish caught and sold or consumed, estimated value	—	—	40
Silk, cloth, limestone, forest products and small manufactures, estimated value	—	—	60
			Total = 42, 37

Population of Assam (excluding Manipur) in 1921-22: 7,606,230 Average money value of annual income per head 1921-22, nearly Rs. 56 Or per occupied house Rs. 266

Note by Llyod : "No attempt has been made to estimate the shares of income taken by the trader, the money-lender and the rent receiver on the one hand and the cultivator and wage-earner on the other" (ibid).

* "The average income of the people cannot be estimated with any exactitude in terms of money in an agricultural country. By a rough calculation from the outturn of crops grown and the other product of the province in 1921-22, with the prices prevailing at the principal marts it might be estimated at the equivalent of about Rs. 56 per head per annum, but in any case the cultivators who form the great bulk of the population are less dependent on money rates than on the amount of outturn of rice and other crops for their food supply" (Lloyd, *ibid*, p. 181).

NOTES AND REFERENCES

1. *Report on the Census of Assam, 1881*, p. 115
2. Alice and Daniel Thomer (1974). *Land and Labour in* India, Bombay, P. 72.
3. *ibid.* p. 73.
4. *Census Report 1881, op. Cit.* p. 116.
5. *ibid.*
6. E. A. Gait, (1892), *Census of India*, 1891, report on Assam, p. 293.
7. B. C. Allen (1902), *Census of India 1901*, Vol. IV Assam Part I Report, Shillong, p. 169.
8. C. S. Mullan, *Census of India, 1931*, Vol. III Assam, Part I, Report, Shillong, p. 116.
9. (a) J. M. Swiney, *Census of India 1911*, Vol. III *Assam Part I, Report*, p. 168.
   (b) G. T. Lloyd, *Census of India 1921*, Vol. III Assam Part I Report, p. 185.
   (c) C. S. Mullan, op. cit., p. 136.
10. G. T. Lloyd, *op. cit.*, Appendix G, P. XXXV.
11. R. B. Vaghaiwalla, *Census of India, 1951*, Vol. XII, *Assam Manipur and Tripura, Part I – A Report*, p. 102.
12. *ibid.* p. 103.
13. *ibid.* p. 103
14. J. B. Ganguly (1994), "Structural Changes in Assam's Economy, 1826-1947", H. K. Barpujari Endowment Lecture delivered in the Dibrugarh University, (unpublished MS), p. 163.

15

IMPACT OF THE SECOND WORLD WAR (1939 – 1945) ON ASSAM'S ECONOMY

Normal life in Assam was severely disrupted by the Second World War (henceforth 'War'). It assumed serious proportions in 1944 when the Japanese came up to Kohima town in Naga Hills District of Assam.[1] Earlier, Singapore fell on 15th February, Rangoon on 7th March and Andamans on 12th March 1942 to the invading Japanese army. Thousands of Indian evacuees from Singapore, Malaysia and Burma region came to Assam on foot traversing the hazardous mountain passes and jungle-covered hilly paths. Some of them also reached Assam by other means of travel, such as, air and sea, Many evacuees subsequently left Assam for their homes. Yet the heavy movements of the evacuees in addition to those of the army resulted in intense pressure on the transport system, communication, trade, commerce, etc. The Government and non-government agencies like the tea plantation companies were involved in providing shelters and relief to the fleeing masses from the war front. Obviously these developments seriously dislocated economic activities. Many non-Assamese wholesale and retail traders fled to their home provinces.

Assam was made the war base for resisting the Japanese forces' advance and to drive them away from their conquered territories in South Asia. A field army of six divisions was mobilized in Assam under the British Command. The American armed forces also operated from Assam to help China in fighting the Japanese[2].

The military operations, or course, strengthened the basic

infrastructure since roads, airfields, camps, hospitals, etc were built and the railway communication system improved. This entire system was placed under the control of the American army. (See supra, Chapter 12 for more details).

Assam joined the "Quit India" Movement launched in 1942. People in some parts of Assam, such as, Nowgong became very active in disturbing the lines of military movement. The Government unleashed drastic repressive measures like firing, putting many freedom fighters in jail and imposing collective fines on the people.

These events further upset normal economic activities entailing economic hardships for the common people.

1. War-Time Inflation

Prices all over the country started rising with the outbreak of War. Inflationary pressure became more and more acute as the war went on. The wholesale price index in India (1914-15=100) rose from Rs. 88,15 in 1938-39 to Rs. 221.90 in 1946-47 (see table 15.1 below):

Table 15.1
Wholesale price index of India (1914-15=100) 1938-39 to 1946-47.

Year	Wholesale Price Index
1938-39	88.15
1939-40	88.14
1940-41	96.90
1941-42	119.00
1942-43	162.80
1943-44	180.10
1944-45	182.40
1945-46	199.10
1946-47	221.90

Source : Joint-stock companies in British India and the Indian States, Government of India, Rajat Ray, Industrialization in India, p. 39 Quoted in *Banglar Arthik Itihash* Subodh Kumar Mukhopadhyay by Bengali), p. 175. See note No. 3.

Prices in Assam went up even higher as it was directly involved in the ongoing mobilization of armed forces, their movements, hectic construction of roads, military camps, aerodromes, etc and also because of a rise in public expenditure on procurement of goods for meeting war needs, and rapid rise in employment opportunities as more and more youths were recruited into the army, civil defence like units of air-raid precaution, civil supplies and rationing department, etc. There was also an increase in the number of workers engaged by the constractors for construction works and movement of supplies. There was a scarcity of essential consumption goods, particularly foodgrain. In 1942-43, many non-Assamese wholesale and retail traders left Assam for their respective homes away from the war zone. Amalendu Guha noted that the resulting disruption of markets led to looting of several *hats* (markets) in parts of Goalpara in November 1942[4].

For overcoming possible breakdown of the normal trade operations the Government had to intervene by directly undertaking commercial operations. Noted managing agency firm, M/S Shaw Wallace and Co. Ltd., was appointed by the Government for conducting wholesale purchase of salt, sugar, wheat, flour and standard cloth from outside on Government account. Similarly another resourceful firm M/S Steel Brothers Ltd. was appointed for purchase of other essential commodities like rice, paddy and mustard oil from the local market. These measures were taken for ensuring supplies of necessary consumption goods and stabilizing their prices. But such actions could not stop hoarding, black marketing and profiteering. No wonder, the price of salt the most essential commodity of public consumption went up to eight rupees a *seer* (a little less than one Kg.) in 1943.[5] The Annual Report on the Land Revenue Administration of the Assam Valley Division for the year 1943-44 noted that the average increase in prices was not less than 300 per cent[6].

The agriculturists benefited from the rise in prices of foodgrain and other agricultural products but such gains were nullified to some extent as they had to pay higher prices for non-agricultural products. In table 15.2 the comparative indices of prices of agricultural and non-agricultural goods for selected years are given.

Table 15.2
Weighted Index Numbers of Agricultural and Non-Agricultural Prices for the years 1939 to 1947 (1873=100).

Year	Weighted index of agricultural prices	Weighted index of Non-agricultural prices
1939	153	112
1940	147	111
1941	166	132
1942	194	181
1943	421	281
1944	340	233
1945	334	221
1946	353	223
1947	414	252

Source: Dharma Kumar and Tapan Ray Chowdhury (ed), 1983, *The Cambridge Economic History of India*, Volume 2, Cambridge University Press, Cambridge, London, p. 904.

Price rise in comparative perspective *Vis-à-vis* agricultural and non- agricultural goods indicates that the agriculturists were net gainers. Those earning fixed income like the salaried government and non-government employees and the industrial workers were the worst sufferers. Their salaries and wages did not rise to match the inflationary rise in prices of all commodities. In the Brief Summary of the Annual Report on the Land Revenue Administration of the Assam Valley for the year 1943-44 it was observed that the difficulties of the poorly paid Government servants were too marked because the Government did not provide them with adequate relief even as price increased by not less than 300 per cent. The same report, of course, noted that supply of war materials-bamboo, thatch, etc yielded additional income to the villagers and cultivators[7].

In reviewing the economic and social conditions of the decade 1941-1951, Vaghaiwalla, Superintendent of Census Operation 1951, observed that various control orders effected in the beginning of the decade helped check price rise but not for long. Soon these orders resulted in the supplies going underground and it became a problem for the people to obtain their necessaries at controlled prices. Supplies of rice in the market fell as the growers themselves consumed more rice. And another reason they could earn higher income by selling less quantity of rice at higher prices. The growers also resorted to hoarding of food grain. The situation aggravated at the end of the war. "The rationing was introduced in most of the towns regarding rice, Kerosene oil, cloth, sugar, mustard oil, and Dal. Sugar, cloth and Kerosene oil rationing was later extended to rural areas also"[8]. The rationing system, it is observed in the report, led to increased black marketing, profiteering and hoarding. The extent of such economic evils depended upon the level of 'efficiency of the district authorities to enforce the control orders'[9].

One redeeming feature of the war-time economy of Assam was the increased volume of industrial production, especially of mineral oil, coal and tea for meeting war needs. It led in turn to increased demand for labour that pushed up wage rates. The tea garden labourers got their wages partly in the form of food grain. Increased productive activities gave a fillip to trade and commerce after the economy recovered from the initial stage of disruption of such activities in the wake of exodus of many wholesale and retail traders to their home provinces.

2. Public Health

The war period was marked by deterioration in the public health condition. In 1942, there was a very high incidence of death from Cholera. "The reason for its appearance was mainly aftermath to (sic) (1) movement of troops, (2) passing of evacuees from Burma through the Indo - Burma road and Silchar - Bishnupur route and (3) the labourers who were generally recruited from other province in India and who might have brought infection from their native villages"[10], In the following year (1943) scarcity of foodstuffs became acute which led to fall in their consumption level and consequently a deterioration of the health of the people[11].

3. Mushroom Growth of Commerical Banking

During the war period to mobilize savings out of increased incomes of the people and thereby to meet the growing needs of credit of the contractors, traders and other small entrepreneurs, a number of commercial banking companies started their operations in Assam. This was something like a mushroom growth. Prudent banking principle of advancing credit only against financially viable investment proposals was not scrupulously followed. Moreover, high interest rates were imprudently offered to attract deposits. Such unsound banking operations naturally resulted in a number of bank failures as the war period boom came to an end. Many depositors were ruined. Some loan advances were made against inappropriate assets which could not be disposed of to realize the loans advanced against them. No wonder, many such investments flopped.

4. Cooperative Banking

In the cooperative banking sector, increased incomes of the agriculturists should have helped them to pay off their debts to the cooperative societies. The Census Report for 1951 drawing upon the Reserve Bank of India's publication "Cooperation in Assam – A New Experiment" observes that in the initial period of the war years there were 'extremely satisfactory collections in some of the central banks' but soon these stopped. 'A downward tendency was evident'[12].

Non-credit cooperative society movement, however, got a stimulus during the second phase of the war. A number of consumers' stores, milk societies, central wholesale stores and industrial societies were started. To overcome problems resulting from paucity of foodstuffs and other necessaries and as a mean of counteracting the evils of black marketing and hoarding by traders, people started their own cooperative consumer stores. The growth of non-credit societies in Assam during the year 1941-42 to 1945-46 is shown in Table 15.3.

Table 15. 3
Non – Credit Societies in Assam (1941-45).

Year	No. of Societies	No. of Members	Share Capital Rs.	Working Capital Rs.	Sale Rs.	Profit Rs.
1941 - 42	19	1,609	31,001	133,122	406,110	18,455
1942 - 43	43	2,634	46,686	158,219	516,298	25,018
1943 - 44	609	57,357	759,589	943,850	3,522,812	174,767
1944 - 45	1,229	135,380	2,651,002	10,317,647	13,012,842	299,793
1945 - 46	1,403	130,850	3,026,148	10,624,766	36,727,733	425,722

Source : R. B. Vaghaiwalla, *Census Report for 1951*, P. 35

The non-credit societies were 'a war-time creation'. They practically served as 'distributing agencies for controlled commodities'. It was not a concerted move by the consumers to run general stores to meet their own consumption needs at fair prices to curb the power of the profiteering retailer. "Therefore, when the controls were lifted their purpose also seemed to have ended and many of them went into voluntary liquidation while most of the others declined gradually"[13].

The favourable impact of the war on the cooperative movement whether in the sphere of credit societies or in that of non-credit societies was a transitory phenomenon. At the end of war, according to the Registrar, the cooperative societies in Assam had "dwindling assets, increasing liabilities, waning public confidence, a falling off in the number of members, decreasing influx of fresh finance, a shrinking of business and an all-round stagnation[14].

5. Bengal Famine of 1943 and the Spurt of Immigration

About 1.5 million people died in the Bengal Famine of 1943 (for more details vide Chapter 16 below) which brought about a spurt of immigration of destitute landless rural agricultural workers (mostly Muslims) from Bengal into the neighbouring districts of Assam.[15]

To enable the immigrant Muslim agriculturists to settle in Assam and take up land for cultivation the Bengal Legislative Council passed a resolution on 16 July 1943 urging the Government of India "to remove all restrictions imposed by the Assam Government on the land-hungry, emigrant cultivators from Bengal"[16]. The fourth Saadullah Ministry was in power in Assam from 25 August 1942 to 23 March 1945. This Ministry adopted a resolution on land settlement taking advantage of the "grow more food" campaign launched by the Government of India in order to overcome the wartime food shortage in the country. The new land settlement policy was announced aster passing a resolution on 24 August 1943. Accordingly 'distribution of wastelands in proportion to needs of different communities in Nowgang' was resumed. For this purpose 'dereservation of select grazing reserves' was also resorted to. Secondary, surplus professional grazing reserves in Kamrup and Darrong, if any, could be dereserved. Thirdly, surplus reserves also in "all the submontane area, and in Sibsagar and Lakhimpur" could be opened up "for settlement of landless indigenous people".

This policy greatly encouraged the flow of Muslim immigrants into Assam in the name of 'grow more food' campaign. It was so palpable that even the Viceroy of India remarked that this campaign had turned into a 'grow more Muslim' campaign in Assam[17].

The land settlement question continued to be a contentious issue in the post-war years. An all-party conference held in December 1944 recommended that thirty per cent of the available wastelands should be kept reserved for meeting the future needs of the indigenous people. The remaining wastelands might be given to the 'landless sons of the soil' and the pre-1938 immigrants. It was also proposed to have a system for ensuring reservation of land for tribal people in the belts specially reserved for them[18].

Accordingly, the Government adopted a new resolution on wasteland settlement in January 1945. A plan was formulated for the settlement of wastelands in Goalpara, Kamrup, Darrang and Nowgong in favour of landless persons (i.e persons who owned less than 50 bighas of land) of all categories. A ceiling of 30 bighas (10 acres) of land per family was fixed. An important decision related to the constitution of tribal belts. The basis of estimating the requirement of land for tribal people would be twice the area already under their possession plus some more land as a provision for their future needs as and when their population would grow. Similarly, for meeting the needs of future rises in general population 'thirty per cent of all cultivable wastelands in each district, as of 1940 was to be reserved'. Under this land settlement policy, lands under 'Professional Grazing Reserves' were to remain untouched"[19].

This land settlement and immigration continued to be a burning issue in Assam. After prolonged negotiations between political parties in July 1945 the land settlement policy was officially announced. "A landless family was now redefined as one possessing less than twenty bighas of land. All grazing reserves were to be maintained intact and all encroachers were to be indiscriminately evicted therefrom, as a matter of policy. In short, the principles agreed upon in the December Conference were, in all respects, fully restored"[20].

This decision did not satisfy the immigrants' lobby. It moved an amendment of the announced land settlement policy. They urged the Government to allow settlement of land in favour of immigrants "who had already sown at least one crop.............irrespective of their arrival dates in the Brahmaputra Valley or of the legality of their squatting on grazing reserves"[21].

This issue of settlement if immigrant peasants in the so called wastelands and / or *char* (sandbanks) continued to dominate Assam's political economy till the end of the colonial rule.

NOTES AND REFERENCES

1. Most of the houses in Kohima and the neighbouring villages were destroyed or damaged when the Allies subjected this area to heavy aerial bombardment in order to dislodge the Japanese from their hill strongholds into which they had dug themselves'. Even by 1951 the district had not fully 'recovered from the ravages of the war', R. B. Vaghaiwalla (1954), *Census of India,* 1951, Vol. XII: *Assam, Manipur and Tripura,* Part IA Report, Shillong, p. 54.
2. Amalendu Guha (1988), *Planter-Raj to Swaraj, Freedom Struggle and Electoral Politics in Assam 1826-1947,* People's Publishing House, New Delhi, p. 278.

3. Subodh Kumar Mukhopadhyay (1991), *Banglar Arthik Itihash* (Economic History of Bengal), K. P. Bagchi and Co. Kolkata, p. 175.
4. Amalendu Guha, *op. cit.* p. 279.
5. *ibid.* p. 279.
6. *A Summary of the Report on the Land Revenue Administration of the Assam Valley Division for the year 1943-44*, Government of Assam, Section I Para 3.
7. *ibid.* Para 4.
8. Vaghaiwalla, *op. cit.* p. 36.
9. *ibid.*
10. *ibid.* p. 37.
11. *ibid.*
12. R. B. Vaghaiwalla (1954), *op. cit.* p. 35.
13. *ibid.*
14. Quoted in *ibid.*
15. *ibid.* p. 32.
16. Amalendu Guha, *op. cit.* p. 281.
17. *ibid.*
18. *ibid.* p. 284
19. *ibid.* p 285
20. *ibid.* pp. 290-91.
21. *ibid.* p. 291.

16
THE POLITY AND ECONOMIC HISTORY OF COLONIAL ASSAM THE SUMMING UP.

1. Constitutional Evolution of the Politiy

The British rule over Assam over a period of 121 years (1826-1947) was the most eventful period in Assam's socio-economic and political history. From 1826 to 1873 the areas of Assam newly annexed by the British were administered by the Agent for the Governor General in the Northeast Frontier of Bengal which was then a division of the Bengal Presidency. In 1874 Assam was formed into a separate Chief Commissioner's Province but without any legislature of its own. The area of the province included Assam proper, Cachar, Goalpara, Garo Hills and other hill districts. In 1905 Assam's constitutional position was upgraded to that of a Lt. Governor's Province and in 1906 Assam got its legislative council under the Councils Act of 1892. The number of Council members was 15 out of which only two were indirectly elected by the local boards and municipalities subject to the approval of the Lt. Governor. Powers of the Council were extremely limited. Organized political movements particularly the Non-Cooperation Movement of 1920-21, for people's rights to have representation in governance of the province resulted in reformation of the constitution of the local self-government bodies and also of the Assam Legislative Council. Some limited provisions for representation of non-official members were made. Legislative functions were expanded following the Government of India Act of 1919 under which the system of 'Dyarchy' was introduced.

Devolution Rules made under the India Act 1919 provided for separation of administration and revenue sources into two categories – Central and provincial. This enabled the provinces to run their own administration with rights to raise revenue by levying taxes on the provincial sources of revenue in accordance with the budgets passed by the provincial Legislature. However, transfer of financial resource from the Centre for certain purposes continued[1].

In Assam two ministers accountable to the Legislative Council were to advise the Governor on the administration of the 'transferred subjects'. Regarding administration of the 'reserved subjects', the Ministers had no powers. The governor was advised by two executive councillors in the administration of the 'reserved subjects'. The Legislative Council had no control over these subjects. The provincial government was totally responsible to the Central Government in matters concerning administration of these subjects.

"The area of transferred subjects was more limited in Assam, to begin with, than in other provinces. The departments of Public Works, excise and fishery were gradually transferred there only after 1925-26, excise as late as in 1926-27. Transferred departments accounted for only 30.2 per cent of the total budgeted expenditure of 1927-28 and 36.7 per cent of that in 1935-36"[2].

Under the Government of India Act 1935 (which became effective in 1937) a federal constitutional structure for British India was introduced. The legislative powers were divided into three categories, namely, the Federal, Provincial and Concurrent. Matters such as external affairs, currency and coinage, navy, military and air forces and census were in the Federal List. The Provincial List included police, provincial public service and education. The subjects listed in the concurrent category over which both the central and provincial legislatures had their jurisdictions included criminal law and procedure, civil procedure, marrige and divorce and arbitration.

The powers of the provinces to enact and enforce laws were subject to various limitations. The governors were the executive heads of provincial governments and ordinarily before exercising their powers they were to take advice of their ministers who were responsible to the legislature. In certain matters, however, the governor could act using his discretion' or guided by his own 'judgment without taking ministerial advice. Such powers were more extensive in the case of the Governor of Assam. Under section 93 of the Act the governor of any province could take over the whole administration of the province into his own hands if he thought there was a breakdown of the constitution. He could also veto any law passed by the legislature.

The hill areas of Assam were divided into two special categories. Termed as 'excluded areas' and 'partially excluded areas'. The Balipara and Sadiya Frontier Tracts in the north-eastern frontier hills, the Naga Hills district, the Lushari Hills district and the North Cachar Hills subdivisions were designated as excluded areas which had no representation in the legislature. These were administered by the Governor using his 'discretion', that is, without any reference to the cabinet. But funds for public expenditure in these parts of the province came from 'the provincial pool of resources'. 'Partially excluded areas' included the Garo Hills district, Khasi-Jaintia Hills district (excluding Shillong), and the Mikir Hills. People of these districts elected members to the legislature and their administration also was primarily the responsibility of the ministers. But the governor had the power to override a ministers' advice in respect to these areas if necessary in order to maintain 'peace and good government' which was his ultimate responsibility.

"More than a fifth of the province's total expenditure budget was non-votable – some items of it not even open to discussion. On certain specified subjects, a private bill or resolution could be introduced in the legislature only after it had obtained the Governor's sanction"[3].

Political parties, mainly the Indian National Congress and the Muslim League, became more and more involved in electoral politics and ministry formation even though the electorate constituted a very narrow and fragmented base.

The composition of the Assam Legislative Assembly under the Government of India Act 1935 shown that out of a total of Assembly seats, 84 territorial constituencies were distributed as follows: "Non-Muhammedan General including

Schedules Castes' (47): Muhammedan (34); Women (1); European (1) and Indian Christain (1). There were 24 special constituencies earmarked for Backward Plains Tribes (4); People of Backward Hill Areas (5); European Planters (7); Indian Planters (2); Commerce and Industry (2) (European: 1 and Indian: 1) and Tea Garden Labour (4). In such a legislative structure, "European planters and their allies emerged not only as an important but also as the most organized group. They held the balance between the Congress and Non-Congress Camps"[4].

2. Economic Measures of Popular Ministry

Even within the limited legislative and executive powers enjoyed by the Ministry – whether formed by the Congress or a coalition of parties and independents and nominated members headed by the Muslim League – several measures were taken which had a bearing on the economic life of the people. In 1938-39 land revenue assessed until then was reduced by 33 per cent. As a result, the revenue burden was eased by Rs.28 lakh. This benefit which rose up to Rs.40 lakh in 1939-40 and in 1940-41could be attributed to a remission of 50 per cent granted to smaller estates paying Rs.16 or less and 20 to 30 per cent to other estates.

The programme for progressively prohibiting opium consumption was undertaken by the popular ministry. Finally, a total prohibition against opium consumption was effected on 1 March 1941. This measure resulted in the annual fall in revenue. In 1927-28 the fall amounted to a little over Rs38 lakh and to over Rs.10.07 lakh in 1938 – 39.

To make up the loss of revenue on account of these measures, the following new tax laws were taken up for enactment in 1939[6]:

(i) The Assam Sales of Motor Spirit and Lubricant Taxation Act, 1939.

(ii) The Assam Sales Tax Act 1939, But it was not implemented as it was likely to divert sales of goods to the neighboring province of Bengal where there was no Sales Tax.

(iii) The Assam Amusements and Betting Tax Act 1939.

(iv) The Assam Excise (Amendment) Act 1939; and

(v) The Assam Agricultural Income Tax Act 1939.

The enactment of agricultural income tax laws was strongly and persistently opposed by the planters – European and Indian alike. To meet some of the objections of the local peasants who were rich the exemption limit of agricultural income was raised from Rs.2000 to Rs.3000 per annum. Even this was further diluted by the Saadulla Ministry[7]. It was as late as 1937 that the popular ministry assumed limited powers of taking decisions on economic management of the province. Until then the colonial government was very much dominated by the planters whose role in legislating Assam's socio-economic structure was remarkable. It was very persistent dominance which promoted the planters' interest above ail other sections of population. It is on this ground that Amalendu Guha termed the colonial regime as the *'Planter-Raj'*.

3. Economic History of Colonial Assam:The Summing Up

Despite promoting planters' interest, the colonial rule over a period of 121 years made an end of Assam's long period of isolation from other parts of India and carried out programmes of modernization in social, political and economic spheres.

Back in the 1820's and 1830's the colonial rulers established a civil government after suppressing the prevailing chaos since the Ahom regimes failed to maintain law and order and ensure security of people's life. The foreign rulers built up a functional bureaucratic set up. The total change meant a revolutionary transition that was welcome by the people of Assam at large who tasted an environment of peace and security of life and property after a long time. The colonial government, of course, took many unwelcome and oppressive measures that hit people very hard.

The revenue system was reorganized for the purpose of appropriating as much surplus of income generated in the economy as possible. The paik system was replaced by the ryotwari system excepting for Goalpara district where the zamindary system was retained. Land revenue rates were revised upward from time to time. Later a free-hold land-holding system mainly for the benefit of the planters was also created. The land grants made by the Ahom rulers free of revenue or at half rates were by and large retained. The restructured land system meant an end of the feudal order and the emergence of classes of peasant proprietors, sub-tenants, rentiers, share-croppers and, of course, the capitalist farmers such as the planters.

The majority of the peasant proprietors were small landholders owning only between 5 and 5.5 acres of land. They had very little accumulation of capital for investment in intensive cultivation. Therefore, the growth of agricultural output in the province occurred mainly through extensive cultivation and also through improved farm practices introduced by the immigrant peasants who even introduced new food and cash crops.

Capitalist farming for production of tea entailed employment of wage labour, appropriation of 'surplus labour' by various means and inflicting extreme forms of deprivation on the workers most of whom were recruited from outside Assam as indentured labour.

Slavery was abolished in 1843. It was a welcome step in releasing the nine per cent of Assam's population (slaves and bondsmen taken together) from sufferings and indignities.

In the mid-nineteenth century the foundation of the industrial sector primarily led by tea was laid. Trade and commerce – both internal and external – flourished. Modern systems of transport by road, river and rail were developed. Communication systems providing postal, telegraph and telephone services were built up. Financial institutions like commercial banks, cooperative societies and insurance companies slowly came up. People became familiar with these services and were benefited by them.

Development of these infrastructural services, besides the growth of literacy and education, resulted in growing specialization in economic activities of the people, occupational diversification, accumulation of capital and investment in some new spheres that resulted in higher rate of production but at an extremely slow pace in the unorganized sector which comprised the masses of Assam's population.

Foreign capital flowed into Assam for development of industries, such as, tea, mineral oil, coal and plywood industries and for developing river and rail transport services. Indian capital was also invested in industries like tea, edible oil, rice-husking and a few others.

Indigenous manufacturing activities in cottage and small – scale units, such as, cotton and silk-weaving, brass, copper and bell-metal utensils were somewhat affected but the process of 'deindustrialization' was not very much in evidence. It was because some of these industries survived competition with imported manufactured goods, since demand for these products was associated with Assamese culture and tradition and also because consumption of some of these items was high.

One of the darkest spots of foreign capital induced industrialization was the severest form of exploitation of labour, particularly the tea garden workers. In Guha's words they were no better than "wage-slaves".

The promotion of industrialization process under colonial dispensation suffered from the structural weakness, erected as it was on a very narrow base, and being mainly export dependent. It lacked the organizational strength to boost sustained and widely dispersed growth of industrial production and income. Besides, no meaningful linkage with agricultural production obtained. The overall rate of growth of Assam's economy was therefore low and distribution of wealth and income was highly unequal.

Investment in human resource development was inadequate for providing appropriate educational and training facilities for the wider section of population. Health services were provided but no social movement was organized for motivating people, particularly workers to accept modern health care practices and to participate in inoculation and other preventive measures. The tea industry had no stake in investing in education and health services for its workers. Government also did not tax planters for mobilizing revenue to be spent on these programmes.

Forests, an important economic resource of Assam, required to be conserved for ensuring sustainable economic development of the province. The Department of Forests was established by the Government and Assam Forest Regulation was promulgated for management, control and development of this resource to meet the economic needs of people, industry and government. But in the process, traditional free access of the rural and hill people to forests was withdrawn or restricted as mobilization of forest revenue received priority. By contrast, the planters and the timber merchants were treated with more favour in respect of use of forest resources. The overall forest policy did not quite prioritize the objective of regeneration and afforestation programmes.

Demographic development in the colonial period was marked by growth of population on account of immigration of land – less peasants from Bengal, tea garden workers from other provinces, Nepali graziers, professionals and civil servants from Bengal and other parts of India.

Immigration of settlers pursuing occupations in all the three sectors of the economy – primary, secondary and tertiary – continued unabated during the colonial period. As a result not only was the growth of population augmented, but distribution of population among different ethnic, linguistic and religious groups also changed markedly. This was one of the significant results of the colonial model of Assam's economic growth. Population ratio of non-indigenous ethnic, linguistic and religious groups visa-a-vis the total population of Assam increased substantially. As a result the socio-political tension affecting Assam's economic growth assumed critical proportions towards the end of the colonial rule.

In the concluding Chapter of his book *A Theory of Economic History*, John Hicks emphasized the importance of maintaining social identity while aspiring for 'Development'. The process of development is helped by the absorption of immigrant workers to ease the problem of labour shortage yet if in the process the different social units which have 'value' are put into 'a melting pot' much is lost. Therefore he advocates 'Absorption, which is consistent with the maintenance of social identity'[8]. He considers economic history 'as a part of social evolution much more widely considered'[9].

By way of a brief epilogue it may be said that the problem of preserving identity of the indigenous population groups has been a protracted one, socially disturbing at times right from the time of colonial period till to-day. Immigration of different ethnic, religious and linguistic groups did not always occur because of economic necessity for boosting productive activities. We cannot rule out its political implications, furthering political interests of different ethnic, religious and linguistic groups.

NOTES AND REFERENCES

1. Durga Das Basu (1983), *Introduction to the Constitution of India*, Prentice Hall of India Private Limited, New Delhi, pp. 1-11, contains the information about constitutional development in the pre-Independence period.
2. Amalendu Guha (1988), *Planter-Raj to Swaraj: Freedom Struggle and Electoral Politics in Assam 1826-1947*, People's Publishing House, New Delhi, p. 149. For many other factual details of constitutional development discussed here, I have depended on this work.
3. *ibid.* p . 218.
4. *ibid.* p . 219.
5. *ibid.* p. 233.
6. *ibid.* p.233.
7. *ibid.* Pp. 234-35.
8. John Hicks (1969), *A Theory of Economic History*, Clarendon Press, Oxford, pp. 160-61.
9. *ibid.* p, 167.

17
ECONOMIC HISTORY OF STATES

B. Manipur

Introduction

The fertile valley of Manipur measuring about two thousand square kilometres lies on the east of Assam. It has the Naga Hills on its north, the Mizo Hills on South west and Myanmar on South-east. The Meiteis have been living there at least since the beginning of the first millennium. The recorded geneological tree of seventy-four Meitei Chiefs / Kings traces the origin of the dynasty to 33 A. D[1]. It was initially a small clan principality and gradually over the centuries rose as a powerful monarchal state comprising the valley of Manipur and the surrounding hills (covering an area of twenty thousand square kilometres) inhabited by the Nagas, Kukis and a few smaller ethnic groups. Through conquest some Meitei Kings extended the boundary of their Kingdom up to the river Chindwin in the east enclosing the fertile valley of Kabaw (now in Myanmar).

The Meiteis have a rich cultural heritage. The written Meitei language and literature have a long history. Their state chronicle *'Cheitharal Kumbaba'*, written in Meitei dates back to the first century A. D. Manickchand, a Manipuri writer, opines that it was possible for the Meiteis to develop their written language because of their early contact with the Chinese[2].

The King of Manipur, Meidingu Loiyumba, who ruled from 1074 A. D. to 1112 A. D., promulgated the first written constitution of the Kingdom termed as *'Loiyumba Shinyen'* in 1110 A. D. This constitution codified the customary laws, codes and conventions and defined Meitei polity embodying the concept of absolute monarchy. It also specified the systems of administration of justice, land revenue collection, extraction of free labour called 'Lallup', etc. Categorization of administrative departments, duties and functions of the King and the queen, royal etiquette, titles and decorations generally conferred on the nobles and even the standard time to be observed was laid down in the constitution. An important feature of the royal edict was to divide the Kingdom into six *pannas*. This arrangement facilitated getting free service under the *Lallup* system. Later Kings in succession added new provisions to the *'Loiyumba Shinyen'*[3].

The Meitei people were men of determined character imbued with indomitable martial spirit; many of them were skilled horse-riders who fought as fierce cavalrymen in wars. Men could keep on fighting prolonged battles being away from home. This was possible because they did not have to worry about their womenfolk, who were industrious, enterprising, business-minded and adept in weaving, agricultural and horticultural farming and selling and buying goods in the market. In fact not only would they do all household chores but also work in the agricultural fields. They ran shops in markets where surplus produce was sold and goods for family consumption bought. The practice of polygamy was common, particularly among those who could afford to maintain more than one wife. This custom helped the process of growth of Meitei population. The Meiteis were also proud of their ethnic identity and culture and had a strong feeling of allegiance to their Chief/King, which strengthened their ethnic solidarity and ensured security against hillmen's and Burmese attacks.

All these features of Meitei character combined with a strong political structure and economy placed them quite ahead of other ethnic groups living in the surrounding hills in terms of social, political, economic and cultural development. Therefore, they succeeded in dominating over the people of the surrounding hills, namely, the Nagas and the Kukis. But over the centuries there occurred a fusion of certain traits of Meitei culture and of several ethnic groups of hill-dwellers. As a result the Kingdom of Manipur emerged as one distinct political entity with the territorial spread extending from the Manipur valley to the surrounding hills. There were times when the territorial boundary of the Manipur Kingdom included parts of Burma which was possible through conquest by some powerful Manipuri Kings. Just as well at times the boundary shrank when the Burmese counterattacks could not be repulsed. The history of Manipur is replete with incidents connected with Meitei-Burma conflicts and invasions and counter-invasions, none of which continued for more than a few years at a stretch. And despite such violent disruptions, the basic territory of the Kingdom of Manipur covering the valley and the surrounding hills remained almost stable. The latest invasion of Manipur by Burma took place in 1819 which ended with the conclusion of the Treaty of Yandabo in 1826 between East India Company and the King of Ava (Burma). In liberating his country from the Burmese occupation, the young Manipuri Prince, Gambhir Singh, played the decisive role with his 500 member Manipur Levy raised with the assistance of the British. Under the treaty he was recognized by Ava as the King of Manipur.

NOTES AND REFERENCES

1. Naorem Sanjaoba (Ed) (1988), *Manipur : Past and Present,* Vol. I, History, Polity and Law, Mittal Publications, Delhi, pp. 477-79.
2. Kousam Manikchand, (1988), The Evolution of the Meitei State, Published in Sanajaoba, *ibid,* p. 146 and p. 158.
3. Gangmumei Kabui (1988), "Glimpses of Land and People of Ancient Manipur", published in Sanajaoba, *ibid,* p. 307.

18
THE EVERYDAY LIFE PATTERN AND THE MATERIAL LIFE OF THE PEOPLE OF MANIPUR

Gambhir Singh came into power as the King of Manipur in 1826. He had to undertake the task of rebuilding Manipur's economy that was devastated by the Burmese invaders. Before we trace the economic changes and progress achieved in improving the economic conditions of the people of Manipur since 1826 an account of the everyday life pattern of these people in that period of history should be in order. For one thing the market economy did not yet evolve in Manipur in full form. In the words of Braudel, underneath the market economy there lay a 'shadowy zone' of the *'material life'* of people or 'infra-economy', that is, 'the informal other half of economic activity, the world of self sufficiency and barter of goods and services within a very small radius'[1]. Description of the material life is "a sort of 'weighing up of the world' ...., an evaluation of the limits of what was possible in the pre-industrial world. One of these limits is the enormous place then occupied by 'material life'"[2]. We need portray 'the images of daily life' – that exemplify the material life of the people.

1. Daily Bread : Rice, Fish and Dal

The Meiteis living in the Manipur plains acquired the technique of growing rice a long time back. The rich alluvial soil flooded by the numerous rivers and waters of lakes in their respective valleys were highly suitable for growing rice. No wonder, productivity per unit of land as well as labour was much higher than that in the case of the upland rice grown by the hillmen on their swidden farms (shifting cultivation plots). Rice plants, as mentioned by Braudel[3], originally grew in dry countries and later were adapted to 'a semi-aquatic cultivation'. In the latter system as we know the yields were much higher which accounts for its popularity. An important ecological feature of rice growing is that the roots of a paddy plant need 'rich supply of oxygen'. Therefore, "however static the water in a rice field may appear, it is always in motion at some time so that oxygenation is possible. Hydraulic technology has therefore to be used alternately to create and suspend the movement of the water"[4].

Rice growing in the valleys with rivers flowing through them and their lakes is obviously associated with fishing in the water-bodies. Therefore, rice and fish make a common combination of diet of the rice-growers. The Manipuris were no exception. In the dry season some grains and pulses were grown, roots of which fixed oxygen in the soil and thus enriched it for growing rice subsequently. This system of rotation of crops naturally evolved in rice growing areas. This development largely influenced the basket of food items of the Manipuris. The diet of an average Manipuri adult consisted of rice, fish and dal (pulses). Since their conversion to Hinduism of the Vaishnava cult they have ceased to eat egg or meat of any animal whatsoever. Butter or ghee and milk were very rarely consumed.

The diet of the children, particularly of male sex, up to the age of nine when they are ceremoniously initiated into donning the sacred thread according to the Hindu custom could eat meat or egg. But after that ceremony they strictly excluded egg or meat from their diet.

2. Varieties and Mode of Rice Cultivation

About nineteen varieties of rice were cultivated; a few of which were early varieties that ripened in three months but the late varieties, yields of which were much higher, took about six months to be ready for harvest. Cultivators grew much more of the late varieties than the early ones. There were at least fifteen late varieties raised in Manipur. Cultivation of late varieties followed the method of transplantation. Seeds were first cast in the seed bed which was prepared by repeatedly ploughing and harrowing and irrigating so that it might become a plot of liquid mud. On this bed the chosen seeds which had just germinated after being moistened and kept covered in a basket were broadcast. When these took roots and sprouted three or four leaves they were transplanted in the prepared fields which were soft and muddy. The seedlings were pulled up by hand in bunches and the roots were washed clean of mud and then inserted by hands in the muddy field one by one in rows. Broadcasting of seeds in the seed bed usually took place in May and transplantation was done in June-July and the crops ripened by November. Seeds of early varieties were sown broadcast on the fields prepared. The sowing season normally started in February and harvests were reaped in May. The ears of rice corn were cut by iron sickle and heaped in the ground for drying. When dry, these were threshed by hand by beating them on reed-mat. Rice in husk was finally unhusked by using winnowing fans and then stored in the granary. Rice straw had no use for the Manipuries excepting for burning as fuel for cooking. Husking of rice was done in wooden hollow stands by pounding with wooden mortars.

No manure or fertilizers were normally used. Yet the yield was quite high and this made it possible for Manipur to be self-sufficient in rice with provisions for emergency and against natural calamities causing partial or severe crop failures. "The fertility of the soil", according to Brown "which continues without manure to yield good crop, is doubtless owing to the fact that the rivers flowing through the valley are in the rainy season enormously loaded with mud, which becomes annually deposited in the rice fields"[5].

3. The Importance of Rice

Braudel has noted that compared to wheat rice growing has certain advantages. Rice is a more complete food stuff than wheat. For the rice growing population, 80% to 90% or even more of their dietary need is met by rice but it is 50% to 70% only in the case of wheat eating population. Unhusked rice can be stored for a longer period than it is possible for wheat.

In respect of susceptibility to attacks of malaria, rice

growers in the plains are still better off than the swidden cultivators on the hills. In the plains rice fields are irrigated by muddy water of the rivers carrying silts. As a result the fertility of the rice fields gets restored; moreover, malaria-carrying mosquito avoids muddy water but favours the clear water in hills and mountains. Therefore in the highlands, malaria was endemic which kept the population growth in check while population went on thriving in rice growing areas in the river valleys.

As highlighted by Braudel[7], culture of rice-growing (in the plains) influences the socio-political and economic life and institutions of the people concerned. Rice cultivation involves 'enormous concentration on work' through mobilization of 'human capital' and erection and management of irrigation system under the supervision of some dominant superior authority. This would not be possible without a 'stable society' and 'state authority'. Extension of rice cultivation into new areas has to be in an orderly manner which calls for state control. Rice growing villages formed into clusters in order to deal with the collective requirements of irrigation and to ensure security of life and property including the rice crop. Braudel's survey, revealed that successful operation of rice-fields was associated with 'high population and strict social discipline'. The Meities of the Manipur valley tending rice-fields irrigated by muddy waters of the rivers and building embankments for protecting rice-fields from the ravages of high floods manifested such social discipline and supervisory state authority. No wonder then the Meities were so dominant in their relationship with tribesmen of the surrounding hills.

Braudel further notes that the most important aspect of comparative advantage of growing rice in the valleys was that the growers usually raised two or sometimes even three crops of rice in the same plot every year. Or instead of rice, some other crops, such as wheat, barley, vegetables, beans, pulses, could be harvested as the second or third crop in between two rice crops. "The rice-field is thus a factory" observes Braudel[8].

Braudel has estimated that in the late 18th century France average wheat yield per hectare was five quintals. But the yield of rice from an equal area of rice-field (obviously in a rice producing country such as China) often amounted to thirty quintals of rice in husk; after milling the quantity came down to twenty-one quintals of husked rice. One kilogram of edible rice produces 3500 calories, so the total amount of calories per hectare of rice-field comes to 7.35 million calories as compared with only 1.5 million calories in the case of wheat per hectare. An equal area of land used for stock-raising yields 150 kilograms of meat that contributes only 0.34 million animal calories. Citing these comparative figures Braudel points out the 'enormous advantage of the rice-field and of vegetable foodstuffs' and observes: "The Far Eastern civilizations' preference for vegetarianism certainly does not spring from idealism"[9].

The greatest advantage of rice lies in the possibility of a second harvest of it from the same field and so 'a large and densely settled population' could thrive. Certainly rice production in valleys could provide 'a degree of security of food supply' to the growers. This accounted for the demographic growth in the rice-growing region such as Manipur.

The rice economy of the Meities in Manipur placed them in an advantageous position compared with the other ethnic groups living in the hills around the Manipur valley. The former had a higher rate of population growth. Consequently they enjoyed numerical superiority to the hillmen. This had an effect in the sphere of military activities, for in those days the size of an army was of critical importance. Besides steady population growth in the Meitei community sustained by the stable rice economy served as an autonomous factor in boosting agricultural development through intense agricultural practices.

In sharp contrast with the practice of the hillmen, using a substantial part of rice they produced to brew rice-beer the Meiteis did not divert any part of the produced rice for making any such drink which for them is taboo.

The Kings of Manipur consistently discouraged growth of external trade in rice grains since they disallowed any export of these foodgrains out of Manipur. With the excess amount of rice produced in any season they built up stocks of rice to meet the shortfalls, if any, and to prepare for further contingencies. The kingdom could not rely on import of rice from outside for meeting such exigencies as the trade routes were ill-developed and moreover, importing of rice from outside involved high cost. Pursuance of such a food policy helped to ensure food security for the people of Manipur.

Next to rice, fish - both fresh and dried - were an important item of the Meities' daily diet. The rivers of the Kingdom and the big lakes like Logtak, Ekop and Waithand abounded in a variety of fishes – big and small. As recorded by Brown there were some professional fishermen who also served as the cavalry soldiers of the Rajah. Many of them were dwellers in the vicinity of the lake Waithan. The number of persons who lives by fishing was 1400 according to the same source[10]. Catching of fish by non-professional fishermen, such as, farmers and their family members mostly for self-consumption was also common. In the Imphal market fishes were sold and bought in plenty. Some dried and fermented fish came from Cachar and Sylhet in British India.

The supreme importance of rice and fish in the diet of a Manipuri is borne out by the fact that on military expeditions and long marches the troops ate only rice and fermented fish. Johnstone has admired the cheerfulness of the Manipuris and their good-humored disposition even on a long and trying march defying the feeling of fatigue. This is what he observed when the Manipuri fighters joined the British force on its march to Naga Hills led by Johnstone. He has further praised them for their abstemious food habit as they "live chiefly on rice and fish, which is often rotten, from preference"[11].

The Manipuris seldom consumed milk, butter or ghee in those days. Sweetmeats were consumed occasionally. These were prepared for self – consumption. Some sweetmeats could also be obtained from the market.

4. Salt

Salt is the basic ingredient for cooking meals in all societies. Manipur being a landlocked country it had to depend on the natural salt springs for the supply of salt and occasionally on imports from Cachar and Sylhet in British India or from Burmah. R. B. Pemberton in his Report on

Manipur 1835 noted that Manipur valley was rich in several salt springs on its eastern side bordering the foot hills. Normally salt production from these salt pits exceeded the demands of the valley's population. The tribal people of the surrounding hills obtained salt from the valley in exchanges for the hill products, such as, tobacco, ginger, cotton. Salt obtained from the different springs vary in quality. The best quality salt was obtained from the springs of Wueekhong and the royal family's needs for salt were satisfied by the products of these springs alone. All salt springs were the property of the king and salt manufacturers had to pay 20 per cent of the total quantity of water drawn from the springs as tax to the King. The villagers who specialized in the art of manufacturing salt by using indigenous technology took part in cultivation also, but only to a little extent. And they got rice and other agricultural products from the agricultural farmers and fish from the fishermen by selling their salt to them. Such exchanges were mostly of barter type.

Pemberton has commended the Manipuri technology of processing water from salt springs into salt. This process yielded from 1/19 to 1/20th of the weight of springs water as salt. But at Newcastle, where salt was derived from sea water by solar evaporation, 30 to 40 tons of sea water yielded one ton of salt.[12]

Food habits in those days were very simple as already mentioned. Ordinary leafy and green vegetables were extensively grown in the kitchen gardens mainly for self-consumption. But some surplus produce was also sold in the market. Almost every Manipuri house did have within its boundary some open courtyards including a tank. Vegetables were extensively grown in the courtyard grounds and fishes reared in the tank. The European officers who resided in Manipur as army officers, political agents, members of survey parties and in various other capacities introduced the cultivation of many European varieties of vegetables, such as, peas, potatoes, cabbages, carrots, radish, beetroots and turnips. Pemberton has noted in his report (P. 31): "Almost all the garden produce of Europe is now found in the valley...... The potato and pea particularly, have proved so acceptable to the people, that they are now almost universally cultivated and exposed for sale in the different bazaars of the country"[13].

An important source of vegetable protein in Manipur was the tree bean. One species of permanent tree bore bunches of long, flat beans which were relished by the Manipuris. These beans cooked for eating, are tasty, nutrient and rich in protein content. In Manipur variety of fruits were found: they were applies, apricots, raspberries, strawberries, oranges, limes, pomegranates, guavas, mangoes, jackfruit pine-applies, and so on. But excepting for oranges and pine-applies, in the cultivation of which much care was taken, other fruits were of inferior quality. But Manipur was quite famous for the high quality pine-applies and oranges grown on the low ranges of hills in the southern extremity of Logtak lake[14].

The diet of an average Meitei consisting of rice, fish, pulses, beans, vegetables and seasonal fruits was a balanced one. Manipuris were also fond of taking part in sports and games such as, boat race, polo and hockey, (indigenous style) wrestling, horse riding. They also took part in martial sports sword fighting, spear fighting and wrestling. These features account for the vigour and valour of the Manipuris.

5. Stimulants and Drugs

The Meitei men and women have been habitual takers of betel leaves and betel nuts with lime even as almost their entire supply was imported from the neighbouring district of Cachar in British India. The Manipuris took to Pan (betel leaf) chewing probably after they came in contact first with hillmen and then with the people of Cachar who had this habit and were in a position to meet the growing needs of the Manipuris. These items accounted for a considerable part of Manipur's trade with Cachar. Smoking tobacco was also very common among the Manipuris. A. part of the supply of tobacco leaves was obtained from the hill farmers. The Meiteis were, however, not addicted to opium.

6. Dwelling Houses

Plans, sizes and designs as also locations of dwelling houses, materials used and organization of labour employed to build them were well-planned. These evolved in process of adaptation of styles of living within the parameters of community's beliefs and ethos, their physical features and with the physical features and demographic condition of the territory. Levels of technological knowledge, cultural attainments and economic developments are all reflected in the organization of the housing sector. The housing sector is an important building block of any economy. The size and importance of this sector in the economy of a country depend on demographic growth, size of population, costs of building materials used and labour employed for building houses, total area of land covered by this sector and the wider agricultural and other productive activities.

People of ordinary means built their houses using materials like bamboos, reeds, mud mixed with cowdung and thatch. The framework of a hut was made of bamboos, its walls with locally grown reeds which then were plastered over with mud mixed with cowdung. The roofs were covered with thatch. People who were better off used timber and bamboo for erecting the structures of their houses which had the same mud-plastered walls and thatched roofs. As for size, their houses and courtyards were, of course, much bigger and quality of materials used was better than that used by ordinary people. Even the royal palace was not built of bricks. It was also mud-walled but its roof was made of corrugated galvanized tin sheets. "Some of the approaches to the Raja's dwelling house were made of brick" observes Johnstone[15]. Manipur being an earthquake prone region, it would be risky by having ordinary brick-built houses. Moreover the larger section of the population could not also afford the high costs of building houses with bricks. But several temples built had brick-walls and thatch-roofs excepting for one in the palace covered with tin roof and another a gilded one.

The plans of the houses of different classes of people had some common features. Every house was east-facing having an open verandah in that direction. There were no windows in the walls. Light and air could enter through just two doors one opening into the verandah and the other into the north wall near the north-west corner. The big open verandah served as the place where all activities took place in the day time excepting for cooking which was done inside the room which had no partition. The bedside of the head of the family located near the south wall was screened off by mats to ensure privacy.

Every house had a fenced in compound containing gardens of fruit and vegetable plants and a small pond. The water in the pond was kept clean as it was used for drinking. Washing was not done in the pond. For such activities water would be lifted from the pond and used in a manner that would prevent the soiled water from falling back into the pond.

7. Economics of the Housing Sector

The housing sector manifested an essential element of Manipur's self-sufficient economy. For building houses, excepting for the palace and temples only locally available materials – bamboo, timber, thatch, mud, cowdung, etc were used. Supply of these needs did not normally involve any market transactions. People of ordinary means built their houses with family-labour and / or labour of the neighbours on mutual co-operation basis. The well-to-do people could engage labour on payment of wages. But the wage rate was not determined by market forces; customary rates prevailed. For building royal houses, temples and public buildings free labour was employed under the Lallup system. Galvanized iron sheets used for roofing palace buildings and temples has to be imported either from Cachar (British India) or from Burmah.

Plans and designs of houses were useful and practical rather than decorative. These were also cost-effective in terms of both resources and time required for their construction. The houses could be quickly rebuilt following devastations caused by natural calamities or destructions perpetrated by invading marauders from across the border. The houses were environment – friendly and in pleasant harmony with the natural surroundings. The compounds added to the wealth of the community/state in the shape of recurring annual yields from the kitchen garden, orchard and tank.

8. Dress and Fashion

Like his house the dress of a Manipuri was also simple, utilitarian, economical and made of materials internally produced. Only some woollen products, not worn by the masses of people, were imported from outside[16]. A common Manipuri man put on a dhoti, kurta or shirt and occasionally a white sheet of cloth as a wrapper. He also wore a turban on his head. In the winter some people used quilted and padded coat'. These were all textile products of local manufacturing.

A woman's dress consisted of *fanek*, that is, a piece of cloth worn round the body 'under the armpits and over the breast, and tucked in by hand at the side of the body'[17]. It is made of cotton and silk of bright colours with stripes of different hues. Over the *fanek* the body is covered with white muslin without veiling her face. In the winter full sleeved and tight-fitting jackets made of bright-coloured velvet or satin were worn. These materials were also locally produced. In fact Manipuri women wove cotton cloth, cotton rug (*Khesh*), muslin and silk with dexterity.

The Manipuris generally preferred the dress materials turned out by their women to any imported stuff. Even the Rajah and his court patronized the local creations of art and handicrafts[18].

Johnstone has admired the dress of Manipuri gentlemen. In their sparkling white dhuti, kurta and turban they appeared elegant, dignified and of manly bearing. Brown has appreciated the dress of the women describing it as "picturesque and pleasing"[19], even though the dress materials had simple designs and were unostentatious. The women's dress beautifully matched their industrious habit and graceful demeanor.

The spirit of unostentatious living was also manifested in the range of ornaments worn by women. Of course there was a general restriction on wearing gold ornaments other than earrings without the permission of the King. Wearing of gold-embroidered clothes was also prohibited. Ornaments made of metals other than gold included earrings, necklaces, bracelets, nose rings, etc. Manipur men also wore ornaments. Brown observes: "The Manipuri generally wears small rings of gold in his ears when he can afford it, and the well-to-do among them have necklaces of coral and gold and hollow chased armlets of gold called "Khiji" on their wrists. They are very fond of carrying flowers in their earrings or in holes in their ears, and in their head-dress"[20].

The Manipuris abhor liquor and all manner of intoxicating drugs. Among the Muslim settlers in Manipur some were addicted to opium. Poppy was grown in parts of their area of inhabitation.

9. Hillmen's Economy

In the early part of the 19th century the area of the territory under the rule of the Raja of Manipur was estimated at 7000 square miles (18130 sq. kms), of which 650 sq. miles (1684 sq. kms) constituted Manipur valley of rich alluvial and fertile soil and the remaining 6350 sq. miles (16446 sq. kms) consisted of hilly and mountainous terrain surrounding the valley[21]. The dwellers on these hills were numerous tribal people belonging to the major groups, namely the Nagas and the Kukis. The total population of hillmen was 74000[22]. The Naga Hills lie on the north of Manipur valley. And the Naga tribesmen, who live in compact villages, generally occupy the hills in the northern part of Manipur adjacent to the Naga Hills, now known as Nagaland. The Kukis originally living in the Lushai Hills (Present day Mizoram) and the adjoining areas continued to migrate northwards for a long time past. They settled in the southern hills in Manipur and even beyond on the border with Burma (Myanmar).

The population of the Kukis was a few thousand only till 1850s when a large number of Kukis migrated to Manipur. William McCulloch was the political Agent in Manipur at that time. He played an active role in settling the Kukis in areas bordering both Burma and the Hills where lived the Nagas in Manipur.

The hill ranges generally run from north to south and the heights of the ranges higher in the north gradually decrease towards the south. These are densely covered with forests excepting for the sides of the hill ranges facing the Manipur valley. Virgin forests on this side have suffered depletion because of the practice of shifting cultivation.

Animal husbandry was also an important component of the hillmen's economy. The hillmen reared buffaloes, cows, mithuns (*Bos frontalis*) goats, pigs, fowls, ducks, etc[23]. Some animals served as beast of burden and some as source of meat. Cows were not generally milched as the hillmen did not take milk.

Both the Nagas and the Kukis mainly practised Swidden agriculture in the hill forests to produce rice, their staple food, vegetables, oilseeds (sesame), pepper, ginger, potatoes of small size and inferior quality, maize, sweet potato, cotton, etc. They collected edible forest products including plentiful of yam, as well as firewood and building materials. Hunting games in the forest and fishing in hill streams were also among their important productive activities for meeting their subsistence needs.

Such common features notwithstanding, detailed structures of organizations of social and economic activities of the two tribal groups were markedly different from one another. The Naga villages are comparatively old, more stable nearly permanently located with well-demarcated boundaries. Besides practising shifting cultivation, many Naga families, particularly the Tangkhul Nagas living in the hills east of the Manipur valley, practised wet-rice cultivation in the terraces cut on the hill slopes. These were fortified by building stone walls on the lower side and irrigated by diverting hill stream through small irrigation channels skillfully constructed for the purpose. System of terrace cultivation was basically different from that of Swidden cultivation. It involved application of higher technology by which means the same terrace plot could be cultivated on a permanent basis provided it was maintained properly. And it depended on the recognition of ownership of the terrace plot by individual families. The nature of private ownership of terrace land was quite different and more explicit than that of Swidden cultivation plots. In the case of the former an individual enjoyed the rights of use, occupation and transfer. But in the latter case, only rights of use and occupation were enjoyed by an individual household.

The specific advantages of terrace cultivation are threefold. In the terraces wet-rice varieties are raised by transplanting paddy plants. This results in much higher rate of production of rice per hectare than that under Swidden cultivation. Secondly, the quality of grain of wet-rice varieties grown in terraced farms is better than that in the latter case.

Thirdly, since the terraces are generally located near their homes, the hillmen can better protect the crops from destruction by wild animals and harvest their crops at ease in shorter period of time.

The Naga villages having locational stability could follow land-use plan in accordance with the community's perception of sustainable use of the valuable resource of land. According to T.C. Hodson, "Each Naga Village possesses a well-defined area of territory not only of cultivated and terraced land but of *Jhum* and waste land as well"[24].

This was possible because of the Naga system of land management and distribution. Traditionally all the villagers had access to village land reckoning it as community land. The Chief of the village distributed land for Swidden cultivation among the villagers in consultation with the village elders. No villager could be deprived of his access to Swidden land and ousted from the village by the chief on his own. Only the village council of elders could take such a decision to punish any villager for committing any serious crime for defiance of village council's directive, if any. There was no system of payment of any rent to the chief by a villager for enjoying access to Swidden land. Of course every hill farmer had to pay a house tax to the government every year.

Compared to Naga village the Kuki villages in the hills of Manipur in the nineteenth century were less stable as the Kukis continued to migrate further northward. Moreover, the art of settled cultivation was still not acquired by them. They were almost wholly dependent on Swidden cultivation for subsistence. The Kuki village chief was very powerful. The entire area of village land was owned by him. He allotted plots of forest land to individual families on receiving payment of rent in kind. He had the power to eject from the village individual families who were unable to pay the high amount of rent charged by him. He was also the religious leader of the villagers. All these features reflected the existence of an autocratic system of rule of the Kuki chief. And in this respect the Kuki village organization was vitally different from the Naga village organization.

Moreover, an average Naga villager was economically better off than an average Kuki villager. This was so firstly because individual ownership of land was recognized which ensured an incentive to produce more. Secondly, the Naga villagers had already adopted some diversification of production activities as they practicised both swidden (shifting) and settled cultivation. Thirdly, they made planned use of village land for ensuring better and sustainable use of the same. Finally, the villagers were free from any exaction of rent by the village chief.

The hillmen's economy in the Manipur hills was not an insular subsistence economy. They produced cash crops like oilseeds, cotton, pepper, ginger etc. Parts of such produces were traded with the Manipuris to procure salt, iron tools and agricultural implements, fire-arms, glass beads, utensils, brass and bell-metal ornaments, livestock, Manipuri quilts, cloths, etc. The hillmen also exported to the plains forest products and a few household industry products like cloth, mats and baskets. The manufactures of their household industries and trading of goods are non-swidden economic pursuits of the hillmen. These activities augmented their incomes and resulted in acquisition of some assets. Normally the hillmen did not dispose of their surplus rice, if any. They developed techniques of building rat-proof and weather-proof granaries and pots for storage of grains to meet the shortage of grains in the wake of crop failure due to natural calamities which were not infrequent in the hills.

10. Sources of Energy

Sources of energy harnessed by a people indicate the level of technological development achieved by it. And this sets a limit to the possibilities of expansion of productive economic activities and further incomes. The earliest source of energy in all societies was the human engine. Next came the harnessing of animal power to relieve human power from performing many strenuous activities and also to raise human productivity in many spheres.

(i) Animal Power

The Manupuris harnessed buffaloes and also bullocks for productive agricultural activities and also for driving carts. But the buffalo was 'most highly prized' becasuie 'one buffaloe performs nearly double the quantity of work that two

Bangalee bullocks are capable of executing.'[25] Pemberton has estimated that in 1835 there were about three thousand buffaloes in the whole valley. This buffalo population was not enough to meet the demand of the farmers. Therefore, 'the less wealthy cultivators', observes Pemberton, 'are compelled occasionally to avail themselves of the services of the despised bullock, which in Muneepur attains a size and symmetry of figure very superior to those of the Bengali cattle.'[26]

The Manipuris were quite famous in that period of history for their wealth of ponies. They were of small height, normally about 12 hands (4 feet). But they were very strong and hardy. Manipur raised a formidable cavalry using the ponies as mounts. Riding their ponies the Meiteis played the game of *Sagot Kungju* which was the forerunner of the game of polo that the British officers developed taking the cue from it. Manipur's ponies were in great demand outside Manipur. Unrestricted export of ponies from Manipur, however, made them almost extinct finally.

Elephants caught in the forests were tamed and trained mainly for the King and nobles to ride. These were also used for transporting timber and other loads. Ivory was used for making artistic crafts and it was also exported.

(ii) Heat Energy

Heat energy is most commonly used for cooking food, heating rooms in the winter, iron smelting and in manufacturing several articles, such as, salt, tools, weapons and other useful items - iron, gold and silver jewellery, metal as well as earthen pots and utensils, etc. Woods as the main source of heat energy was used as a fuel wood and charcoal. Manipur had large forest wealth and hence the supply of wood as the source of heat energy was adequate to meet the growing demand for it.

For purpose of lighting, vegetative products such as oil extracted from oilseeds and wood, mainly pinewood, were used. Bee-wax was also a source of light energy.

Later mineral oil, which had to be imported from Burmah and Assam, became another important source of energy. Acetylene gas was used for the lighting arrangement in and around the palace and the approach road to the palace.[27]

11. Transport System

Level of development of the transport system is crucial for the expansion of productive activities and also creation of wealth and augmentation of income in a country. The system covers the network of roadways, waterways, railways, airways, etc. and various other means of transport. In the nineteenth century, roads in Manipur were only a few and only some of its rivers were navigable. Foot paths across the open plains and through forest served as the most common lines linking different parts of the kingdom for movement of persons and transporting goods.

The main road was that which linked Silchar in Cachar of British India with Imphal, capital of Manipur covering a distance of about 165 kms. This road was completed only after Anglo-Manipur relations became closer following the trade and defence agreement entered into by the two parties in 1833 (vide, Chapter 20). The construction of this road was a joint venture of the British and Manipur governments. The technical expertise and supervision was the responsibility of the engineers of the British Government while Raja Gambhir Singh made available labour force for the work. After 1865 the maintenance of the road became the responsibility of Manipur government. Bullock carts could ply on this road carrying full loads. This road became the vital channel for flow of goods and movement of persons and livestock between Cachar and Manipur. Armies also moved along this road up to the border of Burma. The road crosses some rivers, the larger ones of which were spanned by cane hanging bridges during the rainy season.

Within the boundaries of Manipur there were only two other roads : one connecting Imphal with the foot of the hills and the other connecting Imphal and the salt wells.

This road network was quite meagre for promoting productive activities and trade. Most of the transportation of goods from one place to another was handled by human labour. Even when armies moved their ration, ammunition, baggage etc. were carried by labour. For this purpose the King engaged labour under the *lallup* system, that is, without making any payment. On many an occasion the British authorities asked the Raja to provide them with large gangs of free labour to aid the movement of British troops for mounting military expeditions on the hill areas. The whole arrangement was a locking in of huge human labour force for unproductive activities.

Transporting goods by boats in the navigable rivers was of insignificant proportion. Canoes hewn out of single trees of great size were used for the boat races during Manipuri festivals and state celebrations. Building of boats was, in fact, a skilful manufacturing activity carried out by the Lois who were concentrated in a few villages.

Palanquins, locally termed *dolais*, were used for passenger traffic mostly within Imphal town. But this mode of travel could be used only by the Raja, members of the royal family, nobles and high officials.

12. Manufactures

(i) Cotton Textiles

The Manipuris produced a number of consumer and simple capital goods both for internal use as well as for export. Cotton textiles woven by Manipuri women included Khesh cloth of coarse quality, muslin of fine quality worn as scarfs by women, muslin of a little inferior quality used for turbans and jackets and a variety of colourful dress materials. Johnstone, who served as political agent in Manipur, acclaimed Manipuri women as highly skilled weavers who in many cases completely killed out the manufacture of cloths formerly peculiar to certain of the hill-tribes, over whom the Manipuris had obtained mastery by superior intellect.[28]

(ii) Silk Textiles

Manipur produced a considerable quantity of silk textiles. Pemberton has praised Manipuri silk cloth for their strength, and the brilliancy of their colours. Petticoats, jackets, and large scarfs were made of silk cloth for use as dress by both women and men. Embroidered silk cloth was in great demand in Burmah. Silk cloths were also exported to Cachar in British India.

Leaves of mulberry plant were the sole feed of the silk worms. Mulberry plantations were raised in just five villages on the western and north-western borders of the valley close to the hills. Silk culture was the exclusive occupation of the

Lois, reckoned as a low professional caste. This fact stood in the way of extension of silk culture in Manipur. For, any family which would take up silk culture would lose its social status and become a *Loi*. About three hundred persons were engaged in silk culture in the 1870s.[29] Each such person had to pay a tax of three hundred rupees for pursuing this profession. Of course they were exempted from rendering from free labour service under the *'lallup'* system. The weavers of silk cloth were a separate professional class known as "kubo". The kuboes wove silk textiles by procuring raw silk from the *Lois*.

(iii) Iron tools manufacture

Iron ore was found in Manipur in the form of Titaniferous Oxydulated Ore in the beds of small streams south of Thobal river and in the hills near Lengatel. As mentioned by Pemberton in his report of 1839 the manipuris had developed indigenous technology to locate iron ore deposits in hills and river beds and to smelt iron from ore and manufacture a number of tools and implements. It was easy to discover the whereabouts of iron deposits in the hills as grasses covering them almost invariably look withered an indication of their existence. For hitting the iron ore deposits in river beds a unique technique was used. At the end of the rainy season when the river bed becomes siltless, a skilled workman thrusts his iron spear into the ground and lifting it out of the bed checks if the iron spear head has any small particles of iron ore adhering to it. If so, it was concluded that iron ore existed there. The iron spear head can attract iron ore particles only if it acquires magnetic property. And it so does presumably because when it is not in use, the owner keeps it away by vertically inserting it into the ground in his courtyard. According to Pemberton's estimate the proportion of recovery of iron from ore through the smelting process amounted to fifty per cent which was quite satisfactory.

The iron works were run mainly in three villages under the direction of one chieftain named Boodhee Rajah. These works turned out axes, hoes, ploughshares, spear and arrow heads, long iron blades used as *dao* with wooden handle, etc. This profession was limited to a few families only whose members inherited the skill.

(iv) Leather manufactures

By the middle of the eighteenth century the Manipuri artisans learnt the technique of tanning leather. It involved extracting the tanning chemicals from the barks of trees found plentifully in the local forests. The end product of leather was of very good quality with which a number of articles were made, such as, saddles, shoes, belts, pouches, etc. mainly for the use of the army men. Commonly, hides of deer and calves were processed into leather for such manufactures.

(vi) Pottery

Manipuri potters produced cooking and other utensils using metals, such as, brass, copper, bell-metal, clay and even stone. Various pots such as cooking pots, water pitchers were also made of clay. Even sandstone was used to make eating bowls which were 'artificially blackened.' Such stone pots were beutifully polished.

(vii) Jewellery

Metal jewellery works were a small cottage level industry in which some artisans were self-employed. They turned out gold ornaments, such as rings, bracelets and necklaces. They also made armlets of brass and bell-metal which were chiefly bought by the hill men.

13. Professional skills of the Manipuris

Manipuri artisans acquired admirable skills in several fields. Their professional skills as carpenters was highly prized in Cachar and Sylhet in British India. Brown has observed that the good Manipur carpenters were capable of 'turning out first rate works', and could 'imitate English work successfully.'[31] Manipuri turners produced artistic wood carvings and articles of ivory. They could also turn out articles of silver, glass and knew the art of electroplating. In praise of their technical skill, Brown has said that Manipuri artisans could 'make good serviceable locks' and could 'at a pinch repair and clean a clock.' James Johnstone has also noted the high calibre of the Manipuri artisans, who were patronized by the Kings in their pursuit of mechanical arts. In his words : "He (Maharaja Chandrakirti Singh) had a great taste for mechanical arts of all kinds, and a vast fund of information which he had acquired by questioning....... He had glass manufactured in his workshops, and once sent me a petroleum lamp, every portion of which was made by his own artificers" (1987 : 70-71). He further mentions : "I had several pieces of silver work made to try the mettle of the Manipuri silversmiths, one bowl, a most perfect copy of a Burmese bowl with figures on it in high relief, was beautifully executed."[32]

Manipuri artisans gifted with highly artistic and technical skills were almost exclusively employed for the production of articles to meet the demand of the royal court. In fact many of them worked in the palace workshop where articles were fabricated in accordance with the Rajah's preferences, and under his guidance and instructions. It was a situation of monopolistic demand of the king for the services of the most skilled workers of the different professional groups. Such groups constituted exclusive caste like formations. Because of this exclusiveness number of such skilled artisans remained very limited and so also the quantum of their outputs.

The state, nevertheless, followed the policy of protecting and patronizing Manipur's cottage industries. The government levied customs duties on all articles imported into the state and also on a few articles exported out of Manipur. These duties were the most important source of King's revenue in terms of money. The British government approached the Rajah through the political Agent to withdraw the import and export duties so that the volume of trade between British India and Manipur could be augmented. During his tenure as Political Agent, Johnstone succeeded in persuading the Manipur Durbar to lower the rates of import duty in the case of goods which were not produced in Manipur.

As for the import duties on cloth, Johnstone endorsed the Durbur's policy in consideration of the fact that the imported coarse cloths 'entered into competition with the excellent manufactures of Manipur' which he wished to see preserved in all their integrity.[33] Johnstone even appreciated the fact that while in Assam indigenously manufactured chintzes were lost for lack demand in the face of cheaper mill made products which were available in plenty, in Manipur the production of colourful and fine cloths was kept up, thanks to a Native Court encouraging production of such fineries, urged by tradition and taste.[34]

14. Money and Exchange

In the mid-nineteenth century, a large number of Manipuri households left far behind the subsistence mode of production. Imphal grew into an urban centre. Its population in 1881 was 60,000. People living in Imphal, besides the king and his nobles and their families, depended on supplies of many goods produced in the rural areas. In some spheres labour specialization in the production process of goods emerged. Some groups of producers produced exclusively non-farm items of goods. As a result the process of exchanging goods for goods in some cases, and of exchanging goods for money in certain other cases evolved in Manipur's economy. Transaction of goods took place in the markets spread over different parts of the valley. The market places were in the open, that is they had no roofs over them or on shop houses built in the market. Only women had access to the market both as sellers and as buyers. The citizens and the traders also required money to meet certain claims of the king including his claims in regard to a few taxes and duties.

Obviously monetary transactions could not take place without coins or currency notes. But no system of banking and issuance of currency by an authority existed. Coins - *'sel'* issued by the Raja and British and Burmese silver rupee and smaller coins, such as, four-anna and two-anna pieces circulated in the market. As Brown has noted, the rate of exchange of 'sel' for British or Burmese rupee varied between 420 and 450 'sels' for one rupee (1975 : 89). 'Sel' was made of bell-metal weighing about sixteen grains. Bell metal was imported from Burma in the form of gongs etc. and also occasionally from British India. Amount of 'sel' coined by the Raja depended on the demand for it. It was offered to the members of the public in exchange for goods or other coins in circulation. Burmese rupees would be obtained by exporting goods to that country. The supply of British rupees came from trade transactions and from expenditures incurred by the British civil and military establishments located in Manipur. The British government also started paying 'a monthly stipend of five hundred Sicca Rupees to the Rajah of Manipur' with effect from 1834 as compensation for making over the Kubo valley of Manipur to Burma. Manipuri women, who carried out trade in the market, were very familiar and attached to the bell-metal coin 'sel'. Therefore, when about 1865 the Political Agent in Manipur made an attempt to introduce copper coins getting a large quantity of the same supplied by the British Government, it failed. Manipuri women in the bazaars positively refused to have anything to do with copper coin and so it had to be returned.[35]

Monetization of economic transactions in Manipur was already quite extensive. The impact of market forces of demand and supply on the value of money was also evident from the fact that around 1878 or 1879, Manipur was afflicted by a monetary crisis. James Johnstone was then the Political Agent in Manipur. According to him, speculators in Imphal hoarded 'sel' in order to push up its value in terms of silver rupee. Though a large number of transactions was rupee-based, prices of goods quoted were always in terms of 'sel' and amount of rupee to be paid for any good was calculated by converting the number of 'sels' into number of rupees at the prevailing rate of conversion of rupee vis-à-vis 'sel'. Therefore in that situation value of rupee in terms of 'sel' fell drastically. It created panic and 'the bazaar was in an uproar, and business ceased.' The crisis was overcome by minting and issuing a large quantity of 'sel' by the Manipur Government on the advice of the Political Agent. The exchange rate between 'sel' and rupees that had gone down to 240:1 rose to 400:1 and the market transactions came back to normalcy.[36]

This incident could be taken as an indication that the linkage between the economy of Manipur and that of British India already reached a significant level. During this crisis initially the transectors having rupees in their possession suffered. And mostly the British subjects, such as, Indian traders and the civil and military staff of the British Government positioned in Manipur had to offer rupees to purchase goods in Manipur. So they suffered since the purchasing power of rupee fell. No wonder, the political agent took up the matter up with the King of Manipur and pursuaded him to issue a large quantity of 'sel'. The king also fixed the exchange rate which was 400 'sel' for a rupee. Had he not done it, ultimately Manipuri producers would have also suffered as effective demand for their products would continue to remain low causing fall in price and employment opportunities.

NOTES AND REFERENCES

1. Fernand Braudel (1986), *Civilization and Capitalism 15th - 16th Century,* Vol. I, The structures of Everyday Life : The Limits of the Possible, William Collins Sons & Co. Ltd., London, p. 24.
2. *ibid.* p. 25
3. *ibid.* p. 145
4. *ibid.* p. 145
5. R. Brown (1975), *Statistical Account of Manipur and the Hill Territory under its Rule,* first published in 1874, reprinted in 1975, Sanskaran Prakashak, Delhi, p. 87.
6. Braudel, *op. cit.*, pp. 145-158.
7. *ibid.* p. 149
8. *ibid.* p. 151
9. *ibid.* p. 151
10. R. Brown *op. cit.*, p. 8-9
11. James Johnstone (1987), *Manipur and the Naga Hills,* Reprint edition by Gian Publishing House, Delhi, p. 98
12. R.B. Pemberton (1993), *Report on Manipur, 1835,* reprinted in Naorem Sanajaoba (ed.), *Manipur, Treaties and Documents (1110-1971),* Mittal Publications, New Delhi, p. 30.
13. *ibid.* p. 31
14. *ibid.* p. 26-27
15. James Johnstone, *op. cit.*, p. 108
16. R.B. Pemberton, *op. cit.*, p. 35
17. R. Brown, *op. cit.*, p. 78
18. James Johnstone, *op. cit.*, p. 116
19. R. Brown, *op. cit.*, p. 78
20. *ibid.* p. 78
21. R.B. Pemberton, *op. cit.*, p. 23

22. R. Brown, *op. cit.*, p. 5
23. *ibid.* p. 85
24. T.C. Hodson (1984), *The Meitheis*, Reprint edition, Neeraj Publishing House, New Delhi (first published by David Nutt, London, 1908), p. 57.
25. R.B. Pemberton, op. cit., p. 31
26. *ibid.*
27. Gangmumei Kabi (1991), "Imphal - A short Historical Account", published in Lal Dena *op. cit.*, p. 204
28. James Johnstone, *op. cit.*, p. 97
29. R. Brown, op. cit.,p. 90
30. P. B. Pemberton, *op. cit.*, p. 29
31. R. Brown, *op. cit.*, p. 90
32. James Johnstone, *op. cit.*, p. 220
33. *ibid.* p. 116
34. *ibid.*
35. R. Brown, *op. cit.*, p. 89
36. James Johnstone, *op. cit.*, p. 123.

19
MANIPUR'S POLITICAL - ECONOMIC SYSTEM UNDER THE RAJAS

Until the British occupation in 1891, Manipur was constitutionally a monarchal state. The Raja enjoyed almost absolute power to rule. The constitution of Manipur was nothing but the codification of the royal edicts. He dictated and enforced the terms and conditions for enjoyment of a limited measure of civil liberty and property rights by his subjects. These were conditional upon the different inputs of production, such as, labour supply including self-labour, land and other natural resources, outputs turned out by them as well as upon different items of immovable and movable assets of individuals and groups of individuals. The nature, extent and effectiveness of enjoyment of property rights granted to people largely acted as their own incentives to produce beyond the subsistence level. The King benefited from increased volumes of production of goods and services, which brought him revenues in the form of taxes – both in cash and in kind – duties, levies, etc. that went up. He devised administrative, bureaucratic and military structures to keep up the system and ensure collection of land revenue, taxes, duties, levies and free labour services as much as possible.

What served people as the incentives to production and the rendering of services by them – both civil and military – to the King were not only dependent on the prospects of the share of the fruits of their labour they would enjoy but also on their ideological commitment to serve the King. But the absolute power of the monarch to collect revenues from the earning of his subjects was similarly, somewhat moderated by ideology. There were other limitations as well of the King's power. He had to appoint agents as administrative, judicial and military functionaries to run the state and realize taxes, revenues and labour services on his behalf. It was not quite possible always for the King to constrain his agents fully whose interests did not completely coincide with that of their master. No wonder, at times the King's agents colluded with the subjects to appropriate parts of the revenue collected by them instead of handing over the entire collection to the King. As the monopoly firm's powers to monopolize profits are constrained by the threat of potential competitors to enter the industry, the King's monopoly of power could not but be limited because of the threat of invasion by neighbouring states and / or 'potential rulers within his own state'I.

Powers of states tend to change with the growth of population and 'developments in military technology'. With the acquisition of more power the King seeks to enlarge the size of his Kingdom by conquering other lands so that he can earn higher volume of monopoly rents as growth in size causes growth in territorial specialization and exchangeII.

A King's power to conquer other lands is dependent on his power to mobilize his army men and army officers for the purpose given the military technology at their command. In Manipur besides the prospects of material rewards to be reaped from such ventures and few punishments to be suffered for lacking fighting ability and suffering defeats, the ideology of the people too served as an inspiration to fight for their King and the state. Before the emergence of the nation states, ethnic loyalty, religious faiths, etc influenced the group behaviour in support of or opposition to their rulers.

The structures of political and economic institutions built by the Kings of Manipur over the centuries crumbled as Manipur was devastated and depopulated during the Burmese occupation of the Kingdom from 1819 to 1826. On becoming the King of Manipur in 1826 Gambhir Singh had, therefore, to rebuild the system without, of course, any marked deviation from the traditional structure. The salient features of the renovated structure are known from the writings of Brown (1975), Hodson (1975), Johnstone (1987), McCulloch (1859) and some Manipuri scholars[1]. Brown,

Johnstone and McCulloch have recorded their accounts as they observed them in operation during their respective tenures as Political Agents of Manipur in the post-1826 period.

1. The System of *Lallup*

The Command structure of the King over manpower, for harnessing it for both military and civil services, represented the most basic and vital component of the political-economic system. It was so both for the rulers and for the ruled. The system of *lallup* was devised to make it compulsory for every man aged between 17 and 60 years to render free services to the state for ten days in every forty. As an individual attained the age of 17, he became entitled to have one *purree* of cultivable land (roughly 3 acres or 1.21 hectares of land) for his own support. He had, however, to pay tax in kind to the King for that piece of land. The system had some flexibility; an individual could avoid rendering *lallup* service for the required period when his turn came by providing a substitute for him or making payment of a certain sum of money to someone or to a group of *lallup* workers who would agree to do the work assigned to him under *lallup*. This money was not payable to the state but only to the workers who substituted for him.

Also, a man suffering from serious illness or afflicted with permanent disability before attaining the age of sixty was exempted from *lallup* duty. For such exemptions, of course, the permission of the authority had to be obtained by furnishing satisfactory evidence of permanent illness and/or disability.

According to Brown, *lallup* system was first introduced during the reign of Paikhomba (1666 – 1697)[2]. Originally it was meant for drafting the able-bodied subjects for military duties under the King. Hodson, therefore, interpreted the system as a synonym of 'military organization'[3]. Actually all civil and military duties were covered by the system. And in times of peace emphasis was placed on public works. *Lallup* workers were also commissioned to meet the personal needs of the King, members of his court and nobles, relating to building and maintenance of the palace and running of workshop. The tribal subjects living in the hills were also required to render free *lallup* services for enjoying access to forest and hill lands for shifting or terrace cultivation in accordance with their traditional community management system. Military duties did not simply mean fighting; carrying military supplies, ammunitions, etc. was also covered by the *lallup* system. Many public works, such as, construction of public roads, bunding of river banks, channeling the flow of streams for irrigating paddy fields, were managed with *lallup* labour.

Under the royal edict that codified the constitutional structure of the statc, Manipur valley was divided into six *pannas* or divisions to facilitate administration and management of the *lallup* system and its functioning.

Besides *lallup,* there was also the system of division of professional functions or occupations among the specified households known as *yumnak_mashin.* Some families were assigned the work of maintenance of temples and worshipping of deities (as priests), some were categorized as weavers, some dyers, some artificers, goldsmiths, blacksmiths, carpenters, brass and bell metal workers, etc. Different surnames of the families were accordingly decreed by royal edicts. The seven *salais* (clans) were divided into 538 *yumnaks* or surnames[4].

A significant modification of the *lallup* system particularly related to military organization was effected by Gambhir Singh when he raised (with the assistance of the British) and commanded the Manipur Army for successfully defeating the Burmese in the campaigns of 1824-26. Gambhir Singh maintained this highly professional and well-equipped military unit outside the operation of the *lallup* system.

2. The Lois; the Kei-roi-thau

Manufacturing pottery, silk-culture and silkcloth manufacturing, boat-making, salt-manufacturing, iron-smelting, distilling of yu (country liquor), cutting of posts and beams of timber, making canoes, cutting grass for the Raja's ponies, etc were exclusively operated by the *Lois* caste having the status of the lowest caste or division in the society. About their origin Hodson states as follows: The Lois lived in the villages which were some distance away from Imphal. These villages had been under subjection of the Meiteis for a long lime. There is one *Loi* inhabited village called Sengmai on the Manipur-Kohima cart road about nine miles off Imphal. They moved there from the south. Fayeng Loi, "preserves a tradition that they once occupied the site of the Konung or Fort from which they were driven out by Pakhungba, which means the rise of the Meitei power. Andro Loi, a village in the vicinity of Fayeng, claims the same orgin"[5].

Some of the Loi villages were used as penal colonies or places for deportation as a punishment for the captives taken during raids on Naga villages, or for the vanquished Manipuri rebels against any ruling King or by opponents of the movement for embracing Hinduism initiated by Gharib Nawaz, etc. Curiously enough, the Loi villagers were comparatively prosperous in the state, 'for the reason that, untramelled by caste prejudices, they are able and allowed to practise industries which were denied to the Meitheis'[6].

Another class of people named *Kei* (originally slaves of the Raja) also suffered on account of their very position in the society. Their duties were to provide and pound rice for the Raja's household. Earlier this task was not that heavy or unbearably burdensome. But later, that is, in the 19th century, the supply of rice under this arrangement became insufficient. To resolve this problem, a new system called *Kei-roi-thau* or work of *Keis* and *Lois* was introduced. It was not confined to supply of rice alone; any work or the supply of any other article could be demanded under orders of the Raja. This arbitrary and oppressive system was commonly resented.

3. Occupational classes of population

Within the *lallup* system the structure of each of the occupational divisions of the population was built by royal edicts. These divisions were not absolutely rigid, some flexibility having been permitted in order to meet the needs of the King and his household and also of his court. Occupational divisions were linked with hierarchical groupings of population on ethnic lines. McCulloch's study shows that the population of Manipur was divided into the following descending order of hierarchy: the Meithei, the Phoongnai, the Tengkhul (Naga), the Ayokba (captured slaves made to work for the Raja), the Kei, the Loi and the

Mahommedans. The Meithei population was divided into four groups called 'Punnahs', in order of superiority. They were 'Kaphum', 'Lai phum', 'Ahulloop' and 'Niharoop'[7]. Persons belonging to these *punnahs* had to do their assigned duties for every ten days in forty.

The Phungnai 'class' was grouped into two Pannas, one group served as the bearers of *hukas* (smoking devices) of the Raja and of other royal dignitaries, the other group worked as watchmen. Each such group was further divided into several sub-groups exclusively for attending to the needs of the King, the queens and of other close relations of the Raja. 'The real servant class' performing these multifarious duties belonged to the Phungnai class. For organizing and overseeing their work there were seven grades of officers.

The Meitheis belonging to different Punnahs performed under the *lallup* system duties exclusively, such as house-building, bridge-building, boat making, including collecting timber for such building activities. Some of them worked as artificers, goldsmiths, silversmiths, blacksmiths, carpenters, workers in brass and bell metal utensils and manufacturers of royal clothes. And some worked as keepers of Raja's elephants, ponies etc. and as suppliers of firewood.

The Brahmins were also required to perform duties for the king and the state under *lallup* system. They cooked for the Raja and his god Govindjee. 'In fact, excepting the lowest description of service, there is scarcely any which is not performed by some part of the Meithi population'[8].

McCulloch further notes that all the heads of the Punnahs were appointed by the King who selected them from among his trustworthy favourites 'without reference to their origin'. No fixed pay was paid for any such duties. But some officers were entitled to *loce-il*, that is, to services of an attendant or a number of attendants, who were required to perform any work that the officer concerned might ask them to do. The *loce-ils* naturally abhorred this kind of servile attachments to such officers and some of them secured freedom from bondage of this nature by paying a sum of money to a person of his choice who would be willing to work as a *loce-il* in his place.

Like ordinary classes of workers the officers in charge of

different activities were also divided into distinct classes each having a specific ethnic name. For example, "In the villages or hamlets occupied by Lois, especially the twelve salt villages, the chief village official is the *hanjaba,* but then these villages are under the care of the Thumjaorungba or overseers of salt, a *lallup* department of some importance"[9].

4. Ethnic groupings of the Meitheis

The Meitheis comprised an amalgam of seven clans, or *Saleis,* namely, Ningthaja, Kumul, Luang, Angom, Moirang, Khabananba and Chenglei. Each of these clans comprised a number of sub-clans called Yumnaks, which varied from 115 in the case of Ningthaja, or royal clan, to 17 in the case of Khabananba. Originally there were ten saleis, three out of whom with the passing years in history became extinct. Each salei was originally under a headman designated as the *Ningthou* or King of the clan. Within a clan, inter-marriage was not permissible. In the past each clan "occupied definite areas, as we know to have been the case with the Moirangs who still preserve a considerable degree of independence and autonomy and are mainly settled in the immediate vicinity of their eponymous village"[10].

There was noticeable similarity in the organization of hill-tribes who had sub-divisions bearing Meithei names, such as Ningthaja, Kumul, and Luang. The Lois, notes Hodson (ibid), were divided into clans 'in much the same way and intermarry with other Loi villages if the industry of those villages be identical with that of their own'. The Meitheis living in those Loi villages which originated as penal settlements were accorded a higher status than the ordinary Lois. They could grasp 'a chance of asserting their fidelity to Hinduism'.

5. Slavery in Manipur

Another institutionalized form of employment of labour without having to pay wage was the system of slavery. Brown, McCulloch, Hodson, et al have observed that slavery in Manipur was of milder form and not comparable with that in the western countries in respect of harshness in treatment of the slaves. Mainly there were two classes of slaves in Manipur : (i) some had to become slaves in order to repay the debt taken from their would-be masters. And they remained so until the debts they incurred along with interest were fully repaid; (ii) A similar kind of bondage could be the fate of a person who in a state of utter helplessness, needed money to defray some unavoidable expenses for which he would approach a man of resources and offered himself to be his slave. These slaves, or more appropriately, bonded labourers would be fed and clothed by their owners. There were cases of parents in abject poverty selling their children for money to avoid starvation. Such slaves lived almost as members of the family and they were generally treated well by their masters. Cases of ill-treatment have been also there, or how else could one explain the instances of slaves running away from their owners' houses? Some even escaped into British Indian territory where they were immediately set free.

Some people became slaves because, poor as they were, that was the only way open to them to escape paying compensation decreed by a court of law for committing some specific crimes. When a thief was caught but the stolen goods could not be recovered from him, he and other members of his family could be seized and sold. They would be performing duties as slaves until these became equal in monetary worth to the worth of the stolen goods. A defaulting debtor and the members of family might face similar fate. Also, any culprit involved in a case of adultery, who was unable to meet the claim for damages, would be subjected to slavery[11].

The Raja himself had battalions of slaves numbering from 1200 to 1500. The social classes of such slaves after they were liberated came to be known as *Ayokpa, Tengkul* and *Kei.* When rulers changed, the slaves of the outgoing rulers, according to the traditional practice, were redistributed among the incoming rulers. Sometime in the 1860s, the King ordered that the slaves would remain the property of their owners under all circumstances[12].

All slaves in Manipur were broadly grouped into two classes: "the one, the absolute property of the buyer, called *meenai chanaba* (meaning "to belong to and be fed by a man"), the other *asalba*, or a slave for such time as the money paid to him, or advanced on him, may not be paid back"[13].

As always, slavery in any form depresses labour efficiency

and productivity. It does not only severely restrict civil liberty but also narrows the space of choice of the persons in bondage and thereby hampers development.

6. *Singlup* (Wood Club) or Village Panchayats

In the villages in the Manipur valley there were 'wood clubs' called singlups headed by the village chief. These clubs, according to Brown, were somewhat similar to the panchayats in Bengal. For the *singlup* adjudicated minor disputes among the villagers. One of the main functions of the *singlup* was to provide a kind of social security for the very poor and destitute villagers. Food and succour were provided for the utterly impoverished villagers by the *singlup*. In their sickness they were looked after by the same body and after their death, provision of wood etc for cremation and performance of the last rites was taken care of by the wood club of the village. Evaluating the functions of the wood club Brown concludes: 'although many of the inhabitants are very poor, actual starvation or fatal neglect is rendered impossible'.[14]

7. The Land System

The British Political Agents like Brown, McCulloch, et al have characterized the land system of Manipur under the Rajas as one based on the basic premise that all the land belonged to the King and he had the absolute right to allow anyone any amount of land to be used for any specified purpose on terms and conditions to be laid down by him. At the same time he had the right to withhold this permission. The system of land-holding prevalent in Manipur is noted as follows.

Under the *lallup* system each adult male got one *puree* or 3 acres of land for cultivation on payment of the prescribed tax in kind. This way land was directly cultivated by the individuals for their livelihood, and this way they contributed to the augmentation of revenue of the state. The Rajas also made grants of land to officials and favourites either for a specified period of time or for life time. In some cases such lands granted to them were heritable by the recipients' descendants. On such lands also normal rate of tax in kind was payable. However, the King's relations, Brahmins, and sepoys were exempted from paying land tax up to a fixed proportion of land specified in each case, but for land above that limit tax was payable.

According to Brown's estimate about one-third of the total area of land was cultivated under the direct system, more than one-third was held by the members of the ruling family, Brahmins and sepoys and the rest, less than one-third of the land, was in the possession of the village headmen, officials, etc 'who held it by favour from the raja'[15].

The rate of tax payable in kind to the Raja was variable in kind even though theoretically it was a fixed one. Brown observed that tax actually varied from two baskets to thirteen baskets of paddy for each *purree* (3 acres) of land. One basket contained roughly 60 pounds or approximately 27 kg of paddy. "It is said that", writes Brown, "two baskets which nominally should only be taken from every one alike, is realized from favourites, and that the average from others may be set down at twelve baskets yearly; this is seldom exceeded, except in rare emergencies, as war, etc. This, again, will apply to land cultivated for the raja or held by those subject to lallup"[16].

The system of letting out land to tenant cultivators by the intermediaries, such as, the officials, family members of the King, Brahmins, who received grants of land from the King but did not cultivate the fields themselves, was also there. In these cases appropriation of rent from the tenants was 'more severe', as it could be as high as twenty-four baskets (that is, 648 kg.) for one *purree* (or 3 acres) of land[17].

As Brown estimated (ibid;86), depending on the quality of land, one *purree* of land in those days yielded between 100 and 200 baskets (i.e., 13 thousand and 26 thousand kgs.) of paddy[18]. The average annual yield per *purree* or 3 acres of land was estimated at 150 baskets or 4050 kg. In such a condition appropriation of 13 baskets or 351 kg of paddy might not appear too high but as the rate of rent formally proclaimed by the state was 2 baskets or 54 kg of paddy, every extra basket taken was an undue exaction which became an issue of grievance as noted by Brown during his time (1867-1875 A. D.). But such resentments did not assume serious proportions as in the absence of any proper survey of land and maintenance of land records on the basis of such a survey, the tillers of the land in many cases actually held land, the area of which was more than the standard measure. Brown recorded that sometimes the actual size of a holding was nearer double that of the standard measure.

Realizing the importance of conducting survey of land, a decision was taken by the King in 1868 to take up the work of land survey. But people did not like the move. There were charges that the surveyors were prone to bribery, many of whom were not also properly qualified for surveying land. Several surveyors were actually punished for accepting bribes for manipulating survey results.

8. The Role of Civil Society in Regulating the Land System

The land holding system discussed above was clearly inequitous and oppressive for the ordinary tillers of land. These shortcomings affected the incentives to them to produce more and bring more land under cultivation. The whole system was based on the premise that the King was the sole proprietor of all land. The British Political Agents like Brown and McCulloch and many others as well accepted this position as the true reflection of reality. Hodson, however, questioned such a stand taken by the British officers. He asserted that the people themselves were not in agreement with this theory 'in the blunt and unqualified manner in which it is stated by the native authorities, most of whom were interested witnesses'.[19]. He opined that all non – arable land were communally and jointly held and managed, and only the cultivated fields were individually held. He cited some evidences in support of his stand. For example, villagers protested strongly against 'the unrestricted alienation of land by Manipuris to Muhammedans and other persons of alien descent' and vigorously denounced the 'speculative tricksters', who took out leases for the waste lands near outlying villages and charged exorbitant rent for grazing or grass cutting'[20]. Hodson found the Manipuri village system quite strong and effective.

The community's role in maintaining the sacred groves and managing the access of the people to the common village lands which were not individually held seems to have been an effective one. This was an indication of the role the civil society played in containing the absolutism of the state power.

The inequitous, unjust and corrupt land system thwarted the extension of agriculture in Manipur valley. About one-half of the valley land was cultivable out of which only one-fourth was under cultivation[21]. The oppressive system of *Kei-roi-thau*, that is, the power of the state to demand of any individual to provide rice and other articles for the state was also a disincentive to bring more land under cultivation even though more irrigation works were completed under the King's orders with a view to extending agricultural activities to new areas. People's voice or the will of the civil society ultimately prevailed and the system was modified which encouraged people to bring more land under cultivation, as noted by Brown.

"It has been ascertained from all sides that within the last few years, more especially, cultivation has been considerably increased; water-courses have been extensively constructed, the survey is being still carried on, and with more satisfaction to the people, and the *Kei-roi-thau* has been so modified as to be no longer a cause of dissatisfaction to the cultivators"[22].

9. Position of Women in Society, Economy and Civil Society

The Meitei women have been the solid bastion of traditional Meitei culture and civilization. The Meitei Kings were engaged in almost constant warfare with the neighbouring powers and the hill men of the hills flanking the Imphal Valley. Under the *lallup* system, every Meitei male aged between 17 and 60 was required to render free services to the King for ten days in every forty. Besides, every male member could be conscripted by the King for waging wars with other powers. This was possible because the Meitei women, who were extremely industrious, used to perform the productive activities related to agriculture, animal husbandry, cottage industry and internal trade, besides the domestic chores. These constituted the mainstay of the Meitei economy and that was why the role of women was of vital importance in keeping the superstructure of Meitei state going and expanding.

Rice was the main agricultural crop which was grown

mainly by using the method of transplantation of seedlings. Women worked in the paddy fields from early morning, preparing fields, sowing seeds, nurturing seedbeds, transplanting seedlings, weeding, etc. These activities were generally performed by women of a particular village in groups, in accordance with the system known as *Khutlang*[23]. For harvesting crops, which called for mobilization of a large work force, men joined women to complete the work quickly. Kitchen gardening for growing vegetables both for self-consumption and for exchange fell within the sphere of women's activities.

They did the work of feeding domestic animals such as, cows, buffalos, ponies, goats, fowls, ducks and pigeons and took care of them.

Meitei women have been traditionally very good spinners of cotton yarn and weavers of cloth. Every woman irrespective of the family's political and economic status, took part in these activities. Every family's common requirement of cloth was met by these materials prepared by women of the family on their own looms.

Selling surplus agricultural, horticultural and household industrial products and buying goods for family's consumption and meeting other needs fell within the exclusive domain of women. In fact the markets were run by women themselves. As the Meitei women worked more hours in farming than men it was a "female farming system' as defined by Ester Boserup[24].

The gamut of women's activities further included 'embroidery,' rice pounding, fishing and helping in house-buildings etc[25].

Traditionally Meitei women value cleanliness. They keep their houses spick and span and the courtyards clean. Clothes and utensils are regularly washed. The level of sanitation and hygiene in Meitei villages is therefore generally good.

Despite the important role played by Meitei women in productive and other activities which constituted the core of Meitei culture and civilization, their status in society was not commensurate with that. They had little say in the decision-making process whether in the affairs of the family or those in larger spheres of society and the state. The position of women in society was affected by the custom of polygamy, common among the well-to-do Meiteies. The treatment of women by their husbands according to Brown brought in a kind of 'domestic slavery' for them. He observes: "Women are really the slaves of their husbands; they are sold in satisfaction of their debts, and it is said that men often pawn their wives to purchase some office or even a pony"[26]. Meitei personal law weighed heavily against the interests of women. Personal law was based on the *Puyas*, i.e., the accepted law or the command of the ancestors. This has been stated in detail by Sanabam Raghumani in his paper, "Mee tei Personal Law' which claims:

"The husband is the master and is entitled to deal with the women in the light of his title inherited in his cattle or slaves"[27]. Inheritance of ancestral property was traced through the male line (P. 343). A Woman's property in Meitei law could consist of the presents given by her parents at the time of or after her marriage, "Movable property", records Raghumani, 'is woman's real property' (P.341). Any property (movable) given to a wife by her husband after her marriage with him could be retained by her at the time of divorce from her husband. A piece of property purchased with a woman's own property remains her property. The basic deprivation of women related to the fact that they had no title to land even as the 'female farming system' obtained conspicuously in Manipur.

Without playing down social infirmities of Meitei women, it may be asserted that the energy, skill, the spirit of enterprise and hard-working habits of the Meitei women found release in their all pervasive activities and were expressed in increased production of goods and services in the farm and non-farm sectors and in spheres of trade, as they were not confined behind any 'purdah' and they enjoyed the rights of free-mixing and unrestricted movements in the fields, roads and markets. Women's contributions to the growth of Meitei economy as reflected in increased production of goods have been very high. Their participation in trade and exchange served as an important incentive to production of surplus over family's own consumption needs. And this propelled growth and accumulation of wealth to a considerable extent.

Launching of movements organized by women to protest against state policy and to influence state actions and policies at different points of time both before and after 1891 marks an important feature of Manipur's economic history. In the configuration of Manipur's civil society women's mass movements stand out as a landmark in Manipur's economic history.

10. Deficiencies of the System

The architectural core of the political and economic institutions was the extraction of labour under the systems of *lallup* and slavery. Since *all* the male adults of the population were required to work on projects and sites as directed by the royal authorities concerned, there was little scope for assigning work to an individual according to his capability, skill and efficiency. As a result, naturally optimum or near optimum utilization of human resource was never obtained. What is more, this arrangement had a bad impact since it suppressed the spirit of enterprise, initiative on the part of people and acquisition of higher skills and development of technology by them. This aspect has been aptly highlighted by McCulloch:

"Under the operation of *laloop*, a good artificer works along with a bad one, and receives no more thanks for his work than if it were as bad as that of his less skilful associate. He becomes disgusted, and his only aim is to amass quickly, by his superior intelligence, enough to purchase his release from work. This done, he thinks no more of his trade. Thus all are for ever at the rudiments and no progress is made"[28].

James Johnstone, who was Political Agent in Manipur from 1850 to 1886, has praised the operation of *lallup* for building roads, digging canals and execution of 'great public works for the benefit of the state'. He argued that in a sparsely populated 'poor state' where government revenue was meagre and the wage rates were often comparatively high, it was almost impossible to carry out many much-needed public works on payment. Another justification for the system according to him was that the cultivating farmers had spare time on their hands which was profitably utilized and 'for the benefit of the community at large'[29].

It is true that many public works were completed by

utilizing compulsory labour under *lallup* but the proportion of labour put to such works was in most of the cases less than that for meeting personal and private needs of the King, the members of his household, royal court and officials. Many a time *lallup* labour was employed for carrying arms, ammunition and provisions of the army. Even for the British army movements such unpaid labour was employed. In fact, the practice of getting work done without payment was built into the whole political and economic system so that the value structure of labour power suffered distortion. Labour exploitation was much more harmful to the development of human resource potential than the benefits derived from the execution of some public works.

11. Wealth Accumulation

In an agrarian economy land is the basic item of property which the people would primarily like to possess. In this respect the position has been regulated as an adjunct to the system of *lallup*. Under that system the average size of a farm was around 3 acres of land which yielded very little surplus after paying the land tax and other charges levied by the King from time to time. Therefore, the possibility of accumulation of wealth by the agricultural farmers was very limited. Only a few farmers could afford to acquire cattle – an important productive asset complementary to that of farm land. The total stock of cattle wealth was meagre and stealing of cattle was 'a common offence in the country'[30]. In the manufacturing sector also the artisans were subjected to strict restrictions on occupational mobility and to taxation so that saving of income and accumulation of wealth could not but be negligible.

Prospects of accumulation of wealth largely depend on the environment of peace and security in the society. The political and social organization of Manipur state was overwhelmingly geared to launching wars against the neighbouring hill-tribes and defending against the Burmese invading armies time and again. The economy of Manipur was repeatedly devastated by the Burmese invaders, the latest disaster they suffered from their invasion being that of 1819 to 1826. Such a milieu cannot be conducive to the accumulation of productive wealth. People, who could afford, turned to hoarding their savings in the form of gold or in forms of other precious durables which could be kept hidden from the marauding invaders and King's officials. This happened on a considerable scale in Manipur.

Once while riding along the road near Imphal, Johnstone noticed 'a deep hole freshly dug in the side of a hill'. On enquiry he learnt that during the Burmese invasion a number of Manipuri refugees before fleeing their country buried their treasures in such a manner as would not be discovered by the invaders or others. On return to his homeland a refugee or perhaps his descendant dug up holes 'in search for treasure buried during the Burmese invasion by a relation, who had left an exact description of the spot as a guide to any of his descendants who might return'[31].

Rules of inheritance of private property, movable or immovable, also reflect the general climate of accumulation of wealth.

Hodson noted that the chronicles of Manipur did not help to ascertain the rules of inheritance of private property. But he maintained that land was regarded as held at the will of the ruling power of the state. Regarding movable property, the general practice, it seemed to Hodson, was 'to provide for the sons during the life time of the father'. After his death it was the youngest son who was 'the heir general if at the time of father's death' he was still living in the ancestral home[31].

Manipuris generally tended to be improvident because it was 'politically unwise to possess the reputation of wealth in a country where the conditions of life are as unsettled as they still are in many respects in Manipur, and those who held high offices, had to spend freely to maintain their position which might be at any moment taken from them and disposed of to a higher bidder'[33].

These were the reasons why credit supply was so limited. There was no institutional arrangement for dealing in credit. Both demand for and supply of credit were on a personal level. Demand for credit was hardly related to productive activities. It was mostly for meeting emergent needs, such as those for basic necessaries for survival and social obligations to observe rituals and religious ceremonies. In such circumstances, the rate of interest was obviously very high. The Government, of course, legally compelled the debtors to fulfil their obligations. Hodson noted that if the amount borrowed was not repaid within a year the debtor had to pay a hundred per cent interest on it. He further observed that 'either as a result of this rule, or even perhaps as the cause of it', the Manipuris had a 'bad reputation for neglect of their obligations'[34]. And as already noted, when making a study of the system of slavery, in many a case an insolvent debtor would meet his obligation by becoming the 'slave' of this creditor. The law of the country as was enforced by its courts permitted this practice.

NOTES AND REFERENCES

1. Douglas C. North (1981), *Structure and Change in Economic History*, W. W. Norton & Company, New York, London, pp 25 – 27

II. *Ibid.* p. 208

1. (i) R. Brown (1975), *Statistical Account of Manipur*, reprint edition, Sanskaran Prakashak, New Delhi.

   (ii) T. C. Hodson (1984), *The Meitheis*, reprint edition, Neeraj Publishing House, New Delhi.

   (iii) James Jnonstone (1987), *Manipur and the Naga Hills*, reprint edition, Gian Publishing House, New Delhi.

   (iv) W. McCulloch (1859), *Account of the Valley of Munnipore, and of the Hill Tribes*, Calcutta (our references are based on the quotations in others' works).

   (v) Gangmumei Kabui (1988), *Glimpses of Land and People of Ancient Manipur*, Published in Naorem Sanajaoba (ed), *Manipur : Past and Present*, Mittal Publications, Delhi.

2. R. Brown, *op. cit,*. p. 83.
3. T. C. Hodson, *op. cit.* p. 59.
4. Gangmumei Kabui, *op. cit.*, p. 307.
5. T. C. Hodson, *op. cit.*, p. 65.
6. *ibid.* p. 10.
7. *ibid.* p. 63.
8. W. McCulloch, *op. cit.* quoted in Hodson, *ibid*, p. 63.
9. T. C. Hodson, *ibid*, p. 72.
10. *ibid.* p. 73.

11. R. Brown, *op. cit.*, p. 91
12. *ibid.*
13. *ibid.* p. 90.
14. ibid. p. 92.
15. ibid. p. 86.
16. *ibid.* p. 86.
17. *ibid.* p. 86.
18. *ibid.* p. 86.
19. T. C. Hodson, p. 87.
20. *ibid.*
21. B. Brown, *op. cit.*, p. 86.
22. *ibid.* pp. 86-87.
23. Ksh. Bimola Devi, "Manipur Women – A Study", published in Sanajaoba (ed), (1988), *op. cit.*, p. 167.
24. Ester Boserup (1970), *Women's Role in Economic Development*, George Allen & Unwin, London, p. 16.
25. Bimola Devi,, *op. cit.* p. 167.
26. R. Brown, *op. cit.*, p. 77.
27. Sanabam Rahgumani (1988), "Mee tei Personal Law", Published in Sanajaoba (ed) (1988), *op. cit.*, pp . 329-348.
28. Quoted in T. C. Hodson, *op. cit.*, p. 22.
29. James Johnstone, *op. cit.*, p. 114.
30. T. C. Hodson, *op. cit.*, p. 88.
31. James Johnstone, *op. cit.*, p. 126
32. T. C. Hodson, *op. cit.*, p. 77.
33. *ibid.* p. 78
34. *ibid.* pp. 89-90.

20
ECONOMIC RECOVERY AND GROWTH FROM 1826 TO 1891

Manipur's economic recovery at the end of Burmese occupation in 1826 proceeded alongside streamlining of the administrative structure and some liberalization of *modus operandi* of economic transitions as carried out under the British influence and even pressure at times. The British policy *vis-à-vis* Manipur was shaped by the objective of seeing Manipur as a strong defence base against aggressive designs of Burma on the eastern parts of British India. They also sought to use the territory of Manipur to open an overland trade route to Burma and therefrom to the Yunnan Province of China. In pursuance of these policies the East India Company's Government became increasingly involved in nurturing closer political and military ties with the King of Manipur and reached an agreement with him to facilitate and promote flow of trade between British India and Manipur and also Burma with Manipur's co-operation.

1. British-Manipur Trade and Defence Agreement of 1833

The Anglo-Manipuri relations in this period culminated in signing a trade and defence agreement between the British Government and Gambhir Singh as the King of Manipur on 18th April, 1833. The Rajah of Manipur agreed not to obstruct the 'trade carried on between the two countries by Bengali or Mannipore merchants' and not to exact heavy duties or to make a monopoly of any article of merchandise. He further agreed not to prevent 'the Nagas inhabiting the Kalanaga and Noon-jai Ranges of Hills from selling or bartering ginger, cotton, pepper and every other article, in fact the produce of their country, in the plains of Cachar, at the Banskandu and Oodharban bazaars, as has been their custom.' Under a previous agreement the British Government transferred to the Rajah of Manipur its control over these two ranges situated between the eastern and western bends of the Barak river.

With the help of the King of Manipur the British Government took up the project to construct a road from the eastern bank of the Jiri river, which separates Manipur from Cachar, to the valley of Manipur via Kalanaga and Kowpoom hills. This, claimed the British, would boost the intercourse that was already in existence between the territories of the British Government and those of the Rajah. This would be beneficial to both the Rajah and the people of Manipur. Therefore, the Rajah was required under the agreement 'to furnish a quota of Nagas to assist in the construction of the road.' More importantly, the Rajah assumed the responsibility for maintaining the road after it was completed so as to enable bullocks with goods loaded on their backs to pass during the cold and dry seasons alike. He also agreed to render every assistance that the British officers in charge of constructing this road might require.

The other part of the agreement enjoined that the Rajah, in the event of a war with the Burmese necessitating the movement of government troops through Manipur into Burma, would provide the British with hill porters to assist transporting the ammunition and baggage of troops. Moreover, 'In the event of anything happening on the Eastern Frontier of the British territories, the Rajah will, when required, assist the British Government with a portion (sic.) of his troops.'[1]

The road constructed to connect Cachar with Manipur facilitated movement of goods and persons between these two areas; it also opened up the possibility of trade with the Burmese. The resulting growth in business transactions and exchange of goods and services led to an increase in productive activities and in occupational specialization among the Meiteis. The raising of the Manipur Levy was an important step toward introducing professionalism among soldiers as against the earlier system of *Lallup* under which the adult male Manipuris were to render free military service as and when the King required it. Gambhir Singh was allowed to maintain an army of 3000 troops who were trained and equipped by the British Government. This development made a further dent into the traditional system of exacting free military service.

Manipur's economy had passed through a long period of near stagnation after the death of Garib Nawaz in 1749, since the Kingdom was gripped by a state of relentless political instability, strife and unrest. The situation severely worsened when the Burmese invaded Manipur in 1819 and continued to devastate and plunder Manipur's resources and assets up to 1826. The people of Manipur dubbed the period from 1819 to 1826 *Chaki Taret-Khuntakba* (Seven Years' Devastation). Manipur's population fell to about 10,000 persons, as many men were killed or taken away as slaves by the Burmese. Many fled Manipur and took refuge in Sylhet, Cachar and other neighbouring areas. Agricultural production decreased drastically and much of the fertile valley lands became uncultivable having had an overgrowth of grasses, weeds, bushes, etc.

Eight years of peace and stability during the reign of Gambhir Singh were the years of reconstruction of Manipur's economy. Many of those who fled Manipur returned to their homeland, increasing areas of agricultural land were reclaimed and brought under cultivation by clearing weeds, grasses, etc. The damaged roads were repaired, new roads were constructed, old markets reopened and new markets opened, trade flow between Cachar and Manipur and that between Manipur and Burma increased in volume as some of the trade restrictions were withdrawn. The Nagas were allowed freely to bring down again their cash crops like ginger, cotton and pepper with a view to exchanging them for goods they were in need of in some designated markets, such as, Banskandi and Udharban bazaars. Construction activities were undertaken on a wide scale to rebuild the villages that were destroyed. Moreover, the king also built a new capital at Langthabal about 8 kilometers south of Imphal. Besides the King's palace, the headquarters of the Manipur Levy was also located there.

The basic parameters of Manipur's political and economic institutional structure remained more or less the same excepting for some minor changes carried out under the British Government's instructions. Added to this were the resilience, industry and ideological commitment of the people to work hard for collective good of the Kingdom of Manipur that helped rebuild Manipur's economy within a short period. The signs of economic growth could well be seen in the growth of population, movement towards further specialization and diversification of productive activities, raising of new crops, increasing volume of monetization of transactions, commercialization of agricultural production, increasing volumes of internal and external trade, etc.

The only setback to the economic progress of Manipur was the handing over of the Kabaw Valley by the British Government from the possession of Manipur to that of Burma in 1834 with effect from 9th January. It is a fertile valley covering an area of 1200 sq. miles and is even greater in size than the Manipur Valley having an area of 650 sq. miles. As a state grows in size, it achieves economic growth also as a consequence of 'growth of territorial specialization and exchange'.[2] And the opposite happens when a state shrinks in size. Although the level of territorial specialization and exchange in Manipur of Gambhir Singh's time was low, yet the Kabaw Valley having good timber forests besides fertile cultivable lands had significantly augmented resource base and volume of agricultural and cottage industry products. Payment of a fixed amount of six thousand rupees by the British Government to the Manipur Rajah to compensate for this loss was clearly inadequate in the short run and in the long run it became insignificant as its value eroded on account of inflation. Moreover, Manipur was deprived of the gains resulting from rise in revenue yields as the economy of that part prospered. Significantly, Maharaja Gambhir Singh suddenly died on the very day the valley was transferred to Burma.

2. Posting of British Political Agent in Manipur, 1835

The British intervention into the affairs of Manipur did not stop with the transfer of Kabaw Valley in 1834. In the following year, that is 1835, the Governor General of India appointed a political agent and posted him to Manipur. He was to ensure safeguarding of British interests in Manipur and also to mediate between Burma and Manipur in order to avoid any border disputes between the two.

Over the years the *de facto* powers and influences of the Political Agents grew as they had to intervene in settling disputes among the princes over succession to the throne. The ruling raja often looked to the Political Agent for support in retaining his throne. As representative of the powerful British Government whatever the stand taken by the Political Agent and his opinions and views on the affairs of the state carried some weight.

The process of modernization and liberalization of institutional frame overarching the organization of economic activities were initiated by the Political Agents. The degree of effectiveness of such interventions obviously depended on the personality, character and tact of the Political Agent concerned in articulating suggested changes before the Raja and his Durbar.

After the death of Gambhir Singh in 1834, Manipur became the scene of intermittent feuds and bloody conflicts among the different claimants for succession to the throne. This state of turmoil, instability and near anarchy continued unabated until Chandrakirti Singh, son of Gambhir Singh, who was an infant in 1834, 'succeeded gaining possession of the throne' in 1850 and was recognized as the Raja of Manipur by the British. Even after this several armed attempts were made till 1866 by some members of the royal family to dethrone Chandrakirti Singh, who with British backing succeeded in overthrowing these challenges.

During India's War of Independence in 1857 Chandrakirti Singh took an open and unequivocal stand for supporting the British with his troops and officers in suppressing that movement. In recognition of his services and express loyalty to the British Government the King was presented with 'a dress of honour, a sword and a belt'. Since then, Anglo-Manipur relations grew closer as years passed. Chandrakirti was ultimately Knighted.

During the long reign of thirty-five years (1850 to 1886) Chandrakirti Singh had to deal with repeated and frequent raids and attacks committed by the neighbouring tribal groups, such as, the Angami Nagas, Mizos, Sootie Kukis and Chasad Kukis. In suppressing these onslaughts, he got help and guidance from the British. Also, with the latter's active involvement, the King succeeded in settling border disputes with the Mizos, Nagas and Burmese. He provided troops, coolies and provisions for the British during the second Anglo-Burmese war, which ended in the defeat of the Burmese and annexation of Burma to British India in 1885.

In those troubled times Chandrakirti Singh somehow was able to maintain the territorial integrity of Manipur state. The economy of Manipur during that turbulent period naturally took on the nature of a war economy. As a result, expansion of productive activities through application of all available manpower under the *Lallup* system was restricted. However, the growing interactions between the respective political agents and the King led to some minor institutional reforms – like easing restrictions on internal and external trade, building new roads, opening of one school, provision for training facilities for the artisans to enable them to acquire new and better skills, orderly settlement of the immigrant Kukis, etc. These measures directly or indirectly strengthened the economic base of Manipur.

As already noted in Chapter 19 land survey work was started in 1868. The persons engaged in conducting survey of individual plots were accused of taking bribes for manipulating the measurement of the actual area of a holding. Several such persons were punished having been found guilty of this corrupt practice. People, therefore, generally were opposed to the survey work for this reason. Brown observed that the reason for such opposition was that many individuals actually held land for cultivation measuring larger than the area to which they were entitled under the *Lallup* system. Finally the king ordered some modifications of the system so that it could be carried on 'with more satisfaction to the people.'[3]

Similarly bowing to popular resentment, the rigorous

rules of *Kei-roi-thau* (power of the state to demand of any individual to provide rice and other goods produced by him for the state) were also relaxed. These measures led to the extension of cultivation and consequently, increased agricultural production in the state.

In terms of the trade and defence agreement of 1833, a road was built from Cachar to Burma border via Imphal. During Assam's Chief Commissioner Elliot's visit to Manipur in 1879-80 a decision was taken to open a cart-road from Manipur to Kohima, headquarters of Naga Hills.

In 1881 construction of the cart road from Imphal to Mao on the northern part of Manipur bordering Naga Hills was completed. It was Johnstone, the Political Agent, who persuaded the King to agree to the construction of this vital road. This road ultimately joined the road that was built from Manipur border to Kohima, headquarters of the Naga Hills, and therefrom to Dimapur, the nearest rail station on the Assam-Bengal Railway.

There was also improvement in the condition of the Cachar-Imphal Road. Johnstone took the initiative in obtaining supplies of wire-ropes and tools required and also in securing services of engineers from the Government of India in order to replace in stages the twelve cane suspension bridges by wire-rope suspension bridges. The third important road was the one that connected the valley of Imphal with the Chindwin Valley in Upper Burma.

Development of these road communications and the British Government's policy prevailing upon the King, thanks to its Political Agent, to ease restrictions on imports and exports of goods helped augment Manipur's external trade. And with the growth of trade rose the incomes of people such as the producers, traders, workers, professionals, transport operators and administrators. Such a development augured well for the people at large since it not only opened up wider scope for choice for them but also enhanced their capabilities.

Particulars about the composition and volume of trade for the year 1873-74, (that is, before road communication through Naga Hills was established), as given in Administration Report of Manipur Agency for that year[4] indicate a fairly significant level of development of Manipur's external trade that flowed mainly along Imphal-Cachar road. The government levied a duty on all exports even as certain items of products were not allowed to be exported at all. These were : printed silk dhoti, laced pugree (head gear), *ningthon phi* (Manipuri shirt), and of course rice. Cows and bullocks were not exported even though there was no statutory ban on export of them. Excepting for a few items, imports of goods were subjected to an import duty. Accordingly, specific duties at varying rates were imposed on the imports of betelnut, American cloth, long cloth, Mull Mull, satin, swiss cloth, steel, carpet, brass, copper, thread, paper, soap, iron pan, nails, velvet Shantipur dhoti, Jaypooree chadar (wrapper), woollen chadar, and umbrella. But imports of books, bottles and phials, shoes, *namabali* (a wrapper on which are printed the names of gods), Vrindaban brass stamps and conches were duty free. An *ad valorem* duty at the rate of one anna (roughly 6 paise) per rupee was payable on imports of the items named as follows : looking-glass, *hooka* (hubble bubble), *hooka* stand, dyes, spices, pepper, sandal wood, cards, lace, buttons, sugar, tamarind, wooden box, iron dao, axe, knife, padlock, saw, and needles.

The more important items of export from Manipur in 1873-74 were ivory, wax, silk, dyed yarn, mosquito net, *saloo phanek* (woman's garment), bed sheets, Maring *phi,* lai *phi, chadar* (wrapper), *Kumlang phurit* (black readymade shirts), *thouree phi, lai-yeng* (silk wrapper of superior quality), thread carpet, *lasing phi* (padded cloth), silk dhoti, *silk phanek,* buffaloes, ponies and elephants.

In 1873-74, export duties on the following were at the rate stated itemwise : Ivory Rs. 5 per maund (1 maund = 37.32 kg.), wax Rs.2.5 per maund, silk 0.18 per seer (1 seer = 933.10 grams), pony Rs.20 each, Manipuri he-buffalo Rs. 9 each and she-buffalo Rs.10 each and Burmese buffalo of both sexes Rs. 9 each.

A perusal of Manipur's external trade reveals that even though the agricultural sector was the most important one, as nearly hundred per cent of the population took part in agricultural production activities for subsistence, none of the agricultural products was exported. Of course there was a ban on the export of rice even when surplus rice was produced. Hardly any other field crop was produced in excess of the local demand to be offered for export. Given the communication constraints and absence of facilities for preservation of perishable crops and lack of external demand for any other farm product, there was indeed no incentive to the farmers to produce extra for meeting external demand.

Fluctuations in crop productions were, however, caused by variable weather conditions – favourable or unfavourable. Significantly, one of the important items of export in the farm sector was livestock, namely, buffaloes and ponies. These were exported to Cachar. Such exports were prompted by external demand. So strong was the demand for ponies that to meet it the stock of these precious animals fell very low by 1877 when the ministers consulted the Political Agent (Johnstone) about it and obtained his consent to stop export of ponies for some years.[5] The relative importance of livestock export is evident from the fact that in 1868-69 out of the total amount of export duty of Rs.3533 collected by the government on exports to Cachar an amount of Rs.2900 was on exports of buffaloes; - Manipuri buffaloes accounted for (Rs.1500), Burmese buffaloes for Rs.500 and Manipuri ponies Rs.900.[6] In 1873 Brown recorded that trade in buffalo was stopped as its population fell owing to the outbreak of murrain, a highly infectious and malignant disease of cattle. Every year under licence given by the government, elephants were caught from Jiri Forest and some other wooded hill tracts, such as, Laimaton Range of hills. In 1868-69 sale of elephants caught in Jiri Forest fetched Rs.7000 for the government of Manipur.[7] Elephants were bought mainly for the purpose of taking them out of Manipur. This was indeed an important item of export from Manipur.

Revenue earnings from import duties were much less than those from export duties. For example, in 1868-69, while duties on exports to Cachar yielded Rs.3533, duties on imports from Cachar amounted to Rs.1975.50 only.[8] Political Agents implored the Raja to allow the essential goods not produced in Manipur to be imported and made available to meet the demands of the people of Manipur at affordable prices. "On the whole the duties on almost every article" observes Johnstone, "were lowered during my term of office, and the imports largely increased. Indeed, but for the cumbersome system of levying the custom charges, there would have been no grievance at all, and as it was, they hardly added anything to the cost of the articles when sold in Manipur, many of which could be bought for little more than the price paid in Cachar, plus the charge for carriage."[9]

Manipur's handloom industry run as household units began thriving again in the post-1826 decades. During this period, cotton and silk textile products and coloured yarns were among some major items of export. Exports of such articles boosted the growth of handloom industry.

Since Manipur was rich in forest wealth, forest products like wax and ivory were exported in considerable quantities. It appears, timber extraction from forests and its export did not yet become a significant phenomenon. In 1868-69, licence fee paid to the government for cutting wood, bamboo and cane amounted to only Rs.406.[10]

Manipur levied customs duties on all goods imported into the state and on some of the goods exported to British India. These duties constituted Manipur's major source of revenue earnings in cash; of course, the import duties provided some protection to local industries. Since the Government of India wanted to augment the flow of India-Manipur trade, James Johnstone, who served as Political Agent in Manipur from 1877 to 1886, persuaded the King and his Durbar to lower the rates of import duty on the articles not produced in Manipur. In the case of cloth, Johnstone "strongly advocated the duties being kept up, where, as in the case of coarse cloths the imports entered into competition with the excellent manufacture of Manipur which I wished to see preserved in all their integrity."[11]

Johnstone has recorded in his memoir that during his term of office in Manipur duties on almost every article were lowered resulting in the increased volume of imports of goods into Manipur from India. The systems of levying customs charges were somewhat cumbersome according to Johnstone which caused some resentment. The actual incidence of the duties was not, however, heavy since many an article imported was sold at a price just a 'little more than the price paid in Cachar, plus the charge for carriage."[12]

3. Revenue of The State

In the last phase of Chandrakirti Singh's reign total revenue of the state including the sum of Rs.6370 paid by the British Government every year to compensate for the loss of revenue sustained on account of ceding Kabaw Valley which was to an extent between twenty five and thirty thousand rupees. The receipts from different sources in 1868-69 were as follows (annas and pies ignored)[13] :

Table 20.1
Manipur's Revenue Receipts for 1868-69

1.	Duties on imports from Cachar	Rs.	1975
2.	Duties on exports to Cachar	Rs.	3533
3.	Duties on exports to Burma	Rs.	100
4.	Licenses for cutting wood, bamboo cane etc. from the Jiri Forest	Rs.	406
5.	By sale of elephants caught in the Jiri Forest	Rs.	7000
6.	Revenue realized from the Manipuri inhabitants of the valley varied between	Rs.	12000 and 15000 per annum
7.	Annual compensation paid by British Government for ceding Kabaw Valley	Rs.	6370
		Total	**Rs.31,384 to Rs. 34,384**

In 1873 collection of export duty was somewhat less than the normal amount since export of buffalo was stopped 'owing to the murrain in the country' (Brown, ibid). However, as thirty elephants were caught from the Limatol range of hills, proceeds from the sale of these elephants more than compensated for the loss in revenue by the stoppage of the trade in buffaloes.'[14] Data about annual expenditure of the government during these years are not available. Since hardly any savings or public debts of the government accumulated over these years, it is obvious that the amount of annual public expenditure was almost equal to that of revenue. The break-up of public expenditure is not available but circumstantial evidence would suggest that the major expenditures were under following heads: civil administration, military establishment and weaponry, civil list and material costs of public works including renovations of the royal palace.

4. Monetary Crisis

For the trading activities, in the absence of any banking system in operation and in absence of paper money, only coins were used as medium of exchange. The King of Manipur issued a coin called '*sel*' which served exclusively as the unit of account though the Indian rupee was also in circulation. In actual practice "large sums were paid in rupees, but the amount was always reckoned in '*sel*'.[15] In 1878-79 the normal rate of exchange was 480 *sels* for 1 rupee. But this rate, depending on the relative supply and demand of the coin occasionally fluctuated. With the increased volume of business transactions the demand for *sel* expanded. But some speculators hoarded *sel* so that its supply became short in relation to demand and under the pressure of the market forces the exchange value of *sel* went up. It hovered around 240 *sel* for a rupee. This fall in value of the rupee drastically reduced the purchasing power of those having rupees in their possession. Panic gripped the market and 'the bazaar was in an uproar, and business ceased.'[16]

Johnstone was the Political Agent in Manipur at that time. He met the King and explained to him "the very great injury" that this monetary crisis was causing the state's economy. As a remedy he advised the King to issue large quantities of *sel* to augment its supply in the market. It was done and the exchange value of the rupee was finaliy fixed at 400 *sels* for one rupee. This restored normalcy in business transactions in the country.

5. Food Shortage in 1879

Almost about the same time, that is in 1879, Manipur faced a shortage of rice, its production having been affected by natural forces. Price of rice in the market went up causing discontent among people. But by releasing rice from the stock maintained by the state the shortage was overcome and price of rice stabilized.

6. Development of Education and New Skill Formations

Creation of educational opportunities and training facilities for new skills was an important development during the tenure of Johnstone as Political Agent in Manipur. The first school was, however, started in 1872 'at the suggestion of Major-General W.F. Nuthall', the then Political Agent. To encourage pupils to attend school, the Government of Bengal sent books[17], maps, etc. worth about 400 to 500 rupees for their use. The King and his Durbar were not, however, enthusiastic about this move for the obvious apprehension that with the spread of education among people, the pressure for social, political and economic reforms would mount. As a result, the school was nearly closed.

The proposal for starting a school at Imphal was revived by Johnstone. He succeeded in obtaining the consent of the King to establish an English school in 1885. In the beginning, of course, only a small number of students attended the school. But their number slowly increased. Development of the modern institutional form of education had come to stay even though, contrary to expectations, women's education did not at that time make any headway.

As time passed some unfounded apprehensions about women's education died down and from the 1890s an increasing number of students – both boys and girls – began attending schools as more and more schools were opened.

Johnstone also took the initiative in persuading the Raja to agree to send some Manipuri artisans to Kanpur for training in the art of carpet weaving and manufacturing of leather goods of higher quality. About their achievements Johnstone observed : "............these men had long been making use of their knowledge in Manipur, and I found that first rate cotton carpets and boots, shoes and saddles of English pattern, had been manufactured for the Maharajah, the workmanship being in all cases creditable, and in that of the carpets most excellent."[18]

The Political Agent took an active interest in introducing simple technological improvements on labour productivity and in achieving qualitative improvements in the products turned out by potters, silver-smiths, gold-smiths and so on. The technical skill of Manipuri silversmiths impressed Johnstone very much. In his own words : "I had several pieces of silver work made (by them) to try the mettle of the Manipuri silversmiths, one bowl, a most perfect copy of a Burmese bowl with figures on it in high relief, was beautifully executed."[19]

It is difficult to get an accurate estimate of Manipur's population until the report of the regular census taken in 1872 is gone through. One's estimate of Manipur's population till then must be approximate or nearly accurate, considered in the light of three referential sources. These are : (1) B.R.Pemberton's Report on the Eastern Frontier of British India, 1835 (2) The Bengal and Agra Guide and Gazetteer for 1839 and (3) R.M. Martin's Statistics of the Colonies of British Empire, 1839. Their estimates of area, population and density of population are given below[20]:

Table 20.2
Manipur's Estimated area and Population as Recorded in

	Pemberton's Report 1835	The Bengal & Agra Guide and Gazetteer 1839	R.M. Martin's Statistics of the Colonies of British Empire 1839
1. Area in sq. mile	7,000	8,000	6,200
2. Population : Persons	20,000	30,000	50,000
3. Density of population (persons per sq. mile)	2.86	3.75	8.06

Source : *Census of India 1961 : Report of the Population Estimates of India*, Vol. V,: 1831-1840, Edited by Durgaprasad Bhattacharya, 1994. Govt. of India, New Delhi, p. 173.

During the Burmese occupation of Manipur from 1819 to 1826 its population severely declined as many people were killed or taken away as slaves by the invaders and a large number of Manipuris fled and took refuge in different parts of British India, including Cachar, Sylhet, Dacca and Nadia in Bengal. However, as the war ended many of the refugees returned and immigration of people other than Meiteis into Manipur from the West also took place, largely because the growing British-Manipur relations led to an increasing flow of trade and also because of the stationing of troops, officials and staff in Manipur by the British. All these brought about a steady rise in the State's population.

According to the Census of 1872, Manipur had a population of 126,000 and that of 1881, 221,070. So the average annual rate of increase between 1872 and 1881 was 7.5 per cent, while this rate between 1881 and 1901 (Population : 284, 415) was 2.8 per cent. Moreover, the level and spread of productive activities in the 1830s as recorded by the different authorities could not have been possible with 2.86 density of population (Pemberton's estimate), or 3.75 (Bengal & Agra Guide) or even 8.06 (as estimated by Martin) per sq. mile.

In 1840, there was an outbreak of cholera in Manipur which reduced the population by more than 3000 persons. Despite this fall in population at the normally possible rate of growth of population it was unlikely to rise from 50,000 in 1839 (Martin's estimate) to 126,000 in 1872. Therefore, the population estimates of the 1830s were flawed being underestimates. Bhattacharya too comes to such a conclusion.[21]

The technology of productive activities, whether in farming or in non-farming sectors, such as transport and cloth manufacturing – both cotton and silk – salt at salt-well pits, iron tools and weapons by smelting iron from locally available ores, pots and utensils – both earthen and metallic – leather goods etc. was highly labour-intensive, that is to say, labour-capital ratio was very high. Therefore, the level and growth of economic activities were critically dependent on the growth of labour-supply, that is, growth of population. Rise in the rate of acquisition of knowledge and skills by

Manipur's people also had influenced population growth in the state. But in the nineteenth century conditions in Manipur, the quantitative growth of population was proportionately of much more importance.

Ester Boserup[22] contends that in the pre-industrial economies, growth of population promotes technological change by making it possible to raise capital formation and volume of investments in expanding production. In such an economy, population growth is taken as an autonomous change.

In the light of these considerations, it is presumed that the steady increase in population from the 1830s to 1890s was an indication of the steady progress in productive activities. This trend was strengthened by certain other changes in the structure of Manipur's economy. Under the British persuasion some administrative reforms and easing of restrictions on the processes of transactions were carried out. Flow of internal and external trade increased. A few crops – vegetables and fruits – were introduced. A school was started in 1872. Later in 1885 a new English school was established in Imphal by James Johnstone, the then Political Agent in Manipur.

7. Level of Urbanization

Agricultural and allied activities were the mainstay of Manipur's economy. Therefore, the process of urbanization was almost absent. Viewed in terms of population, Imphal, the capital of the Kingdom, where resided the Raja, the Chief Officials, the Political Agent, etc. could be reckoned the only town in Manipur. Imphal's population was 35,000 as estimated by Brown in 1873. But according to the 1881 census it was 60,000. Excepting for the population concentration other usual features of an urban centre were absent. Referring to Imphal, Brown writes: "This village, for it is nothing more, covers a large extent of ground and contains a population of 35,000. The houses are constructed of wood and bamboo; some of them, however, especially within the enclosure where the raja resides, are of large size and height. Of brick buildings there are very few and comprise the raja's powder magazine, a gateway, a curious pair of symmetrical buildings forming part of the sides of the road leading through the centre of the raja's enclosure ..... and a few Hindu muts scattered here and there throughout the capital."[23]

Besides being an administrative centre, Imphal was also growing as a commercial centre. All road links of Manipur with Silchar, Naga Hills and Burma were connected with Imphal. Kooak Keithel (crow bazar) was at a place where the road from Silchar touched Imphal. The two most important markets in Imphal town were the women's market at Khawairamband and the Sadar Bazar. In 1869, Imphal was ravaged by a severe earthquake. All the brick buildings were razed to the ground. The Khawairamband market was also extensively damaged. But it was soon reconstructed. And in 1872 three new markets were opened, one at Singjamei, the second at Sanjenthong and a third of Heirangoithong.[24]

8. Epidemics

The rate of population growth was affected by the outbreak of cholera and of small pox in epidemic form every few years. The cholera epidemic in 1880 was particularly severe.[25] The Political Agents took the initiative in procuring vaccines and preventive and curative drugs from India in order to control epidemics. Despite official approval of a vaccination campaign to control the spread of small pox, the citizens were initially reluctant to participate in it. Over the years on the insistence of the Political Agents and having had experience of the preventive effects of small pox vaccination, people at large cooperated with the vaccination campaigners. As a result the epidemic of small pox was effectively controlled in Manipur.

To prevent the outbreak of cholera epidemic, the Political Agents persuaded the King and his Durbar to launch a campaign for raising public awareness about sanitation, cleanliness and keeping drinking water sources free from contamination. The cholera epidemic of 1880 was exceptionally severe. Import of appropriate medicines for the treatment of cholera patients by the doctors of the civil hospital established in the Political Agent's Residency also helped to control the cholera epidemic in the state to some extent. All these measures helped ensure positive rate of population growth.

9. Manipur's Economic Progress Under Chandrakirti Singh: A Summing Up

During Chandrakirti Singh's reign (1850-1886) Manipur enjoyed for long an unprecedented spell of peace and stability. This made it possible for the Raja and his Durbar to relax the rigidity of state regulations concerning economic activities to some extent. This happened, of course, under subtle and persuasive pressure of the Political Agents. As a result, outputs of farm and non-farm sectors increased, trade and commerce gradually emerged as a significant sector of economic activities and Manipur showed signs of expanding economic opportunities.

An important economic landmark in this period relates to the beginning of production of wheat as a new crop in Manipur. In 1870 growing of wheat in the cold season was started on an experimental basis in the state. In that year total production of wheat amounted to 25 maunds (933 kg.). Wheat was mainly consumed by the King, the nobles and family members, besides, of course, the British officials and some Indians located in Manipur. Since the experiment succeeded, the area under wheat was extended and by 1872 production of wheat increased to 250 maunds (9330 kg). Soon it became a problem to find more suitable fields for its cultivation in the cold season.[26]

Manipur, however, experienced widespread destruction of houses and buildings including the royal palace. There were damages to the Imphal-Cachar Road, large landslips, floods, uprooting of trees, etc. caused by the severe earthquake of 1869.[27] Though formidable, it was a temporary setback. Gradually Manipur rebuilt its damaged infrastructure and revived the production potential.

The overall picture of economic wellbeing of the people of Manipur in the 1870s is portrayed by the Political Agent (James Johnstone) in the Annual Administrative Report of Manipur Agency for 1877-78 (P. 13) as follows :

"After very careful observation I cannot but express that, strange as it may appear, the Manipuris generally seem to be quite as well off as the inhabitants of an average British district. Abject poverty is unknown." [28]

NOTES AND REFERENCES

1. Naorem Sanajaoba (Ed.), (1988), *Manipur Past and Present* Vol. I *History, Polity and Law,* Mittal Publications, Delhi, Appendix XV. pp. 466-67.
2. D.C. North (1981), *Structure and Change in Economic History,* W. W. Norton & Co., New York, p. 208.
3. R. Brown (1975), *Statistical Account of Manipur,* first published in 1874, reprinted in 1975 by Sanskaran Prakashak, Delhi, p. 87.
4. As quoted in R. K. Jhalajit Sing (1965), *A Short History of Manipur,* O.K. Store, Poona Bazar Road, Imphal, pp. 241-43.
5. James Johnstone (1987), *Manipur and the Naga Hills* (Reprint), Gian Publishing House, New Delhi, p. 117.
6. R. Brown, *op. cit.*, p. 88.
7. *ibid.*
8. *ibid.*
9. James Johnstone, *op. cit.*, p. 117.
10. R. Brown, *op. cit.*, p. 88.
11. James Johnstone, *op. cit.*, p. 116.
12. *ibid.*
13. R. Brown, *op. cit.*, p. 89.
14. *ibid.*
15. James Johnstone, *op. cit.*, p. 123.
16. *ibid.*
17. R. Brown, *op. cit.*, p. 93.
18. James Johnstone, *op. cit.* p. 220.
19. *ibid.*
20. Durgaprasad Bhattacharya (Ed.), (1994), *Census of India 1961: Report of the Population Estimates of India,* Vol. V : 1831-1840, Govt. of India, New Delhi, p. 173.
21. *ibid.* p. 176.
22. Ester Boserup (1965), *The Conditions of Agricultural Growth,* George Allen & Unwin Ltd., London.
23. R. Brown, *op. cit.*, p. 2.
24. Gangmumei Kabui (1991), Imphal – A Short Historical Account, published in Lal Dena (ed.), *History of Modern Manipur, (1826-1949),* Orbit Publications, New Delhi, p. 199.

25. Jhalajit Singh, *op. cit.*, p. 254.
26. *Annual Administration Report for 1873-74*, p. 13, quoted in Jhalajit Singh, op. cit., p. 245.
27. R. Brown, *op. cit.*, p. 95-98.
28. *Annual Administration Report of Manipur Agency, 1877-78*, p. 13, quoted in Jhalajit Singh, *op. cit.*, p. 260.

21
ECONOMIC CHANGES AND GROWTH FROM 1891 to 1947

Treating Manipur as their protectorate, the British Government intervened on several occasions to settle disputes among the scions of the royal dynasty over rival claims to the throne. Such an intervention in 1891 led to the fierce Anglo Manipuri War which resulted in the defeat of the Manipuris. Thereafter on 27 April 1891 the British virtually took over the administration of the Kingdom, even though it was not annexed to the British Indian Empire. The British Government permitted the reestablishment of native rule defining the position of the Raja as subordinate to that of the Queen Empress of India. An annual tribute of Rs. 50,000/-imposed on the Raja and his successors was to be paid to the British Government. It was further stipulated that the native state's existence *qua* native state would be 'dependent upon the loyalty and good conduct of the raja and his successors'.

In pursuance of this decision, they crowned the five year old prince Churachand Singh King of Manipur in April 1892,and a regency administrative council was constituted under the overall control of the Political Agent, Major Maxwell, while at the same time the minor King was sent to Mayo's College, Ajmer, for his education. The Political Agent was also made the Superintendent of Manipur State. Churachand Singh returned on completion of his education and attaining adulthood in May 1907, officially took over the administration of the state as the Raja of Manipur .Of course the de facto powers of administration were in the hands of British officers[1].

The British authority frequently prevailed upon the Raja and his Durbar to acquiesce in the constitutional, administrative and institutional changes that the former proposed to bring about.

The very arrangement of regency administration during the period from April 1892 to May 1907 enabled the British authority to introduce straightaway several administrative, judicial and basic structural changes in the state system. These changes had either direct or indirect impact on the manner of management of Manipur's economy. Such reforms had bearings on the scope and opportunities, which opened up for people's participation in economic activities, production of goods and services and distribution of the products among different sections of population.

On April 29, 1892, that is, the day of the investiture of the minor Raja Churachand Singh, Maxwell, the then Political Agent in Manipur and Superintendent of the state, announced the abolition of the system of slavery, proclaiming that "all persons at present in slavery to private individuals shall cease to be slaves in five years from the 29th April (1892), or any previous date on repayment of the purchase money"(for particulars about the system of slavery, vide, chapter 19 section 5 and also chapter 3 section 3.

The system was so deeply ingrained in the socio-economic structure of Manipur, particularly in rural areas, that it continued to operate there in some form or the other till the British paramountcy over the state came to an end in 1947[2]. It is obvious that in the absence of determined follow-up actions to liberate the slaves and to enable them to take up productive activities on their own, by providing necessary resources, the system could not be completely abolished. But then certainly, the formal abolition of slavery enabled many such unfortunate persons to breathe the air of freedom from bondage and with human dignity.

Simultaneously, the feudal practice of extracting free service from every male adult subject for ten days in every forty, known as *'lallup'* (vide, chapter 2 section 3 and chapter 19 section 1) was also abolished and in its place a new system of revenue collection was introduced. In accordance with it, in the valley a house tax at the uniform rate of Rs.2 per homestead and in the hill territory Rs.3 per household payable per annum were imposed. In the plains, in addition, land revenue was payable at a uniform rate of Rs.5 per pari (=$2^1/_2$ acres) of land held by a person under the decennial patta system which was introduced by the Regency Administration as in Assam." "According to this settlement, the tenants were conferred a permanent heritable and transferable right of occupancy so long as they paid the revenue due from them. Where a tenant was unwilling to take a ten –year patta annual pattas were issued which, however, would not convey any permanent rights in (sic.) the land held by the tenants"[3].

The records of the Darbar under the Raja indicated that in 1892 –93 the area of land cultivated in the state measured 26,708 'paris', i.e, about 66,770 acres, of which about 25,000 'paris' or 62,500 acres of land were available for settlement of the ryots leaving aside 4,250 acres that had been already granted to the Raja's officials and the police personnel. Granting each prospective tenant 2.5 acres of land on an average, under the new system, 25,000 pattas could be distributed. The Political Agent's report for 1892-93 reveals that the Government planned to distribute 24,000 pattas. The actual number of pattas distributed that year was much less, only 14,000 (1892-93: 8). About 25 per cent of settled land went into the hands of non- cultivating owners like the Brahmins, Rajkumars and State Officials. They in their turn sublet their lands to actual cultivators[4].

The system of realization of revenue in cash created for the tenants problem of meeting the government demands, as many of them could not yet earn enough amount of income in cash. This problem was compounded by the lack of land survey records and inadequacy of revenue collection system. Therefore, a survey of all lands was undertaken in 1898. When it was completed the actual areas of cultivable land proved to be measuring much more than what was earlier estimated. This also helped to detect the concealed acres of land cultivated by tenants. For the purpose of land revenue collection Manipur valley was divided into 4 divisions ('pannas') each of which was placed under one revenue-collecting functionary named *Lakpa*. He was entitled to a commission of 10 per cent of the revenue collected amounting up to Rs. 6,000/- and 5 per cent of collections exceeding that amount. This system yielded higher amount of revenue collection. But this also meant that quite substantial amounts of commission on land revenue went into the pockets of the *lakpas*. To enhance the state's share, the system of commission payment was replaced by that of appointing them on fixed salaries.

The changed land settlement system resulted in expansion of the total areas under cultivation from 90,000 acres to 1,41,104 acres in 1907[5].

The new land revenue system marked the end of the royal claim that all land belonged to the King in perpetuity and any individual could enjoy the right to use any land for any purpose as permitted by the King but without any right to transfer to any other individual. Patta- holding tenants could enjoy permanent right to hold any plot of land on payment of revenue to the state as required. This right was both heritable and transferable. Thus land, like any other commodity, became an exchangeable item. This change opened up the possibility of sub-letting land either on rent payment or on sharecropping basis. But such possibilities could arise only at a later stage in the event of land becoming scarce with the growth of population.

More importantly, the new system had not only augmented the amount of land revenue mobilized by the government but it had also facilitated the on-going process of monetization of transactions in the economy. The system of paying tax in kind and the barter system of exchanging goods and services are economically unsound, inefficient and growth hampering. Under the new system of collection of land revenue and house tax in cash, these two items emerged as the most important sources of revenue earning for the government. In 1903-04, out of Manipur's total revenue of Rs.395 thousand, land revenue alone yielded Rs.277 thousand and house tax, 46 thousand and the two together brought in Rs. 323 thousand or 81.77 percent of the total revenue[6].

In the earlier regime, the King and the Durbar members

and judicial functionaries, and the sepoys, 'to whom more than two-thirds of the whole land was granted (by the King) were exempted from paying land revenue'[7]. This practice was a necessary offshoot of the policy of non-payment of cash remuneration to the administrative and judicial functionaries as well as army personnel. In the new regime the system of paying remuneration for any service rendered to the state instead of making land grant freed considerable area of land from the possession of nobles and states officials, allowing for settlement of the cultivating tenants. This promoted agricultural production by expanding the area under cultivation.

Shortly after the subordination of Manipur by the British in 1897, the old palace compound was converted into a cantonment to which the Cantonment Act 1889 became applicable. The British Reserve was created in Imphal covering an area of 310 acres including the cantonment site. This was done purportedly to provide security for the British subjects living in Manipur who were often involved in clashes with the local people. Besides the cantonment, the Residency, the state police station, the post and telegraph office, the state treasury, the civil hospital, the state jail, the civil bazaar, etc were located within the Reserve. Later, with a view to extending the area of the British Reserve, some more area outside Imphal (at Kamgshup) was purchased by the British[8].

By establishing the civil jail, treasury, a civil hospital and a post office besides installing a telecommunication unit within the British Reserve the process of modernizing administration of law and justice, treasury management, provision of health services, postal and telegraph services etc were initiated. Expertise and efficient services of the Europeans appointed as state engineers, civil surgeons, and so on helped develop services for the better social condition of the people of Manipur. "Their efforts to improve the little state ", writes Jhalajit Singh, "in their respective spheres within the meagre resources placed at their disposal are worthy of admiration"[9].

The only hospital at Imphal town had 14 beds for treating indoor patients. In1904 all-told10, 000 cases were treated of which 300 were indoor patients and 400 were treated surgically. A total expenditure of Rs.4000/- was made on the hospital that year (Imperial Gazetteer, vol. VIII 1908: 195)[10].

In order to prevent the outbreak of small pox, a vaccination programme was taken up without making it legally compulsory. The people of Manipur who dreaded this disease were by and large cooperative. Only the Kukis resisted this move in the initial years. Their opposition gradually died down. The success of the drive could well be measured by the fact in 1903-04, 58 per 1,000 people of Manipur were successfully vaccinated. This was 'considerably above the proportion in Assam as a whole'[11].

The other important social development relates to the educational facilities offered. In 1885 the Johnstone Middle School was opened at Imphal. By 1903-04,the number of primary schools in the state went up to 29 including 2 located in the hills. The total number of students attending schools as on 31st March 1904 was 46 in the middle stage, and as many as1583 in primary schools[12].

During the period of administration of Manipur by the Political Agent, the system of financial management in the form of an annual budget was introduced. It indicated expected revenue earnings from different sources and approved amounts of public expenditures to be incurred on different items in the fiscal year. The principal items of revenue and expenditure in the budget for 1903-04 (Actuals) were as follows[13].

Table 21.1
Manipur's Budget for 1903-04(Actuals)

		Revenue (Principal item Rs. in thousand)		**Expenditure (Principal items) Rs. in thousand**	
1.	Land revenue	277	1.	State Works	148
2.	House Tax	46	2.	Civil list	50
3.	Fisheries	24	3.	Tribute to Govt. of India	50
4.	Forests	26	4.	Police	60

(Condt...)

	Revenue (Principal item Rs. in thousand)		Expenditure (Principal items) Rs. in thousand
5. Salt	6	5. Land revenue (administration)	28
6. Compensation received from Govt. of India for transferring Kabaw valley	6	6. Education	15
7. Others	10	7. Others	37
8. Total	395	8. Total	388

The system of showing the estimated annual financial transactions of the government in the form of a budget was a very important step towards streamlining the management system of the state's economy. From the budgetary trend some idea about the growth of production and the distributive aspect of such growth could be formed. The budget for 1903-04 clearly brings out the fact that the incidence of nearly 88 per cent of the state's revenue collections (on account of land revenue, house tax and fisheries) fell on the common people whose main occupations were agriculture and allied activities. Nearly 26 per cent of total expenditure was incurred on personal and household expenses of the Raja (civil list) and on payment of tribute to the British Government, which was quite a heavy burden on the people of Manipur.

The Budget allocations for state works (Rs.148 thousand) and education (Rs.15 thousand) were, however, helpful in furthering physical infrastructure and in the human resource development that could promote social and economic development of Manipur in the long run. In the prevailing conditions of subsistence level economic activities of the people, the main source of capital formation and investment should be public savings resulting from surplus revenue budget and from investment of that surplus for creating productive assets in the economy. But this prospect was bound to be nullified, as it was, by the fact that the state had to pay an annual tribute of Rs.50,000/- to the British Government.

1. Abortive plan for establishing a silk producing firm

In1902, Messrs A.Wright & Company, Calcutta, put up a proposal for establishing a silk rearing and spinning mill in Manipur and sought to enjoy the monopoly right of producing silk in Manipur. They were keen on entering into an agreement with the Manipur Durbar to formalize this arrangement. In the British officers' circle there were reservations about granting monopoly right to develop silk industry to a private firm. To settle the issue, the Director of Land Records and Agriculture, Assam (Hennikar), was deputed to Kashmir to study the conditions that favoured a state monopoly of silk growing there and to suggest if granting of monopoly right to a private firm would be beneficial to the growers and rearers of silk-worms, and cocoons and to the people of Manipur as a whole. Hennikar favoured granting monopoly right to the private firm subject to the condition that the Manipur state would retain powers of control and of inspection. This was approved by the British authority.

An agreement was signed by the parties concerned on 29 November 1906. This would be in force for a period of 30 years in the first instance. "The raja agreed that he would grant the land that might be necessary for the successful operation of the factory, free of land revenue. He also agreed that the state would not levy any tax or duty on any cocoons, silk or silk waste exported by the firm. In case of dispute, the decision of the Lieutenant Governor of Eastern Bengal and Assam would be final (and) binding on both parties"[14].

The British economic policy *vis-à-vis* the native states was not to provide any financial grant or to extend any direct support for mobilization of capital from the money market for investment in developing industries, social overheads, etc. The British officers, however, exercised supervisory and advisory role in regulating directly or indirectly, all financial and commercial deals between the native states and commercial and industrial firms coming from outside. The proposed plan for a silk rearing and manufacturing unit to be started by M/S A. Wright & Company, however, did not ultimately materialize presumably because they could not obtain any financial support or guarantee either from the Manipur Durbar or from the Government of India. Another reason might be the disturbed political climate in Manipur at that time, which dissuaded the Company from starting any industry in Manipur.

2. Women's Agitation 1904

Resentment against several oppressive measures taken by the British authority to extract free labour, fines and against other forms of exploitation of them was brewing since the British occupation of Manipur in 1891. It finally flared up into an organized agitation launched by the women of Manipur in 1904.

Immediately after the occupation of Manipur the British officers had not only disarmed the whole population but also used the members of the Manipur Army as unpaid coolies to fetch rations from Khuzuma, seventy two miles south of Kohima, for the British troops stationed in Manipur. Secondly, even as the Political Agent (Maxwell) pronounced the abolition of the *Lallup* system in1892, for the construction of Mao-Manipur road, nearby villagers were made to work on that project without any payment. Besides, Manipur was made to bear one –half of the cost of construction of the same road.

Thirdly, in addition to the annual tribute of Rs.50,000/- which the British authorities received, they also decided to realize a fine of rupees two and a half lakh from the state as a punishment for the disturbances of 1891. It was particularly alleged that at that time when the British had abandoned the residency, the Manipuri soldiers looted about one lakh and forty-eight thousand rupees from the treasury in the residency.

The fourth cause of resentment was attributable to the British policy of encouraging duty-free export of rice from the state to Kohima. This alarmed the people at the possible rise in prices of rice and a shortage in supply of rice for them in the event of a fall in its production. Such apprehensions were aggravated by the event of 6 July 1904 when all the 28 sheds containing 300 seats of Imphal's Khawairamband Bazar (Sena Keithel) were 'burnt to the ground'. This all-women's market was the principal centre of internal trade and commerce of Manipur. Its loss severely affected the system of business transactions, which those women carried out.

On 15 July two bungalows of the British officials were 'destroyed by fire' at night. Again on 4 August a third bungalow was gutted by fire. The British authorities considered these clear cases of arson. Some members of the Manipur gentry, particularly of the Rajkumar family, were suspected to have been involved in instigating such crimes.

The Political Agent and the Superintendent of the state passed orders on 30 September 1904 asking the Manipur inhabitants of Imphal to rebuild the destroyed bungalows by using teak wood, which was to be collected from the Kabaw valley by giving free labour for this purpose. To enforce obedience of the people of Imphal to these orders, it was further proclaimed that in the event of non-compliance, a punitive force would be stationed at Imphal the costs of which would be realized from the local people. Such punitive measures angered the people who held protest meetings and decided to flout the unjust orders. These agitations were suppressed by the British authorities with a heavy hand and the leaders of the movement arrested and put on trial.

Finally, Manipuri women power confronted the British power on the contentious issue of reconstruction of the damaged British buildings by the people of Manipur by rendering free labour and providing the building materials free. On 3 September 1904 thousands of women, collected at the Khwairamband bazaar, which was kept closed for this purpose, and marched to the residency to see the Political Agent and Superintendent of the State, Major Maxwell. They continued to mount pressure on the British authority staging demonstrations for several days despite police action against them. Many demonstrators were injured. But they succeeded in nearly paralysing the normal life in Imphal. In the face of such stubborn and organized agitation by the women, the British authority had to finally withdraw the orders requiring the Manipuris to rebuild the gutted buildings free of cost. This success was a great boost to the process of empowerment of Manipuri women. And women continued to play a very important role in business, farming and manufacturing (at the household level) activities in the state.

In 1907 Churachand Singh was formally installed as the Raja of Manipur. The Governor General of India in his proclamation on this occasion, advised the Raja to note that his position as a ruler was given to him not for his own sake or to enable him to derive means of pleasure for himself, "but as a sacred trust to be used for the benefit and welfare of your subjects". At the same time the British Government promulgated the Manipur Administration Rules for the creation of the Manipur State Durbar consisting of 3 Manipuri officers as members and the Raja as its President. One British officer was appointed by the Government its Vice-President, who actually played the pivotal role relegating the Raja's position almost to that of a titular head. Functions of the government were divided among several departments and placed under the respective members for administration for carrying out the decisions taken by the Durbar. The financial matters of the government were directly or indirectly controlled by the British Government[15].

Under the 1916 amendment of the Administration Rules proclaimed by the British Government, the King was delinked from the Durbar and formally placed above it. In his place the British officer who in the earlier arrangement functioned as the Vice-President, was made the President. Though formally no decision of the Durbar became valid without the approval of the Raja, the real power behind the Durbar's decision-making process was the Political Agent even though he was not an express part of the administrative structure. The system of drawing up of state budget annually was formalized under these Rules. The Durbar prepared the budget showing revenues and expenditures under separate heads for the Manipur valley and the hills. But the budget proposal before being operative required the prior approval of the Government of India, which had powers to modify the budget estimates.

The most critical part of the British dictate in reshaping the organizational structure of the King's regime was to take away the effective powers of the King and his Durbar to administer the hill areas which were an integral part of

Manipur state, The Political Agent and the Assistant Political Agent (Vice-President of the Durbar) were directly and effectively involved in the administration of the hill areas and the hill people. Of course, to assuage the Raja's feelings of resentment it was laid down that the President of the Durbar (that is, the Assistant Political Agent) would administer the hill districts on behalf of the King. By this arrangement a clear-cut separation of the Manipur plains from the Manipur hills was effected. The professed purpose was to take special measures for the development of the tribal areas and the people who were much behind the Meiteis in terms of the social and economic development.

Nine- tenths of the territorial spread of the Kingdom of Manipur consisted of hills, while only one-tenth of plains. The Meiteis and a scattering of some immigrant groups from outside and some tribal settlers coming from the hills lived in the plains. The hill villages were exclusively inhabited by tribal people belonging to two broad groups, namely, the Nagas and the Kuki-Chin tribes.

Direct British intervention in the administration and development of hill areas of Manipur brought about significant changes in socio-cultural values and attitudes of the hill people and consequently in their economic pursuits as well. These developments were both the causes and effects of changes in the matrix of social interrelations between the Meiteis who were heretofore the dominant ethnic group and the Naga and Kuki-Chin tribal people of the Manipur state. Until the conversion of Meities to Hindu beliefs and rituals, social and cultural interfaces between them and the tribal people were growing. Consequently, some kind of a 'Meitei-centric social mobility', of the tribal people as manifested in their adoption of Meitei values, customs and beliefs was taking place. This process was even leading to the entry of small groups of tribals into the fold of Meitei social formation[16]. But then it was damped by the obscurantist attitude of the Hinduized Meiteis. And the British policy of patronizing and guiding the process of change and modernization of the administrative structure in the hill areas sharpened this ethnic divide, This trend was further boosted by the growing involvement of the Christian

Missionaries in the conversion of the Kukis and Nagas to Christianity.

The concomitant economic changes were marked by the growth of population, development of human resource through spread of literacy and education among the tribal youths, new kind of farm practices and processing of farm and forest products, growing volume of monetary transactions involving exchanges of commodities and labour services and some degree of diversification in occupational pattern. Such changes, though perceptible, were taking place at an extremely slow pace.

The British recognized the tribal chiefs and refrained from interfering in matters concerning the powers and privileges enjoyed by the chiefs in their respective jurisdictions. Rather, the Chiefs were authorized to collect house tax and help mobilize forced labour (Pothang) as and when called upon to do so by the government. " The Pothang was of two kinds — Pothang Bekari and Poothang Seakhai. According to the first, the people were under obligation to carry goods or baggage or to make bridges or roads and build new bungalows without payment for the officials touring the hill areas. According to the second system, each household was to subscribe money, chicken eggs or other domestic animals to feed the touring officials free of cost"[17]. These obnoxious practices of exacting labour in the hills went against the proclaimed British Policy of ending exploitation and oppression, which the hill people suffered in the pre-1891 regime of the Raja. However, some development of physical infrastructure in the hills could be achieved by employing free tribal labourers in such projects. But often, free labour in the hills was used for carrying provisions, ammunition and baggage of army personnel when movement of troops took place to suppress rebellions in the Naga Hills, Mizo Hills, etc.

The Raja of Manipur and the tribal chiefs functioned as willing partners of the British colonial administrators in their modernization programme and the process of carrying it out in Manipur. It would, they believed, augment revenue collections, and help maintain armed police and military units to ensure Manipur's internal and external security. These changes, however, promoted some social and economic development of Manipur.

Raja Churachand Singh's rule from 1907 to 1941 was politically and economically quite eventful for Manipur. Opportunities for the younger generation gradually opened up to acquire literacy and education. Introduction of modern system of medical treatment and launching of anti-epidemic vaccination and inoculation programmes brought down the rate of mortality and that of morbidity. Consequently, there was a rise in population in the Manipur plains in particular.

Installation of a water-works unit for supply of filtered water for drinking to the inhabitants of Imphal in 1913 was an important step toward controlling the spread of water-borne diseases, which were so common in the town. And Imphal was the most densely populated part of the valley. In 1911 a little over one-fourth of Manipur's population—74,650 out of 346, 222 persons—lived in Imphal.

In 1909 the state engineer Mitchell prepared a plan for drawing water form the Maklung and Polok rivers flowing in the western part of the Imphal valley with a view to supplying safe drinking water to the people of Imphal. The estimated cost for the project amounted to Rs.2, 67, 000. When the scheme was completed in 1913, the total cost however, went up to Rs.2, 97, 079. The Government of India gave a loan of Rs.20, 000 at the rate of 4 per cent interest for this project, which was inaugurated by Raja Churachand Singh in July 1913[18]. Until the completion of the water-works, the citizens of Imphal had to use river and tank water for drinking. But these sources were mostly polluted and unsafe. Even before this water-works project got under way, in 1906 Maxwell, Political Agent, got the Ningthem Pukhri (big tank) located in Wangkhei division of Imphal cleared of reeds and weeds and dredged so that this might serve as a source of clean drinking water for the inhabitants of Imphal. It was a huge water body measuring 730ft in length, 645ft in breadth and 32ft in depth. A scheme was also drawn for taking water through pipe from the pond to the market areas[19].

3. Demographic Development

With the Raja's approval improvements in sanitation and public health measures were carried out aided by the active involvement of the British officers under the overall planning and management of the Political Agent. These steps made it possible to check deaths due to epidemic to some extent and to reduce the general level of morbidity of the state's population. Such developments, besides the prevailing environment of peace and stability, were reflected in the growth of population during the first half of the 20th century.

In 1901 Manipur's total population according to the Census for that year was 284,465 including the tribal population of 100,000. The total population rose up to 346,212 in 1911 registering a decadal rate of growth of 21.7 per cent. Density of population increased from 34 to 41 per sq. mile. In the table below the trend of Manipur's population growth is indicated.

Table 21.2
Growth of Population of Manipur: 1901-1951
(Area : 8628 sq. miles)

Census Year	Total Population	Tribal population (per cent of total population within brackets)	Decadal rate of growth population (per cent)	Density of population per sq. mile
1901	284,465	100,000 (35)		33
1911	346,222		21.71	41
1921	384,016		10.92	46
1931	445,606	159,566 (35.8)	16.04	52
1941	512,069		14.92	59
1951	577,635		12.80	67

Sources : Respective Census Reports.

Population increased from 284,465 in 1901 to 512,069 in 1941. But the rate of population growth kept on declining in the decades 1911-1921, 1931-41and 1941-51 as indicated in the table above. The fall in the growth rate in the decade 1911-1921 was confined to the hill areas – which suffered terrible 'havoc wrought by the influenza epidemic'. Another factor responsible was the Kuki rebellion of 1917-19 that unsettled the tribal population in the affected area. As per the Census Report of 1931,between 1911and 1921, population of the hills increased by only one per cent as against an increase in the population of the Manipur valley of 16.5 per cent. According to this census (i.e. for 1931) the population of the hills increased more rapidly than that of the valley. While the increase in the hills was to the extent of 21.3 per cent, in the valley it was only by 13.5 per cent .The increase in the hills, as it notes, must be principally due to the good public health of the decade and to the peaceful conditions, which followed the suppression of the Kuki rebellion[20].

Normally population in the valley increased at a faster rate than that in the hills. But in 1921-31 decade, the rate of increase in the valley went down. It was only 13.5 per cent as against 16.7 per cent in 1901-11decade and 16.5 per cent in the period 1911-21. Mullan sought to explain this phenomenon by pointing out that many Manipuris emigrated 'from the more crowded parts of the main valley to areas which were technically within the "hill section" of the state and of course suitable for rice cultivation'. Mullan further referred to the report of the Political Agent telling that time was rapidly approaching 'when there will be no further room for agricultural expansion in the main valley and that settlements of Manipuries are, even now, competing with hillmen for land in the tributary valleys such as those of the Khuga and Chakpi rivers'[21].

By 1931 pressure of population in the valley increased so much that farming operations in the available area of agricultural land could not provide employment opportunities for the rural workers throughout the year. Therefore, seasonal emigration during the cold weather to the plains of Assam and Burma ' in search of trade and employment 'became an annual feature.

The Mean Decennial Growth Rate of Manipur fell from 14.91 per cent in 1931-41 to 12.80 percent in 1941-51 decade. This decline, as mentioned in the 1951Census Report was 'due to devastation caused by the continued involvement of Manipur for long years in World War II when it was occupied by the Japanese armies for quite some time in their advance from Burma towards India and the general shortage of medicine and supplies it gave rise to'[22].

Growth rates of rural and urban population in percentage terms in the different decades were as follows:

Table 21.3:
Percentage Variation of Population from 1901 to 1951

	1901 to 1911	1911 to 1921	1921 to 1931	1931 to 1941	1941 to 1951
Total	+ 21.71	+ 10.92	+ 16.04	+ 14.92	+ 12.80
Rural	+ 27.96	+ 11.95	+ 18.35	+ 14.61	+ 39.39
Urban	+ 3.34	+ 7.17	+ 7.25	+ 16.21	- 97.13

Source: The office of the Registrar General and Census Commissioner of India as quoted in NEC, Basic Statistics of North Eastern Region, Shillong 1980,P.2 [22 (a)].

The above table shows that the growth rate of rural population declined in the 1911-1921 and 1931-41 decade, while the urban population maintained a steadily increasing trend up to 1931-1941decade. The steady growth of urban population, that is, the population of Imphal, which was the only urban centre in the state, indicated an overall positive trend of economic growth. But this process got a severe jolt from the Japanese aggression of Manipur and their besieging of Imphal for quite some time during the Second World War. The urban growth rate fell by nearly one hundred per cent. It was due to the migration of dwellers of Imphal to rural areas for safety. This caused considerable dislocation in Manipur' s economic organization.

4. Literacy and Occupational Distribution

Growth of literacy, educational attainments and occupational diversification over the years are indicative of the quick improvements taking place in the economic conditions of Manipur's people. Modern system of school education began in Manipur only after the establishment of the British Political Agency in 1835. Young children acquired literacy, that is ability to read and write, and of course, after a stage, numeracy, the knowledge of simple arithmetic, that is.

Information about growth of literacy and changing pattern of occupational pursuits of the people can be obtained from the Census Reports. The first census of the population of Manipur had been taken in 1872 along with that of India as a whole. Each report of the census conducted in Manipur under the overall guidance and supervision of the Superintendent, census operation, Assam formed part of the Census Report about Assam, which was included as a volume of the Census of India. The Census enumerations of the population of Manipur in 1872and 1881 were not exhaustive and well organized. Again, the census enumeration papers for 1891 were destroyed during Anglo-Manipur War that year. Therefore, we shall use the Census Reports for 1901 onwards for reviewing the progress of literacy and changes in occupational pattern of the people of Manipur till the end of the colonial period. The results of the 1951 census enumerations will, however, be made use of to form an idea about the levels of literacy and educational attainments, and about Manipur's economic organization and its people's living conditions in and about1947.

5. Growth of Literacy

B.C. Allen, author of the Report on the Census of Assam, 1901, explained the difficulty in enumerating the genuinely literate persons. In his words: "The return of literacy is beset with a certain amount of difficulty. In the first place it is not always easy to determine what the expression should include. A considerable number of people can read and write, but only.... 'with difficulty', and it is not easy to say at exactly what stage the claimant to the title should be described as literate. The standard of knowledge exacted was probably low, as the average enumerator is not a man of great literacy attainments himself, and should be contented with but little in others: but any excess in this direction must have been to some extent corrected in the abstracting office, as literates may have been occasionally overlooked, but never improperly inserted in the tables"[23].

In the case of Manipur – where nine- tenths of the geographical area consisted of hills and the tribal people constituted one-third of the population, the process of conducting census enumerations was even more difficult. Still, for noting the trend in the rise of literacy rate in the state the census figures might be reckoned as satisfactory indicators.

In 1901, only 9 out of every one thousand persons, aged 5 and over were literates. Obviously, literacy among the female population was still at an extremely low level. Only one woman out of every one thousand in each of the two age groups, viz., 15 to 80 years and 20 years and above could read and write. As against this, 19 male persons out of every one thousand in all age groups, 5 and above were literate. In the age groups 10 to 15, 15 to 20, and 20 and above, these proportions were 7, 22 and 31 respectively for males. The school-going boys would normally be in the age group of below 15 and for the beginners some of them might be even older, that is they could be falling in the age group 15 to 20 years. These premises suggest that the development of school education had been still in the nascent stage in Manipur, The level of educational development was even far lower in the case of female children[24].

Literacy rates steadily grew over the years, and in 1931 the position was as follows. For ages 5 and over, 40 persons in every one thousand were literate of whom 78 men in every one thousand and 4 women in every one thousand acquired literacy. In other words, the rate of literacy rose from 0.9 per cent in1901 to 4 per cent in 1931. The trend in the spread of education in Manipur may be noted from the fact that in the school-going age groups 10-15 and 15-20 the number of boys and young men acquiring literacy reached the figures of 48 and 105 per thousand. The corresponding figures for girls and young women were 4 and 6 respectively[25].

Spread of literacy was not limited to any particular community. The numerical positions per thousand aged 5 and over among different religious groups are stated as Hindus –109 males and 8 females; Muslims-109 males and 18 females; Christians-234 males and 40 females; Tribals-10 males and 1 female [25 (a)]. Highest level of literacy among Christians, according to Mullan was attributable to the facts that this religion included the European and Eurasian population and that the Christian Missionaries 'succeeded in imparting a certain amount of instructions to their converts'[26].

Despite the disturbed condition prevailing in Manipur during the Second World War, growth of literacy continued unabated. This is reflected in the Census enumerations for the year 1951. In that year the total number of literates stood at 65,895 of whom 58,933 were male and 6,962 female. Total population in1951 was 577,635 and hence the literacy rate stood at 11.4 per cent. This indicates that over 20 year period that is, from 1931 to 1951 literacy rate increased by more than 7 per cent. This is a significant indicator of the rate of development of human resource which one would consider crucially important in achieving all round social, political and economic progress.

6. Economic Progress as Reflected in Occupational Distribution

Occupational distribution of population throws light on the structure of economic organization of the people of Manipur. The decadal changes in the livelihood pattern of people as revealed by the Censuses, each conducted every ten years had an important bearing on people's economic conditions, which too were changing.

Growth of population and rise in its density pushed up man-land ratio and led to expansion of areas brought under cultivation the scope for which was not unlimited. This factor, which combined with the rise in literacy and spread of education, although at a slow pace, impelled the youths to go in for non-farming occupations. This change was facilitated by some development of the basic infrastructure, such as, roads, transport and communications services, new markets and permanent sheds in markets, schools, health care units, etc. On top of this was, of course, the restructuring of administrative set- up to cope with expansion of administrative services to different parts of the state.

Manipuri women have been traditionally involved in trading activities which received further boost from the new developments and rises in production of agricultural goods and textile fabrics. In such a spectrum of occupational opportunities, the position of trade and commerce became more and more important, and so became various professions.

For the 1901census enumeration the occupations were arranged in eight main classes, i.e., "A-Government, B-Pasture and Agriculture, C-Personal Service, D-Preparation and supply of Material substances, E-Commerce, Transport and storage, F-Professions, G-Unskilled non-agricultural labour, and H- Means on Subsistence Independent of occupation"[27]. Considering the fact that the range of occupational diversification was narrow in Manipur the occupational distributions of population have been classed under five heads, namely, agriculture; industry; commerce; professions and miscellaneous others.

It is not that all persons were actual workers engaged in a particular occupation; some were dependents, and some would pursue more than one occupation. To deal with these realities the enumerators were instructed to show a person as 'dependent' 'whenever the individual in question did not actually work at the occupation shown against his or her name. The rules further laid down that for persons with two or more occupations the chief one only should be entered, except when they owned or cultivated land in addition to another occupation when both should be recorded'[28]. This pattern was more of less followed for the 1911 and 1921 Census also.

Proportions of total population supported by agriculture, industry, commerce and transport, professions and miscellaneous others in 1901, 1911and 1921 were as follows:

Table 21.4
Occupational Distribution of Population of Manipur : 1901 - 1921

Proportion of total population (in percentage terms) supported by (actual workers and dependents)	Census years		
	1901	**1911**	**1921**
1. Agriculture	72.80	77.70	83.93
2. Industry	22.10	14.20	8.80
3. Commerce (including transport)	0.34	4.30	4.50
4. Professions (public force, public administration, professions and liberal arts religion, law, medicine, instruction, letters and arts and sciences)	1.71	2.00	2.16
5. Miscellaneous (proprietors other than of agricultural land) funds and scholarship holders, domestic service inmates of jails, asylums, beggars etc.	3.05	1.80	0.61
	100.00	**100.00**	**100.00**

Sources : i) Census of India 1901, Vol. IV, *Assam,* Part-I Report by B. C. Allen, pp 172-174

ii) *Census of India 1911,* Vol. III, *Assam, Part-I* Report by Mc Swiney, p. 168

iii) *Census of India 1921,* by G. T. Floyd, Vo. III, *Assam, Part-II,* Tables, Table No. XVII, P. 136 ff. Total population of workers and dependents is 374201 which is less than the census population of 384016. Proportions of occupational groups have been estimated on the basis of the total of 374,201.

The data about livelihood categories provided by different censuses are not strictly convincing as the instructions given to enumerators for inclusion of persons pursuing different economic activities in a particular category varied from census to census. However, the figures shown in the table above clearly suggest growing importance of trading activities, transportation of goods and movement of people from place to place as also expanding opportunities for pursuing different liberal professions. Growth of professional activities is obviously linked with the growth of urbanization. During the entire period of Manipur's economic history which is being studied here, Imphal was the only town in Manipur. And as we have noted in table 21.3 urban population grew steadily in the whole period up to 1941. Some anomalies in the shares of commerce and industry taken note of in the Census of 1901 and of 1911 might be explained in the light of B.C. Allen's observations (Census Report for 1901). The low proportion of agriculturists in 1901 (i.e., 72.8 per-cent) "…. is chiefly due to the fact that no less than 34,304 women have been shown as actual workers under the head of weavers and spinners; but there is, as far as I am aware, little export of cloths from Manipur, and, as the total population of that State is only 284,465, it hardly seems probable that over 34,000 Manipuri females can be earning their living by weaving cloths for sale, and the majority of those persons were probably the women folks of agriculturists, who make cloths for home wear, and who in other districts have been included in the cultivating class"[29] (P. 162).

Allen was only partly right in his assessment. For, Manipuri women did produce some quantities of textile fabrics for sale no doubt and many of them were also traders who dealt in both agricultural produce as well as textiles. Therefore the low proportion of commercial population should be ascribed to an under-enumeration. This was corrected in 1911and 1921 censuses showing that this occupation then supported 4.50 and 4.40 per cent of population. About participation of women of Manipur as contractors, priestesses and in writing books, Allen's comments are worth noting. "…There are 12 female contractors, the majority of whom were censused in the Khasi and Jaintia Hills and Manipur, where women are much given to trading on their own account, 1,113 priestesses, and one lady in Manipur who asserted that she made her living by writing books"[30].

Some changes were made in occupational categorization and in the presentation of data for the 1931 census. In the earlier censuses all persons supported by different occupations (i.e., earners, working dependents and dependents) were enumerated and presented in the tables. But in the 1931 Census Report only the actual earners and working dependents in any particular occupation were enumerated and presented. In 1931, 54 per cent of population were non-working dependents while 20.9 percent were working dependents and 25.1 percent earners (principal occupation). Percentages of the total population who were occupied as earners (principal occupation) and working dependents in different sub-classes grouped into five categories in the same manner as for the earlier censuses were agriculture 79.30; industry 13.68; commerce (including transport) 4.12; professions 2.16 and miscellaneous 0.74. In the last category (miscellaneous) the proportion, is much below 1 because, most of the persons in this category were not earners or earning dependents. The trends of growth in trading activities and professional occupations were, however, maintained in 1931. In the Appendix disaggregated figures for total earners (principal occupation) and working dependents with sex distribution in different occupations are given. That will show that there were 2249 male and 84 female earners in professions and liberal arts and 310 males and 63 females were working dependents in that category. These included 41 males occupied in legal profession while there were 394 male and 25 female medical practitioners of whom 31 were registered doctors. Male teachers numbered 377 and female 4. It is further noted that there were 86 male and 81 female beggars, which shows that the problem of destitution was a reality in Manipur. As the occupational diversification and specialization processes proceed along with urbanization, marketization of economic activities and monetization of transactions, the old socio-economic egalitarian order as is generally seen, gradually breaks down. Individuals who cannot find for themselves are reduced to destitution, particularly in the urban area.

Another consequence of the marketization process and the growth of employment in professional services was the fluctuation in the level of employment on account of rising and falling trends in market demand; for goods and services. Therefore, the world-wide great depression of 1929-30s had also had an impact on Manipur's economy. The problems of unemployment, particularly one related to educated unemployment, arose in the state in that period. In 1931 census operation, enumeration of the educated unemployed was undertaken. In Manipur, according to the 1931 census Report, there were 18 educated unemployed of whom 5 were unemployed for less than one year while 13 were unemployed for one year or more. Eleven unemployed were in the age group 20 –24, 6 in the age group 25-29 and 1 in the age group 30-34.

Although the total number of unemployed was not a big one, it, however, gave a jolt to the new generation of educated youths who aspired to take up salaried jobs at the end of their education.

Because of the financial stringency resulting from the outbreak of the Second World War, 1941 census was a much-restricted operation. For that census occupational distribution of population was not enumerated. Therefore, we may turn our attention to the results of the post-Independence period's first census conducted in 1951. The findings of this census may be taken as approximating the realities prevailing about the year 1947.

According to the 1951 Census Report (p. 102 and p.108) livelihood pattern in Manipur in that year was as follows:

Table 21.5: Livelihood Pattern in 1951

Agricultural Classes	Per cent of Population
I. Cultivators of land wholly or mainly owned by them and their dependents	71.2
II. Cultivators of land not owned by them either wholly or mainly (i. e, cultivating tenants) and their dependents.	10.0
III. Cultivating labourers and their dependents	0.2
IV. Non-cultivating owners of land; agricultural rent-receivers and their	2.0
Total agricultural classes	**83.4**

Non-Agricultural Classes

Persons (including dependents) who derive their principal means of livelihood from:

Non-agricultural classes	Percent of population
V. Production other than cultivation	7.0
VI. Commerce	4.2
VII. Transport	0.5
VIII. Other services and miscellaneous sources	4.9
Total non – agricultural classes	**16.6**

Results of 1951 census enumeration of livelihood classes revealed the crucial aspect of inequality in land distribution. There were 57,800 cultivating tenants and their dependents (10 per cent of total population), 11,560 non-cultivating owners of land, agricultural rent-receivers and their dependents.

7. Development of Imphal

Imphal has played a crucial role in the economic growth of Manipur. Following the British occupation of Manipur, urban-rural population divide became an important feature of the demographic development of the state. A slow growing volume of investment was being made in the development of urban services and infrastructure. Migration of population from the rural and hill areas and from outside Manipur to Imphal resulted in steady swelling of the town's population. It increased from 60,000 in 1881 to 72,234 in 1901, from 74,650 in 1911 to 80,003 in 1921, and from 85,804 in 1931 to 99,716 in 1941. But in the wake of the Japanese attack on Imphal during the Second World War, 97 percent of Imphal's population migrated to rural areas. It was a setback to Imphal's development.

Major Maxwell who served as the Political Agent and Superintendent of the state for 15 years from 1891,took the initiative in the development of the town roads, markets, supply of drinking water, etc. The old and famous Women's Market at Khawiromband had thatch roofed sheds for the use of women shopkeepers. These were prone to frequent fire accidents since the sellers would use open kerosene lamps or pine woods for lighting the sheds at night. In 1906 these thatched roofs were replaced by corrugated iron sheets by the Government at a cost of Rs.7, 803[31]. This improvement was hailed by the women traders, as it reduced the risk of fire accidents occurring in the market.

The other market in Imphal, namely Sadar Bazaar, was very crowded and unwieldy. Marketing facilities also needed to be expanded to cope with the needs of the rising number of traders and to handle growing volume of trade. Therefore, a new site was developed on the north of the British Reserve by building a boulevard (a two-lane road having trees planted in the middle to separate the lanes) entailing an expenditure of Rs.1, 435[32]. This has since been renamed Thangal Bazaar. Construction of the market was completed in 1906. It 'involved reconstructing the carters and Naga Serais, and the levelling of a large area of ground, filling in of several tanks and the construction of 1069 yards of metalled roadway'. The market initially had 17 shops but provision was there for further expansion[33]. Since then, some more markets came up in Imphal, which emerged as a growing commercial centre in Manipur.

A hydroelectric plant was built in 1935 at Leimakhong, 14 miles north-west of Imphal for generating electricity by harnessing the water flow of Leimakhong river. From this plant electricity was supplied to Imphal. Electricity for the people of Imphal thus became available in 1935. Of course the palace and its surroundings had the benefit of electricity some years earlier, to produce which a generator run on petrol was installed. Until then the palace and its approach road were lighted by acetylene gas[34].

8. Local Self-Governing Body of Imphal

The central core (nucleus) of Imphal town was the British Reserve. The territorial boundary of the British Reserve covered the royal palace and the fortress, the British residency, the main markets and parts of Thangmeiband and Kabo Leikai of Khurai (one of the four divisions into which Imphal was divided for administrative convenience). The British Reserve was under the direct administration of the Political Agent[35]. The composition of the municipal organization of the Reserve may be noted from the

Administrative Report for 1915-16."There is no municipality in the state. But in the year under report, the control of all municipal work was handed over to the Political Agent. He is assisted by a committee of five members nominated by him. The maintenance charges are provided for partly by a Government grant and partly by a state grant of Rs. 4,000 and the revenue from various taxes incident on residents in the British reserve. These taxes which brought in an average revenue of about Rs. 3,800 were surrendered by the Durbar when the state gave up control over the municipal work"[36]. The fund available for providing municipal services constituted the Imphal Town Fund into which the grant of the Government and the state and the collections from municipal taxes were credited. In 1915-16 the Fund amounted to Rs. 10,373 out of which Rs 9,168 was expended on municipal work. In 1917-18 the income went up to Rs 14,840 and the expenditure to Rs. 15,457. This trend indicated that municipal services in the town were expanding.

9. Political and Economic Changes During The Two World Wars

Manipur's politico-economic development was affected by both the First and the Second World Wars. Even though Manipur was far away from the theatre of the First World War, the state having been under the British colonial domination, had to join the war in support of the British power. Besides contributing a sum of Rs1.34 lakh as war loan the state raised the Manipur labour corps for which 2000 Naga and Kuki hillmen were recruited. They were sent to France in May 1917 mainly for 'digging trenches, carrying loads and building base camps'[37]. In protest against the attempts made by the colonial rulers through the political agent of Manipur to raise another labour corps by enlisting hillmen, the Kukis in particular, who rose in revolt in 1917. The political agent, Higgins, gave orders, directing the Kukis to provide at least one coolie from every two families of each Kuki village. The Kukis made representations to the Commissioners of Surma Valley and hill districts against these orders and argued that since their custom was to bring back home the head of the person who met with his death anywhere outside his home, it would be impossible to observe this custom in the very likely event of a Kuki labour dying in France or any other foreign field. They were, therefore, unable to join the labour corps. This objection was ruled out and the Kuki Chiefs were warned that should they fail to provide the British with recruits for the labour corps the Kukis would be punished for such recalcitrance. This stand of the political agent provoked the Kukis to rise against the British authority. The Kukis, whose rebellion continued for over two years were finally subdued through military strikes on different Kuki inhabited villages in the hills.The rebellion however continued for over two years during which period many Kuki villages were burnt down and razed to the ground. The Kukis also burnt and looted several neighbouring Naga villages and killed Nagas who were suspected to have sided with the British and who did not co-operate with the Kuki rebels.

The Kuki rebellion and the upheavals in the hills of Manipur in the year from 1917 to 1919 were, however, in the ultimate analysis an outburst of the pent up grievances against the autocratic administration imposed on the hill people. The lack of even minimum development of the physical infrastructure in the hills was exposed in the course of military expeditions to the hills. Bureaucratic exploitation and lack of direct contact between the British officials and the hillmen were also responsible for tribal discontent in the Manipur hills. Once they realized these basic causes of Kuki rebellion, the British Government took some important measures for reorganizing the administrative structure in the hill areas of Manipur. These measures had vital consequences on the fiscal arrangement existing between the Manipur state and Government of India.

10. New Administrative and Fiscal Arrangements

Following the new arrangement the administration of the hill areas was placed under the direct jurisdiction of the Maharaja who would decide matters on the advice of the Political Agent 'to a far closer and more intimate degree than in matters connected with the plainsmen'[38].

To ensure more direct British involvement in the administration of hill areas, these were divided into three sub-divisions each of which was placed under the charge of a European Sub-Divisional Officer, who was directly accountable to the President of the Durbar. The Sub-divisional officers enjoyed both executive and judicial powers of original jurisdiction. Appeals against some of their judgements could be made to the President of the Durbar, and in certain cases, if not happy with the President's decision, to the Political Agent. The policy guidance for the SDOs required them to reside in their respective areas "all the year round, open up roads, administer simple justice, set up schools and hospitals, and generally act as –fathers to the hillmen and restore their confidence in the British raj"[39].

The new administrative structure entailed substantial amount of additional public expenditure that was beyond the fiscal capacity of the Manipur state Government to bear. Considering this, the British Government took the following decisions to strengthen the budgetory resource of the Manipur Government:

The annual instalment of repayment of the loan of Rs. 2,75,000 which the State Government took in 1917 was reduced from Rs. 60,000 to Rs. 10,000. The amount of the annual tribute payable by Manipur to the Government of India was reduced from Rs. 50,000 to Rs.5000 for ten years in the first instance. And the annual contribution of Rs. 30,000 used to be made by Manipur towards the maintenance of the Mao-Imphal Road was remitted. They also contemplated separation of the budget provisions for hill people from those for the plainspeople, in the hope that this would prevent diversion of funds meant for meeting the requirements of the hill administrative authority to meet the requirements of Manipur plains[40].

Following the Kuki rebellion the colonial rulers got directly involved in the administration of the hill areas of Manipur. The feudal arrangement was an impediment to the hillmen's progress. The restructured administrative set-up and the new fiscal arrangement made it possible to make more resources available to the hill areas for development of infrastructure. The colonial rulers as also the Christian missionaries took several steps to initiate modernization process that led to social and economic development of the hill people. They received modern education, health-care, and also training facilities for acquiring professional skill.

The resulting changes in social, cultural, political and economic milieu conflicted with the traditional power structures. The feudal and religious authorities in the hills made several attempts to counteract the changes by fomenting agitations and violent protest movements. A few of these movements took the form of anti-British freedom movement. The leaders got some inspiration from the struggle for independence waged by the Indian people against the British rule under leaders like Gandhi and Nehru.

The movement launched by the Zelianerong (Kabui Naga group) led by Jadonang from mid-1920s to 1931 and that by Rani Gaidinliu from 1930 to 1949 had social, religious, economic and political objectives. Gaidinliu organized the Nagas living in Manipur, Naga Hills and North Cachar Hills. The anti-British movement launched by Zeliangrong (Naga tribe comprising Zemi, Liangmei and Rongmei sub-groups) led by Jadonang from the mid-1920's to the middle of 1931 had the objective of building "a Naga Heaven" a 'millennium' on earth where there would be no want, it (would) be a land of plenty"[41]. Jadonang gave a call to the villagers to 'stop paying taxes to the government' and to 'disobey the unjust laws of the state'. This stage of the movement coincided with the Civil Disobedience movement launched by Gandhi in India. Taking a serious note of the movement initiated by Jadonang who was reckoned a Messiah King of the Kabuis and Kacha Nagas'the British Government ultimately arrested him and alleging his part along with fellow-villagers in the murder of four Manipuri traders in Kambiron, a Naga village in March 1930 executed him on 29 August 1931.

Following Jadonang's death , Gaidinliu, a brave Naga damsel of sixteen, ,took up the challenge of leading an anti-British agitation in Manipur, in parts of Naga Hills and in the North Cachar Hills of Assam. She urged her people not to pay house tax, nor render any free labour service, nor even pay compulsory porterage charges as and when imposed on them. She was successful in building a large following for fulfilling Jadonang's dream of establishing a'Naga Heaven', that is 'a country full of God's miraculous bounty where there would be no wants'. Many Nagas discontented with the colonial rule joined Gaindinliu's movement and volunteered to fight under her leadership to drive away the British from their land. The 'army' of these brave men was led by Gaidinliu to start erecting a wooden fortress in Pulomi village to take on the Assam Rifles that was sent by British to quell the rebellion. But before they could complete building, Captain Macdonald got Gaidinliu arrested on 17 October 1932 in a surprise attack on them. She was sentenced to life imprisonment by the Political Agent of Manipur. Her followers surrendered and the movement came to an end.

The abortive Kuki and Naga rebellions were in fact attempts made to preserve Manipur's traditional socio-political and economic institutions in the face of the modernization process initiated by the British. The ethnic identity-based conservatism slowly gave in to the Christian and western values, as conversion to Christianity and modern education among the new generation of youths went ahead steadily. An educated elite class slowly emerged.

Two things, keeping Manipur hills' administrative structure separate from that of the Manipur plains and dilution of the King's and the Durbar's role in the administration of the hill areas, helped preserve the tribals' rights in their lands, forests and in other spheres of natural resources.

The growing educated middle class in the plains and in a smaller measure in the hills started asserting its political and economic rights by limiting the absolute powers of the ruling king who collaborated with the colonial power. This development led to the birth of the first political party in Manipur in 1938 named Nikhil Manipur Mahasabha. Its main demand was for establishment of a responsible government in Manipur having a legislature with elected members and the king functioning only as a titular head. This party was formed mainly to promote political and economic aspirations of the middle class, and that too of its male members.

The other asserting group comprised the Manipuri women, particularly women traders reputed to have a long tradition of launching organized protest movements against those who infringed their rights and interests. The peasants and workers constituted by far the largest segment of

Manipur's population. And it was H. Irabot Singh, a leftist intellectual, who took the initiative to form a party in order to organize this class of people with a view to protecting their interests. The opportunity arose for making this move in the wake of Women's Agitation (Nupee Lan) in 1939.

In the pre-colonial period, internal trading activities were mostly in the hands of Manipuri women. And the volume of external trade was small. The colonial rulers following the policy of free trade encouraged external trade. Thanks to their patronage, a number of non-Manipuri traders did operate in the state. Among such traders the Marwaris were the most resourceful in respect of mobilization of both capital and expertise. Marwari capital was mostly invested in trading, particularly in wholesale trading. Gradually the Marwari traders acquired near monopoly of the wholesale trade in rice, which was the most important product in the agricultural and the non- agricultural sectors taken together. In normal years, the farmers produced substantial quantities of surplus rice by selling which they could increase their income. This possibility virtually remained blocked as in the precolonial period the export of rice was not permitted by the Durbar and the non-rice cultivating producers, such as fishermen, potters, weavers, and salt manufacturers had barter trade transactions with the rice producers. The King and his kin met their requirements of rice through the system of *Kei-roi-thau* (vide Chapter 19). The other non-farming land-holding groups, such as, the nobles, Brahmins, sepoys, village headmen and officials, could meet requirements of rice from rice collected as substitute for rent (see above Chapter 19).

The above pattern of rice production and distribution in the society did not offer any economically significant incentive to the self- consuming rice-producers to produce more rice than what was required for subsistence and for meeting the state-imposed obligations. The colonial rulers abolished the *Lallup* system of land-management and use and imposed a house tax of Rs.2 on each homestead. Besides, land–revenue was also required to be paid by the patta-holders of land at the rate of Rs. 5/- per *pari* (about 3 acres).

In 1939 the British authority prevailed upon the Durbar

to allow export of substantial quantities of rice from Manipur. This helped them to meet the requirements of rice of their troops and non-combatant staff stationed in Manipur, Naga Hills, Assam, etc. Even then export trade in rice when opened resulted in the demand-induced increase in the production of rice, rise in price of rice and the expansion of the volume of rice trade. These developments favoured the rice-farmers to some extent even though there were rises in transaction costs, the major share of which was appropriated by the traders, millers, transport operators, and so on.

The Marwaris established rice-mills which meant an important technological advance in rice-processing. But this caused some displacement of rice-pounding activity in the household sector. Even more importantly, this development altered the pattern of internal rice-trading activity. The middlemen could procure paddy for the rice-mills for processing. Generally there was a nexus between the millers and the middlemen. Or, simply, the millers engaged agents for procuring rice from the village farmers. The millers also controlled the operation of bullock carts either by directly owning them or by hiring them on a priority basis by making advance payment. At a later stage motor lorries were brought into service. All such technological steps raised productive efficiency and the total output of rice and other crops. Additional areas of land were brought under cultivation, which also contributed to the increases in rice production. The total area under cultivation, for example, increased from 1,75,537 acres in 1925-26 to 1,85,213 acres in 1938[43].

Rice could be exported out of Manipur by private traders on payment of what was known as cart tax, according to which this tax was payable at the rate fixed for one cart load of rice. Export operation was permitted for a period of six weeks as fixed by the government. The total volume of export under this system, therefore, remained restricted. But later, when lorries came into use for transporting rice, volume of export went up, even though export operation was permissible, as before, for the fixed period of six weeks.

Rice was also exported in accordance with the agreements entered into between Assam Government and the Government of Manipur. This arrangement made it possible to export rice to the Kohima Civil Station and also to different other places where Assam Riflesmen were stationed.

Rice exports were subjected to payment of export duty, which yielded substantial amount of revenue as volume of export sharply increased after the Marwari traders entered the export business in a big way in 1932. The trend of the rising volume of rice exports is indicated below:

Table 21.6
Rice Exports of Manipur

Year	Volume of export, (in maund), 1 maund=0.37quintal
1897-98	11,206
1898-993	34,436
1922-23	80,000
1925-26	1,55,014
1931	1,05,287
1932	2,77,387

Source: Joykumar Singh, 1991: 145-146

Such changes caused redistribution of income generated by rice production and trade, favouring the traders, particularly the Marwaris, who owned the rice mills as also either owned or controlled the operation of the transport services. Up to some extent such a redistribution of income in the society did not give rise to protests among the Manipuris who were affected by this development. But the situation became grave and intolerable in 1939 following the heavy fall in rice production because of natural calamities[44].

It was because of annual exports of rice that the stock of rice grain, which they built fell to a very low level, or was exhausted totally. On top of this exports further lowered the supply of rice available in the local markets. No wonder, price of rice went up by 60 per cent, that is, from the normal rate of Rupee one and four annas (1.25) to Rs 2 (2.00) per maund (1 maund = 0.37 quintal).

People were alarmed at the shortage of rice in the market. In such a situation the Manipuri women led by the women traders of Tera Keithel and Khwairamband Keithel (market) organized protest movement and demanded the closure of all rice mills. They even tried to stop the bullock carts carrying paddy to the mills. Furthe, they urged the government to stop export of rice. To assert their demands, on 12 December 1939 they surrounded the President of the Manipur State Durbar and some British officials for long hours. They were rescued by Assam Rifles men who beat up the agitators injuring 30 women out of whom 10 had to be admitted to hospital. They also closed their shops in the market which caused a deadlock in retail trading activities in Imphal. To suppress the agitation five women leaders of the movement were arrested and imprisoned for six months. The Political Agent also warned that the existing shop-owners would be dispossessed of their shops, which would be allotted to others in accordance with his preference. Being leaderless the women agitators gradually quietened.

The British government, however, realized the gravity of the economic situation generated by the export of rice. This is evident from the Assam Governor Robert Reid's observations as quoted by Joykumar Singh (1911: 149). "..........the occasion for this was the economic grievances arising out of a rise in the price of rice due to the excessive exports coupled with a genuine fear of a shortage (which) means starvation, because it is impossible to import rice at a price which a Manipuri can pay. The heavy exports in turn were the result of numerous rice mills which have sprung up in Manipur"[45].

The Assam Governor's evaluation of the women's agitation was in fact an acknowledgment of the genuineness of the grievances voiced by the women, for the redressal of which they had to launch the agitation. And the Political Agent of Manipur had to review the policy of permitting export of rice from Manipur. The colonial rulers and the Manipur Durbar became very alert in order to check the rising prices and to ensure availability of rice for the people. In fact, the threat of famine looming large was effectively removed. This was indeed a historical achievement brought about by the Women's agitation of 1939. In recognition of this heroic movement of the Women of Manipur the state observes 12 December every year as the Nupee Lan Day in memory of those women who organized this agitation and suffered injuries and imprisonment inflicted upon them by the colonial rulers. The Nikhil Manipur Mahasabha submitted a petition to the Maharaja in 1938 pleading for constitutional reforms in order to induct a popularly elected and responsible government in place of absolute monarchy. One of the demands was to restrict the amount earmarked for the Civil List, that is, the annual provision of funds for the personal and household expenses of the Maharaja to a fixed proportion of the annual revenue of the state. The other demands, inter alia, related to the mode of appointment of public servants, abolition of the socio-economically pernicious system known as *mangba sengba*, that is, excommunication of individuals for violating any religious ritual and depriving them of their rights to cremate any dead member of the family and to perform *sradh* ceremony as required under Hindu custom. Persons thus excommunicated could get back their social status by spending a considerable amount of money for performing *purification* rites. This was a great economic torture inflicted on the common people of poor means. The petition also called for updating and properly preparing and maintaining land records.

Some of these demands were met by the end of 1939-40. The size of the Civil list fund was restricted to 10 per cent of state revenue and the released funds from the Civil List were to be spent for people's welfare. An Appointment Board was set up for holding examinations to select candidates on merit for appointment to Government departments[46].

It is, however, significant that the Nikhil Manipuri Mahasabha,the first political party in Manipur that came into being in December 1938, did not support the Nupee Lan. The Party was dominated by the well-to-do elite and the educated middle class. The radical group in this party led by Hijam Irabot Singh proposed to support the women's movement. But the proposal was opposed by the majority group. Therefore Irabot Singh and his supporters broke away from the Nikhil Manipuri Mahasabha and formed a new party, which they named the Praja Sanmelani.

Irabot Singh also took the initiative in organizing Manipur's women under the banner of a political party to which they gave the name Mahila Sanmilani. A peasants' party called Krishak Sanmelani was also formed by Singh in Manipur. All the three parties endorsed and supported the Women's agitation for solving the problem of rice shortage in the state.

The demands made by the Nikhil Manipuri Mahasabha and the agitating women exposed the weaknesses and rigidities of the political–administrative structure of Manipur. The system left no scope for popular participation in decision-making process, neither could it reflect the general will of the civil society nor could respond to it. At least Governor of Assam Robert Reid realized the shortcomings of this system and therefore he instructed the Maharaja to undertake substantial extent of administrative reforms in the state.

Irabot Singh and his Krishak Sanmelani besides demanding constitutional changes providing for the formation of a democratically elected government with the King as the titular head, agitated for land reforms and abolition of feudal levies in order to protect the interests of the peasants and workers. They were also for integration of the administrative set up for the hills with that of the plains so that Meitei–Naga–Kuki unity could be preserved.

The movement of the Krishak Sanmelani led by Irabot Singh created a sense of awareness among peasants about their deprivations, to overcome which they voiced protests against the practice of exactions from them in the name of Peon Amin ration and wanted the abolition of *pathang begar* or forced labour. They wanted to limit the system of private exploitation of natural resources, and therefore opposed the system of auctioning hills and natural lakes to the private bidders who could thereby occupy and use them for private gains. They demanded that large-sized land holdings be abolished and that plots of land be allotted to the actual tillers of the soil. The villagers should be given, they asserted, the rights to use the resources in the neighbouring hills. The peasants suffered losses since the traders and public agencies used different measures of weight, and no standard type in their transactions of goods with them. Therefore they insisted that the standard measure of one maund should be equal to 40 seers (37 kg) as current in British India. The rice growers did not get the market price for their products, the government having fixed the price for sale of rice. This mainly benefited the traders and urban consumers. Therefore, the Krishak Sanmelani urged the government to withdraw the system and let the peasants fix the price, the market price for paddy, that is.

All these demands clearly indicate how under the guidance of Irabot Singh, the peasants were seeking to organize themselves for achieving a shift in the distribution of income in their favour, compared to that among the feudal class, traders, middle-class, etc. Of course, the peasants had still a long way to go before they could realize their goal. For the distribution of political, economic and social power was still heavily weighed in favour of the feudal, trading and middle classes. Moreover, before the Krishak Sanmelani could effectively organize the peasants to gain concessions in their favour, the movement lost its steam, as Manipur got itself involved in the Second World War when the Japanese Army and the Indian National Army marched into Manipur in March 1944. Irabot Singh was suspected to have been colluding with Netaji Subhas Chandra Bose, the leader of the I.N.A. movement and was arrested under the Defence of India Rules in 1944 and sent to jail in Silchar in Assam[47].

11. Impact of The Second World War on the Economy of Manipur

The Japanese made the first air raid on Imphal on 10 May 1942. This caused an exodus of the inhabitants of Imphal to villages. The town was again bombed on 20 and 21 April 1943. The third air raid on Imphal was carried out by the Japanese on 16 and 17 March 1944.

The Japanese armed forces and the Indian National Army Units jointly started marching into Manipur's territory from Burma on 4 February 1944 and these forces began their retreat on 26 July, 1944. During this period first Ukhrul and then Shaangshuk, 8 miles south of Ukhrul, fell to the Japanese. The Japanese and the INA advanced towards Bishenpur from the south. Moirang fell on 23 April 1944. A large part of Manipur valley in the south was taken over by the INA and the Japanese forces and they kept the area under their control for nearly five months and kept Imphal besieged by these forces for some time.

The Allied forces resisted the advance of the INA and the Japanese to the Manipur and Naga Hills with the active involvement of the Meiteis, Nagas and the Kukis. Moreover, these places provided the routes through which the evacuees from Burma and some other places in South-east Asia came to India for shelter. The retreat of the British forces in the face of Japanese conquest of these territories as well as the march of the Allied forces to drive away the Japanese from the territories occupied by them in South-east Asia took place through Assam, Naga Hills and Manipur. Naturally, the people of Manipur had to endure disturbances in their normal living conditions and in the pursuit of their economic activities. Production of farm as well as non-farm goods was affected; flow of both internal and external trade choked, shortages of food stuff, industrial inputs, drugs and some other essential commodities caused acute sufferings of the people. Many families also lost some of their movable and immovable properties.

Yet such sufferings did not prompt the people to launch any movement and agitation that could have disturbed the war efforts of the British and Allied forces. At the end of war, the British Government freed Manipur state from its obligation to pay the annual tribute of Rs.50,000 which it had been paying since 1891. This was given effect to from 1945.

For facilitating the movement of troops and military supplies the road from Dimapur to Imphal via Kohima and Mao was widened and improved. The road from Imphal too was extended up to Burmese border (Tamu) via Palel and strengthened and improved. These developments, of course, led to infrastructural improvements in the state.

The Government made good some of the losses suffered by the people in the war by paying compensation. The Krishak Sanmelani, however, continued agitation for raising quantum of war compensation.

The most serious consequence of the war was the fall in the growth rate of population of Manipur, which was from16.04 percent in decade 1921-31 and 14.92 p.c. in 1931-41 decade down to 12.80 p.c. in 1941-51 decade. This has been attributed by Bhagaiwala in his Census Report for 1951 to "devastation caused by the continued involvement of Manipur for long years in the World War II when it was occupied by the Japanese armies (sic.) for quite some time in their advance from Burma towards India and the great shortage of medicine and supplies it gave rise to"[48].

APPENDIX

Occupational Distribution of Population of Manipur: 1931

	Total earners (principal occupation)		Total working dependents	
	M	**F**	**M**	**F**
1. Production of Raw Materials (exploitation of animals and vegetation, pasture and agriculture, cultivation of special crops, exploitation of minerals)	75712	13783	24314	49325
2. Preparation and supply of material substances (industry, transport, trade),	6147	11398	804	18043
of which industry (sub class III) only accounts for:	3032	7347	475	16923
of industry again textiles account for :	134	6789	143	16427
Sub class IV (transport) accounts for:	787	9	59	...
And subclass V (trade) accounts for :	2328	4049	270	1120
Again banks, of Trade, Banks, establishments of credit,etc. account for:	49	2	1	1

(Condt...)

	Total earners (principal occupation)		Total working dependents	
	M	**F**	**M**	**F**
3. Public Admn & liberal arts	3878	103	314	63
a) of which public force (sub-class VI) namely , army, police, etc. accounts for	914	--	2	--
b) of which pub. adm. accounts for :	715	19	2	--
c) of which Professions and liberal arts (sub-class VIII) account for:	2249	84	310	63
and (Ci) of (C) Law accounts for	41	--	--	--
and (Cii) of (C): Medicine	394	25	39	9
including registered medical practitioners:	31	...	1	...
(Ciii) of (C) Instruction (teachers)	377	4	4	...
4. Miscellaneous (persons living on their income, domestic service, insufficiently described occupations, unproductive, such as, inmates of jails, asylums, alms houses, beggars vagrants, prostitutes)	763	131	178	27

In 1931 there were 86 male and 81 female beggars while there was no prostitutes at all.

Source : *Census of India 1931*, Vol III *Assam Part II Tables*, Table X.

NOTES AND REFERENCES

1. K. Ibochuba (1998), Anglo-Manipur Relations (1762-1947), published in Nasrem *Sanajaoba (ed), Manipur Past and Present, Vol. I, History,* Polity and Law, Mittal Publications, Delhi 1988, p. 108.
2. Gangmumei Kabui (1991), Socio-Religious Reform Movement and Christian Proselytism, published in Lal Dena (ed), *History of Modern Manipur (1826-1949),* 1991. Orbit Publishers, New Delhi, p.98.
3. Lal Dena, *op.cit.* , p. 77.
4. S. N. Pandey (1994), Transformation of Land Settlement in Manipur under Colonial Rule, published in J. B. Bhattacharjee (ed) Studies in the Economic History of North East India, Har-Anand Publications, New Delhi, p. 118.
5. *ibid.* p. 119.
6. *Imperial Gazetteer of India,* Vol. VIII (1908), p. 195.
7. Lal Dena, *op. cit.*, p. 76.
8. K. Ibochuba, op. cit., p. 108.
9. R. K. Jhalajit Singh (1965), A Short History of Manipur, O. K. Store, Poona Bazar Road, Imphal, p. 301.
10. *Imperial Gazetteer, op. cit.* p.195.
11. *ibid.* p.195.
12. *ibid.* p.195.
13. *ibid.* p. 195.
14. Lal Dena, *op. cit.*, p. 86.
15. M. Ibohal, (1988). The Outlines of the Constitutional History of Manipur, published in Naorem Sanajaoba (ed), *op. cit.*, p.296.
16. R. K. Ranjit (1988), Emergent Ethnic Processes in Manipur, published in Naorem Sanajaoba (ed), op. cit., p.87.
17. Lal Dena, *op. cit.*, p. 81.
18. Gangumei Kabui (1991), Imphal—A Short Historical Account, published in Lal Dena (ed), *op.cit.* p. 207.
19. *ibid.*
20. C. S. Mullan, *Census of India,* 1931-Vol. III-Assam–Part I – Report, (printed in 1932), p.29.
21. *ibid.*
22. R. B. Vaghaiwalla, *Census of India 1951,* Volume XII, *Assam, Manipur and Tripura, part I-A, Report,* p..39.

22. (a). *North Eastern Council, Basic Statistics of North Eastern Region*, Shillong, 1980, p.2.
23. *B. C. Allen, Census of India 1901, Volume IV*, Assam, Part I, Report, p 97.
24. *ibid.* p.102.
25. C. S. Mullan, *op. cit.*, p.160.
25. (a). *ibid.* p.161.
26. *ibid.*
27. B. C. Allen, *op. cit.*, p. 161.
28. *ibid.* p.161.
29. B. C. Allen, *op.* cit., p. 162.
30. *ibid.* p.168.
31. Gangmumei Kabui (1991), *op. cit.*, p.206
32. *ibid.* p.206
33. *ibid.* p.206
34. *ibid.* p.204
35. *ibid.* p.202
36. Quoted by Kabui in *ibid.* p.208.
37. Lal Dena, 1991, *op.cit.*, p.126.
38. *ibid.* pp.132-133.
39. Quoted in *ibid*, P133.
40. *ibid.* pp.133-34.
41. Gangmumei Kabui (1991), *op.cit.*, p.137.
42. *ibid.*
43. Jaikumar Singh (1991). Women's Agitation of 1939, published in Lal Dena (ed), *op.cit.*, p.146.
44. *ibid.* p.148.
45. *ibid.* p.149.
46. R. K. Jhalajit Singh, *op. cit.*, p. 309.
47. Lal Dena, *op.cit.*, p.181.
48. R. B. Vaghaiwalla, *op.cit.*, p.39.

22
ECONOMIC HISTORY OF STATES

C. TRIPURA

1. Introduction

Until Tripura's integration into the Indian Union in 1949 it was a princely state known as 'Hill Tipperah' because of its predominantly hilly terrain. Roughly two-thirds of its total area of 10,477 sq kms are hilly. Six principal parallel hill ranges run from north to south covering the entire state. The average distance between any two hill ranges is about 20 kms. The hill ranges are of moderate heights, the highest peak of the highest hill range named the Jampai hills is about 975m high. Besides the six main hill ranges there are two minor ranges in the southern part of the state known as Deotamura and Taka Tulshi. There are also innumerable hillocks (locally termed *tilas*) spread almost all over the state alternating with marshy valleys, locally called *loonga*. About three thousand sq kms. of area in the western, southern and northern parts of the state bordering Bangladesh are flat tracts of fertile land suitable for settled wet rice cultivation. Many *loongas* (marshy valleys) also contain cultivable lands. The soils in the hilly parts are mostly of the laterite formation while that in the valleys, river basins and *loongas* are of the alluvial type.

The original settlers comprising the different tribal communities of the Mongolian origin came to Hill Tipperah from the east. They practised shifting cultivation in the Tripura hills, where extensive areas under bamboo forests were very suitable for shifting cultivation. The economy based on shifting cultivation hardly generated any surplus and accumulation of capital. They lived in isolated hill villages without interacting with other economic systems and cultures. Such state-less socio-cultural tribal formations were not, of course, static entities. Over time, on account of endogenous and exogenous forces of change, the system started generating some surplus, such as cotton and sesame, which were exchanged for food-grains and other necessary products of the plains.

Even though no definite year could be ascertained as to when Tripura became a monarchial state, there are evidences which would suggest that the state formation process started in the early 15th century.[1] Maha Manikya, alias Chhengthung Fa, was probably the first Tripura Chief who succeeded in establishing his domination over most of the tribal groups living in Hill Tipperah and became the ruling King of the territory.

In course of time the Tripura Kings became very powerful and they extended the boundary of the kingdom to the west beyond the Tripura Hills and occupied a large part of Bengal. But the Mughals finally threw them back by waging repeated wars against the Tripura rulers, leaving them finally with a Zamindari estate named 'Chakle Roshnabed' in the plains bordering Hill Tipperah, for which an annual rent payable to the former was fixed at Rs. 5,000/-. A similar arrangement continued even after the British came on the scene.

Tripura's contact with the British began in 1760 when Mir Kashim, the then Nawab of Bengal, sought the help of the East India Company to forcibly subdue Raja Krishna Manikya of Tripura who defaulted *vis-à-vis* payment of revenue of Chakla Roshnabad. The Company's *fauz* who easily suppressed the defiant Tripura ruler, ultimately occupied Chakla Roshnabad and became its owner in 1765 when it was vested with the Dewani rights. In 1793 Chakla Roshnabad was permanently settled in favour of Rajdhar Manikya, Raja of Tripura. Since then the British recognized the Raja of Tripura as the independent ruler of Hill Tipperah and a Zamindar of Chakla Roshnabad as an "integral portion of an impartible Raj"[2].

The area of the zamindary estate falling within the plains of the British districts of Tipperah, Noakhali and Sylhet in the province of Bengal was 1,476 sq Km. The Zamindary yielded an annual income that exceeded the total revenue earnings of the King from the Hill Tipperah area. For example in 1871-72 the gross rental from the Zamindari amounted to about Rs. 6 lakh whereas the total revenue of the State of Hill Tipperah from all its sources was only Rs. 1,50,000.[3]

In the early decades of the nineteenth century, very little or no significant change in the economic sphere took place. The hill people carried on with the traditional economic pursuits and produced some surplus of cotton, til (sesame) etc. and collected several forest items, such as, bamboo, timber, wax, lac, which were mainly exported. These exports yielded custom duties to augment the revenues of the state while collections of the same from Chakla Roshnabad continued to be an important source of revenue.

In the decades following the annexation of Assam (1826) and consolidation of British rule there Tripura's north-eastern border villages along with those adjoining the eastern frontier of Bengal were the scenes of repeated plundering and arsoning carried on by the Kuki tribal raiders. The reigning Kings of Tripura during those years were Kasi Chandra Manikya (1826-29), Krishna Kishore Manikya (1831-50) and Isan Chandra Manikya (1850-62), who were either unable or allegedly reluctant to contain the Kuki Lushai marauders. But at the height of such onslaughts and plundering the Kukis burst into fifteen villages in the plains of Tipperah (in British India lying in the west of Hill Tipperah) for plundering and burning, and killed as many as 185 British subjects, besides carrying off one hundred captives.[4]

The British suspected that the Tripura Rajas, who grumbled about the unilateral fixation of boundary of Sylhet and that of Cachar with Tripura by the Government in 1822 and 1826 respectively had a hand in engineering such Kuki Lushai raids on the villages of Tipperah. The conditions worsened as Birchandra became the *de facto* Raja in 1862 and was shaky about wielding his authority to maintain peace and order in the state.

The Government also formulated a policy of establishing friendly relations with the Kuki-Lushai tribesmen. It was also felt that the policy and the dealings of the Tipperah Raj with these tribes should synchronize with that of the

Government. With this in view it was decided to appoint a Political Agent for Hill Tipperah to be posted at Agartala. There was yet another reason why this step was taken. The Agent was to induce the Raja to open out his country and carry out reforms for ensuring an 'enlightened administration'[5].

The office of the Political Agency was abolished in 1890. But the twenty years of the tenure of this office (1871 to 1890) marked the most eventful period of effecting administrative, social, political, fiscal, economic and other reforms in the state. All these changes had significant impact on the economic development of Tripura. Birchandra Manikya was the reigning monarch during that period. His rule spanned a total period of 34 years, that is, from 1862 to 1896. Tripura's history of economic growth in the colonial period should therefore be outlined from the beginning of Birchandra Manikya's rule.

2. The Economic Scenario in the Pre-colonial Period

As already stated, the state formation process in Tripura took shape in the fifteenth century when Mahamanikya *alias* Chhengthung Fa, succeeded in establishing his claim as a King to the territory of Tripura that not only included the hilly portions of the state but also a substantial area in the plains in the west from Chittagong to Sylhet. Mahamanikya's rule covered the period from C. 1415 AD to C. 1431 AD[6].

For three centuries since the emergence of Tripura as a monarchial state immigration of population from the west, mainly Bengal, continued. The Manipuris and some tribal communities, such as, the Chakmas and Maghs from Chittagong Hill Tracts and Khasis and a few other Bodo-speaking tribes from Assam came to settle in Tripura from the east. Such immigrations led to the growth of population in the state and also expansion of economic activities. The immigrants from the west were the peasants, artisans, persons employed by the *Rajas* for performing administrative, police, military, religious and other state-sponsored duties. Such waves of migrants led to increased economic activities, capital formation (albeit at a slow pace) and technological improvement all of which helped the growth of agrarian and manufacturing sectors, mainly in the plains.

In the hilly part of the state most of the tribal households continued to subsist on shifting cultivation. Yet they were required to pay taxes on their jhum products besides house tax (*Ghar-Chukti Kar*). They had also to render free labour services to the Raja. The economic conditions of the tribals improved just marginally as their economic transactions with the plainspeople expanded. Of course, such economic contacts also adversely affected the tribal communities since they were increasingly becoming dependents on the non-tribal *mahajans* (moneylenders) for crop credit (*da dan*) at high and often uneconomic rates of interest. Such developments engendered the process of transfer of tribal land to the non-tribals.

The *Rajmala*, or the chronicle of the reigns of the Tripura Rajas, contains detailed accounts of the wide-ranging productive activities of non-tribal immigrant skilled artisans of different professional castes. Their products included cotton and silk textiles, leather goods, ivory, gold and silver ornaments, wood carvings, iron tools, brass and bell metal utensils, etc. Bamboo and cane crafts were extensively turned out in the hills as well as in the plains. Two emissaries of the Ahom King, named Ratna Kandali and Arjundas Bairagi, visited Tripura three times between 1709 and 1715. Their book, *Tripura Buranji*[7] is replete with their accounts of Tripura's manufactures, trade fair, etc.

Udaypur, the then capital of the Tripura Rajas, was a thriving centre of manufacturing activities of the weavers, carpenters, goldsmiths, blacksmiths, washermen, and so on. The Udaypur market was a busy business centre having many permanent shops where various manufactured products of Tripura were transacted. The emissaries during one of their visits to Tripura stopped over at a tribal village, named Rangrung, situated on the eastern frontier of Tripura and adjacent to Cachar and Manipur. This village was a flourishing trade centre where people from different parts of Tripura and from Cachar and Manipur assembled to exchange their surplus products. People from Cachar brought for sale mainly goats, ducks, poultry birds, dried fish, rice, salt, oil, molasses, and tobacco leaves. The Manipuris sold gold, plates and jars made of bell-metal and / or brass and warm clothes. The traders of Tripura offered copper, salt, oil, molasses, tobacco-leaves, betelnuts, dried fish, etc. These accounts show that in the early 18th century Tripura had a thriving economy thanks to the patronage of the kings and the environment of peace and order prevailing in the state.

Tripura's political and economic decline set in with the annexation of the plains which formed an inalienable part of the state to the Bengal Suba in 1729, when the King of Tripura, Dharmamanikya was decisively defeated by Mir Habib, the Naib of Murshid Quli II, who was the Mughal governor of Dacca. Dharmamanikya took refuge in the hills.

The Nawab of Bengal renamed the occupied plains lying in the west of Hill Tipperah 'Chakla Roshnabad'. Chakla Roshnabad was finally converted into a zamindari under the Mughals. Dharmamanikya made peace with the Nawab of Bengal and regained his throne in 1733 as the ruler of Hill Tipperah. He was also given the zamindari right over Chakla Roshnabad at an annual revenue of Rs. 50,000.[8]

This event, however, failed to bring peace to Tripura. The period from 1733 to 1761 when the British intervened in the affairs of Tripura was marred by palace intrigues over succession to the throne and disputes with the Nawabs of Bengal regarding payment of revenues, etc. The plundering and destructive Kuki raids on several parts of Tripura made life of the people so miserable and insecure that they deserted in large numbers such vulnerable areas. There might be another reason for the large scale exodus of people as explained by Maharaja Birchandra Manikya to the Political Agent, C. W. Bolton. During the Muslim rule, "bad government drove numbers of people into this state" while the establishment of 'good government' by the British had induced many of such immigrants to go back to their homes in Bengal.[10] Such instability, turmoil, disorder, violence and an atmosphere of insecurity led to the emigration of many settlers in Tripura who came from outside. Udaypur, the centre of economic prosperity, became so disturbed and vulnerable to Kuki raids and internecine violence that the capital had to be shifted from there to Agartala. Exodus of professionals, artisans, farmers, traders, officials, etc. caused the decrease in population and an all-round slump in economic activities.[9]

This downward swing continued for more than a hundred years and the period of recovery did begin during the reign of Birchandra Manikya (1862-1896) when Tripura's modernization process began under the compelling pressure of the British Government. Tripura's economic history in the colonial period thus covers the period from 1862 to 1947.

NOTES AND REFERENCES

1. J. B. Ganguly, 1994, The Economic Content of the State Formation Process in Medieval Tripura, *Studies in the Economic History of North East India*, J. B. Bhattacherjee, ed, Har-Anand Publications, New Delhi. pp. 29-31.
2. Dipak Kumar Chaudhuri, 1999. T*he Political Agents and the Native Raj - Conflict, Conciliation and Progress, Tripura between 1871 to 1890*, Mittal Publications, New Delhi.
3. *ibid.* p. 68.
4. *ibid.* p. 30.
5. *ibid.*
6. *Nalini Ranjan Roy Chowdhury,* 1983. Tripura Through the Ages, A Short History of Tripura From the Earliest Times to 1947 A. D., Sterling Publishers Pvt. Ltd., New Delhi, p. 14.
7. S. K. Bhuyan, ed., 1962. Tripurar Buranji (in Assamese), Guwahati.
8. *Kailash Chandra Singha, 1985. Rajmala or the History of Tripura* (in Bengali), the edited version, Mahadeb Chakraborty, Jyotish Datta, Ratna Das and Vishmadeb Bhhattacharyya, eds., Barnamala Prakashni, Agartala, Tripura, p. 115.
9. Dipak Kumar Chaudhuri, op. cit. pp. 175 - 176.
10. Dipak Kumar Chaudhuri (ed), 1996. *Administration Report of the Political Agency, Hill Tipperah,* Vol. I, Report for 1877 - 78, p. 119, Tripura State Cultural Research Institute and Museum, Government of Tripura, Agartala.

23
THE POLITY, PEOPLE AND THEIR MATERIAL LIFE: "THE LIMITS OF THE POSSIBLE"
(Pre- and Early-Colonial Period)

The long line of hereditary Rajas of Hill Tipperah, titled 'Manikyas', formally enjoyed absolute power to rule, as all executive, judicial and legislative powers were concentrated in their hands. The British administrators coming into contact with the Rajas of Tripura highlighted the despotic powers enjoyed by them. According to A. Mackenzie, "the Rajah who is an ordinary Bengali zemindar on the plains, reigns an independent prince over 3,000 square miles of upland, and was for many years a more absolute monarch than Scindia or Puttiala, - owing no law but his sovereign will, bound by no treaty, subject to no control, safe in his obscurity from criticism and reform"[1].

There was no formally enacted law excepting for some royal proclamations and decisions of the Durbar headed by the King. Raja was the supreme appellate judicial authority for all criminal and civil cases and wielded powers of awarding, as well as remitting, all kinds of punishment including capital punishment. All civil, police, military and judicial appointments were controlled by him. Hill Tipperah was an isolated small feudal state where the majority of the subjects were tribals belonging to different ethnic groups without any political awareness of organized state structure. Traditionally the tribal people, particularly those of the major tribal communities known as 'Tripura tribes', were loyal and respectful to the Rajas and other members of the royal family. The old Tripura, Deshi Tripura, Jamatiya, Noatia and Riang tribes were covered by the appellation 'Tripura tribes'.

By the end of eighteenth century, Tripura's isolation started dissolving and the absolute powers of the monarchal regime also began eroding on account of some historical changes occurring in and around the state. The British, in the course of extending the boundary of their empire to the east, reached the western frontier of Hill Tipperah, which they could have easily annexed to their empire. But they did not, presumably, because Hill Tipperah's resources, were meagre and also for the reason they wanted to make use of this frontier state for coming to terms with the fierce hill tribes on the north-eastern frontier. Even though Hill Tipperah was not a part of the British empire, its rulers could not remain indifferent to what was happening in their immediate neighbourhood. Particularly so, as when with the coming of the British all-round changes took place in administrative, political, economic, judicial and cultural spheres in Bengal.

Secondly, being the zamindar of Chakla Roshnabad under the British, a Tripura Raja had to depend on the latter for settlement of disputes over succession to the zamindari as well as to the throne of Hill Tipperah.

Even internally, almost every reigning Raja of Tripura had to contend with chronic palace intrigues and conspiracy to dethrone him. Much of his time, energy, and resources were spent on fighting legal battles in the British courts to secure his succession to the throne and at the same time to safeguard his royal privileges. Moreover, the Rajas had to encounter some of the tribes who frequently troubled them by revolting against their rule.

Political power as wielded by the rulers is inextricably related to the economic base of their state. This base was extremely narrow and weak for the rulers of Tripura. They had very little scope for manoeuvring their actions in the face of British pressure. The main source of income of the Raja was the revenue earned from the Chakla Roshnabad zamindari under the British which amounted to more than six lakh rupees annually[2] as against the total revenue of the state, amounting to less than two lakh rupees, from all the sources within Hill Tipperah, such as, land revenue, family tax, excise and custom duties. In 1876-77 such taxes totalled an amount of Rs.1, 82,632[3]. The backbone of Hill Tipperah's economy was the total output of hill farmers practising shifting cultivation and their forest products a good deal of which they exported. The hillmen's economy was stationary, with no accumulation of capital. Settled cultivation in the plains was restricted to narrow stretches of land bordering the British districts of Tripura, Noakhali, Sylhet and Chittagong. In 1876-77 land revenue collected from plains-farmers amounted to only Rs.31, 421.[4]

Hill Tipperah was populated predominantly by tribal communities consisting of the Tripura tribes besides the Hallams and Kukis. Most of them dwelt in small villages located in the forest lands in the hills, mounds (locally called *tila)*, foothill areas, etc. Only a few of them lived in the plains. Normally each village (called *para* or *bari*) consisted of 15 to 20 households. A '*para*' was commonly named after the village chief. All members of a household lived in the same house built of bamboo walls, bamboo or wooden posts and thatch roof. The structure rested on a platform made of bamboos which was built about 2 to 3 metres high from the ground. They attached a bamboo or wooden staircase to their house for climbing it or into its room, or for getting down to the ground from the house. Each house had some open space on the platform in front of the main room of the house for lounging, gossiping, meeting people, etc. The elevated structure of the house was considered safe against attacks of wild animals that abounded in the forest. The villagers invariably built their granary outside their village periphery to keep their food stock safe from fire hazards which the tribal hamlets faced occasionally.

The exact size of the tribal population could not be ascertained until the census was taken in 1901. Some of the Political Agents, however, estimated Tripura's population on the basis of the number of tribal households paying house-tax to the King. They then multiplied that figure by the estimated average size of each tribal family to arrive at their own estimate. Captain E. G. Lillingston in his Report for

1873-74 accordingly formed an estimate of the total tribal population, which was 22, 475. According to him an average tribal family comprised 5 members. This total estimate included the tribal population of 9305 of Kailashahar Sub-Division, which was separately enumerated by the Sub-Divisional Officer of Kailashahar. The whole exercise was wide of the mark as some tribal families in each village were exempted from payment of house-tax. The average size of the tribal family was also greater than a family consisting of 5 members as the enumeration of Kailashahar indicated.[5]

C. W. Bolton, Political Agent of Hill Tipperah, in his Administration Report for 1876-77 presented a more realistic estimate of Hill Tipperah's total population, which was 91, 759[6]. This was divided into two segments: (i) 36, 035 persons living in the plains and (ii) 55, 724 in the hills. The community-wise divisions of population were as follows:

Table 23.1
Population of Hill Tipperah, 1876 – 77

Population of the plains				**Population of the Hills**
Bengali	Hindus	6, 663	Tipperahs	31,751
"	Muslims	19,504	Jamaliyas	5, 104
	Manipuris	7,187	Noatias	
	Christians	119	Riangs	4, 625
Assamese &	Gurkhas	80	Halams	6, 391
	Mughs	373	Kukis	4, 955
	Tipperahs	1,809		2, 898
	Total	36,035		55,724

Grand Total : 91,759

Both the estimates were on the low side. For, the 1901 census returned the tribal population of 91, 679.

The tribe- wise break-up of hill population in 1901 is given below[7]:

Table 23.2
The Tribe- Wise Break-Up Of Hill Population In 1901

Tribe	Population
1. Tripura (including Riang, Noatia and Jamatiya)	75, 781
2. Chakma	4, 510
3. Kookie	7, 547
4. Halam	2, 215
5. Mog	1, 491
6. Lushai	135
	91,679

The tribal population of Tripura increased somewhat with the immigration of tribals, like the Chakmas and Mogs, from Chittagong Hill Tracts for settling down in Tripura. Even then it might be presumed that the tribal population of Hill Tipperah in the 1870s could not be less than nearly fifty thousand since the rate of natural growth of tribal population had been quite low in that period.

The Imperial Census of India was first taken in 1872 and the second census was taken in 1881. Since then Census enumerations of population had been conducted every ten years in British India as also in the princely-ruled states, including Tripura. Population of Tripura and its decadal growth rates indicated by these census enumerations are noted below:[8]

Table 23.3
Population Of Tripura And Its Decadal Growth Rate: 1872– 1901

Year	Population	Decadal increase	Percentage of decadal growth
1872	35, 262	——	——
1881	95, 637	+ 60, 375	171%
1891	1, 37, 442	+ 41, 805	44%
1901	1, 73, 325	+ 35, 883	26%

The census operations of 1872, 1881 and 1891 were marked by under-renumeration of population because of difficulties in communication with the remote hill villages, illiteracy of the people, and general aversion to enumerations for fear of being subjected to increased imposition of taxes and duties by the Government. In this regard, L. S. S. Omally in his census Report for 1921 aptly observed:

"The first Census of the State was admittedly incomplete and that of 1881 was also probably inaccurate. So that the abnormal increase of 171 percent recorded in 1881 and the very high rate of growth of 44 percent returned in 1891 must be discounted. The first reliable Census was that of 1901 according to which the number of inhabitants was 26 percent more than (that) ten years before".[9]

In 1901, of the total population of 1, 73, 325, 91, 679 persons were tribals who constituted 52.89 percent of the total population. Only a miniscule minority of the tribal population – about a few thousand – lived in the plains while the rest lived in the hill villages. Population of the plain-dwellers was about eighty thousand persons.

Much of the hilly terrain of Tripura was under bamboo forests where the hill people practised slash and burn or shifting cultivation locally known as *jhum-_chash* for growing their main food crop, rice, besides some minor food grains like corn, millet, maize, *kaon,* etc. In some places tapioca and sweet potatoes were cultivated. *Jhuming_*was a system of mixed cropping for, in the same *jhum_*field along with paddy, other crops, such as, oilseeds, cotton and vegetable, were cultivated simultaneously. Of course, these crops different as they were, matured on different dates and these were harvested in that sequence. Pumpkin, brinjal, chilli, gourd, melon, etc. were the main vegetables grown in the jhum fields. Their main oilseed, sesame, and their main fibre crop, cotton, were the two important jhum crops. Sugarcanes were also produced on a small scale by the *jhumias.* Since the *jhumias* were addicted to smoking some quantity of tobacco was grown in their courtyard/kitchen gardens. Some of the *jhum* crops, such as, vegetables,oilseeds, cotton and even a few fine and amorous grains, mainly *Kaon,* were grown not only for self-consumption but also for sale. The system of shifting cultivation in most cases was less productive per unit of labour-year as well as per unit of land than in the case of settled plough cultivation system in the plains. They, however, grew some surplus of cash crops for sale to meet their subsistence needs and to pay taxes to the Raja. The surplus of oilseeds, cotton and some grain produced in the *jhum,* some minor forest products collected by them, such as, bamboo, lac, honey, wax, wild animal products, like skins and hides, ivory and a few items of their household industry products, viz, mats, baskets, were exchanged for cash to pay taxes, redeem debts and procure necessaries from markets in the plains.

By the time Maharaja Birchandra ascended the throne and willy nilly initiated the process of modernization in Tripura, many of the *jhumia* families had already lost much of their traditional self-sufficiency in economy. The system of jhuming in forest lands caused denudation of forests and erosion of soil on the hill slopes resulting in decrease in soil fertility as well as productivity of *jhum* farming. Even then the jhumia families were required to pay house-tax and excise duties on some of their crops. Duties were also imposed on the traders-cum-money lenders (*mahajans*) for their crop-credit (locally known as *dadan*) and at times even for meeting current consumption needs.

An average tribal family's diet consisted of rice, green leaves, vegetable, tubers, arums, obtained from the *jhum* and/or collected from forests, one or two pulses and beans, fresh fish caught from nearby streams and dried and fermented fish partly home-processed and partly procured from market, eggs and meat (such as, chicken, pork, flesh of hunted animals). They did not take milk or milk products. The Hinduized group of Tripura tribes did not take beef. Their cooking process was simple, hygienic and would ensure nourishment. They boiled rice but did not throw away the gruel, which was allowed to be soaked into the boiled rice. Use of fat and hot spices other than chilli – both green and powdered – was uncommon. Consumption of rice beer was indeed very heavy, so also smoking of tobacco by men, and opium by some tribesmen. They used wooden, earthen and metal pots, depending on availability and affordability, for cooking and as receptacles. They also used banana leaves, which served as eating plates and cut bamboo pieces for storing water and cooking some items of food. Also they made use of hardened gourd shells as bottles for both storing and fetching water from the streams. This short description of food habits and simple mode of living of the tribal people of Tripura indicates that they were very much dependent on their own farming activities and free collections from forests for their living. Naturally then they remained outside the pale of market mechanism to a great extent. This made their economy simple and stationary, and they felt no urge either to grow more for improving their living standard.

Many tribal families were economically too hard- pressed even to carry on with their austere living. The common run of tribals living in hill villages were cut off from the outside world. They were illiterate, habitually easy- going, improvident and unambitious. For most of them taking to settled plough cultivations in the plains was taboo. Their jhum-based economy was basically a static one, which precluded all urge to save and accumulate. In such an environment of the zero- growth economy, the majority of them wallowed even in a very low level of living without raising any grumbling voice. It looked as if they enjoyed a sort of 'bliss of ignorance' as one Political Agent had observed after visiting their villages.

Such a frozen society, however, started melting, albeit at an extremely slow pace as Birchandra Manikya began the process of modernization in administrative, fiscal, judicial, land and other revenue management systems pressured as he was by the British government. The tribal communities' living in isolation also began dissipating. The pattern and direction of such changes in the lifestyle of both the tribal and non-tribal population of Tripura shall be studied in chapter 24.

In the plains of 'Hill Tipperah' lived mainly the members of the royal family and their kin, members of the feudal nobility, civil and military officers and men and their families, the settled cultivators belonging to Bengali, Manipuri and a few Assamese and Gurkha families, besides some tribals who settled down in the foothills and valleys for practising settled cultivation. Some Christian families of Portuguese origin, who migrated from Chittagong about seven generations earlier settled down in a village called Mariamnagar near Agartala.[10]

Cultivation was the occupation of almost all the settlers in the plains other than those in the employ of the Government, members of armed forces and a few professionals. There were hardly any professional artisans; of course, for the tribals, Manipuri and Assamese women spinning and weaving of cotton textiles was a part of their routine household chores. There were also no traders among the local population who could be classed professional. Trading operations were in the hands of the professional traders hailing from the neighbouring districts of Bengal. Illiteracy was nearly universal. No wonder then, there was no middle class in the society. In the hills all the households had access to forest lands for *jhuming* and for growing their foodgrain and crop. In the plains also land was available for cultivation on favourable terms of land settlement. Therefore, there was no class of landless wage labourers skilled or unskilled. For supply of such labour Hill Tipperah had to depend on workers brought in from neighbouring districts of Bengal. To meet the requirement of labour, Tripura Raj imposed the system of *taithung* in the hills and in the plains impressment of labour according to which *raiyats* were under compulsory obligation to render free service to the state when required for public use. This was one of the factors that discouraged immigration of the cultivating class from neighbouring districts even though settlement of lands was obtainable on easy terms.

The *taithung* system imposed the obligation on hill-men and women of any village to provide free labour for carrying luggage of the touring officials, and if required, for clearing jungles for opening paths to facilitate their movement to the next village, where another batch of workers would render *taithung* service.

There was the system of slavery, which mainly served the interest of the *Thakurs*, who were members of the nobility. They indulged in purchasing hill men as slaves mainly for attending to their domestic chore. Generally the hill men facing economic hardships sold themselves for either a specified or even an unspecified period of time to the *Thakurs* for liquidating debts. A hill man often sold himself along with his wife and children. If a hill man died or fled before completing his tenure of slavery, his children had to serve as slaves of that master. This pernicious system continued until it was abolished under pressure of the British Government in 1878 in the teeth of opposition from the *Thakurs.*[11]

The small size of population in the plains and chronic shortage of labour restricted the area of land brought under cultivation to only about 100 sq miles. And even this became possible because of the system that allowed the British Indian subjects from the adjacent districts of Bengal to cultivate and grow crops as Ziratia tenants within the boundary of Hill Tipperah without having to settle down in the state. They entered Hill Tipperah and stayed there during the cultivating season and took back the crops after harvesting. They were, of course, required to pay the usual land revenue charges to the Raja.[12] In times of food scarcity in the state the Durbar imposed restrictions on them stipulating that none of them would be allowed to take back with him grown paddy in excess of the quantity each Ziratia tenant's household needed for self-consumption.

Two varieties of rice, *Aman* (autumn rice) and Aush (summer rice) in the proportion of roughly 3:1 were grown by the cultivators in the plains. They also grew in their homestead lands sugarcane, though not in plenty, a few varieties of pulse and vegetable, tobacco, etc. Even though the technology of production was poor and the cultivators depended on rain water for irrigation they were self- sufficient in rice they produced which was their staple food. In normal years, which were free from natural calamities and pest attacks affecting crop-production, some surplus of rice was produced which could be exported. All the subjects of the Raja, whether living in the hills or in the plains, were entitled to collect forest products for self-consumption free of cost. Economic conditions of the plainsmen were satisfactory at the subsistence level. They were free from indebtedness and had lands of their own. No wonder there were no beggars in the state and the crime rate was also very low.[13]

Transport and communication system was utterly undeveloped. There were only a few unmetalled mud roads, the only wheeled means of transport was bullock cart. People covered distances mostly on foot, and would carry loads of goods on head; palanquins were used by some who could afford them but only on ceremonial occasions. The King and his kin rode elephants for moving from place to place. Some rivers, namely, the Gomati, the Howrah, the Khowai, the Manu and the Muhuri, were navigable by boats not carrying heavy loads. Bamboo, timber and some other forest products were floated downstream to bring them to the plains. Elephants were used for moving heavy timber loads from the forests to the river points. Sawing of trees and timber was done by using long saws.

The members of the feudal nobility were known as the *Thakurs*. They were the sons of the reigning Raja and the descendents of the Rajas preceding him and also others intimately related to the royal family helping to establish and strengthen the dynastic rule of the Tripura Rajas. Among the *Thakurs,* however, the *Kartas* were highest in the hierarchy. They were the male descendents of the reigning Raja.

The highest administrative posts were occupied by the *Kartas* and the posts somewhat lower in the hierarchy, including those which were judicial were reserved for the *Thakurs*. These were not salaried positions since the *Thakurs* were fully supported by the state. Moreover, collection of a few taxes and duties was assigned to the *Thakurs* on very attractive terms. This practice rendered the revenue structure and the system of revenue administration very uneconomical, inefficient and inequitable. It created a powerful and exploitative rentier class.

The main heads of revenue collections were: land revenue, house tax, taxes an forest produce, duties on cotton, sesame and a number of other items including opium, wine, etc. Besides, duties on exports and imports, royalty on elephant catching, catching of birds and small wild animals, cesses imposed on social ceremonies like marriage, etc. also yielded some revenue. As already mentioned the net income from the zemindary estate of Chakla Roshnabad was the most important source of income of the ruling Rajas until the fiscal system was thoroughly reformed. House Tax was collected by village chiefs and was directly paid to the Raja on a particular festival day when the chiefs assembled in the capital and were entertained to a great feast given by the Raja. This practice was followed in order to strengthen the bonds of loyalty of the hill subjects to the Raja. The task of collection of other farmers' revenue was assigned to sub-farmers. Many of these sub-farmers were the Bengalis of the neighboring districts. These tax-farmers were very influential and powerful. The whole system was wasteful and regressive; moreover, it created a powerful and exploitative rentier class.

Public expenditures out of the state's revenues were made mainly on the Raja and his family's maintenance, their marriage and religious ceremonies, pilgrimage to holy places, tours and travels within and outside the state all of which involved extravagant expenses. Next in importance was the expenditures incurred on the salaries and perquisites of civil and military staff and the members of the feudal nobility, and on procurement of office and military equipment and weaponry. Expenditure on public works like roads, canals, bridges and on education, public health drainage and sanitation, etc. was most casual and of insignificant proportion to the total amount of public expenditure. Some investments were, of course, made by different Rajas for the purpose of building temples, tanks, royal palaces and for building a few unmetalled *Kuchha* roads. In fact, there was no system entailing preparation of annual budget estimates in order to guide expenditure. What is more, there was no provision for keeping the Raja's private finances separate from those of the state government. Therefore, the fiscal management of the state was highly arbitrary and regressive in nature.

In a primitive economy like that of Hill Tipperah one source of capital formation could be the growth of population and labour supply. Ester Boserup has explained why in the case of primitive communities, population 'growth necessitates a high rate of investment' to be mobilized by the cultivators for maintenance of their larger families by reducing 'the periods of leisure enjoyed by them' and activating their idle labour hours for increasing production. This process did not depend on the cultivators' ability and willingness to reduce consumption in order to save and invest but on the effective incentive to additional work by the increased number of family members.[14] This source of capital accumulation remained untapped in the hill villages, as the growth rate of the tribal population in the hills was nearly zero. But when the hill farmers took up settled cultivation in the plains (mainly in foot-hill region) they were able to create capital. But such a trend was extremely feeble in the nineteenth century. The other prime source of capital generation could be the immigration of settled cultivators from outside the state. Even this trend became manifest only from the beginning of the twentieth century.

"The Limits of The Possible:"

In all spheres in Hill Tipperah, such as, population, both in terms of quantity and quality, productive utilization of natural resources on a sustainable basis, technology of production, state of physical infrastructure, the limits of the possibility of raising people's productivity and expanding the area of their choices were extremely attenuated. As already noted, density of population was very low, only 16.5 per sq. km. for the entire state. It meant that large areas were uninhabited by people and so were under forest, jungles, marshes, bushes, etc. where wild animals and insects roamed. This was a clear picture of an utterly undeveloped and economically backward state. Not only was the size of population small, but its composition was such as would make the quality of human resource very low. Technology of production was primitive, and the physical infrastructure required for expanding productive use of available resources was almost non-existent.

The slender limits of the scope for expanding economic performances were further compounded by the feudal, profligate, static, corrupt, conservative, inefficient and despotic administrative structure of the state.

NOTES AND REFERENCES

1. A. Mackenzie, 1995. The North-East Frontier of India, reprinted edition of author's book titled, *History of the relations of Government with the hill tribes of the north-east frontier of Bengal,* first published in 1884. Reprinted by Mittal Publications, New-Delhi, p. 272.
2. Kailashchandra Singha, 1985. *Rajmala or Tripurar Itibritta* (in Bengali), reprinted edition, edited by Mahadeb Chakraborty, Jyotish Datta, Ratna Das and Vhishmadev Bhattacharyya, Barnamala Prakashani, Agartala, p. 195 (of 4th Part, 6th chapter)
3. Dipak Kumar Chaudhuri (ed), 1996, *Administration Report of the Political Agency, Hill Tipperah (1872-1878),* Vol.I, Government of Tripura, Agartala, p.137.
4. *ibid.*
5. *ibid.* pp. 39-40
6. *ibid.* p.112.
7. Asitchandra Chaudhury, *Census Report. 1310 Tripura Era, 1901 A.D.* (in Bengali), republished by the Tribal Research Institute, Government of Tripura in 1995, p.18.
8. Asitchandra Chaudhury, *ibid,* p.(v)
9. *ibid* p.(Vi)
10. Dipak Kumar Chaudhuri (ed), op.cit. pp. 105-06.
11. *ibid. Administration Report, 1975-76,* Para 13 and Admin. Report, 1976 -77, Para 10.
12. Mahadev Chakravorti, 1994. The Ziratia Problem of Tripura, published in J. B. Bhattacharjee, ed. *Studies in the Economic History of North East India, Shillong,* pp.384-403.
13. Dipak Kumar Chaudhuri (ed), 1996.*Administration Report of the Political Agency, Hill Tipperah (1878-79 – 1889-90),* Vol. II, Government of Tripura, (Report for 1881-82) p. 81.
14. Ester Boserup, 1965. *The conditions of Agricultural Growth: The Economics of Agrarian change under Population Pressure,* George Allen and Unwin Ltd, London, p.88 (vide, also the Preface P. XIII of this book).

24
STRUCTURAL CHANGES IN TRIPURA'S SOCIO-ECONOMIC FORMATIONS IN THE LATE NINETEENTH CENTURY

Tripura state's formation was somewhat unique in the sense that even though the rule of the independent Rajas of Tripura covered only the hilly terrain and narrow strips of plains in the northern, western and southern parts of the state bordering British India, they also held a permanently settled zamindari estate known as Chakla Roshnabad. It was situated in British India and spread over the districts of Tripura, Noakhali and Sylhet. The zamindary estate bordered Hill Tipperah on its West. The importance of this zamindari in the state structure is evident from the fact that, even though it was a part of British India, it was also an "integral portion of an impartible Raj". Therefore "the normal Zamindary rules", asserts Chaudhuri, "were not applicable to it". Thus, on the one it could not be auctioned like other zamindaries, even in default of Government revenues, because it was 'impartible', on the other, it was always beyond sale, because none other than the Raja of Tripura could acquire its proprietorship. It was the zamindari of a specific Raj, and the succession to the zamindari was always dependent on the succession to the Raj"[1].

The income earned from the zamindari, mainly as land revenue from the tenants, most of whom were the Bengali cultivators was the most important source of the Tripura Raja's income without which maintenance of civil and military establishments and some basic physical infrastructure, so essential for sustaining the rule of the Rajas over Hill Tipperah, could not have been possible.

Hill Tipperah's internal economic formation represented a tribal formation that was based on the practice of the primitive method of shifting cultivation. Of course, being a part of the state of Tripura, the hill farmers produced not only foodgrain mainly for self-consumption but also other crops like cotton, oilseeds (sesame) and some vegetable and collected commercially useful forest produce which they sold to transactors from outside. Such exports were subjected to payment of duties to the Raja. The tribal households were required to pay house tax to the Raja. Therefore the economic system was a sort of mixed bag though its management structure built by the Rajas was a feudalistic and medieval one.

Changes in these formations were first initiated under the inducement of the British in the 1870s by Birchandra Manikya who ruled Hill Tipperah from 1862 to1896. During his rule the British for the first time appointed their Political Agent in Tripura in 1871. This development was made in pursuance of the British Government's policy of enjoining on the rulers of the princely states to carry out reforms in the native systems of administration of law and justice, land settlements, public finance, etc. The Political Agents particularly urged upon the rulers to build up proper fiscal management structure in order to expand the revenue base for increasing state's income and curb unwarranted profligacy of the rulers with a view to enhancing public expenditures on basic infrastructure, etc. Emphasis was also laid on the need for providing modern medical and public health services as well as educational facilities for the subjects. Another significant objective was to advise the Raja of Tripura to open up the state's nearly closed economy by expanding the range and volume of economic transactions with the outsiders. The office of the Political Agency of Tripura was abolished in 1890 but a system of remote control by the British Government was indirectly exercised even after 1890. The Raja was required to submit an annual report on his administration to the Government. Of course the tenure of the Political Agency from 1871 to 1890 was marked by several effective measures adopted for paving the way for Tripura's transition, although at a slow pace, from the medieval to the modern milieu. In this respect the Political Agents had not only succeeded in swaying the Raja's decision in favour of change and his methods of going about it, but also actively took part in overseeing the running of schools, the Agartala Municipality, the state-run hospital /dispensary, etc.

The Political Agents wanted to bring about reforms in the chaotic, uneconomical and oppressive system of fiscal management prevailing the state. They repeatedly suggested to prepare annual budget estimates and to raise revenue earnings by rationalizing the taxation structure and the system of collection of land revenue, taxes and duties on the one hand, and effecting economy in non-productive current expenditures on the other. The largest amount of expenditure incurred by the Raja was on meeting his personal and household establishment expenses. The Raja lavishly spent the state's revenue income on these accounts. Besides, he had to spend large sums of money on fighting the legal battles for safeguarding his throne.

The fiscal mismanagement reached a critical stage as the total expenditures incurred by the Raja per annum went on exceeding the total annual earnings from Hill Tipperah's internal sources and that from the zamindari. As a result the King had to borrow substantial amounts of fund from different sources and even had to defer the payment of salaries to the public servants. The Raja was also constrained to take advances from the tax and land revenue farmers to tide over the crisis. The Political Agents sought to advise the Raja to carry out fiscal reforms. But they were not furnished with the information about the Raja's accumulated debt burden as it was considered a 'State secret'. Therefore they had to depend on their own sources for estimating the amount of debt burden. Such estimates might not have been very accurate but perhaps were not far off the mark. The Political Agent in his Report for 1877-78 estimated that the Raja's debt burden amounted to 5 lakh of rupees[2 (a)]. What was more, this debt burden was steadily increasing over the years. The interest liabilities also were ruinous for the state exchequer as the rates of interest varied from 30 to 70 per cent per annum. Borrowing at such exhorbitant rates had to be resorted to mainly for the purpose of paying revenue tax to the Government on account of the Chakla Roshnabad zamindari.

By 1884-85 the financial condition of the state reached a disastrous level as the total debt burden exceeded eleven lakh of rupees as estimated by the Political Agent. The manner of management of this debt burden, as revealed in the Political Agent's Report for that year[2(b)], was also unusual and uneconomical. Nearly half of the total debt amount of Rs.11 lakh represented the salaries and allowances of officers, pensioners and other categories of Government staff besides the amounts of purchase made from the shopkeepers and other tradesmen on credit (without interest) to meet the personal requirements of the Raja and his family. For the balance of the debt burden about Rs. 80,000/-had to be paid annually as interest calculated 'at the rate of 12 per cent per annum'[2(c)].

The Political Agents, one after another, advised the Raja to introduce the system of preparation of annual budgets showing total revenues and expenditures of the state. But it was not done until 1891-92. From 1873-74, however, the practice of preparation of annual statements of revenues derived from all sources was started. Total expenditures of the state were not revealed obviously to keep the Raja's personal and private expenditures a closely guarded secret. At Tripura's level of economic development in the late nineteenth century, it was of great importance that the state's financial resources were properly managed for facilitating capital formation by the government and development of infrastructure and providing some incentives to the private sector to save income and accumulate.

The data about Tripura's revenue earnings from 1873-74 onward throw much significant light on the economic activities and growth of the state. Though figures for the total public expenditures were not available for the years prior to 1891-92, the Political Agents in their annual reports gave some information about public expenditures on education, health, municipal services, etc. Social development dependent on such state financed efforts was vital for propelling economic growth by raising the quality of human resource.

1. Education

In 1872 there were only two schools in the whole state one was located at Agartala and the other at Kailashar. The former with 40 students on its roll was known as the Maharaja's School as it was patronized by the king who provided a small monthly grant of Rs.30/- only that was quite insufficient for paying salaries to teachers and meeting other costs of maintenance. The students were the sons of officials and government employees and of talukders. They all belonged to 'the better classes'. The Political Agent in his Report for 1873-74 mentioned that monthly deductions were made from the salaries of *amlahs* (government staff) which came as voluntary subscriptions for the maintenance of schools. The school of Kailashar in the North Sub-division was opened by the Superintendent of Kailashar in 1871 with 8 or 9 students on the roll. It received a state grant of Rs.15/- per month. The Political Agent noted that the number of students increased to 25 or so in 3 months. School education in the state that got started in the 1870s was an important move towards modernization. The state grant to Kailashar School was raised to Rs.180/- per month in 1873-74. School fees cellected from students partly met the total expenses for running the school.

The number of schools of different standards located in different parts of the state and the strengths of student enrolment in these schools had grown for some years since 1874-75. In the beginning all the schools were for boys only; the first school for girls was started in 1876 in a Christian village known as Marriamnagar near Agartala.

Progress of school education in the eighties had a downward slide. The number of boys' schools fell from 31 in 1880-81 to only 16 in 1889-90 and the strength of student enrolment (boys) went down from 692 in 1882-83 to 493 only in 1888-89.

The picture of girls' education was even more dismal. The total number of primary schools for girls was 4 in 1879-80 having 64 students on the roll. But there were only 2 primary schools in 1884-85, which had only 26 students on the rolls. From the reports of the Political Agents it could be ascertained that such a regressive trend in the growth of school education was on account of the facts that the schools suffered from financial stringencies as both the state authorities and the people who mattered were indifferent and callous about the need for educating their children. There was also a lurking fear in the minds of many guardians that education among their children would alienate them from their families and the social and religious moorings.

The system of school inspection was unsatisfactory, and neither the teachers were paid their salaries on time, nor the stipendiary students got their stipends regularly.

In fact the state had no defined education policy nor had it any official structure for properly overseeing the opening and running of schools. May be, the Raja was apprehensive of the consequences of the spread of education among his subjects that would lead to the emergence of the middleclass which could be vocal, articulating people's needs and grievances and raise questions about the Raja's unfettered powers and official privileges and so on.

Even though the Political Agents were much interested in getting the Raja and his Kin – the *Thakurs*, involved in providing educational facilities for the tribals, nothing effective was done to induce the tribal parents to send their children to schools in the plains or to open schools in tribal villages.

The scenario of educational development somewhat changed for the better after 1890 when Umakanta Das was appointed by Birchandra as his Minister with the consent of the Government. Das, who was a member of the Bengal Civil Service, was first appointed an Assistant Political Agent in 1878. The number of primary schools steadily increased from 36 in 1896 (the last year of Birchandra's rule) to 43 in1897, 47 in1898, 63 in 1902, 88 in 1903, 91 in 1904, 99 in 1905 and 137 in1908. It happened during the reign of Birchandra's successor, Radhakisore Manikya, who effectively promoted the modern system of education and of health services, besides agricultural production. In the next chapter these developments will be studied.

2. Medical and Health Service

General conditions relating to health, hygiene and sanitation in Agartala 'town' and adjacent villages were very unsatisfactory and no wonder, there used to be outbreak of cholera almost every other year. The Political Agent in his report for 1873-74 recorded that one dispensary – a charitable one –was opened in 1873 by the Raja. On the advice of the Political Agent, the service of Dr Stork, Medical Officer of Comilla, was placed under the Tripura Raja in 1873. For treatment of patients the Raja provided medicines, and Dr Stork his service gratis. But the unit did not have adequate furniture and other equipment. In that year, however, as many as 3034 outdoor patients were treated in the Hospital.

In April and May 1873 cholera broke out in an epidemic proportion in Agartala town and adjacent villages and many people deserted their homes in panic. Dr Stork treated the patients using medicines supplied by the Raja. By 1990 the number of charitable dispensaries rose to four—'one at the headquarters station of each of the four sub-divisions of the state.' There was also an additional charitable dispensary attached to royal palace which distributed free medicines to the general public as also to the members of the Raja's household. It had two departments – one for allopathic and another for homeopathic treatment of patients. This dispensary was kept open day and night and heavy work was done in it.

Dr Stork resigned and left Agartala in October 1874 and since then Bengali doctors had run the dispensaries and treated patients.

To prevent cholera, pox and dysentery epidemics improvements in the sanitary conditions in Agartala and nearby areas were badly needed. 'The place was over-run with jungle, and after a little rain all the surrounding country' became 'an unhealthy swamp'. That was why the Political Agent strongly felt that municipal matters should be properly organized to deal with these problems.

The Agartala Municipality was instituted in 1871 with the Political Agent as its Chairman. The Raja paid a grant of Rs. 3,100/- "which was spent on building a bridge, making roads through the bazaar, repairing sheds for market days, etc". Subsequently, the Municipality became much ineffective. The Political Agent in his Report for 1873-74 resented that the sanctioned money for that year was not given to the Committee, the overseer did not receive his salary for some months and payments for works done were outstanding for a considerable period of time. To set the municipal matters right, a Municipal Act was framed in 1873-74, which came into operation on 9 April 1874 (1st of Baisakh).The Act contained some sensible rules regarding sanitary matters"— and under it taxes could be levied on "the rate payers, assessed according to their circumstances, and the extent and value of the property proposed to be protected". The town was divided into eight wards and a chowkidar appointed.[3]

But even in1875 the Municipality remained practically inoperative. This made the Political Agent observe, "It is my intention to advocate that this sham institution be abolished. In a place like this, where the Raja's word is law, and where all dread his power in a manner almost slavish, it is absurd to suppose that any institution can flourish which is based on a system of self-government".[4]

Till the end of the Political Agency, which came off in 1890 the Municipality's achievements were extremely limited; the problems of drainage, conservancy, and unsatisfactory conditions of town roads continued. But a beginning had been made in developing the municipal service in the state and in the prevailing feudal environment that was a significant step indeed towards reforming the administrative structure.

3. Post Office

Development of postal and tele-communication services was of vital importance for ending Tripura's isolation from the world outside and for facilitating the process of modernization. On October 1, 1875 a post office was opened for which the Raja made a monthly grant of Rs.40. The Political Agent served as its ex-officio Post Master. It became very useful for the people and the volume of postal transactions handled by this post office expanded from year to year. In the Administration Report for 1889-90 it is mentioned that in 1889-90 an amount of Rs.90,553 was remitted from this post office in money orders and Rs.5,840 in insured covers, as against Rs.83,785 and Rs.3,815 respectively in the previous year. The amount of money orders paid from this post office in 1889-90 was Rs.34,480 against Rs.31,116 reported last year.[5] "The Imperial Postal Department proposed to have a few additional post offices established in the interior of the state. The Durbar did not view the proposal with favour, but to remove public inconvenience undertook to effect the delivery by its own establishment of all covers intended for parties living far in the interior of the hills which the postman could not conveniently visit"[6]. This arrangement obviously restricted the access of the people in the interior places to other postal services, like purchasing stamps, sending money orders.

The Political Agent in his note dated 5 July1890 proposed to open telegraphic communication between Brahmanbaria and Comilla and to provide a branch line to Agartala and a through connection to Cachar. But this proposal took time to materialize.

4. Communcations

Land communication facilities within the state were utterly undeveloped and those between Agartala and the nearest towns outside the state were almost non- existent. In 1875 the Political Agent noted that Agartala was almost cut off from the rest of the world for want of land communication. Communication by water also was open only in the rainy season. Within the state there were no roads at all and there was 'only an apology for one ' in Agartala town. To visit Kailashahar in the north of the state it was necessary to make a long detour by the rivers through Tripura and Sylhet districts, which took about 15 days. In that year a survey work was undertaken for the purpose of constructing a road to connect Agartala with the road that links Comilla with Brahmanbaria in Tripura district of British India.[7] Subsequently construction of this road was completed as also communication facilities of moderate standard only were opened up in the sub-divisional stations. But for lack of funds allotted for improvement of roads, conditions in the interior areas were worse and extremely bad. "Hill paths were of course cut as usual during the winter to allow the hill peons and sepoys to pass from the capital of the state to the several posts and offices in the interior, and also to the principal hill villages. These paths were cut by the hillmen themselves free of cost. The work, however, was done according to the instructions and under the supervision of the local officers of the state".[8]

5. Economic Growth

During Bir Chandra's rule the process of modernization of the socio-economic structure was just a beginning and its pace was extremely slow and its gamut restricted to a narrow range. The Raja was not at all very enthusiastic about steering changes in the traditional, primitive and regressive socio-economic and political institutions. Most of the structural changes were reluctantly effected by the Durbar under pressure of the British authorities. For example, the pernicious system of slavery and of *Sati* (burning of Hindu widows) was abolished in 1877 and1889 respectively following persistent urgings of the Political Agents, although the Government abolished both these systems in India much earlier, that is, in 1843 and 1829 respectively. The most important areas of reform related to the introduction of annual budgets of the state's income and expenditures and the systems of revenue collections and items of taxation, opening of schools for education of children, establishment of medical dispensaries for treatment of diseases and fighting epidemic diseases, constitution of the Agartala Municipality, building roads within the state as well as roads to connect Agartala with Comilla- Brahmanbaria road, opening of postal facilities, etc.

Even though these changes were inadequate for improving the living conditions of people to their potential heights, they had, however, promoted some measure of economic growth of the state. The total area brought under settled cultivation was expanded as there was immigration of population, although at a very low rate as yet and land revenue rates were made attractive for encouraging settled plough cultivation to spread. This move not only attracted immigration of farm population from outside but also encouraged some tribal and non-tribal resident farmers to reclaim waste lands in the plains for settled cultivation. In the 1870s only an area of 100 sq. miles out of the total cultivable area of 1500 sq. miles was under actual cultivation.

Therefore, the scope for expanding the area of settled cultivation was still quite considerable.

6. Land Revenue System in 1870's

The Political Agent's Report for 1878-79 indicates that sizable portions of lands in the plains were given by the Rajas to various persons by way of favour or in consideration of services rendered. These landed estates accounting for nearly one –fourth of the total cultivable lands represented Devottor, Brahmattor or service lands. About one-eighth of agricultural lands was, 'dug for purposes of tanks'.

"By granting *taluki pottahs* (*pattas*) to enterprising cultivators", writes the Political Agent, "the state has reclaimed a considerable portion which is now under cultivation. Besides *taluks*, there are under them *dar-taluks*, and under *dar-taluks*, and the *ryoti jotes*. Some of the *taluks* are permanent, while others are *meadi*. Ryots have occupancy rights, which however, they can enjoy only as long as the enjoyment does not tend to mar the interest of any one of the Thakurs who are the principal talukdars" (italics added to mark the local terms).[9]

Over the years the system of land tenure evolved as follows: The Raja was the sole proprietor of lands and enjoyed the right to distribute land rent-free if he so pleased, or rent-paying of different terms and conditions. Among rent-paying tenures there were *jangal-abadi* leases, the usual conditions of which were that the land would be *rent-free* "for a period of from four to ten years, according to the nature of the jungle, then to be subject to rent at the rate of 2 or 3 annas per bigha, gradually increasing till it reaches a moderate amount, " which was less than the rate paid for adjoining lands in the British districts of India.[10]

Some lands were leased out on *ijara* basis for a period varying between one and seven years. The *ijaradars* were somewhat like revenue farmers. (They acted as agents for the state). The *talukas* were given as *quami* on rent fixed on permanent basis, *miyadi* or *taskhichi* on rent subject to revision after the given periods. All such landholders were permitted to let out lands to the actual cultivators or *raiyats*.

The *raiyats* could also sub-let their *raiyati jots* to the under-*raiyats* called *korfa* tenants. The common practice was to let the *korfa* tenants to cultivate land on crop-sharing basis (barga system).

In the Koilashahar sub- division certain Brahmins claimed that they were the zamindars as they held land on permanent and hereditary basis at fixed and invariable rates of rent.[11]

There was a unique class of non-resident tenants, known as Ziratia tenants, who were British subjects residing in the adjoining districts of British India, and were mostly living in Chakla Roshnabad (Raja's zamindari in Tripura, Sylhet and Noakhali districts). They cultivated land in Hill Tipperah as raiyats without occupancy rights. They remained in Hill Tipperah during the cultivating season and returned to their homes after harvesting their crops and paying the usual dues to the state. On rare occasions when Tripura faced food shortage the state imposed restrictions on the Ziratia tenants to take out of the state paddy in excess of what was actually needed to meet the consumption requirements of their families.

The pattern of land revenue system and the lower rates of rent than those obtaining in the neighbouring Indian districts favoured immigration of farming and farm-related occupational groups from outside although at very moderate rates. Considerable expansion of cultivation by reclaiming waste lands was effected partly by the immigrant tribal farmers taking to plough cultivation and partly by the Manipuri settlers, who were very industrious and efficient. Numerically the Manipuri settlers in the plains constituted the second largest group after the Bengalis.

Taking advantage of *jangal-abadi* terms of settlement of waste-land reclaimed for cultivation, some members of the indigenous tribal communities, particularly the Tripura and Jamatiya tribes, also slowly started taking to settled plough cultivation in the plains, as an occupation subsidiary to their occupation of shifting cultivation. They often engaged immigrant Bengali Muslim workers for farming operations.

A growing number of Mogs and Chakmas came from the Chittagoang Hill Tracts for settling in Tripura. They also took to settled plough cultivation in the valleys.

The overall impact of such changes was the rise in agricultural output and income of the rural population. This trend was also favoured by the rising trend in the price of rice, the main crop produced by the cultivators. The Political Agent noted that the price of rice had been increasing since 1882-83 with the increasing demand from outside and also withdrawal of 'any restriction upon the free exportation of the grain'.[12]

The Political Agent also observed that both the skilled and unskilled labour had to be brought in from the neighbouring districts as the local residents were 'pretty well off with their agricultural profession' and did not therefore want 'to work for hire'.[13]

That there were positive trends of economic growth was also borne out by the fact that the trade of the country was slowly improving, as was clear from the fact that nearly all the old markets were gradually flourishing and new ones were being 'established in hitherto unimportant places'. The Political Agent further stated that "at each of the head-quarters stations, and almost at each of the police thannas and outposts", there was then a standing market, which was attended by Bengalis and hill people. To quote him: "This is a state of things which was not in existence seven years ago. The purchasing power of the people has evidently increased owing to the generally good harvests which they have obtained successively during the last few years".[14]

External trade was also flourishing yielding greater amounts of revenue as the system of farming out collection of tolls and export duties from the river and land points from where forest produce like bamboos, canes, thatching grass, canes, timber, etc. and the *jhum* products like cotton, *til* (sesamum), etc. would be exported was being replaced gradually. This was done on the advice of the Political Agents by the state government which undertook to manage directly some of the *ghats* (there were nine *ghats* in all called *Khas* -

management). In the late nineteenth century, taxes directly imposed on the volumes of cotton and *til* produced by the farmers and export duties on cotton and *til* were the largest source of revenue for Hill Tipperah. Production of these two crops was also the hill people's main source of money income for paying taxes and purchasing commodities they needed from the market. Cultivation of cotton and *til* was prohibited in the plains, so that the tribals could enjoy the monopoly lover producing these crops, which were their main sources of money income. Of course, they had to pay one –fourth of the quantities of cotton and *til* produced by them as taxes to the state.

In the late 1880s, trade in cotton suffered a setback. The Political Agent noted this development in his report for 1884-85 in which it was stated that the volume of cotton exports fell as production of jute in the adjoining Indian districts steadily increased and as trading in jute became more profitable for the traders from those districts, mainly handling cotton exports from the hills of Tripura, had switched over to jute business. The Political Agent estimated that about one –third of the quantity of cotton available for export remained undisposed of at the end of the year (1874-75).

In absence of demand, the *Kheda* operation for catching elephants remained almost suspended, and consequently revenue earned from sale and exportation of elephants also fell. Yet, the total amount of revenue and total earnings from external trade were on the increase, not only on account of the revision of the structure of taxes and duties and replacement of farming out system by that of *Khas* management but also because of the growth in total output of commodities in the plains as well as the hills. Though the total output figures are not available for that period, from indirect evidences like the trends in revenue earnings and volumes of exports, etc. it might be concluded that Tripura's economy registered a positive trend of growth in the late nineteenth century. In table 24.1 source– wise revenue earnings of Tripura for selected years are given.

Table 24.1
Source-Wise Revenue of Tripura for Selected Years (in Thousand of Rupees)

Year	Land Revenue	Family Tax	Forest Produce	Cotton & Til	Kheda Royalty	Other Sources	Total
1873-74	38.65	24.67	27.33	45.69	18.02	08.99	163.35
1874-75	38.78	24.22	40.40	47.18	24.00	12.35	186.93
1875-76	34.95	24.42	43.10	47.45	37.45	26.12	213.47
1887-88	38.26	28.18	88.41	128.18	7.50	46.82	337.35
1888-89	52.01	20.98	81.85	96.37	4.95	41.35	297.51
1889-90	53.97	28.43	78.95	100.18	5.55	45.32	312.40

Source: Dipak Kumar Chaudhuri, 1999, p.147. Compiled from the Administration Reports for the relevant years.

In table 24.2 proportions of different sources of revenue to the total revenue are given for the same selected years.

Table 24.2
Proportions of Different Sources to Total Revenue (in Percentage Terms)

Year	Land Revenue	Family Tax	Forest Produce	Cotton & Til	Kheda Royalty	Other Sources	Total
1873-74	23.66	15.10	16.73	27.97	11.03	5.50	100.00
1874-75	20.75	12.96	21.61	25.24	12.84	6.61	100.00
1875-76	16.37	11.43	20.19	22.22	17.54	12.24	99.99
1887-88	11.34	8.35	26.21	38.00	2.22	13.88	100.00
1888-89	17.48	7.05	27.51	32.39	1.66	13.90	99.99
1889-90	17.28	9.10	25.27	32.07	1.78	14.51	100.00

Source: Dipak Kumar Chaudhuri, 1999. p. 148. Worked out from Table No.3.1

'Other Sources' include, buffalo mehal (charge for grazing buffalo) collections from cattle pounds, chowkidari tax, Kazia mehal (amount payable by the Kazi of Agartala against his earnings for registering Mohamedan marriages), rents from markets, excise duties on liquour, opium and *gaja*, fines, court fees, stamp duties, registration fees proceeds from jails, fees for summary orders on settlement of debts, sale proceeds from unclaimed property, especially unclaimed timber, etc.

Increase in revenues from land revenue, forest produce, cotton and sesame (til), and from 'other sources' resulted from the expansion of productive activities in agricultural sphere and increased collections of forest produce and also increased volumes and values of exports (see table 24.3 given below). The second highest sector of growth (viz. forest produce), of course, could jeopardise the long–term prospects of growth unless appropriate forest conservation measures were adopted. Creation of the department of forest for scientific management of forest resources was yet to materialize.

Tripura's main items of export in the late eighteenth century were: Cotton, Sesame (*til*), forest produce, such as, timber, thatching grass, bamboo, cane, elephants, singing birds, mats, baskets, charcoal and a little quantity of cotton carpets made by the Kukis (called Poeris), etc. and also dugouts made by the Riangs and Chakmas in their hill habitats which were flowed down by the rivers, Gomati and Fenny to the neighbouring Indian districts.

Rise in the total value of exports from 1880-81 to 1889-90 may be noted from table24.3 which follows:

Table 24.3
Value of Exports from Tripura: 1880-81—1889-90

Year	Total value of exports (Rs.)
1880-81	4,71,718
1881-82	4,99,504
1882-83	5,60,180
1883-84	5,83,628
1884-85	6,26,000
1885-86	6,00,000
1886-87	6,25,000
1887-88	7,82,000
1888-89	6,41,000
1889-90	7,48,000

Source: Dipak Kumar Chaudhuri, 199,p.179 (Compiled from the Reports of the Political Agents for the relevant years).

The products of the shifting cultivators and collections from forests were almost all the items of export from Tripura. The settled cultivators could offer only a little quantity of rice and uncleaned molasses for export.

7. Distributive Aspects of Growth

The tribal producers' contributions to Tripura's economic growth in the given period were relatively much greater than those of the other sections of population, and they were also subjected to relatively greater tax burdens than the rest. For, they paid house tax, which constituted 9.10 per cent of total revenue in 1889-90; taxes on cotton and til produced by them accounted for 32.07 per cent of the total revenue in that year. They also paid a part of the tax of forest produce. The Political Agent pointed out in his report for 1886-87 that some Mog and Riang families emigrated from Tripura to Chittagong Hill Tracts to avoid paying 'the high rates of the family tax and the cotton and the til duty'.[15] The impact of such emigration on the size of total population, however, was marginal. The producers in the plains paid only the land revenue, the rate of which was officially kept very low to attract more settlers. No wonder, the amount of land revenue contributed to the total revenue earned in 1889-90 was only 17.28 per cent. The large part of the income generated in the export trade sector went to the traders from the adjoining districts of India who controlled this trade and also many of the farmers collecting export duty were from outside Tripura. This affected the prospects of capital formation that might result from increased income in the State.

Growth of population due to fall in death rates, as medical and health services improved, and as well as immigration of population was in that period an important factor in enhancing capital formation and growth. The estimated population of Tripura was 95,637 in 1880-81 which increased to an estimated figure of 1,37,442 in 1890-91 and finally to 1,73,325 in 1901. Growth of capital formation resulting from rise in population and change in the technique of cultivation from shifting to settled cultivation pushed up investments in reclamation of waste lands and expansion of area under settled cultivation.[16] This trend was marked by a rise in total amount of land revenue. It increased from Rs. 34,717 in

1880-81 to Rs. 53,973 in 1889-90.[17] From the reports of the Political Agents it has been noted by Chaudhuri that the spurt in land revenue collection was attributable to the reclamation of waste-lands, particularly in Kailashahar and Udaypur sub-devisions by the immigrant Bengali and Manipuri settlers respectively. It was also observed that in some areas even some tribal households 'began to take lease of waste-lands and strarted plough cultivation'.The Jamatiyas of Udaipur took up plainsland for their habitation as well as for practising settled cultivation. They were encouraged by the state by providing them with cattle and agricultural implements.[18]

NOTES AND REFERENCES

1. Dipak Kumar Chaudhuri (1999). *The Political Agents and the Native Raj,* Mittal Publications, New Delhi, p. 2 and Note No. 3 on p.7.
2. (a) *Administration Report of the Political Agency, Hill Tipperah, for 1877-78* (para 10); (b) *Administration Report for 1884-85* (para 43), reproduced in Dipak Kumar Chaudhuri (ed), 1996, *Admn. Report of the Political Agency, Hill Tipperah,* Vol.I and Vol. II, published by Govt. of Tripura.
2. (c) Dipak Kumar Chaudhuri (1999), *op.cit.* p. 79-80.
3. Dipak Kumar Chaudhuri (ed),1996,*op.cit.* Vol.I, p.47.
4. *ibid.* Vol.I. p. 66.
5. *ibid.* Vol. II, p.255.
6. *ibid.* Vol. II, p. 255.
7. *ibid.* Vol. I, p. 53.
8. *ibid.* Vol. II, p. 256.
9. *ibid.* Vol. II, p. 20.
10. W. W. Hunter, *A Statistical Account of Bengal* Vol.VI 1876, reprinted in 1973, Delhi, p.505.
11. Dipak Kumar Chaudhuri (1995), Vol. II, p. 20.
12. *ibid.* p.141.
13. ibid.
14. *ibid.* p.143.
15. *ibid.* p.193.

16. The process of capital formation induced by population growth in certain given conditions has been discussed in chapter I.
17. Dipak Kumar Chaudhuri (1999), p.122,
18. *ibid.* pp.112-113.

25
IMMIGRATION OF POPULATION, INSTITUTIONAL CHANGES, ECONOMIC GROWTH AND FLUCTUATIONS (1901 to 1934)

The modernization process that was initiated by Birchandra Manikya, on the advice of the Political Agents, was continued by his successors even after the office of the Political Agent was withdrawn from Agartala and the District Magistrate of Tripura District of Bengal began acting additionally as the ex-officio Political Agent. During this period experienced officers from Bengal cadre were appointed one after another as Minister or Dewan or as some top-ranking officer. This arrangement resulted in structuring the systems of administration, law and justice, land settlements, education, health services, etc. on modern lines following the pattern prevailing in Bengal Province. Birchandra was succeeded by Radhakishore Manikya in 1897 and after his death in a car accident in Varanasi in 1909, his son Birendra Kishore Manikya ascended the throne in the same year. Both these rulers showed an interest in carrying out reforms and incurred public expenditures on building infrastructure and royal palaces, besides promoting education, health and police services and on mobilization of armed forces, etc. This trend necessitated increased amount of revenue and income for the state Government which could be possible mainly through increase in collections of land revenue and export duties on cotton, sesame, jute, forest produce and a few other items produced in the state. Fulfilment of this objective was dependent on two factors: (i) institutional reforms and migration of population from outside (mainly Bengal) for settlement in the state and (ii) reclamation of waste lands for expansion of the area under cultivation in the plains.

Offer of attractive terms for land settlement encouraged immigration of agrarian population to some extent, and offer of employment in the civil, police and military services under the government also helped. Opportunities provided for joining different professions as teachers, doctors, lawyers, etc. also ensured inflow of population from outside. But for Tripura's economic development, some basic institutional changes were also called for. The adequate functioning of the competitive market mechanism and entrepreneurial involvement in expansion of productive activities and trade transactions – both internal and external – much depended on the enactment of clearly defined laws for protection of private property, enforcement of contractual obligations and freedom of choice in economic decision- making within the limits prescribed by law, etc. For this purpose an appropriate judicial system and an effective law-enforcing body, the police department, needed to be set up. Moreover, it also required setting up several government departments to deal with the problems faced by different productive sectors and to provide the producers in those sectors with incentives and opportunities to adopt higher technologies of production for both increasing and diversifying their outputs.

With Tripura still being ruled by the Rajas who wielded almost absolute power and with the feudal nobilities comprising the *Kartas* and *Thakurs* around them, it was still a far cry from putting in place such institutional arrangements to the fullest extent. Some steps were, however, taken to enact written laws, codes, such as, the criminal procedure code, the civil procedure code, a police guide and a Limitation Act.[1] The old practice of dispensing justice by the rulers in accordance with their sense of equity and good conscience was done away with and the government established two magisterial and one civil courts of original jurisdiction in the Headquarters (Agartala) and above them an appellate court and a court for hearing special appeals from the two criminal courts of original jurisdiction. One of these dealt with the cases involving the hill tribes and the other with those involving non-tribal subjects. The special appeals were heard by the Maharaja himself. This arrangement was subsequently modified by creating the Khas Appeal Adalat with two judges sitting on its bench and the Yubaraj instead of the king presiding over it. Referring to the Bengal Administration Report for 1888-89 Roychoudhury maintains that this arrangement improved the conditions of the subordinate courts and also of the jails.[2] Under an Act of 1908 two classes of courts were constituted for trying civil and criminal cases respectively. There were "the *Khas Adalat* with its original and appellate sides and thirteen or fourteen other courts of Magistrate- Munsiffs exercising original jurisdiction only".[3]

The police administration was much strengthened and improved during Radhakishore Manikya's time by dividing the state into several police thanas and tehsil circles and appointing one Superintendent of Police as the head of the police force. For proper administration of the state it was divided, first, into seven and later into ten sub-divisions placing each of them under the charge of an officer designated as the Magistrate Collector. The modernized system of civil, judicial and police administration helped maintain peace and order and also collection of revenues. Such changes along with the opening of more and more educational institutions, expansion of medical and health services and development of communication facilities encouraged and enabled an increasing number of persons from outside to migrate to Tripura for settlement and to pursue their respective occupations.

Increasing educational and medical facilities were both the causes and consequences of immigration of population into the state. That there was expansion of educational facilities might well be noted from the fact that in 1896 there were only 36 schools at primary level and by 1909 the number increased to 137. Besides, schools at higher levels were also opened, the Umakanta Academy as a Higher English School at Agartala having two branches – one at Kailashahar (for the northern part) and the other at Belonia (for the southern part). In 1910-11, there were 4 Middle English Schools, 1

Higher Vernacular School for boys and 1 Higher Vernacular Schools for girls (the Tulshibati Girls' school) at Agartala . In that year the total number of students attending different schools was 4908 including 255 girl students[5(a)].

In 1902 one college was started at Agartala to provide free higher educations for 'whosoever was fit' for receiving it. But this 'highly flourishing Agartala College' had to be closed down in 1904 as reported in the newspaper Amrita Bazar Patrika dated 20th August 1904.[4] But in order to keep opportunities open for higher education for the students, the then Raja Radhakishore Manikya sanctioned money for the Victoria College at Comilla in Tripura District, for constructing a suitable building to augment its capacity to admit students. He also sanctioned an annual grant of five thousand rupees for that college. Radhakishore Manikya developed friendly relations with Rabindranath Thakur and liberally provided financial help for establishing the Santiniketan Brahmacharya Vidyalaya and sanctioned annual grants for Visva Bharati. The king also extended financial assistance to Jagadish Chandra Bose, the noted scientist, for carrying out his scientific research. Even the Bengali poet Hemchandra Bandyapadhyay, who was blind, was granted an annual pension. Bengali was made the official language of the sate. These good acts of the Raja of Tripura made him popular among the Bengalis who in large numbers continued to immigrate into Tripura for settlement, attracted as they were by the terms of land settlement and job prospects.

In 1897-98 the Department of Agriculture was set up with the main objective of providing opportunities for the shifting cultivators in the hills to take to settled plough cultivation. The Department provided *taccavi* loans and agricultural inputs for the willing hillmen. Of course, hardly any dent could be made in their age-old habit of *jhuming*[5(b)].To augment drinking water facilities, a number of tanks were excavated or kept clean throughout the state.[6]

Considering the potential of sericulture in the state, Jogesh Chandra Chaudhuri, a qualified person, was sent to Japan in 1909-10 for studying the operational details of sericulture. A sericulture farm was established at Kashipur and experiments on the suitable variety of worm and its feed plants were conducted. The experiments were not successful and ultimately the Kashipur farm was closed down.[7]

Although the State Government's hope for the development of sericulture was somewhat belied, prospects of Tripura's industrial development brightened up in the second decade of the twentieth century after allowing private entrepreneurs to start tea plantations after reclaiming waste lands. A young chemist of Tripura, named A.C. Bhattacharyya, after a chemical analysis of Tripura's soils, reported that these were suitable for tea cultivation. Some young entrepreneurs of Bengal, who were enthusiastic over starting new business and industrial ventures by forming joint- stock companies in the post-First World War years, became interested in undertaking tea plantations in Tripura after obtaining settlement of wastelands for this purpose. It was in 1916 that Birendra Kishore Manikya for the first time allowed settlement of waste lands for tea plantations. In the same year the Hirachara Tea Garden – the first one in Tripura was established in Kailashahar (North) Division. In fact there were altogether 4 settlements of waste lands for tea cultivation, 2 in Kailashahar and 2 in Dharmanagar Divisions. Regarding the terms of settlement, the Administration Report for 1916-17 states as follows:

"The *Jama* in each case is enhanceable every 20 years and is Rs. 8 per drone (6.5 acres) with a Nazarana (one – time payment) amounting to a Year's revenue. The total approximate area of the grants is 8000 acres (2000 acres each) or 1260 drones which will bring in a revenue of about Rs.10,000 a year, after 3 years of exemption. Rs.7, 040 has already been received on account of Nazarana. The terms secured included the payment of an *ad valorem* export duty or royalty of 2½ percent on the Calcutta price".[8]

By 1930 the number of tea estates reached 50 covering an area of 3,394 hectares and producing 12, 49,374 pounds of tea. The total number of labourers working in the tea gardens was 5, 451 including 2, 555 women. Most of these labourers were tribals who migrated from Bihar, Orissa, Madras and Madhya Pradesh. Very few of the indigenous tribal people of Tripura worked as tea garden labourers.

All the 50 tea estates were owned and run by the Indian entrepreneurs most of whom were Bengali. Many of them formed joint- stock companies for this purpose.

Development of tea industry boosted employment opportunities, income and exports. In 1929 the total quantum of tea exports was 17, 110 maunds (about 633070 kg) valued at Rs. 6, 84, 400 But the industry was affected by the Great Depression of 1930s. Therefore in 1930 quantity of tea exported came down to 15,310 maund (about 566470 kg,) and the total value to Rs.4, 59, 300.[9]

An important aspect of the development of tea industry in Tripura was the immigration of tribal population from different parts of India, which changed the demographic structure of population of the State.

The Medical Department was established in order to open and run dispensaries and hospitals and to take preventive measures against epidemic diseases like cholera, pox, plague. The modern system of medical treatment received a real breakthrough in 1903 when the Victoria Memorial Hospital was established in Agartala. The State's vaccination programme against epidemic diseases was implemented only in the plains area as, to go by the Political Agent's observations, the hill people resisted being vaccinated[10].

Improvement in the state of Public health and prevention of epidemic diseases much depended on the effective functioning of the Agartala Municipality as the size of urban population was rising and Agartala was the only town in the whole state. Since the highest density of population was in the town, the Municipal services, such as, management of drainage system and maintenance of congenial sanitary environment required to be strengthened. In this regard an important step was taken to prepare a Municipal Bill which received the assent of the king in 1912-13 and the Act became effective in the same year. In accordance with the Act the Municipal Committee was constituted with 4 official and 3 non-official members all of whom were nominated by the Government.[11]

The Public Works Department set up by the State Government was an important institutional event that helped to plan and execute buildings and construction works so essential for the development of the basic infrastructure of the state's economy. In Radhakishore Manikya's time (1897 to 1909) constructions of several buildings, bridges, roads, etc. were undertaken. The royal palace at Agartala was severely damaged by the earthquake of 1897. Therefore a new building, big and imposing, was built as the new royal palace which was named Ujjayanta Raj Palace. The work was executed by the noted firm of engineers, Messrs. Martin & Co of Calcutta. But it also involved excavation of huge tanks, laying gardens, turfs with flower-beds. etc. The buildings came up in Agartala for the Victoria Memorial Hospital, the temple of Lord Jagannatha, the State Museum and one school.

His successor Birendra Kishore Manikya also patronized those engaged in building activities. It was he who got another palace, known as Kunjaban Palace, built on the north of the Ujjayanta Palace in beautiful sylvan surroundings.

In 1913-14 constructions of the road from Amlighat to Sabrum, the buildings for Tulshibati Girl's School, one temple for Goddess Durga and another for Laxmi and Narayana, etc were undertaken in Agartala. In 1915-16 a masonry bridge on the river Muraichhera in Kailashahar division and one dispensary building with corrugated tin-roof on it were constructed at Kailashahar in 1915-16. Costs of these works were borne by two Muslim gentlemen of that area.[12 (a)] In 1916-17 the important public works that were completed included the Carmichael bridge over the river Howrah near Agartala on the Agartala-Udaipur road, the Sonamura-Udaipur road, Sonamura School house, Kailashahar post-office, etc. In August 1919 the new government secretariat building at Agartala was opened by the Governor of Bengal, who also laid the foundation stone of the High Court building there. Two important roads, one from Agartala to Bishalgarh and another at Birendranagar were 'put into fair order' in 1920-21.[12(b)]

For executing public works and those related to the construction of palaces, large amounts of money were required to be spent. This was possible because the revenue income of the state steadily increased mainly on account of greater yields from land revenue as well as duties on cotton, til, jute, tea, forest produce, etc.

The Government encouraged the Jhumias to grow more cotton and of better quality. In 1918-19 an unsuccessful experiment was made for growing Dharwar variety of cotton in the dry season. It was later found that this variety grew well in the rainy season. The hill-farmers were supplied with seeds of this variety of cotton for growing it on their jhums. The results were reported to be encouraging in 1923-24.The Administration Report for 1923-24 pointed out that this cotton grown on the Tripura hills was sent to the Government Economic Botanist at Dacca, the Central Cotton Committee, Bombay, the Banga Laksmi Cotton Mills, Messrs Kettlewell Berllen & Co. and the Dhakeswari Mills at Narayangunj (near Dacca). Reports from these sources were encouraging although the selling price of Tripura Cotton was Rs.5 per maund less than that produced by the Bombay growers. This was due to 'unclean picking'. Encouraged by this trend in 1924-25 seeds of Dharwar long-stapled variety were distributed to 2000 jhumias at higher altitudes ranging from 15 to 600 feet. At this time the state had about 19, 000 acres under cotton with the Jhumias.[13]

Rising rates of population growth mainly on account of the immigration of Bengali settlers, led to the continuous expansion of areas of waste land under cultivation. In many respects economic activities in the hills and plains were interdependent: therefore, expansion and growth in the latter had corresponding effects on the former. Some hill- farmers following examples of the Bengali cultivators took to settled plough cultivation in the valleys. We may now turn to review the trends of immigration of population along with their impact on Tripura's economic development. The Bengali settlers consisted of both the educated middle-class people as well as landless peasants. Those educated were instrumental in the formulation and execution of the programmes of the modernization process in Tripura. A suitable administrative structure was required to be built up for expanding educational, medical, civil, police and military services, construction and maintenance of public works, management of forests, etc. Therefore services of bureaucrats, teachers, doctors, engineers, foresters, security personnel, etc. were needed to keep the programmes going.

Such services through private initiative could be possible as immigration of people seeking self-employment opportunities as teachers, doctors, lawyers, etc. continued.

In the Census for 1901 it was enumerated that there were 43, 894 immigrants who constituted 25.38 per cent of the total population of 1, 73, 325 persons. Most of them came from the neighbouring districts of Bengal. No wonder Bengali-speaking population in 1901 formed 40 per cent, 'Tipperah' (*Kag_Barak*) speaking population 44 per cent, and the Kuki-chin speaking group 16 per cent of the total population.[14]

Distribution of population in terms of some important livelihood classes in 1901 was as follows:[15]

Table 25.1
Distribution of Population in Terms of Livelihood Classes

Sl. No.	Livelihood classes	Workers	Dependents	Total
1.	Government service	699	501	1200
2.	Landlord	631	2,103	2734
3.	Tenant farmers	30,102	44,797	74,899
4.	Agricultural labour	411	151	562
5.	Shifting cultivators	46,027 *	34,248	80,275

* Including 9,260 having subsidiary occupation of settled plough cultivation.

Most of the landlords, tenant farmers and agricultural labourers were Bengali settlers, besides some Manipuris. There were 12, 851 Manipuris in Tripura in 1901. In the government service also the educated Bengalis predominated. Excepting for some important top positions reserved for the close kin of the King, the Bengali educated graduates were appointed for most of the administrative and judicial posts. The Imperial Gazetteer noted that in 1903-04 there were 99 primary schools, 2 special schools, 1 secondary school and one Arts College. Almost hundred per cent of the teachers of these institutions were Bengalis. For in 1901 only 4, 274 persons were literate, out of whom 291 persons knew English,

3, 511 Bengali, 111 Hindi, 15 Oriya and others 313.[16] There were 10 charitable dispensaries in the state and the total number of medical practitioners was 81, many of whom were Bengalis.

Immigration of population continued during the following decades also. In the Report for 1931 census the trends of growth of total, immigrant, emigrant and natural population have been shown as follows:[17]

Table 25.2
Growth of Total Population Alongside Immigrant, Emigrant and Natural Population

Year	1901	1911	Decadal Increase (%)	1921	Decadal Increase (%)	1931	Decadal Increase (%)
Total population	1,73,325	2,29,613	32.5	3,04,437	32.6	3,82,450	25.6
Immigrant population	43,894	81,6631	86.0	96,386	18.0	1,14,383	18.6
Emigrant population	152	1,372	-	358	-	6,543	-
Natural Population	1,25,583	1,49,322	15.2	2,08,409	39.6	2,74,610	31.3

The rulers of Tripura followed the policy of encouraging immigrants to come and settle down in Tripura for its all-round development. Tripura's economic development during the period from 1901 to 1931 may be estimated from the growing trends of expansion of areas under cultivation, outputs of crops and manufactures of those items for which data are available, the revenue yields from different sources, volumes and values of exports and imports, etc. In the absence of figures for state domestic products these indices will be used for this study.

The most critical factor for the expansion of cultivated area was the progress in land settlement area. In 1901 and 1902 the settlement of total area was done by following different modes of settlement, such as permanent settlement of waste lands, and Tashkhisi settlement of cultivated lands (permanently held estates, revenue rates of which were enhanceable after every 20 years) and Jotedari settlement of cultivated and waste land (enjoying Raiyati right on payment of rent). Under these heads taken together total areas settled in 1910 and 1911 were 15, 327 acres and 21, 996 acres yielding Rs,40, 884 and Rs.36,264 as revenue respectively. The average rate of rent in 1911 was less than that in 1910 on account of the fact that most of the lands settled were situated far into the interior of the state and were fresh reclamations. Observing this fact the Administrative Report for 1902-03 also pointed out that good arable lands along the borders of the state were then mostly under cultivation.[18]

Every year settlement of new areas under different modes continued. By 1916-17 total area settled measured 434 square miles representing 79.63 per cent of the total cultivable area of 545 sq. miles in the plains.[19] Of course, the entire settled area was not actually cultivated. With the increase in area of settled land, total area brought under cultivation also rose. In 1931 the position about cultivable area, and area actually cultivated for growing different crops stood as follows:[20]

Table 25.3
Areas of Land under Different Modes of Cultivation

Total area of Tripura (sq.mile)	Total cultivable area (sq.mile)		Area suitable for shifting cultivation (sq.m)	Actual area of settled cultivation (sq.m)	Actual area of shifting cultivation (sq.m)
	plains land	plateau land			
4,116	545	401	2000	471	114

Distribution of total cultivated area under different crops in 1931 is indicated below (all in sq. miles):[21]

Table 25. 4
Cultivated area under Different Crops (sq. mile)

Paddy	Jute	Sugarcane	Mustard	Tea	Miscellaneous other crops	Total	Total area actually cultivated by shifting cultivators
410	10.2	7.6	8.0	12.3	22.9	471	114

Although the area under rice cultivation in the plains accounted for 87 per cent of the total cultivated area, the progress in growing new crops, such as jute, mustard, sugarcane, some grams and pulses (included under the head, 'miscellaneous other crops') and tea was achieved through diversification of agricultural production, and better utilization of cultivable land by following the system of rotation of crops. Production of cash crops like jute, sugarcane, oilseeds, grams, et al raised the prospects of higher incomes for the cultivators. Moreover, production of tea, as noted earlier, led to the utilization of waste lands for industrialization which meant higher income per unit of land, more employment opportunities, increased tempo of immigration and increased revenue earnings for the state.

Impressed by such agricultural development and expansion of economic activities in the plains and also realizing the need for conservation of forests for ensuring better economic utilization of forest wealth of the state, the rulers of Tripura took some measures for inducing the hill farmers to abandon *jhuming* and take to settled plough cultivation in the plains which they thought would help improve their economic condition. The measures taken were offering *takkavi* loans, and providing agricultural inputs like agricultural implements, bullocks and seeds. A programme for publicity was launched in the hills to bring home to the hill farmers the benefits of settled cultivation as against shifting cultivation. But year after year in the annual administration reports it was lamented that very few of these farmers responded to such incentives offered by the government, for which reason the pace of progress in the transition from shifting to settled cultivation was rather slow and unsatisfactory.

Moreover, Tripura's agriculture-based economic expansion suffered periodic fluctuations as amounts of output were 'extremely weather-sensitive'. Hill-farmers experienced crop-failures on account of storms and gales and rat menace following the flowering of bamboo plants, which normally occurred in about every ten to twelve years.

In the plains, the settled farmers had to contend with damages of crops on account of floods and soil erosion in the river valleys. Inundation of agricultural fields by rivers in spate was quite frequent. Flood waters caused deposition of sands on farmlands making the soil quite barren and unfit for cultivation until the sands were removed, a task which was quite labour-intensive and costly, Such fluctuations in the productive activities were inherent in Tripura's ecology.

The progress made in the agrarian economy may be noted from the following table that indicates the quantities of different agricultural and forest products exported from Tripura in 1930-31.[22] In the last decade of the nineteenth century, from 1880-81 to 1889-90, that is, Tripura's chief exports were cotton, sesame (til) forest produce (timbers, thatching grass, canes, bamboos, etc), elephants, singing birds, boats, bamboo-mats, baskets, charcoal, and occasionally cotton rugs woven by the Kukis. The total value of exports amounted to Rs.4, 717 lakh in 1880-81, which increased to Rs.7. 480 lakh in 1889-90.[23] By contrast, by 1931, the number of commodities exported increased as also the total value of exports which amounted to Rs.73. 0 lakh for agricultural commodities and Rs.21.12 lakh for forest produce.

Table 25.5 (a):
Exports of Agricultural Products in 1930-31

Names of crops	Quantity (in maund)	Value (Rs.)
1. Paddy and rice	26, 18, 870	52, 37, 740
2. Jute	73,662	3,68, 310
3. Mustard	31, 376	1,56, 580
4. Molasses (gur)	1,05, 200	4, 20, 800
5. Cotton	17, 583	1, 75, 830
6. Sesame (til)	23,210	69, 630
7. Tea	15,310	4,59, 300
8. Fruits and vegetables	——	72, 000
9. Fodder	1,20,000	30,000
10. Cattle	20,000 Nos.	3,00,000
11. Hides of animals	600	4,000
12. Bones of animals	700	170
13. Oilcake	5,000	15,000
	Total =	**73,09,360**

Table 25.5 (b):
Exports of Forest Produce in 1930-31

Item	Quantity	Value (Rs)
1.Timber	5,13,365 cubic foot	7,96,714
2.Bamboo	12,76,172 bundles	8,05,444
3.Sungrass (chan)	10,93,190 bundles	3,04,474
4.Firewood	4,03,627 bundles	83,917
5.Bamboo mat	1, 50,000 nos.	7,500
6.Umbrella handle	20,000 bundles	6,000
7.Others	——	1,08,876
	Total =	**21, 12, 925**

Source: for both the tables: Somendra Chandra Debbarma, Census Report for 1931 (in Bengali), 1997edn, Pp. 103- 104.

Among the items of export, paddy, tea, molasses and mustard were the more important products from the plains while cotton, sesame and forest products were from the hill areas. A review of the items of exports and their quantities and values reveals that the agrarian economy of Tripura began flourishing even though the process was somewhat thwarted as some of the items of exports were affected by the Great Depression of 1929-1933. The export scenario as it was then indicates that some processed items of agricultural, animal husbandry and forest produce were exported. These were tea, molasses, oilcakes, hides and bones, bamboo mats, umbrella handles, etc. Increased production of existing and new crops, and processed agricultural items and their export generated additional income not only for the producers but also for the Government, as yields from taxes under different heads and duties increased remarkably. This opened up the possibility of expansion of physical infrastructure, that is, the social and economic overheads like, roads, bridges, buildings, educational institutions, hospitals and dispensaries, postal and telegraph services, municipal services, etc. Actual achievements in these fields may be assessed on the evidence of the trend of growth of revenue earnings of the Government and that of expenditures incurred on developing the overheads.

The table (No. 25.6) enclosed shows the amounts of gross revenue collections from different sources for 1901-02, 1910-11 and 1930.31. Total revenue collections amounted to Rs.7.06 lakh in 1901-02 and it increased to Rs.10.93 lakh in 1910-11 and to Rs. 13.92 lakh in 1930-31. The most important revenue-yielding items were land revenue, toll on forest produce, tax on cotton and oilseeds, excise duties and stamps and court-fees. This trend confirms that there were growth of population, extension of cultivation to new areas by reclaiming waste lands, and some diversification of economic activities as well. Net revenue collections from the Chakla Roshnabad zamindari also increased over these years excepting for the year 1930-31, on account of the great depression that affected the cultivators of Chakla Roshnabad. However, the increased income at the disposal of the Raja (see table 25.7) was not expended rationally for building the social overheads and for development of human resource by expanding educational and health care facilities for promoting people's welfare.

Table 25.6
Gross Revenue Collections,1901-02, 1910-11 and 1930-31

Sl. Nos.	Heads of Revenue	Gross Collections (Rs.) 1901-02	1910-11	1930-31
1.	Land Revenue	2,21,875	3,20,707	4,40,180
2.	Family Tax in the hills	40,684	48,462	37,204
3.	Toll on forest produce	2,13,348	3,09,905	3,60,030
4.	Toll on forest on the Feni River	2,968	5,998	30,524
5.	Tax on Cotton & Oil seeds	98,314	2,01,840	1,07,281
6.	Elephant &buffalo grazing Mehal	6,470	8,745	6,024
7.	Proceeds from reserved *Sal* Trees	1,495	15,705	5,500
8.	Royalty on Elephants caught	6,312	7,625	4,099
9.	Kazai Mahal	988	1,336	——
10.	Excise	8,011	15,531	92,302
11.	Stamps & court-fees	25,968	40,975	82,738
12.	Law & Justice (fines)	4,482	3,647	4,865
13.	Process fees	5,336	8,987	14,830
14.	Adda Mehal	10,874	15,688	19,769
15.	Registration	2,910	6,559	11,045
16.	Jail	1,190	1,231	1,400
17.	Cattle pounds	3,548	4,900	5,219
18.	Thatching grass Mehal	8,677	8,397	5,789
19.	Rents of markets	3,452	5,815	6,668
20.	Nazars	13,279	30,486	37,733
21.	Education	——	——	16,581
22.	Tea Export duty	——	——	12,742
23.	Jute Export Duty	——	——	27,978
24.	Recovery of personal advances	——	——	5,062
25.	Depreciation contribution	——	——	——
26.	Interest on bank deposits	——	——	1,549
27.	Miscellaneous	25,139	31,277	55,597
	Total =	**7,06,359**	**10,93,816**	**13,92,709**

Source: Relevant Tripura Administration Reports, vide, Note No. 5, P. 57, p. 414 & p. 1495

Rise in general administrative expenses (Table 25.7) was due to the expansion of administrative machinery for strengthening the system of governance and the employment of more civil servants. The reason for the increase in administrative expenses was explained by the Political Agent. It was due to "usual grade increments and creation of a few posts required with expansion of work, and to the payment of a special allowance, graciously granted by His Highness as compensation for the high prices of provisions". Expenditure on education was quite meagre as there was no plan and programme for expanding educational facilities for the common subjects. Whatever increase there was in respect of this item over the years was largely due to the education of the princes. The other two causes were the creation of new teaching posts and 'high prices allowance'. Expenditures on public works were quite nominal considering the utterly undeveloped physical infrastructure like roads, bridges, water-supply, and irrigation facility. The lion's share of total expenditure was made on defraying the King's household expenses, his privy purse, travelling expenses of the King and his family and maintenance grants to the Thakurs. The expenditure structure is a typical example of the feudal manner of management of the state's financial resources even when the state's economy got more and more integrated into the British colonial economy of India and through that the external trade relations of colonial India:

Table 25.7
Total Receipts and Main Items of Expenditure for Tripura (St)

	1901-02	1910-11	1930-31
1. Total Receipts including that from the Zamindari and including opening balance	19,49,791	26,31,756	37,43,914
2. Main items of expenditure for Tripura State:			
i) General Administrative charges	2,00,276	2,42,221	5,79,206
ii) Public Works	2,91,357*	1,65,358	2,45,067
iii) Municipality	-	7,723	10,000
iv) Education	68,837	56,521	1,34,669
v) Medical & sanitation	23,564	42,620	70,663
vi) King's household expenses, privy purse, maintenance of Thakurs, traveling expenses, etc.	4,58,250 ***	3,90,153	4,35,846

* Including that for the Municipality**** Including expenses of the king's attending Delhi Durbar.
Sources: Administration Reports of the relevant years, vide, Note No. 5 pp. 58-59, P 416 and P. 1496.

Three important items of Tripura's export formed parts of India's total export, namely, cotton, tea and jute. In the years of the Great Depression, volumes and values of all these exports of Tripura slumped along with India's (see Table 25. 8: below) . Since cotton was grown in the hills the fall in income inflicted by the depression was most heavy on the poor shifting cultivators who had practically no accumulated assets or stocks of grain to fall back upon in times of crisis such as this. These cultivators used to take crop advances partly in cash and partly in kind, such as, food and other necessaries for their survival during the lean months when their stocks of food grains ran empty, and their *jhum* crops were not yet ready for harvesting. During the depression years many of them were unable to repay crop advances and faced difficulties in taking fresh crop advances. The number of defaulters in regard to house tax liability increased. In fact the complex situation caused widespread tribal unrest in some parts of Tripura hills, particularly in the Khowai Division in West Tripura.

The Political Agent in his Administration Report for 1932-33 observed: "The all –round economic depression had its adverse effects both on the Raj and the people in general. Kashipur Farm (silk-rearing) was abolished. The infant tea industry was in a deep crisis and two tea estates prayed for relinquishment of portions of their tea settlements with remission of arrear dues .No public funds were available for public works*[24]. There was an outbreak of *Kalaazar* throughout the State. As a result of the world–wide financial crisis .... retrenchment both in staff and offices were (sic) effected throughout Tripura, causing the abolition of the Kulai Tahasil office and the dispensary .... .In the Maharaja's Match Factory at Agartala , only the match boxes and sticks were made and not the finished matches due to the want of machineries (sic) required"[25].

* Foot note : Total receipt of the State including that from the zamindaries was Rs.37.43 lakhs in 1930-31, (see Table (25.7 above) and it fell to Rs. 22 lakhs in 1933-34.

Table 25.8
Exports of Jute , Cotton (ginned) and Tea in 1929-30 and 1930-31

Item	Quantity exported		Value (Rs)	
	1929-1930	1930-1931	1929-1930	1930-1931
Jute (mds)	83,440	73,662	5,81,080	3,68,310
Cotton (mds)	22,950	17,583	3,44,250	1,75,830
Tea	17,110	15,310	6,81,400	4,59,300

Source: Ranjit Kumar De (ed),(2000), The Statistical Account of Tripura, Uppal Publishing House, New Delhi, P.32.This Account is based on Memorandum of Statistics Relating to Agriculture, Forests, Exports 1930-31 and 1937-38, Tripura Government.

During this period, however, at Agartala "a telephone system connecting important public buildings and residences was under construction. Also a "temporary telephone line was constructed from Agartala to Chandra Sadhupara, a village at the foot of the Baramura hills at a distance of 18 miles".[25]

For countering the unrest of the people, particularly of the tribal shifting cultivators of Khowai who were the worst hit by the depression, the King visited Kalyanpur in Khowai and met the affected people to ascertain the causes of their sufferings. He realized the extreme vulnerability of the shifting cultivators whose economy was much dependent on the production and sale of cash crops like cotton and oil seeds, on their jhums, and decided to create a tribal reserve in that area in 1930-31for the exclusive settlement of the members of the Tripura, Noatia, Jamatia, Riang and Halam tribes there and for inducing them to take to settled plough cultivation. This was known as the Kalyanpur Reserve, which comprised an area of 70,400 acres. Subsequently the total area reserved was raised to 1,248,000 acres in 1941. The task of settling the hill people was placed under the charge of a minister. The progress in settlement of shifting cultivators was not, however, as expected.

The sufferings of the people during the depression years and lack of adequate relief measures provided by the Government inspired widespread discontentment and unrest. Presumably it was to deal with this situation that some sort of a flag march of the military was conducted in1931-32. The Political Agent reported: "In the midst of economic crisis, the Military Forces of Tripura comprising the First and Second Bir Company with State Band, signaling party and other followers marched out on extensive area of the State".[27]

One significant anti-depression welfare measure undertaken by the government related to the creation of a Khawai Improvement Fund through mobilizing an amount of Rs. 6,772 from the zamindars, lawyers and businessmen. The fund was to be administered by the Khowai Improvement Committee consisting of the representatives of the donors and the members of the Tripura tribe for the construction of roads and provision of drinking water facilities.[28]

The Government took several measures to reduce public expenditure. Pasting of economy slips on used envelopes for reuse was practised. Rates of remuneration for examiners of answer scripts were reduced and moderators for different examinations were required to perform their duties without any remuneration. T.A. and D.A. rates for officials were also reduced. The financial crisis became so acute that in 1933 the government had to prepare a revised budget in the middle of the financial year.[29]

In 1931, the Government opened a department for banking in the State Treasury and mobilized term deposits from the public by offering rates of interest payable twice a year at 6 p.c., 6.25 p.c. and 7 p.c. for one, two, three and four year terms respectively.

By 1933-34, "gradual recovery from the effect of worldwide depression and economic slump became perceptible". Amount of land revenue collection slightly increased because of 'the better paying capacity of the *Talukdars* than that of the *jotedars'*. But the sufferings of the hill people were not yet over. Output and export of tea increased resulting in the improvement of the financial conditions of the tea gardens.[30] Total quantity of jute exported in1937-38 was 1,61,346 mds valued at Rs. 7, 26, 060. Quantity of cotton (cleaned) exported was 16,440 mds in the same year the value of which was Rs. 1,23, 300. The quantity of tea export went up in 1937-38 to 2, 84, 660 lbs valued at Rs. 10, 45 830. The value of exports of forest products also went up to Rs. 4, 66, 540 in 1937-38.[31]

Increase in immigration of population and expansion of area under cultivation by reclaiming more and more waste lands also got a spurt. But the woes of the people were not yet over. In October 1934-35 ' a terrible flood inundated the whole of Agartala town' and the flood-affected people had to take shelter in the palace and some public buildings. Moreover, the deadly disease of cholera broke out in a virulent form in some parts of the state.[32]

NOTES AND REFERENCES

1. Nalini Ranjan Roychoudhury (1983), *Tripura Through the Ages*, Sterling Publishers Private Ltd., New Delhi, p. 81
2. *ibid.* p.82.
3. *ibid.* p. 82.
4. *ibid.* p. 56.

5 (a) Mahadev Chakravarti (Ed), 1994, *Administration Reports of Tripura State since 1902* (in 4 volumes), Gyan Publishing House, New Delhi, Vol. I, p. 24.

5 (b). *ibid.*

6. *ibid.* p. 26.

7. *ibid.* p. 26.

8. *ibid.* Vol II, p. 623 and Somendrachandra Debbarma, *Census Bibarani* (in Bengali), Census Report for 1931, reprinted by Tripura Government in 1997, p. 108.

9. *ibid.* Vol. I, p. 26.

10. Somendrachandra Debbarma, *op. cit.*, pp.108-109.

11. Mahadev Chakravarti, *op. cit.*, Vol. II, p.381.

12. (a) *ibid.* p. 384.

12. (b) *ibid.* p. 387.

13. Bani Prasanna Misra, (1976), *Socio-Economic Adjustments of Tribals, Case Study of Tripura Jhumias*, People's Publishing House, New Delhi, p. 56.

14. *Imperial Gazetteer of India*, Vol. XIII, 1908, Extracts as published in *Census of India, 1961*, Vol.XXVI, Tripura, Part- I (c), 1967, p. 506.

15. Asitchandra Chowdhury, *Census Report of Tripura for 1901* (in Bengali) reprinted by Tribal Research Institute, Tripura, in 1995, p. 19.

16. *ibid.* pp.16-17.

17. Somendrachandra Debbarma, op. cit., p. 34.

18. Mahadev Chakravarti, *op.cit.* vol. I, p. 54.

19. ibid. P.623 and Somendrachandra Debbarma, *op. cit.* p. 98.

20. Somendrachandra Debbarma, *ibid.* pp. 98-99.

21. *ibid.*

22. *ibid.* p. 103.

23. Dipak Kumar Chaudhuri, (1999), *The Political Agents and the Native Raj*, Mittal Publications New Delhi, Table 8.1, prepared on the basis of the Reports of the Political Agents for the relevant years, p. 179.

24. Earlier, in 1923, the proprietors of the tea gardens had approached the government for remission of payment of revenue on account of their financial difficulties. An advisory committee was set up to examine and report on the actual conditions of the tea gardens. On the basis of that report the Raja passed an order rejecting the prayer for complete exclusion from payment of revenue and allowed seven tea gardens to defer payment of revenue by one year. If these gardens merited further consideration in regard to managing the gardens efficiently, collection of revenue would be postponed for three more years. Of course, interest would be charged on the revenue dues at the rate of 6 p.c. per annum, vide Suprasanna Bandyopadhyay (ed), (1971), *Tripura State Gazette Sankalan* (in Bengali), Education, Directorate, Govt. of Tripura, Agartala, p.124. This is not a part of the note No – 25 below.
25. Mahadev Chakravarti, *op, cit.* vol. IV, p. 1559 and p. VI for the data in the foot note.
26. J.B. Ganguli, 1969, *Economic Problems of the Jhumias of Tripura*, Bookland (P) Ltd Calcutta, p. 66.
27. Mahadev Chakravarti, *op. cit.* p. 1559.
28. J. B. Bhattacharjee, "some Documents of Economic Situation in Tripura, 1929-1936: A Study of the Impact of Great Depression" published in J. B. Bhattacharjee (ed), *Studies in the Economic History of North East India*, Har-Anand Pulblications, New Delhi, (1994) p. 376.
29. ibid. p. 380.
30. Mahadev Chakravarti, *op. cit.* p. 1559.
31. Ranjit Kumar De, ed (2000), *The Statistical Account of Tripura*, Uppal Publishing House, New Delhi, p. 70 and pp 96-97. This Account has been compiled from the Memorandum of Statistics Relating to Agriculture, Forests and Exports, 1930-31 and 1937-38, Tripura Government.

26
ECONOMIC RECOVERY AND EXPANSION, WAR-TIME SCARCITIES AND INFLATION AND REANG UNREST (1934 - 1945)

Economic recovery in the post-Depression years slowly picked up from 1934. The vital booster to Tripura's economic expansion and growth was the immigration of population, leading to reclamation of more and more waste lands for extension of the cultivated area. The Government therefore encouraged migration of population into the state. It actually monitored the progress in the immigration of population that pushed up the rate of population growth. During the ten-year period from 1932-33 to 1942-43 the total population of Tripura increased by 1,30,560 persons, that is, from 3,82,450 in 1932-33 to 5,13,010 in 1942-43.[1] This increase has been attributed to the 'influx of labour from the neighbouring British districts' and that of 'up-country coolies', particularly since 1933-34.[2] This phenomenon indicates that the demand for labour in the state increased as productive activities in the plains and plantations went up.

Growth of population augmented the process of reclamation of waste-lands for extension of cultivation to new areas which resulted in the increase of land revenue collections. No wonder, the amount of land revenue including road cess collections doubled, as it increased from Rs. 4.18 lakh in 1932-33 to Rs. 8.44 lakh in 1942-43[2(a)]. In fact Tripura's post-depression recovery was further followed by war-impacted expansion, inflation and scarcities.

Economic expansion and growth was reflected in the

substantial rise in the income of the government as collections not only from land revenue but also from taxes and duties on commodities, such as, cotton, oilseeds, jute, rice and forest produce went up as their exports increased. Tables are given at the end of this chapter. Even the amounts of Family Tax in the hills 'increased considerably on account of 'the improved paying capacity of the hill people'[3]. In 1939-40 collection of this tax amounted to Rs. 77.8 thousand. But in the subsequent years their economic conditions deteriorated, and therefore, amounts of this tax yields varied between Rs. 42.7 and Rs. 62.4 thousand.

The recovery of the nascent tea industry was helped by the International Tea Agreement of 1933 into which India also entered as a participant and in terms of the Agreement the Government passed the Indian Tea Control Act, XXIV of 1933. In 1934 the Tripura Government too adopted some of the provisions of this Act in order to regulate the extension of the area under tea plantation.

The Tripura Tea Control Act of 1348 TE (1938 A.D) laid down that "all acts of the licensing authority appointed under the Act would be subject to the control of the Minister of the Government of Tripura who might cancel, suspend or modify any such act as he thought fit"[4].

The Tea Control Amendment Orders were passed in 1941 (Order No. I of 1351 T.E). At that time appeals from tea estates of Tripura against the orders of the India Tea Licensing Committee relating to production of crop and export quota were dealt with by the Central Government or the High Court of the State. Submissions against the orders of the Committee dealing with extensions were to be made to the Minister.

"Under the provisions of Clause 7 of the International Tea Agreement, the total area of land permissible for extension that could be made during the currency of the Agreement was 52 acres. After considerable correspondence, however, it was decided (in 1940) that 200 acres out of the unutilized area of 981 acres available for extension in Bengal would be allotted to the Tripura State. The total area available for extensions in Tripura was therefore 252 acres.

"The Tripura Tea Control Act having provided for an appeal to the State Government from orders of the Indian

Tea Licensing Committee in respect of the distribution of the area of 252 acres for new extensions in the State, it was suggested by the Committee and agreed to by the State Government, that out of the area, 152 acres should be distributed at the first instance, keeping 100 acres in reserve to meet the requirements of any orders passed in appeals to the State Government. An allotment was made accordingly (November, 1941) on the basis of this arrangement"[5].

From table 26.3 it might be noted that in 1939-40, the year the Second World War started, export of cotton was of the order of 68.9 thousand maunds, an all-time record. This was possible presumably because of the increased world demand due to the outbreak of war which could be adequately met as there was sufficient stock of cotton accumulated during 1939-40 and 1942-43 but not in the year 1941-42. Tea export remained stable over the years. Tripura alone exported large quantities of rice during the years 1940-41 to 1942-43. In 1941-42 also the export of rice was to the tune of 7.8 lakh maunds. Another important item of export was timber which ran up to 5.14 lakh cft to 6.02 lakh cft. Duty collected on this export yielded nearly 2 lakh rupees. High levels of export of oilseeds —— both sesame and mustard – were also maintained during these years.

As a result of the growth of population, expansion of area under cultivation and growth of production of commodities and their exports, revenue under important heads and total revenue collections increased considerably (see Table 26.2). The amounts ranged between Rs. 17.98 lakh (1940-41) and Rs.22.85 lakh (1942-43). In 1939-40 the total revenue collections amounted to Rs. 20.55 lakh.

A consolidated account of select items of public expenditure is given in table 26.4 which shows that the amount of general administrative charges went up substantially: it was more than Rs. 7 lakh in 1939-40 but it went up to Rs. 11.97 lakh in 1945-46. At that level of social and economic development of Tripura the general administration services constituted the most important item of social overhead (i.e. infrastructure) as without expanding and modernizing as also raising the efficiency of the administrative structure productive activities in all the sectors could not be promoted. Yet the other very important need for raising the quality of human resource by expanding educational and medical, health and sanitation services was not given as much importance as it deserved to have. Expenditure on education amounted to a little over Rs. 1 lakh until 1945-46 when it reached nearly Rs. 2 lakh mark. Expenditures on medical and sanitation were less than even one lakh of rupees up to 1942-43 and it however crossed Rs. 1.03 lakh in 1945-46.

Expenditures on public works, an inseparably related aspect of basic infrastructure building, were nearly Rs. 2 lakh until 1945-46 in which year it was Rs. 4 lakh. A road fund was created for financing construction of roads; it amounted to Rs. 1.38 lakh in 1939-40 but it came down to Rs. 57 thousand in 1942-43. The figure for 1945-46 is not available. Substantial expenditure was made on 'Ordinary *Sansar* Charges' and 'His Highness's Nij Tahabil' (Privy Purse) and his tours. This expenditure accounted for Rs. 4.1 lakh in 1939-40 and it was less in 1942-43, only Rs. 3.85 lakh.

The state also incurred expenditure on account of the Second World War and had contributed to the war fund. In 1942-43 war expenditure amounted to Rs. 2.11 lakh and the state's contribution to the war fund amounted Rs. 30 thousand. Indicative of the expansion of productive activities in the post-depression years was the setting up of the Maharaja Match Factory in 1938, which was owned by the Government. It enjoyed monopoly right to manufacture matches in Tripura[6]. Duties collected on matches yielded Rs. 37.6 thousand in 1939-40, Rs. 34.0 thousand in 1941-42 and Rs. 43.4 thousand in 1942-43 (see Table 26. 2 below).

In 1941 the Hotel Khosmahal Ltd was opened in Agartala to provide better hotel facilities for the tourists and other visitors who came to Agartala for business purposes and on official business[6].

In 1939 permission for opening two cinema houses, named Tripurasundari Talkies and Tripura Talkies was granted by the Government with the proviso that screening films would have to be done on payment of Rs. 25 per mensem by each initially for a period of six months.[6]

During the Durga Puja festival an 'industrial exhibition' was held at Agartala as an annual event which provided opportunities for selling cottage industry products and various items of handicraft.

1. War – Time Scarcities and Inflation

From 1940 Tripura became actively involved in providing unstinted all-round support to the British Government in its defence preparedness. In 1940 a Central War Committee, one war committee for each Division were appointed for guiding and coordinating the defence efforts. Orders were passed making it compulsory for the government employees to contribute donations for the war. The amount payable was realized in instalments from their pay-bills[7]. In 1941 the "War Fund" was created[8]. From January 1942 the Government started publishing War Supplement to the State Gazette.

From the War Supplement to the Tripura State Gazette dated 14th January 1942[9] it is noted that 'the entire resources of the State and personal service of the Ruler' were placed 'at the disposal of the Crown'. The amount of donation made by the State to the various War Funds totalled Rs. 57,000 and by the employees Rs. 14,000. Defence Bonds purchased by the State amounted to Rs. 1.75 lakh and by the public through the State Rs. 44 thousand. The Government raised new units of armed forces and the total amount of expenditure incurred on armed forces was above Rs. 5 lakh.

As the war years rolled on and demands for consumer and other goods went on rising the inflationary pressure pushed up prices of goods, particularly rice and other essential items. The War Supplement admitted that 'the sudden rise of prices due to War conditions' necessitated controlling of prices and prevention of hoarding and profiteering by the wholesale and retail dealers in the State.

From this publication it is learnt that a Committee was appointed by the Government with the Sadar Collector as its Chairman, in which some members of the public and representatives of the wholesale and retail dealers were included, to fix the prices of 'necessary commodities of everyday's use'.

From the 'Supplement' dated 30th June 1943 it is noted

that rationing system was introduced in the State for the benefit of the people of poor means. It was laid down that 'Ration Coupons' would not be issued to any person who earned more than Rs. 250 per month 'in a family jointly or separately'[10].

The Government noted that many businessmen refused to sell goods at the controlled prices. Therefore, orders were passed on 6-3-1952 (T.E.) that is, some time in June 1942, that such refusals to sell the enlisted goods, though these were in their stock, would entail heavy punishment such as imprisonment for a period of up to three years and, in addition, even a fine.

The enlisted commodities were: wheat, atta, flour, salt, sugar, kerosene oil, matches, mustard oil, pulses, coconut oil, coal, 'sagoo', betelnut, washing soap, 'soda', paper, medicines and cloth[11].

The management of the war-time economy affected or benefited different classes of people in varying degrees. According to the Consolidated Administration Report for 1943 to 1946, the war-time rise in demand for labour for employment in elaborate military construction works pushed up wage rates as also prices of 'grain all round' that benefited the peasantry. Awards of contracts for construction obviously at high rates enriched the contractor class. 'It was only the landless middle classes with limited and fixed income that were as before brought down to the level of breakdown (Sic.)"[12].

Food scarcity became a serious problem and cause of extreme sufferings of the common people in some parts of India, particularly, Bengal where the disastrous famine of 1943-44 caused an estimated 3.4 million deaths[13]. Jawaharlal Nehru very aptly observed: "It was no calamity of nature or play of the elements that brought this famine, nor was it caused by actual war operations and enemy blockade. Every competent observer is agreed that it was a man-made famine which could have been foreseen and avoided"[14]. Even though Tripura's economy got more and more linked with India's, particularly of Bengal, the State reportedly did not experience any starvation death during 1943-45 as the Administration Report for 1943-45 specifically claimed.

The famine in Bengal caused 'an inrush of distressed people' from that province which gave rise to grave problems. "Prices of rice shot up to even Rs.50 per maund and special measures, with granaries established at many places, had to be adopted for supply of foodstuff at moderate prices to all State employees, pensioners and dependents, involving an outlay of heavy capital expenditure, and a loss incurred that ultimately aggregated over (Rs) six lakhs (Sic.). The only silver-lining was the absence of death from starvation"[15].

Unfortunately in case of Bengal, "Right up to the last moment, when thousand were dying daily in the public streets, famine was denied and references to it in the Press were suppressed by the censors. When *The Statesman* of Calcutta published gruesome and ghastly pictures of starving and dying women and children in the streets of Calcutta a spokesman of the Government of India, speaking officially in the Central Assembly, protested against the 'dramatization' of the situation .... And then, when it became impossible to deny or cloak the existence of widespread famine, each group in authority blamed some other group for it"[16].

Movement of prices of rice from 1938 to 1945 in Tripura in the first part of April each year, that is in the second fortnight of the Bengali month of Chaitra as recorded in Tripura Gazette was as follows: (Table XXVI. 1).

Table 26.1
Movement of Prices : 1938 - 1945

Year	Maximum price of Rice per maund Rs	Minimum price of Rice per maund Rs.
1938	5.00	2.75
1939	6.00	3.00
1940	5.50	3.00
1941	7.00	4.50
1943	22.50	8.00
1944	15.00	6.50
1945	20.00	7.25

Source: Suprasanna Bondyopadhyay, op. cit., Pp. 433-441

The above table indicates that the maximum price of rice increased by 350 p.c. in 1943 over the price prevailing in the pre-war year 1938, while the minimum price rose by 190%. In 1943 in Bengal the price of rice was much higher, it rose from an already high price of Rs. 35 to Rs. 105 per maund[17].

Following the Grow More Food campaign launched by the Government of India, Tripura also adopted the policy of encouraging people to practise intensive cultivation for growing more foodcrops 'with a view to overcoming the difficulties caused by this great war'. The War Supplement to the Tripura State Gazette dated 1 December 1942 carried the message of the King who expressed his "earnest desire that every individual householder with a stern determination shall devote his unstinted energy to the growing of more food productions (Sic) in every inch of land at his disposal". .... It was also his wish that in all plots of vacant land in the private homestead lands and in compounds of the Government office buildings food-crops should be grown[18].

The hectic construction activities in the war-time for defence purposes, however, expanded the communication and medical facilities in the State. An airport was built at Singerbil, near Agartala, and some new roads were constructed, namely, the Comilla – Sanamura – Agartala Road (38 miles), the Agartala – Fatikcherra – Simna Road (30 miles), the Comilla – Agartala – Simna Road (68 miles), and the Agartala Airport Approach Road. The airport and the roads established links with the world outside so that Tripura's isolation was further eased. Tripura's medical and health services expanded with the opening of three full – fledged general hospitals particularly to meet the needs of the army to start with[19].

2. The Riang Unrest of 1942-43

The rationing system introduced in Tripura helped the salaried class and the pensioners located in urban areas to obtain foodgrain at controlled prices. But the rural and hill areas were not covered by the system. In villages in the plains the peasant households had their own stocks of foodgrain and in the hill villages also the resourceful tribal households did not face acute food shortage. But in the tribal villages of some areas in South Tripura, namely, Amarpur, Udaipur, Belonia and Sabroom, many tribal families suffered on account of acute food scarcity. The food crisis occurred because of the procurement of all available paddy by the Government as a matter of priority to meet the demands of the army and of the people of Agartala town. Some of the Chowdhuries (tribal chiefs) allegedly hoarded paddy in their stock to earn more profit from the rising price of paddy[20]. In these affected divisions prices of rice in 1943 were much higher than in other divisions. The price of rice per maund was the highest in Belonia (Rs.22.50). Prices were also higher in Sonamura (Rs.20), Udaipur (Rs.16), Sabroom (Rs.16), and Amarpur (Rs.16), as against Rs.10 in Khowai and Dharmanagar and Rs. 11 in Sadar Division[21]. The worst sufferers of the food crisis were the Riangs, who constituted the second largest tribe after the Tripuras. Very few Riangs took to settled cultivation. In 1931 only 302 Riangs practised settled cultivation as their primary occupation[22]. Although the common Riang families were in distress in 1942-43, they were not spared from payment of house and other taxes. For the Riangs and Noatias the rate of house tax was the highest, it was Rs.5 per family as against Rs. 4 for the Tripuras, Jamatiyas and others. The rates of export duty on bamboo and cane were also higher for the Riangs and the Noatias[23].

As the War broke out the government sought to recruit tribal youths for Tripura's armed forces which were expanded for sending them to the war front. But the Riangs refused to join the army. In 1942-43 when many Raing families suffered from acute food shortage as famine condition developed there, the Riang chief appointed by the king not only extorted house tax but also fines on some pretext or the other. According to a report referred to by Dasgupta a total amount of Rs.20, 725 was exacted as fines from the Riangs[24]. The Riang chiefs raised the rate of subscription as well for *Ganga Puja* (an annual river worship festival observed at the source of the Gomati river) from Rs. 2 to Rs. 4 per family.

All these developments caused extreme resentment and discontent among the common classes of the Riangs who revolted in 1943 under the leadership of Ratanmani Noatia, a *tantrik sadhu*. He had a number of Riang disciples at Bagafa in South Tripura. He organized and led the Riang revolt against the Chowdhuries (chiefs), the Government (the Raja) and the priests for perpetrating economic, social and religious exploitations of Riang commoners. They stopped paying taxes and fines and ceased performing *Puja* by engaging priests and formed a parallel Government. They looted the granaries of some wealthy Chowdhuries and set up community granaries for distributing food to the poor and the needy.

By the end of 1943 the revolt was crushed by the army sent by the Government (i.e., the Raja). About 3000 rebels including 200 women and children were arrested and brought to the capital where the heads of the rebels were shaved and they were compelled to embrace Vaishnavism by denouncing the Sakti cult.

The captured leader, Ratanmani, reportedly met with unnatural death in captivity[25]. Though the revolt was subdued, the smouldering discontent among the Riangs against the Tripura Raja persisted. In 1945, therefore, the King appointed a Special Committee headed by Kumar Nandalal Debbarma and consisting of three other members to enquire into the causes of the Riangs' disaffections and unrest and to recommend measures for restoring peace and order among them as also for effecting all-round improvement in their moral, social and economic conditions[26].

The second world war ended in 1945 and the struggle for India's independence reached a stage when the British Government had to open discussion with the Indian leaders to work out the modalities of transfer pf power in which the future of the princely states had also figured. The Cabinet Mission came in 1946 and announced its plan for an interim government and a constituent assembly. All such developments had an impact on Tripura's future constitutional status. Such political issues overtook the normal functioning of the Tripura Durbar and the Government. Therefore, the committee on the Riangs also could not possibly finalize its recommendations. But then the memory of heroism and reformist zeal of Ratanmani, who championed the cause of the suffering Riangs and preached progressive socio-religious practices, is still cherished by the Riang community.

Table 26.2
Total Annual Collections of Revenue under Different Select Heads from 1939-40 to 1942-43

(Rupees in thousand)

Sl. No	Head of revenue	1939-40	1940-41	1941-42	1942-43
1.	Land Revenue including Road Cess	667.9	577.0	653.3	844.5
2.	Family Tax in the Hill	77.8	42.7	62.4	52.2
3.	Toll on forest produce including income from permit sale and state share of Feni River Tolls	477.5	500.4	441.6	613.9
4.	Tax on Cotton and oilseeds	142.0	66.4	92.5	37.6
5.	Excise	91.4	97.3	90.9	97.8
6.	Tea Royalty	49.4	46.0	53.5	67.4
7.	Jute Export Duty	90.2	63.2	45.1	57.5
8.	Duty on matches	37.6	9.6	34.0	43.4
9.	Miscellaneous	89.9	75.9	70.8	108.7
10.	Total including *all* items	**2055.5**	**1798.5**	**1918.8**	**2285.5**

Source : The consolidated Tripura Administration Report for 1939-40 to 1942-43, Mahadev Chakravarti (ed) *op. cit.* Vol. IV p. 2120.

Table26.3
Quantities of Principal Commodities Exported in 1939-40, 1940-41, 1941-42 and 1942-43

Sl. No	Commodity		1939-40	1940-41	1941-42	1942-43
1.	Cotton	(Mds)	68,964	19,970	33,395	7,250
2.	Til	(Mds)	10,774	24,043	18,708	20,747
3.	Mustard	(Mds)	32,917	35,511	38,430	39,358
4.	Jute	(Mds)	237,430	505,696	90,272	460,008
5.	Rice and Paddy	(Mds)	——	596,720	718,736	360,800
6.	Tea	(Ibs)	32,05,263	32,53,718	33,17,290	33,27,423
7.	(a) Timber including sal and timber exported by the Feni River (State share) (in C.ft).		—	6,02,393	5,14,520	5,90,104
	(b) Amount of Duty collected on timber exports (Rs.)		—	1,09,070	1,04,940	1,90,208

Source : The Consolidated Tripura Administration Report for 1939-40 to 1942-43, Mahadev Chakravarti (ed) op. cit. Vol. IV p. 2116, and 2120.

Table 26.4
A consolidated Account of Select Items of Expenditure of Tripura State in 1939-40, 1940-41, 1942-43 & 1945-46

(Rs. Lakh)

Sl. No	Expenditure on	1939-40	1940-41	1942-43	1945-46
1.	General Administration charges	7.09	7.18	6.45	11.97
2.	Public Works	1.89	1.75	1.78	4.00
3.	Electric lighting	0.25	0.28	0.30	0.20
4.	Municipality	0.17	0.23*	0.10	0.18
5.	Education	1.24	1.31	1.32	1.93

(Condt...)

(Rs. Lakh)

Sl. No	Expenditure on	1939-40	1940-41	1942-43	1945-46
6.	Medical & Sanitation	0.847	0.967	0.855	1.03
7.	Agriculture, Commerce & industries	0.127	0.100	0.040	0.18
8.	Religious Expenses	0.568	0.563	0.588	0.76
9.	Ordinary *Sansar* charges (Maharaja's own and late Maharaja's family, other branches of Raj family, etc)	1.849	1.951	1.668	—
10.	His Highness's Nij Tahabil (Privy Purse) and his tour	2.284	2.297	2.187	—
10.	Road Fund	1.381	1.666	0.571	—
11.	War Expenditure	0.183	0.887	2.114	—
12.	State contribution to the War Fund	—	0.300	0.300	—

Sources : (Cols 3, 4 & 5) : The Consolidated Tripura Administration Report for 1939-40 to 1942-43, Mahadev Chakraborti (ed) *op. cit.* Vol IV. pp. 2123-2125

For Co. 6: Pravas Ranjan Bhattacharjee, (1993) *Economic Transition in Tripura*, Vikas Publishing House, New Delhi, p. 45.

* Including Rs. 2933 spent on sanitation work.

NOTES AND REFERENCES

1. Mahadev Chakravarti (Ed.), 1994, *Administration Reports of Tripura State since 1902* (in 4 volumes), Gyan Publishing House, New Delhi, Vol. IV, Editor's Note, p. VI.
2. *ibid.* 2(a).*ibid.* p. VII
3. *ibid.* p. VIII.
4. *ibid.* p. 2094 (*Administration Report for 1941-42*).
5. *ibid.*

6. Suprasanna Bandyopadhyay (Ed), 1971, *Tripura State Gazette Sankalan 1903–1949* (in Bengali), A. D. Directorate of Education, Government of Tripura, p. (22).
7. *ibid.* p. 330.
8. *ibid.* p. (22).
9. Bandyopadhyay, *op. cit.* pp. 415-17.
10. *ibid.* p. 420.
11. *ibid.* p. 163.
12. B. K. Sen Bahadur (1946), Tripura State Consolidated Administration Report (1943-46), Political Department, Government of Tripura, Agartala, P. 4 as quoted *in Pravas Ranjan Bhattacharjee (1993),* Economic Transition in Tripura, Vikas Publishing House Pvt. Ltd, New Delhi, p. 44.
13. "Estimates of the number of deaths by famine in Bengal in 1943-44 vary greatly. The Department of Anthropology of the Calcutta University carried out an extensive scientific Survey of sample groups in the famine years. They arrived at the figure of about 3,40,000 total deaths by famine in Bengal. .... The official Famine Inquiry Commission .... has come to the conclusion that about one million and a half deaths occurred in Bengal "as a direct result of the famine and the epidemics which followed in its train"" (Jawaharlal Nehru, *The Discovery of India,* 1946, The Signet Press, Calcutta, p. 602: foot note).
14. Jawaharlal Nehru, *op. cit.* p. 603.
15. B. K. Sen (1946), *op. cit.* p. 44.
16. Jawaharlal Nehru, *op. cit.* p. 603.
17. Subodh Kumar Mukhopadhyay (1991), Economic History of Bengal (*Banglar Arthik Itihash*) in Bengali, 20th century (1900-1947), K. P. Bagchi & Co. Kolkata, Table 6.2, p. 101.
18. Suprasanna Bandyopadhyay (Ed), 1971, *op. cit.* pp.417-418.
19. Pravas Ranjan Bhattacharjee (1993), *op. cit.* p. 45.
20. Nalini Ranjan Roychoudhury (1983), *Tripura Through the Ages* (A Short History of Tripura from the earliest times to 1947 A.D), Sterling Publishers Private Limited, New Delhi, p. 62.
21. Suprasanna Bandyopadhyay (1971), *op. cit.* p. 439.
22. Somendrachandra Debbarma, (1933), *Census Bibarani* (in Bengali), Census Report for 1931, reprinted by Tripura Government in 1997, p. 157.

23. Suprasanna Bandyopadhyay (Ed) (1971) *op. cit.* p. (17)
24. Dasgupta, T. M. (1974), *Ratanmani o Riang Bidroha* (Ratanmoni and the Riang Revolt), Gomati, Agartala, 15 October.
25. Nalini Ranjan Roychoudhury , *op. cit.* p. 63.
26. Suprasanna Bandyopadhyay (1971) *op. cit.* pp. 172-173.

APPENDIX

CHANGE AND CONTINUITY DURING THE COLONIAL PERIOD IN TRIBAL AREAS OF NORTH EAST INDIA*

After annexing Assam in 1826, the British began occupying by force the tribal areas bordering Assam plains. But they met with bitter and protracted resistance of the valiant tribal people imbued with the spirit of independence when they were engaged in extending their domination over the different tribal territories. Or course, ultimately the superior military power of the aggressors won and one after another tribal territory, the North Cachar Hills,Garo Hills, Karbi-Anglong, Khasi and Jaintiya Hills came under the colonial rule. The stiffest and violent opposition came from the Naga tribes. Even though a part of the Naga Hills was occupied in 1886, Lhota Nagas were already subdued in 1875, the Angamis in 1870-80 and the Aos in 1889[1]. But the Nagas never reconciled themselves with the administrative status imposed on them by the British.

Consolidation of the tribal areas brought under the British occupation was made nearly complete by the end of the 1880s. These tribal lands were formed into the administrative (hill) districts of Assam. In Chapter 2 we have noted at some length the British policy of administering the tribal districts and of initiating the slow process of their modernization and development. The account of economic formations of tribal communities in the precolonial period forms the content of Chapter 4. British rule involved reforms of tribal customs and institutions, and also wide-ranging structural changes that influenced economic activities.

The system of administration promulgated in the tribal districts was different from that in the plains districts (vide Chapter 2). Constitutional changes in the province for granting some powers of autonomy and self-rule were also not uniform via-a-vis the plains and hills. Under the Government of India Act 1935 Hill areas were divided into two categories, 'excluded areas' and 'partially excluded areas' (vide Chapter 16). However, colonial rule over the tribal areas entailed a rupture with some aspects of the traditional conformation of the tribal socio-cultural and economic milieu.

The traditional tribal land system was somewhat affected with the promulgation of Assam Land Revenue Regulation of 1886. The Government assumed power to make rules for allotment of land to tribes practising *jhum* (shifting) cultivation. Settlement of land for settled cultivation and the rights of settlement holders to transfer, inheritance, etc also came under this Regulation. Government got the power to acquire land and power to make rules for disposal of Government land as also for allotment of grazing grounds, forests, fisheries, etc. Further, the Government acquired the power of imposing Hoe tax or House – tax on the tribal families practising shifting cultivation.

The colonial rule entailed changes in administrative, legal, judicial, revenue, and forest management practices. Modern systems of medical and health care and educational facilities were also slowly extended partly by the government and partly by the missionaries.

With government patronage the Christian Missionaries came to the tribal villages and began proselytizing the tribal people from their traditional faiths to Christianity. They also promoted western values in different ways among the converted people. The Missionaries played a very progressive role in spreading literacy and in providing modern educational and medical and technical training facilities that helped uplift skill formation among the tribals. The tribal people were motivated to give up slavery and some other social evils. The legal measures taken by the government for abolishing slavery have been dealt with in Chapter 3. But this evil system continued in some parts even after the abolition laws were passed. Khawelthanga Sailo, the first Mizo Chieftain set an example by freeing his slaves at a time when the system was widely practised by Mizo Chiefs. In 1906 he embraced Christianity having been influenced by Dr. Fraser, a missionary from England. In 1910, urged by Fraser, K. Sailo freed four slaves[2].

By taking several welfare measures the missionaries helped instill in the tribal people a sense of their own potential, as they got access to the modern institutional infrastructure in that period of their history.

1. Demographic Change

Ester Boserup rightly propounded the thesis (vide Chapter I) that in primitive communities growth of population promotes technological change that leads to increased agricultural production[3]. And during the colonial period, population in the tribal districts steadily rose with improvements brought about in the state of law and order that checked inter-group fightings and killings and with the introduction of modern system of medical service and anti-epidemic inoculation drive. But these were somewhat offset by the fact that the tribals became more susceptible to new diseases like venereal disease and tuberculosis and also fell victims to epidemics which spread more quickly on account of improved communications and growing contacts with 'civilsation'[4].

The total population of the present-day states of Meghalaya (districts of Khasi and Jainta Hills, and Garo Hills), Mizoram (former Lushai Hills district) and Nagaland increased from 5.25 lakh in 1901 to 10.15 lakh in 1951 (Table 1):

Table 1
Population Growth in Tribal Districts 1901 - 1951.

(Thousand Persons)

Census Year	Meghalaya	Mizoram	Nagaland	Total
1901	341	82	102	525
1951	606	196	213	1015

Source : North Eastern Council, Shillong, Basic Statistics of North Eastern Region, 1980, p. 1.

In the Assam Hills Division, according to the 1951 Census Report, population grew by 1 lakh in 1901-1911, by 0.7 lakh in 1911 - 1921 and 1.2 lakh in 1921 - 31 decades. But from 1931 to 1941 population rose by 2.2 lakh and by 1.4 lakh in 1941 - 1951 decade. "All through Assam and its two natural divisions, Hills and Plains and their districts, the growth of the last two decades exceeds the combined growth of the first three decades"[5]. From 1901 to 1951 the total population of Assam Hills increased by 6.5 lakh.

The Mean Decennial Growth Rate of Assam Hills as estimated in the 1951 Census Report, was 15.0 in 1921 - 31 decade, but it came down to 11.7 in 1941 - 51 decade. This rate should actually be 12.8 per cent if the 'omission of a net population of 15000 compared with that in the previous decade' is rectified. But this rate was 22.5 in 1931 - 41 decade, that is, nearly double the rate obtaining in the previous decade. The report observes that the MDGR of Assam Hills has been 'as a rule' lower than that of Assam Plains. The reason is attributed to the facts that communications, medical and public health services in the hills division were even more backward than those in the plains. The level of general economic conditions is very low since 'the sole occupation of the people is agriculture'. Moreover, "..........immigration both of tea garden labourers and of land hungry Muslims of East Bengal was confined to Assam plains"[6].

2. Impact of the Rise in Population

Rise in the growth rate of population was mainly in the rural areas since the level of unbanization was very low in the Hills and Frontier Tracts. According to 1941 Census, only 4.5 per cent of the population lived in 4 towns[7]. The growth of rural population was associated with the growth of agricultural productions to meet the increased need for foodgrains and for exporting of agricultural and forest products to import manufactured and other goods for which demand expanded. Some technological changes for increasing production were also effected. For example, in the Naga Hills emulating the Angamis, some other Naga tribes, where possible, built terraces for settled cultivation. In the Mizo Hills also in some 'suitable localities' the cultivators 'adopted the system of wet rice cultivation'[8].

Another positively important change was the production of new crops and consumption of new food items. The Mizos took to the cultivation of fruit, coffee, tea, etc 'with avidity' which indicated 'a slight rise in the standard of comfort'. They also began drinking milk which effected 'a considerable reduction in infant mortality'[9].

The most important new crop grown in the Khasi Hills was potato. In 1847 Major Butler wrote:

"In the Khasi Hills a large supply of potatoes is annually raised and sold in the Gauhati Market, realizing to the Khasis no inconsiderable profit. The effect of this traffic being to promote a more frequent intercourse with the people of the plains.......[10]. Potatoes are grown 'on long strips running vertically up and down the hills'. They avoided horizontal stripping as it reportedly caused accumulation of water and rotting of potatoes[11].

The shifting cultivators had to pay house tax and the settled cultivators land revenue charges in cash. And for earning cash to meet the government demands they had to produce surplus for sale against cash. This also boosted trade between the hills and plains. In fact, trade transactions in many items of goods – agricultural and non-agricultural –

between the tribals and the plainspeople got a fillip in the colonial period.

Working as agricultural labour mainly in the off-season was an additional source of earning cash to meet government demands and purchase goods not produced in the hills. J. P. Mills in his note[12] stated that gangs of Semas and Aos of Naga Hills went down in the winter to work, in tea gardens 'in order to earn cash for their house tax'. Also they purchased showy articles displayed in the shops, besides distilled liquor drinking of which was their newly acquired habit.

Besides the Naga and Mizo Hills, in some other parts of the hill region also a very slow growing number of cultivators as cultivating owners of land began practising settled wet rice cultivation by building terraces on hill slopes or reclaiming lands in the foot hill plains. Yet the mainstay of the agricultural activities was shifting cultivation. In 1901 the number of shifting cultivators (Jhumias) in Mizo, North Cachar and Naga Hills and the hill tracts of Manipur taken together totalled 2,75,599. B. C. Allen however, pointed out in the Census Report for 1901 that the number of Jhumias would be much more, since a considerable number of them in the Khasi and Jaintia and Garo Hills were wrongly included in the category of ordinary cultivators and not in that of Jhumias[13].

As recorded in 1931 census the total number of Jhumias constituted 11.9 per cent of working population living on cultivation in the province of Assam.

3. Growth of Literacy and Education

In the pre-colonial period most of the tribal communities were at the pre-literate stage. After the British occupation of the tribal areas and the coming of the Christian missionaries there, spread of literacy and education among the tribal people became an inseparably significant aspect of the process of modernization and social and economic development. Some individuals of the colonial bureaucracy and the Christian and other missionaries took steps towards starting schools, spreading literacy and associated activities so as to motivate the people to send their children to schools. Some dedicated Christian Missionaries rendered the local dialects into written languages by introducing Roman alphabet and compiling grammars. Printing of books and dictionaries and even a periodical (*Arunoday*) was a helpful measure for spreading literacy and education. Table 2 showing the levels of literacy in the hill districts in 1901 is given below:

Table 2
Levels of Literacy in the Hill Districts in 1901.

District	Number if literates per 1000 males	Number of literates per 1000 females
Mizo Hills	49	1
North Cachar Hills	74	4
Naga Hills	23	1
Khasi & Jaintia Hills	64	24
Garo Hills	13	2

Source : Census of India 1901, Vol. IV Assam Part I Report, p. 104

The table indicates that the general level of male literacy was very low; it varied from 1.3 per cent in Garo Hills to 7.4 per cent in North Cachar Hills. In fact, the rise in the literacy figure for N. C. Hills was due to the fact that at that time because of the progress in construction of the rail lines in that part, many people from the plains – workers, contractors and traders and their employees lived there at that time. Excepting for Khasi and Jaintia Hills, the rate of female literacy was below 1 per cent.

It was, however, a good sign that the tribal people became more and more interested in sending their children to schools as they valued literacy and education for the development of human resources. This is evident from the growth of literacy level during the 50 year period from 1901 to 1951. Literacy levels as recorded in the 1941 and 1951 census reports are shown in Table 3 below. This social development was a positive factor in expanding productive capacities of the tribal communities and opening up new avenues of livelihood.

Table 3
Literates According to Age Groups Per Mille in 1941 and 1951.

	Aged 5 – 9				Aged 10 – 14				Aged 15 and upwards			
State & Natural Division	**1951**		**1941**		**1951**		**1941**		**1951**		**1941**	
	M	**F**	**M**	**F**	**M**	**F**	**M**	**F**	**M**	**F**	**M**	**F**
Assam Hills	14	6	10	6	31	32	24	10	161	67	156	47

Source : *Census of India 1951, Assam, Manipur & Tripura*, p. 345.

4. Livelihood Pattern

Changes in livelihood pattern of the tribal population are noted from the census reports. We confine our study to the results of the 1901 and 1951 census reports. In the beginning of the 20th century the overwhelming majority of the tribal people were shifting cultivators. The findings of the 1901 census confirm this. In the hill districts 84.6 per cent of the population were agriculturists. In the Khasi and Jaintia Hills the proportion of agriculturists was a little less than 77 per cent. It was so since it was a sparsely populated district and then Shillong's population was mostly made up of non-agriculturists. This fact had a 'very appreciable effect upon the total'. Moreover, as B. C. Allen has also observed, "the Khasi is a fairly enterprising trader, who spends a great part of his time in travelling from one market to another and is not content to subsist entirely on the produce of the soil".[15]

The 1901 census has also highlighted the participation of women in non-conventional professions. For example in the Mizo Hills there were 38 women 'village headmen' including the Mizo Rani. The Report further mentions: "One female is said to be working in a printing press, and four as carpenters. There are 12 female contractors the majority of whom were censused in the Khasi and Jaintia Hills and Manipur, where women are much given to trading on their own account...."[16] Women in Khasi and Jaintia Hills have been traditionally very efficient traders.

For the 1951 census livelihood of people (earners and their dependents) was classified into two broad categories namely, agricultural and non-agricultural classes. Agricultural classes consisted of i) Cultivators of land wholly or mainly owned by them ii) Cultivators of land wholly or mainly unowned iii) cultivating labourers and iv) non-cultivating owners of land and agricultural rent-receivers. Non-agricultural classes included persons (including dependents) who derived their livelihood from v) production other than cultivation; vi) commerce vii) transport and viii) other services and miscellaneous sources.

In the Asam Hills agricultural classes comprised 84.92 per cent of people. The district wise break –up is given in Table. 4.

Table 4
Livelihood Pattern of Population of Hill Districts

Sl. No.	District	Agricultural classes (per cent)	Non-agricultural classes (per cent)
1.	United K & J Hills	67.7	32.3
2.	Naga Hills	94.1	5.9
3.	Mizo Hills	93.0	7.0
4.	Garo Hills	95.0	5.0
5.	United Mikir & N.C. Hills	94.0	6.0

Source: *Census of India 1951*, Vol. XII, *Assam, Manipur and Tripura Part IA, Report*, p. 106.

The break-up of population in the different agricultural classes shows that in all the districts, cultivators of land wholly or mainly owned by them predominate. In Garo Hills the percentage of such cultivators is 89.7, while it is 92.6 in Naga Hills. In the United K & J Hills this percentage is the lowest, 50.5 that is. The percentage of cultivators cultivating land either wholly or mainly unowned is 'nil' in Mizo Hills and only 0.8 in Naga Hills. In the United K & J Hills District it is as high as 8.9. Sub-tenancy has been the trend in ths district on account of the pressure of population[17].

The percentage of agricultural labourers is even more insignificant with the exception of Shillong where such labourers constitute 8 per cent of the population. Everywhere in Assam Hills the number of non-cultivating owners of land and agricultural rent-receivers is totally insignificant; it constitutes only 0.5 per cent.

In respect of production derived from sources other than cultivation, only United K. &. J Hills returns 8 per cent, 'all other districts showing roundabout 1 per cent'. Only 5 per cent of population of United K. &. J Hills get their livelihood from commerce and just 0.6 per cent from transport. "Livelihood class VIII – other Services and Miscellaneous Sources – attain some significance once again in the United K. J District where it supports nearly 20 per cent of the entire population against a percentage varying from 2 to 5 in other Autonomous Districts"[18].

5. The North Eastern Frontier Tracts

The colonial rulers' administration of the North Eastern Frontier Hills as parts of Lakhimpur and Darrang districts of Assam dates back to 1882. In 1914, these hill territories were divided into three sections. One section was constituted by Central and Eastern Section of North-East Frontier Tract with its headquarters at Sadiya. Another section was the Lakhimpur Frontier Tract having its headquarters in Dibrugarh. The third or the Western Section's headquarters was at Charduar. "Subsequent to this, administrative changes were made in 1919, 1921, 1925, 1926, 1928, 1929, 1931, 1943, and 1948"[19].

The first full census of this area (measuring 81,436 sq. Km) was taken in the post-colonial period in 1961 when it was known as The North – East Frontier Agency. Then the population was 3,36,558 and the density of population 4.13 per sq. km. During the colonial period censuses were confined to the plain areas of the different frontier tracts. Therefore the growth of population during the colonial period could not be worked out. But these frontier tracts were very sparsely populated which was because the density of populated must have been even lower than 4.13 per sq. km. For, after Independence NEFA's population increased on account of the immigration (not for settlement in land) of a large number of persons to man administrative departments and various development departments, such as, public works, education, agriculture, industry.

In a sparsely populated tribal area, where the people's main means of livelihood was shifting cultivation excepting for a very few tribes who practised settled wet-rice cultivation (see Chapter – 4) the economy was at the subsistence level and it was almost a stationary one without growth in total production. The colonial penetration into these hills, however, caused some changes in the economic management, such as, monetization of transactions and expansion of trading activities.

The Frontier Tracts were constitutionally kept as "Excluded Areas" and the Inner-Line Regulation was in force in all these Tracts. Therefore the contact of these tribal people with people of the plains was rigidly controlled. Even the missionaries were barred from entering into these tracts for preaching religion or carrying out the process of proselitization.

After the consolidation of the colonial administration of these tracts, selected traders from the plains (mainly Marwaris) and Nepali labourers or ex-armymen were allowed entry into this area. The traders from the plains imported many consumption goods for sale and they purchased locally produced agricultural goods and products of handicrafts and household industries, such as, *daos* and Adi quilts, and collections from forests, as for example, *manjeet* (a dye), *Mishimi Teeta* (Captistia) and rubber.

To promote trade exchanges between the tribals and the plainsmen the Government would organize trade fairs. According to Elwin[20] at Udalgiri annual fairs were held where the Sherdukpens and Akas sold ponies, sheep, dogs, salt, a little gold, blankets, yak's tails, musk, chillies, spices, wax, madder, oranges and walnuts. They purchased English and Assamese cloth, threads, rice, betel-nuts, brass and iron untensils, bar-iron, hoes, etc. About 2000 tribals visited this fair in 1875 and 3600 in 1876. Another fair was organized at

Doimera. In 1876, 'the first year in which statistics were collected, imports did not exceed Rs. 13,000, while at Udalgiri they amounted to over Rs. 25,000, exports being double that amount'.

The most important fair was, however, held at Sadiya[21] where the Miris, Mishmis, Khamptis, came with their surplus products, such as, handicrafts, hand-woven cloth, rubber, elephant tusks and rhinoceros horns. They purchased English yarn, English pottery, salt, brass pots, iron, tea, sugar, oil, *gur*, opium, etc. 'Rubber stood at the head of the list of articles sold by most tribes ....' (For more details see note no 21).

Literacy and education was extremely low as is evident from the fact that in 1947 there were only 2 primary schools in these Tracts.

Even though no complete census about livelihood pattern covering both the hills and the plains is available for the colonial period it is obvious that the people were almost entirely dependent on cultivation (mainly of the shifting model), handicrafts, collections from forests, hunting, fishing and animal husbandry, etc. These facts remained more or less the same around 1947 as elaborated in Chapter – 4.

Of course, there were some sources of surplus cash earnings which were payments by the Government in lieu of *posa*, trading activities and other favourable transactions. This gave an impetus to economic growth. But the rate of growth remained extremely slow. Somewhat paradoxically, in their primitive form of economy, it was the trading activity that was the main factor of economic progress.

All-round developmental activities and large amounts of public investments in the economic infrastructure, education, health, agriculture, industry etc. received a robust boost only after Independence and the conversion of these Tracts into the North Eastern Frontier Agency. NEFA was a centrally administratered Agency and the Central Government was in a position to invest large amounts of resources for its all-round development. The administrative system was also so structured as to be able to implement development projects speedily with the active involvement of the tribal communities at the grassroots level. Of course the existing policy of maintaining the Inner Line Regulation with a view to preserving the tribal identities and the tribe's control over natural and productive resources continued unaffected.

6. Elements of Continuity in The Tribal Areas

Changes in the size of population, growth of literacy and education, emergence of new urban centres, diversification of economic activities, changes in livelihood pattern, etc caused significant changes in the social, political and economic structures in the tribal areas of North East India during the colonial period. But such changes did not result in a complete break with the past. Though the values of modernization informing socio-cultural and economic behaviour were not lost sight of, different ethnic communities in the region continued holding fast to their respective social, cultural and ethical values.

The colonial policy of promulgating the Inner-Line Regulation designed to regulate the entry of people from outside into the tribal areas, e.g., the North Eastern Frontier Tracts, Mizo Hills and Naga Hills, helped preserve the tribal people's identify and their traditional control (to a large extent) over lands, forests, and other natural resources. The individual tribal households and the community were ensured by this measure the use of these as before.

An important stabilizing element was the role of the civil society at the grass root level in safeguarding the interest of the tribals. The role of the village council and of village chief was still effective in regulating the economic, social and cultural affairs of the villagers even though in some cases such authority was somewhat diluted.

The traditional festivals related to the cycle of agricultural production activities (mainly shifting cultivation-based) continued to be celebrated.

In some parts rudiments of inequalities in income and the distribution of productive assets were discernible. But so strong was the ethos of egalitarianism that such economic inequalities could be considered minimal. Social structure was still horizontally homogeneous in the hill villages where the bane of caste system was absent.

Lastly, the traditional role of tribal women in society, especially relating to productive activities, helped preserve continuity and social cohesion in the region.

NOTES AND REFERENCES

1. * For some ideas and views in this Appendix I have drawn upon my paper, "Continuity and change in North-East India during the Colonial Period" published in the *Journal of North-East India Çouncil for Social Science Research*, Shillong, 13-14 December 1999, pp 1-15, which was brought out during the Silver Jubilee Celebration of North-East India Council for Social Science Research, Shillong.

2. * For compiling the data about population change, growth of literacy and livelihood pattern of population of the hill areas of Assam I have used the same secondary sources, namely, the relevant census Reports and the North Eastern Council's Statistics of North Eastern Region, Shillong, 1980.

1. Amalendu Guha (1988), *Planter-Raj to Swaraj : Freedom Struggle and Electoral Politics in Assam 1826-1947*, People's Publishing House, New Delhi, p. 2.
2. The Statesmen of Kolkata dated 4 December 2000 reported that villagers, church leaders and social workers gathered at Maubuang (Mizoram) on 3 December to honour the memory of Khawelthanga Sailo who broke slave shackles in 1910. Slavery in Mizoram dated back to 1750.
3. Ester Boserup (1965), *The Conditions of Agricultural Growth* (The Economics of Agrarian Change under population Pressure), George Allen and Unwin Ltd, London, p. 11 and Foreword by Nicholas Kaldor, p. 7.
4. J.P. Mills, 'The effect on the tribes of the Naga Hills District of Contacts with civilization', Appendix A to the *Census of India, 1931*, Vol. III, Assam Part I – Report by C. S. Mullan, P. (ii): "Improved communications, while they have immensely facilitated internal trade, have undoubtedly spread disease .... Not only have specific diseases, such as venereal disease and tuberculosis, been introduced, but epidemics spread more quickly".
5. R. B. Vaghaiwalla (1954), *Census of India, 1951*, Vol. XII, *Assam, Manipur and Tripura Part IA, Report*, Shillong, p. 40.
6. *ibid*, pp. 40-41.
7. K. W. P. Marar, *Census of India 1941*, Vol. IX: Assam, p. 6 and p. 64.
8. C. J. Helme, "The effect on the Lushais of contact with civilization', Appendix A to the *Census of India, 1931*, Vol. III, Assam, *op.cit.* p. V.

9. *ibid.*
10. Quoted in the *Report of the Committee on Special Multi-purpose Tribal Blocks*, Ministry of Home Affairs, New Delhi, 1960, p. 274.
11. *ibid.*
12. J. P. Mills, op.cit., p. (ii).
13. B. C. Allen (1902), *Census of India 1901*, Vol. IV. *Assam, Part I, Report*, Shillong, p. 163.
14. C. S. Mullan, *Census of India, 1931*, Vol. III, *Assam, Part I – Report*, p. 121.
15. B. C. Allen, *op. cit.* p. 162.
16. *ibid.* p. 168.
17. R. B. Vaghaiwalla *op. cit.*, p. 108.
18. *ibid.*
19. D. Ering (1972), The North-East Frontier Agency, published in K. Suresh Singh (ed), *The Tribal Situation in India*, Matilal Banarsidass for the Indian Institute of Advanced Study (Second Reprint 1990), p. 51.
20. Verrier Elwin (ed) (1959), *India's North – East Frontier in the Nineteenth Century*, Oxford University Press, Madras, Third Impression 1972, p. 353.
21. About the Sadiya Fair, Elwin observes: "The Sadiya Fair catered to the needs of the Miris, Mishmis, Khamptis, Singphos and Abors (Adis), though for some years the Abors did not attend. In 1876, 3000 tribesmen were present and the numbers rose in later years. In 1874, they brought down over Rs. 25,000 worth of their own articles and took home goods to the value of Rs. 17,630. In 1876, the turnover was much greater: they sold Rs. 49,100 and bought Rs.44,475 worth of goods, though the amount fell off considerably in the next few years......................." *ibid.* p. 353.

    "The Report on the Administration of the Province of Assam for 1878 – 79 notes that in 1879 'about 40 Europeans were present, and the usual barter went on between them and the hill people, the latter disposing of all they possessed in the way of arms and ornaments, and of most, indeed, of their clothing. Articles of this nature commanded prices which must have surprised the owners". *ibid.*

BIBLIOGRAPHY

Admn. Report 1921-22.

Agarwal, Bina (1994), *A Field of One's Own, Gender and Land Rights in South Asia,* Cambridge University Press, London.

Alice and Daniel Thomer (1974). *Land and Labour in* India, Bombay.

Allen, B.C. (1902), *Census of India 1901*, Vol. IV, Assam Part-I Report, pp. 162-63.

Banerjee, A.C. (1992), *The New Regime, 1826-31*, In: *Comprehensive History of Assam*, Vol.IV, H.K. Barpujari (Ed), Publication Board, Assam, Guwahati.

Barooah, N.K. *David Scott in North-East India 1802-31: A Study in British Paternalism,* New Delhi, 1970.

Barpujari, H.K. (1970), Problem of the Hill Tribes, North-East Frontier, North Eastern Hill University Publications, Shillong.

Barpujari, H.K. (1993), *The Comprehensive History of Assam,* Vol.V, Publication Board, Assam, Guwahati.

Barpujari, H.K. (1996), *Assam in the Days of the Company,* North East Hill University Shillong.

Barpujari, H.K. (1998), Problem of the Hill Tribes : North - East Frontier, NEHU Reprint, first published 1970.

Barpujari, H.K. (ed), *The Comprehensive History of Assam,* Vol. III, Publication Board, Assam, Guwahati, pp. 146-47.

Barpujari, H.K., *The comprehensive History of Assam,* Vol.

IV contains some papers written by him on different economic aspects for the period, 1826 to 1919.

Barua, Hem (1960), The Red River and the Blue Hills, Lawyer's Book Stall, Guwahati.

Baruah, S.L. (1997), *A Comprehensive History of Assam*, Munishiram Manoharial Publishers, New Delhi.

Baruah, Sanjib (1999), *India against itself, Assam and the Politics of Nationality*, Oxford University Press, New Delhi..

Bengal Revenue Proceedings, 9 August, 1836, No. 47; Jenkins 22 June as quoted by H. K. Barpujari.

Bhattacharjee, J.B. (ed), 1994. Studies in the Economic History of North-East India, HarAnand Publications, New Delhi, pp. 187 -89.

Bhattacharjee, J.B. *Cochar under British Rule in North East India*, Radiant Publishers, New Delhi.

Bhattachrjee, J.B. (2000), Trade and Colony, *The British Colonisation of North East India*, North East India History Association Shillong.

Bhuyan, S.K. (1990), *Anglo-Assamese Relations 1771-1826*, Lawyer's Book Stall, Guwahati, p. 589.

Bolton, C.W. *Political Agent, Hill Tipperah, Administration Report on Hill Tipperah for the year 1877-78..*

Bordoloi, B.N. (1998), Tribal Land Tenure System and land Alienation in North-East India, published in S.N. Mishra (ed) Antiquity to Modernity and Control of Resources among Indian Tribes, Inter -India Publications, New Delhi.

Boserup, Easter (1970), *Women's Role in Economic Development*, George Allen and Unwin, London.

Boserup, Easter (1965), *The Conditions of Agricultural Growth (The Economics of Agrarian Change under Population Pressure)*, George Allen and Unwin Limited, London, and the Foreword by Nicholas Kaldor.

Boserup, Easter (1965), *The Conditions of Agricultural Growth: The Economics of Agrarian Change under Population Pressure*, George Allen and Unwin Ltd., London.

Braudel, Fernand (1986), *Civilization and Capitalism: 15th - 18th century*, vol. I, *The Structures of Everyday Life, The Limits of the Possible* (Translated from the French. Revised by Sian Reynolds), 2nd Reprint, William Collins Sons & Co Ltd, London, Glasgow

Brown, R. (1975), *Statistical Account of Manipur,* first published in 1874, Sanskaran Prakashak, Delhi.

Brown, R. Narrative Report of the Progress of the Survey Party, Naga Hills, Season 1874.

Brown, R. *Statistical Account of Manipur*, first published in 1874 reprinted in 1975, Sanskaran Prakashak, Delhi.

Butler, John. 'Rough Notes on the Angami Nagas'. Journal of the Asiatic Society, 1875, Vol. XLIV, No. 4.

Cambel, T. J. (1898), *Brief History of the Forest Department in Assam*, Published in Home..

Carr, E. H. (1961), *What is History*, Penguin Edition, London.

Coxhead, T.E. Officiating Political Agent, *Hill Tipperah, Administrative Report for 1975-76.*

Dalton, E.T. *Descriptive Ethnology of Bengal* (Calcutta, 1872).

Dasgupta, Keya (1983), "Plantation Economy and Land Tenure System in Brahmaputra Valley, 1839 – 1914", *Economic and Political Weekly*, Vol. XVIII, No. 20, 16 July.

Datta, K.K. (1961), *Survey of India's Social Life and Economic Condition in the Eighteenth Century*, Calcutta.

Devi, Ksh Bimla (1988), Manipuri Women - A Study, In: Sanjaoba (Ed), *Manipur: Past and Present,* Vol.I.

Dove, Michacl (1983), *Theories of Swidden agriculture, and the political economy of ignorance, Agroforestry Systems: 85-89*, The Hague.

Elwin, Verrier (1959), India's North-East Frontier in the Nineteenth Century, Oxford University Press, Madras.

Elwin, Verrier (1969). The Nagas in the Nineteenth Century, Oxford University Press, p. 588.

Elwin, Verrier 1988. *A Philosophy for NEFA, Government of Arunchal Pradesh*, Itanagar.

Engels, F. *The Origin of the Family, Private Property and the State*, Foreign Languages Publishing House, Moscow, 1952, pp. 286-87.

Ering, D. (1972), The North-East Frontier Agency, In: The Tribal Situation in India, ed, K. Suresh Singh, Indian Institute of Advanced Study, Shimla.

Extracts from the article quoted in Census of India, 1931, Report, *op. cit.* p. 127.

Firth, Raymond (1965), *Primitive Polynesian Economy*, Routledge & Kegal Paul, London.

Firth, Raymond and B. S. Yamey (ed.) (1964), *Capital, Saving and Credit in Peasant Societies*, George Allen and Unwin Ltd, London.

Gadgil, Madhab and Ramachandra Guha (1992), *This Fissured Land : An Ecological History of India,* Oxford University Press, Delhi.

Gait, E.A. (1899), *Report on the Census of India, 1891, Assam.*

Gait, Edward (1967), *A History of Assam.* Revised and Enlarged by B.K. Barua and H.V.S. Murthy, Thacker Spink, Kolkata.

Gait, Edward (1997), *A History of Assam,* Lawyer's Book Stall, Guwahati.

Gait, Sir Edward (1997), *A History, of Assam*, Seventh Edition, Lawyer's Book Stall, Guwahati.

Ganguly, J.B. (1993), 'Development of Peasant Farming in the North -Eastern Tribal Region (A study in Tribal Continuities)'. In: *Continuity and Change in Tribal Society*, Mrinal Miri (ed), Indian Institute of Advanced Study, Shimla.

Godwin-Austen, H.H. Report on the Survey Operations in the Naga Hills and Manipur during the field season 1872-73.

Goswami, P. C. (1994), *The Economic Development of Assam,* Kalyani Publishers, New Delhi.

Goswami, Priyam (1999), *Assam in the Nineteenth Century: Industrialization and Colonial Penetration*, Spectrum Publications, Guwahati: Delhi.

Goswami, S.D.Work on *British Revenue Policy and Administration* and works of some other scholars represent such attempts.

Govt. of India, Proceedings of the Revenue and Agricultural Department for December, 1888; Famine Reports on the Condition of the Lower Classes of Population in India, Proceeding 9 and 10 NAI (referred to as Dufferin Enquiry) quoted in Guha.

Guha, Amalendu (1981), Formation of a Working Class in Assam Plantations: A study in Retrospect, In: *Problems of Tea Industry in Northeast India,* Shillong.

Guha, Amalendu (1988), *Planter - Raj to Swaraj Freedom Struggle and Electoral polities in Assam, 1826 -1947,* Peoples Publishing House, New Delhi.

Guha, Amalendu (1991), *Medieval and Early Colonial Assam Society Polity Economy,* K. P. Bagchi & Co., Calcutta.

Haimendorf, C. Von. F. (1962), The Apa Tanis and their Neighbours, A Primitive Civilization of the Eastern Himalayas, Routledge & Kegan Paul, London.

Hamilton, Francis (reprint edn. 1963). *An Account of Assam,* Guwahati.

Hicks, J. (1969), *A Theory of Economic History,* Oxford University Press.

Hicks, John (1969), *A Theory of Economic History,* Clarendon Press, Oxford, p. 3.

Hodson, T.C. *The Meitheis,* reprinted edition, Neeraj Publishing House, New Delhi 1984 (first published by David Nutt, London 1908).

Hungya, P. (1987) 'Land Tenure system in the Hills of Manipur'. In: *Land Relations in North-East India,* B.B. Datta and N.N. Karna (eds), People's Publishing House, New Delhi.

Hunter, W.W. *Statistical Account of Hill Tipperah,* 1876.

Kabui, Gangmumei *Glimpses of Land and People of Ancient Manipur,* published in Naorem Sanajaoba, Manipur Past and Present Vol. I, Mittal Publications, New Delhi, 1988.

Kabui, Gangmumei Socio Religious Reform Movement and

Christian Proselytism, In: Lal Dena (ed), *History of Modern Manipur (1826-1949)*, Orbit Publishers, New Delhi, 1991.

Keya Dasgupta (1988), "Industrialization in the Brahmaputra Valley (1881-1921", *Proceedings of the North East India History Association*, 9th Session, Shillong.

Kumar Dharma (ed), 1983, *The Cambridge Economic History of India*, Vol. 2 (C.1757 - C. 1970), Cambridge University Press, Cambridge, 1983, p. 119-20.

Law Research Institute, Eastern Region, Gauhati High Court, Guwahati Directed by J.N. Das, *A Study of Land System of Tripura*, Guwahati, 1990.

Lloyd, G. T. *Census of India, 1921*, Vol. III, *Assam*, Part-I, Report, p. 167.

Mackenzie, Alexander (1995), *The North -East Frontier of India*, first published in 1884 entitled "History of the Relations of government with the hill tribes of the north-east frontier of Bengal", reprinted by Mittal Publications, New Delhi.

Mackenzie, Alexander "Fate seems rest for the English in India till they stand forth as the Governors or advisers of each tribe and people in the land".

McCulloch, W. *Account of Valley of Manipur and of the Hill Tribes*, Calcutta, 1859, parts of which are quoted in Hodson, 1984.

Mills, A.J. Moffat (1854), *Report on the Province of Assam*, republished by Publication Board, Assam in 1984, Guwahati.

Mishra, S.N. (1983), Arunachal's Tribal Economic Formations and their Dissolution, *Economic and Political Weekly*, Vol. XVIII, No. 43, p. 842

Mullan, C. S. (1933), *Census of India*, 1931, Vol. III, Assam.

Myrdal, Gunnar (1970), *The Challenge of World Poverty: A World Anti-Poverty Programme in Outline*, A Penguin International Edition.

North, Douglas C. (1981), *Structure and Change in Economic History*, W. W. Norton and Company, New York, London.

Pemberton, R. B. (1835), *Report Upon the Countries on the Eastern Frontier of the British Territories*, Reprinted in 1979 by Mittal Publications, New Delhi.

Phookan, Anandaram Dhekial Observations on the Administration of the Province of Assam, Appendix J of A.J. Moffat Mills, Report on the Province of Assam (1854), reprinted by Publication Board, Assam (1984).

Reid, M. (1931), The Indian Peasant Uprooted (A Study of the Human Machine), London.

Report of the Assam Banking Enquiry Committee, 1929-30, quoted in C.S. Mullan.

Report on the Administration of Assam, for the year 1921-22 (reprinted as *Report on the Administration of North East India* (1921-22) by Mittal Publication, Delhi, in 1984, Part II Administration Report, p. 59.

Report on the Administration of North East India (1921-22) (hereafter Admn. Report 1921-22), p. 1.

Report on the Administration of North East India (1921-22): A Mittal Publication, Delhi, 1984 (This is a reprint of the Report on the Administration of Assam, for the year 1921-22), Part II.

Report on the Census of Assam, 1881.

Robinson, W. (1841), A Descriptive Account of Assam, In: V. Elwin, 1969.

Rowney, H.B. (1882), The Wild Tribes of India, quoted in Elwin.

Roy Burman, B.K. (1970), Demographic and Socio-Economic Profiles of the Hill Areas of North -East India, Census of India 1961, Office of the Registrar General, India, New Delhi.

Roy Burman, B.K. *Prefatory Introduction to Alexander Mackenzei*, (1995).

Roy, Sachin (1960), Aspect of Padam - Minyong Culture, North-East Frontier Agency, Shillong.

Roychoudhury, Nalini Ranjan *Tripura through the Ages, A Short History of Tripura from the Earliest Times to 1947 A.D.*, Sterling Publishers Private Ltd. New Delhi, 1983.

Saikia, Rajen (2000), *Social and Economic History of Assam, 1853-1921*, Manohar, New Delhi.

Sanajaoba, Noarem (Ed), (1988), *Manipur: Past and Present*, Vol. I, History.

Stevenson, H.N.C. (1986), *The Economics of the Central Chin Tribes*, (originally published by the Government of Burma in 1943) reprinted by Tribal Research Institute, Government of Mizoram, Aizawl.

The Cambridge Economic History of India, Vol.2 (1983) Cambridge University Press.

The Statesman, "An Assamese", from Jorhat, In: The Letter to Editor" column titled 'Assam' in, Calcutta for May 21, 1886.

Trevelyan, G. M. (1963), *A Shortened History of England*, published in Pelican Books, 1959, reprinted in 1960, 1962, and 1963.

Welsh's Report on Assam, 1794, quoted in Mackenzie (1995).

Woodthrope, R.G. Notes on the Wild Tribes Inhabiting the So-called Naga Hills on our North-East Frontier of India (1881) quoted in Elwin.

INDEX

F

□□□